Big Data Mining and Analytics with Applications

Big Data Mining and Analytics with Applications

Guest Editors

Hongzhi Wang
Chen Ye

MDPI

Basel • Beijing • Wuhan • Barcelona • Belgrade • Novi Sad • Cluj • Manchester

Guest Editors
Hongzhi Wang
Department of Computer
Science and Technology
Harbin Institute of Technology
Harbin
China

Chen Ye
Department of Computer
Science and Technology
Hangzhou Dianzi University
Hangzhou
China

Editorial Office
MDPI AG
Grosspeteranlage 5
4052 Basel, Switzerland

This is a reprint of the Special Issue, published open access by the journal *Mathematics* (ISSN 2227-7390), freely accessible at: https://www.mdpi.com/journal/mathematics/special_issues/Big_Data_Min_Anal.

For citation purposes, cite each article independently as indicated on the article page online and as indicated below:

Lastname, A.A.; Lastname, B.B. Article Title. *Journal Name* **Year**, *Volume Number*, Page Range.

ISBN 978-3-7258-6336-5 (Hbk)
ISBN 978-3-7258-6337-2 (PDF)
https://doi.org/10.3390/books978-3-7258-6337-2

Contents

About the Editors

Hongzhi Wang

Hongzhi Wang is a tenured full professor and doctoral supervisor at Harbin Institute of Technology. He currently serves as the Director of the Massive Data Computing Research Center in the Faculty of Computing, Head of the Data Science and Big Data Technology Program, Director of the Heilongjiang Provincial Key Laboratory of Big Data Science and Engineering, and Head of the HIT Young Scientist Studio. He also holds the position of Secretary-General of the Alumni Association of the Faculty of Computing. As a Distinguished Member of the China Computer Federation and a Senior Member of IEEE, his research focuses on databases, big data management and analytics, and big data governance. He has published over 350 academic papers, including more than 100 SCI-indexed articles, with a total citation count exceeding 6500. He has led more than 20 major research projects, including key projects under the National Natural Science Foundation of China and international collaborative initiatives, and has participated as a key member in numerous national, provincial, and ministerial-level key projects as well as international cooperative research programs.

Chen Ye

Chen Ye is an associate professor at Hangzhou Dianzi University. She serves as a member of the Database Expert Committee and the Big Data Expert Committee of the China Computer Federation (CCF). She earned her Ph.D. from Harbin Institute of Technology in 2020. From 2016 to 2017, she was a visiting researcher in the group of Professor Jing Gao at the University at Buffalo, State University of New York, USA. Since July 2020, she has been affiliated with the School of Computer Science at Hangzhou Dianzi University and is a member of the Perception Computing Laboratory of the Institute of Computer Application Technology and the Key Laboratory of Brain-Machine Collaborative Intelligence. Her main research areas include data cleaning and integration, truth discovery, and crowdsourced data management. As the first author, she has published over 20 papers in top-tier and prominent international conferences and journals. She has participated in multiple projects supported by the National Natural Science Foundation of China (NSFC) and national science and technology programs as a key contributor. She currently leads one NSFC Young Scientists Fund project and one Zhejiang Provincial Natural Science Foundation Young Scientists Fund project.

mathematics MDPI

Editorial

Preface for "Big Data Mining and Analytics with Applications"

Hongzhi Wang [1] and Chen Ye [2,*]

[1] Department of Computer Science and Technology, Harbin Institute of Technology, Harbin 150001, China
[2] Department of Computer Science and Technology, Hangzhou Dianzi University, Hangzhou 310018, China
* Correspondence: chenye@hdu.edu.cn

This is the preface for the Special Issue "Big Data Mining and Analytics with Applications", which was published in the MDPI journal *Mathematics*. Among the 26 submissions received for this Special Issue, the editors selected nine articles and one review paper that successfully passed the peer-review process. They contain original research ideas that have made significant advancements in the theory of Big Data Mining and Analytics with Applications. In particular, the topics discussed in these 10 papers are related to span predictive modeling for spatiotemporal data (e.g., traffic, air quality, crowd flow), data quality and repair, automated data understanding (e.g., table type prediction), advanced clustering and user segmentation, scalable statistical learning (e.g., Bayesian variable selection), and text mining applications (e.g., document classification, fake review detection). Together, they highlight a strong focus on efficient, robust, and interpretable methods for big data mining and analysis across domains.

Contribution 1 presents a two-stage hybrid extreme learning machine for short-term traffic flow forecasting. By combining particle swarm optimization and gravitational search algorithm to optimize extreme learning machine parameters, the model enhances prediction accuracy and stability while retaining the fast training advantage of extreme learning machines. Contribution 2 introduces a modified γ-Sutte indicator for air quality index prediction, which reduces computational complexity by using a shorter sliding window while maintaining high accuracy. Validated on datasets from Taiwan and Laos, the method outperforms existing α-Sutte, β-Sutte, and ARIMA models across multiple metrics, demonstrating both efficiency and transferability. Contribution 3 proposes an automated method for predicting web table column types by integrating CNN with a knowledge base-based voting mechanism. Entities in the table are queried from a knowledge base to identify corresponding categories, expanding the dataset and generating synthetic column samples for data augmentation, thereby enhancing the model's generalization capability. The approach employs a CNN to predict each sub-column and averages the probabilities, while entity description texts extracted from the knowledge base are used to compute keyword coverage as voting probability. The final result is determined by comparing these two probabilities. Contribution 4 implements a two-step cluster analysis methodology to empirically segment travel application users. By employing a log-likelihood distance measure that effectively handles both continuous and categorical variables and utilizing information criteria (AIC/BIC) to automatically determine the optimal number of clusters, this study overcomes the limitations of traditional distance metrics. The resulting identification of four distinct user profiles provides a data-driven framework for understanding real-world usage patterns, offering a methodological contribution to user segmentation in Mobility-as-a-Service research. Contribution 5 proposes the VBSSLQR method, which efficiently performs variable selection in high-dimensional quantile regression by integrating the Spike-and-Slab Lasso prior with Variational Bayesian inference. This approach avoids the computational burden of MCMC sampling and non-convex optimization, enabling scalable and uncertainty-aware variable selection without relying on sub-Gaussian error assumptions. Contribution 6 provides a comprehensive survey on multi-source data repairing, systematically categorizing error types into entity overlapping, attribute conflicts, and value inconsistencies. By organizing existing methods into a unified taxonomy covering entity resolution, truth discovery, and inconsistency repair, this review establishes a clear methodological framework for the field. The survey further identifies key challenges in compound-error repair and semantic-aware detection, offering valuable guidance for future research in multi-source data quality management. Contribution 7 applies the concept of gradient descent to clustering problems to improve the effectiveness of clustering methods. A generic clustering objective function is proposed, enabling more intelligent updates of cluster centroids. To address the slow convergence of gradient descent, Nesterov momentum is incorporated. The method offers greater flexibility by allowing the use of any differentiable distance function in the clustering objective function. Contribution 8 addresses the challenge of efficiently classifying and managing the massive documents generated in educational reform by designing and implementing an automated classification system. After defining classification criteria, constructing a dataset, and preprocessing the data (including tokenization, stop word removal, and part-of-speech tagging), text features are extracted using the TF-IDF algorithm, and the Naïve Bayes algorithm is selected for classification. A software tool is developed to facilitate user interaction, visualizing the distribution proportion of document categories. Contribution 9 aims to eliminate 'water army' in e-commerce platform comment sections by combining TF-IDF and LSI models to identify water army based on behavioral and content features. The processed reviews are further analyzed using a TextCNN model for sentiment analysis, categorizing them as positive or negative. LDA topic modeling is then applied to analyze themes in both positive and negative reviews. Contribution 10 introduces spatial heterogeneity for large-scale crowd flow prediction by employing two fully connected networks to cluster spatial units into different types a posteriori and adaptively. Convolutional layers compress redundant information in historical crowd flow to extract shared patterns of clusters. The temporal evolution of these shared patterns is predicted, and they are mapped back to physical space to derive trend flows. The difference between trends and actual flows is learned to enhance prediction accuracy.

Looking ahead, future research should prioritize the integration of semantic awareness, cross-domain generalization, and uncertainty quantification in big data mining and analytics. Building on the advances in this Special Issue, key directions include the following: (1) developing unified frameworks for compound error repair that jointly resolve entity, attribute, and value inconsistencies using deep semantic representations; (2) designing adaptive spatiotemporal models that explicitly account for heterogeneous dynamics (e.g., in traffic, crowd flow, or air quality) through interpretable, physics-informed architectures; (3) advancing scalable Bayesian and optimization-based methods for high-dimensional data that provide reliable uncertainty estimates without restrictive distributional assumptions; and (4) creating knowledge-enhanced learning systems that seamlessly fuse structured knowledge bases with neural models for robust table understanding, text mining, and anomaly detection in real-world applications. Such efforts will bridge the gap between algorithmic innovation and practical deployment in complex, multi-source data ecosystems.

The Guest Editors extend their sincere appreciation to all of the authors for their valuable contributions to this Special Issue. We are also deeply grateful to the anonymous reviewers for their insightful and professional evaluation reports, which have significantly enhanced the quality of the submitted manuscripts. Furthermore, we acknowledge the excellent collaboration with the publisher, the constant assistance provided by the MDPI associate editors in bringing this project to the end, and the support of the Managing Editor of this Special Issue, Ms. Helene Hu.

Conflicts of Interest: The authors declare no conflicts of interest.

List of Contributions:

1. Cui, Z.; Huang, B.; Dou, H.; Cheng, Y.; Guan, J.; Zhou, T. A Two-Stage Hybrid Extreme Learning Model for Short-Term Traffic Flow Forecasting. *Mathematics* **2022**, *10*, 2087. https://doi.org/10.3390/math10122087.
2. Shih, D.; Hien, T.; Nguyen, L.; Wu, T.; Lai, Y. A Modified γ-Sutte Indicator for Air Quality Index Prediction. *Mathematics* **2022**, *10*, 3060. https://doi.org/10.3390/math10173060.
3. Wu, J.; Ye, C.; Zhi, H.; Jiang, S. Column-Type Prediction for Web Tables Powered by Knowledge Base and Text. *Mathematics* **2023**, *11*, 560. https://doi.org/10.3390/math11030560.
4. Mašek, J.; Štefancová, V.; Mazanec, J.; Juránková, P. The Classification of Application Users Supporting and Facilitating Travel Mobility Using Two-Step Cluster Analysis. *Mathematics* **2023**, *11*, 2192. https://doi.org/10.3390/math11092192.
5. Dai, D.; Tang, A.; Ye, J. High-Dimensional Variable Selection for Quantile Regression Based on Variational Bayesian Method. *Mathematics* **2023**, *11*, 2232. https://doi.org/10.3390/math11102232.
6. Ye, C.; Duan, H.; Zhang, H.; Zhang, H.; Wang, H.; Dai, G. Multi-Source Data Repairing: A Comprehensive Survey. *Mathematics* **2023**, *11*, 2314. https://doi.org/10.3390/math11102314.
7. Shalileh, S. An Effective Partitional Crisp Clustering Method Using Gradient Descent Approach. *Mathematics* **2023**, *11*, 2617. https://doi.org/10.3390/math11122617.
8. Zhang, P.; Ma, Z.; Ren, Z.; Wang, H.; Zhang, C.; Wan, Q.; Sun, D. Design of an Automatic Classification System for Educational Reform Documents Based on Naive Bayes Algorithm. *Mathematics* **2024**, *12*, 1127. https://doi.org/10.3390/math12081127.
9. Li, C.; Zhang, S.; Liu, X. A Study on the Identification of the Water Army to Improve the Helpfulness of Online Product Reviews. *Mathematics* **2024**, *12*, 3234. https://doi.org/10.3390/math12203234.
10. Tan, X.; Chen, K.; Deng, M.; Liu, B.; Zhao, Z.; Tu, Y.; Wu, S. SCS-Net: Stratified Compressive Sensing Network for Large-Scale Crowd Flow Prediction. *Mathematics* **2025**, *13*, 1686. https://doi.org/10.3390/math13101686.

mathematics MDPI

Article

A Two-Stage Hybrid Extreme Learning Model for Short-Term Traffic Flow Forecasting

Zhihan Cui [1], Boyu Huang [1], Haowen Dou [1], Yan Cheng [2], Jitian Guan [2] and Teng Zhou [1,3,*]

1 Department of Computer Science, Shantou University, Shantou 515063, China; 20zhcui@stu.edu.cn (Z.C.); 20byhuang@stu.edu.cn (B.H.); 20hwdou@stu.edu.cn (H.D.)
2 Medical College, Shantou University, Shantou 515063, China; 19ycheng@stu.edu.cn (Y.C.); jtguan@stu.edu.cn (J.G.)
3 Key Laboratory of Intelligent Manufacturing Technology, Ministry of Education, Shantou University, Shantou 515063, China
* Correspondence: zhouteng@stu.edu.cn

Abstract: Credible and accurate traffic flow forecasting is critical for deploying intelligent traffic management systems. Nevertheless, it remains challenging to develop a robust and efficient forecasting model due to the nonlinear characteristics and inherent stochastic traffic flow. Aiming at the nonlinear relationship in the traffic flow for different scenarios, we proposed a two-stage hybrid extreme learning model for short-term traffic flow forecasting. In the first stage, the particle swarm optimization algorithm is employed for determining the initial population distribution of the gravitational search algorithm to improve the efficiency of the global optimal value search. In the second stage, the results of the previous stage, rather than the network structure parameters randomly generated by the extreme learning machine, are used to train the hybrid forecasting model in a data-driven fashion. We evaluated the trained model on four real-world benchmark datasets from highways A1, A2, A4, and A8 connecting the Amsterdam ring road. The RMSEs of the proposed model are 288.03, 204.09, 220.52, and 163.92, respectively, and the MAPEs of the proposed model are 11.53%, 10.16%, 11.67%, and 12.02%, respectively. Experimental results demonstrate the superior performance of our proposed model.

Keywords: intelligent transportation system; traffic flow modeling; time series analysis; machine learning; noise-immune learning

MSC: 05C21

1. Introduction

A pivotal enabler for an intelligent transportation system is the forecasting of traffic flow in the short term [1]. Reliable traffic flow forecasting in real time is aiming to improve traffic operation efficiency and alleviate traffic congestion, which plays a foundational role in guidance implemented and traffic control [2]. An efficient response to traffic congestion can avoid more economic losses and save driving time [3]. Therefore, it has attracted great attention from commercial organizations, public institutions, and individual drivers [4]. However, traffic flow contains seasonality masked by noise and random behavior influenced by external factors, which makes accurate and reliable prediction still a challenging mission [5].

There are different stages of the evolution of traffic prediction methods. A series of models and theories have been constructed in the literature, which is usually roughly classified by time series models, dynamics models, and machine learning models. Random walk, historical average, autoregressive model, and its variants could be categorized as time series models. A simple yet powerful method for making accurate traffic flow forecasting is proposed based on a series of standard structures in traffic flow from the autoregressive integrated moving average (ARIMA) and its variants [6,7]. The Kalman filtering, which forecasts the continuous changing of the traffic flow by simulating the evolution of the traffic flow as a linear dynamic system, is the most typical dynamic mode [8,9]. Nevertheless, complex and nonlinear characteristics of traffic flow could not be handled efficiently by these two kinds of models due to their structure based on the stability assumption. Later, researchers have employed machine learning for forecasting traffic flow with complex and nonlinear features [10,11]. For instance, a k-nearest neighbor regression model based on sample-rebalanced outlier-rejected is developed for the prediction of traffic in the short term [12]. Cai et al. [13] demonstrated that there are more performance advantages of the support vector machine regression model optimized by the gravitational search algorithm than the original support vector machine in traffic flow forecasting. A noise-immune boosting framework was developed by Zheng et al. for forecasting short-term transportation flow [14]. Moreover, the search data-driven optimal models for traffic flow forecasting could be searched by evolutional algorithms [15,16].

In recent years, the popularity of deep learning has increased rapidly in capturing complex and nonlinear patterns in traffic [17–19]. In the early stage, when deep learning is introduced into traffic flow forecasting, stacked autoencoder (SAE) networks [20,21] and deep belief network (DBN) [22] are representative. Then, long short-term memory networks and recurrent neural networks have also been drawn into short-term traffic flow forecasting [23–25]. Luo et al. applied a graph convolution model to make use of the spatial correlation of traffic flow for forecasting [26]. On this foundation, a host of spatiotemporal prediction models is proposed for forecasting traffic in the short term [27–30].

All of the above deep learning models show their robust and significant performance for traffic flow prediction. Nevertheless, the deficiency and low-quality training data may cause these models to fall into local minimum [31,32]. All the network parameters are optimized iteratively based on the gradient descent algorithm according to the principle of empirical risk minimization in deep learning networks [19,33], which greatly improves the computational complexity. Furthermore, determining an optimal network for a tangible road network is based on corresponding expertise knowledge. That is to say, learning a network model f for the nonlinear mapping between the historical traffic flow X and the future traffic flow $\hat{X}$ is the goal of traffic flow forecasting, e.g., $\hat{X} = f(X)$. Nevertheless, the best performance for every dataset is laborious to realize on a single optimal model f^* unless consuming massive computing resources.

The potential of evolutionary algorithms to exploit a model's model is reconsidered to deal with these issues. A *meta* model $\mathcal{F}$ is the learning object of it, and the optimal forecasting model f^* could be obtained from the traffic flow data spontaneously, e.g., $f^* = \mathcal{F}(X, f)$.

In this paper, an uncomplicated but effective hybrid, which applies a data-driven fashion to determining a suitable traffic flow forecasting model, is proposed as an example. The combining PSO and GSA are used as a *meta* model in this example, and the ELM is a base forecasting model. Extreme learning machine (ELM) declared by Huang et al. [34] has been extensively employed for predicting short-term traffic flow with a fast learning rate and simple network structure. On the premise that the activation function of the hidden layer is infinitely differentiable, ELM ascertains the hidden layer biases and input weight by random initialization; then, it employs the Moore–Penrose (MP) generalized inverse for calculating the output weights matrices [33]. The special network structure of ELM could avert or improve some problems such as local minimum, stopping criterion, and learning rate, which are generated by gradient-based learning methods [35,36]. Nevertheless, it is momentous to calculate the optimal hidden layer biases and input weight in ELM [15]. An improper network parameter setting will lead to the problem of overfitting or a decline in forecasting accuracy.

To combat the problem, this article reformulates the extreme learning machine majorized by particle swarm optimization combing gravitational search algorithm, termed a PSOGSA-ELM hybrid model, for traffic flow prediction. During the fundamental idea of our model, a data-driven optimization task replaces the selection of the optimal combination for the hyperparameters of the ELM model, and then, the optimal solution for this task is obtained by a hybrid heuristic swarm intelligent algorithm.

Our contributions to this paper are summarized as shown below:

- We apply the perspective of a *meta* model to rethinking the amelioration of traffic flow forecasting models, with an example about a learning model optimized by a data-driven hybrid evolutionary algorithm.
- We establish a particle swarm optimization combining a gravitational search algorithm optimized extreme learning machine model for forecasting traffic flow in the short term.
- We demonstrate the practicability of our motivation of the data-driven *meta* model by sufficient experiments, whose results demonstrate the outperformance of the proposed model to state-of-the-art models.

The remaining sections of this article are organized as follows. Section 2 reviews the idea of a data-driven meta-model and demonstrates a hybrid extreme learning machine optimized by combining particle swarm optimization and gravitational search algorithm. Section 3 introduces the details of our empirical study on four base datasets gathered from the expressways of Amsterdam, Netherlands. The summary of our study is given in Section 4.

2. Methodology

In this section, an extreme learning machine is applied to establish the traffic flow forecasting model first. Then, particle swarm optimization is employed for determining the parameters of the gravitational search algorithm. Later, the resulting PSOGSA hybrid module is used to optimize the extreme learning machine.

2.1. Extreme Learning Machine

Gradient descent algorithm is applied to renew the parameters in the training process of traditional neural networks. This way, the output result of the neural network can gradually approach the expected one with a decrease in the sum of square errors. There are differences between the conventional feedforward neural network and the extreme learning machine, which is a machine learning algorithm based on a feedforward neural network with a single layer. In ELM, calculating the hidden layer parameters is the approach to determining the output weight, and the hidden layer is built stochastically. This network structure makes the algorithm have faster convergence speed and lower computational complexity, and it also has advantages in fitting ability and generalization performance compared with the traditional gradient-based learning algorithm [37,38]. The standard ELM three-layer structure is shown in Figure 1.

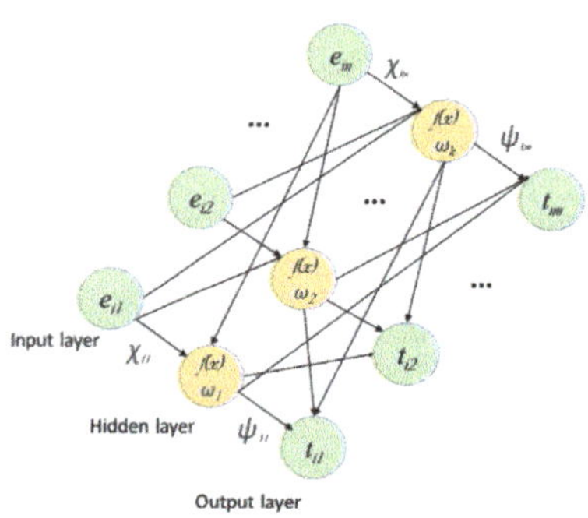

Figure 1. The number of hidden layers in extreme learning machine is only one with three parameters: hidden layer biases ω, input weight χ, and output weight t.

The detailed description of ELM traffic flow forecasting model is as follows. First, the traffic flow at the ath measurement location at the ith time interval could be assumed as $\mu_i^{(a)}$. Then, we employ $\{(e^{(i)}, t^{(i)})\}_{i=1}^{N}$ for representing N traffic flow training samples. After that, the traffic flow at the past and current $\nu - 1$ time interval is set as $e^{(i)} = [\mu_{i-\nu+1}^{(a)}, \ldots, \mu_i^{(a)}]_{a=1}^{A}$, in which A is the number of measurement locations and ν is the time lag. Later, the factual data of the i specimens for the traffic flow prediction model are represented by $f^{(i)} = [\mu_{i+1}^{(a)}]_{a=1}^{A}$. The feedforward neural network with a w_0 hidden nodes hidden layer is demonstrated as:

$$H\beta = T, \tag{1}$$

in which $H = (g_{ij})_{i=1,\ldots,N, j=1,\ldots,w_0}$ indicates the output matrix of the hidden layer. Among them, $g_{ij} = f(\chi_j^T e_i + \omega_j)$ denotes the output of the jth hidden node with regard to e_i. The input nodes and the jth hidden neuron could be linked by a weight vector $\chi_j = [\chi_{j1}, \chi_{j2}, \ldots, \chi_{jn}]^T$. ω_j represents the bias of the jth hidden neuron. The matrix of output weights is expressed as $\beta = [\beta_1, \beta_2, \ldots, \beta_{w_0}]^T$, and we can connect the output nodes and the corresponding jth hidden neuron by the weight vector $j = 1, \ldots, w_0$. To the right of the formula, the objective matrix is denoted as $T = [t_1, t_2, \ldots, t_N]^T$. The operating principle of ELM is to initialize the hidden deviation and input weight randomly. Then, a rational activation function is chosen to ascertain the matrix H. After that, by calculating the least-squares (LS) solution of the linear system, which plays a role in training the feedforward neural network, the output weight ψ could be calculated. The solution procedure is demonstrated as Equation (2).

$$\hat{\beta} = H^{\dagger} T, \tag{2}$$

in which $H^{\dagger}$ denotes the Moore–Penrose (MP) generalized inverse of matrix H.

2.2. Standard Gravitational Search Algorithm

Rashedi et al. [39] proposed a novel heuristic optimization algorithm based on Newtonian laws of gravity and law of motion. In gravitational search algorithm, mutual attraction occurs between all substances under the action of gravity force. Heavier substances that may be close to the global optimal value will make other substances move toward themselves because the heavier substances have greater attraction. Consequently, the solving process of the problem to be optimized is transformed into the process of finding heavier substances [40]. Assume that v substances are distributed in a d-dimensional exploitation space; then, Equation (3) represents the position of the xth substances.

$$\alpha_x = (\iota_x^1, \iota_x^2, \ldots, \iota_x^d, \ldots, \iota_x^v) \; for \; x = 1, 2, \ldots, v, \tag{3}$$

where α_x^d is the location of the xth substances in the d-dimensional space. The xth substance is gravitated by the yth substance at the t_0th iteration, as shown in Equation (4).

$$F_{xy}^d(t_0) = G(t_0)\frac{M_y(t_0) \times M_x(t_0)}{Z_{xy}(t_0) + \delta}(\iota_y^d(t_0) - \iota_x^d(t_0)), \tag{4}$$

in which $M_x(t_0)$ is the inertial masses of the substance x which is affected by gravity, and the force producing substance y is represented as $M_y(t_0)$. δ denotes a tiny appropriate constant and the Euclidian distance between substance x and substance y is $Z_{xy}(t_0)$. $G(t) = G_0 e^{-\zeta(\frac{t_0}{S})}$ represents a gravity constant which gradually decreases during the iteration process, and it is also the controller of the optimized accuracy process. S represents the total iterations, ζ denotes the manually adjusted constant, and the initial value of G_s is G_0. The total gravity acting on the xth substance is the stochastic weighted sum of the force applied from another substance in the dth dimension.

$$F_{xy}^{d}(t_0) = \sum_{y=1, y \neq x}^{v} rand_y F_{xy}^{d}(t_0), \tag{5}$$

where $rand_y \in (0,1)$ denotes a stochastic value employed for increasing the stochastic features of GSA. A global search tactic on the solution space is applied to keep the GSA from sinking into the local minima at the beginning of the optimization process. Then, the global exploitation fades out and local exploitation fades in with the running of the algorithm.

In the process of standardizing exploration and exploitation, the optimization ability of GSA could be improved. After that, the number of the agent is decreased to maintain the balance of exploitation and exploration. Other substances are subjected to gravity from a group of substances with larger mass (λ_{best} corresponding optimal solution) [39]. Equation (6) could strengthen the performance of GSA, whereas by the time function, λ_{best} decreases with the increase of the number of iterations.

$$F_{xy}^{d}(t_0) = \sum_{y \neq x, y \in \lambda_{best}}^{v} rand_y F_{xy}^{d}(t_0). \tag{6}$$

The acceleration of substance x at time t_0 in the d-dimension is shown as Equation (7) based on Newton's second theorem.

$$a_x^d(t_0) = \frac{F_x^d(t_0)}{M_x(t_0)}, \tag{7}$$

where $M_x(t_0)$ is the inertial mass of the xth substance. The velocity and direction of the substance are regulated by the acceleration function. The velocity and position of the substance is updated under the guidance of Equations (8) and (9) in every iteration.

$$v_x^d(t_0+1) = rand_x \times v_x^d(t_0) + a_x^d(t_0), \tag{8}$$

$$\iota_x^d(t_0+1) = \iota_x^d(t_0) + v_x^d(t_0+1). \tag{9}$$

In Equation (9), the position and speed of the substance at the t_0th iteration is denoted as $v_x^d(t_0)$ and $\iota_x^d(t_0)$. Then, we can calculate the inertia mass according to the size of the fitness value. The distance between the substance and the optimal value decreases with the increase of its inertial mass, which demonstrates that the attraction of the substance is inversely proportional to its moving velocity. Later, the inertial mass of the substance is updated as following:

$$m_x(t_0) = \frac{fit_x(t_0) - worst(t_0)}{best(t_0) - worst(t_0)}, \tag{10}$$

$$M_x(t_0) = \frac{m_x(t_0)}{\sum_{y=1}^{v} m_x(t_0)}, \tag{11}$$

in which

$$worst(t_0) = \max_{x \in 1,2,\ldots v} fit_x(t_0), \tag{12}$$

$$best(t_0) = \min_{x \in 1,2,\ldots v} fit_x(t_0), \tag{13}$$

and where $fit_x(t_0)$ denotes the fitness value of the xth substances at time t_0.

2.3. Standard Particle Swarm Optimization

According to the observation of the social behavior of biological organisms, Kennedy and Eberhart propose an evolutionary computation algorithm termed particle swarm optimization (PSO) [41]. PSO explores the best solution in the specified search space through free-flying particles. These particles could be regarded as candidate solutions, and seeking the best particle in the path is the process of seeking the best solution. That is to say, the best solution found so far has the same performance as the independent solution of each particle.

In D-dimensional space, a population composed of N_0 particles can be assumed as $P = (P_1, P_2, \ldots, P_{n0})$, in which the lth particle is denoted as a D-dimensional vector $P_l = [p_{l1}, p_{l2}, \ldots, p_{lD}]^T$. The advantages and disadvantages of the current position can be determined according to the calculation results of the fitness value corresponding to the particle position P_l, based on the objective function. There is a speed representing the direction and the distance of each particle. $\rho = [\rho_{l1}, \rho_{l2}, \ldots, \rho_{lD}]^T$ denotes the speed of the lth particle. The position and speed of the particles are updated in each iteration of the PSO, as shown in the following:

$$\rho_{ld}^{g+1} = \phi \rho_{ld}^{g} + w_1 \kappa_1 (q_d^v - p_{ld}^v), \tag{14}$$

$$p_{ld}^{g+1} = p_{ld}^{g} + \rho_{ld}^{g+1}, \tag{15}$$

in which $Q = [q_1, q_2, \ldots, q_D]^T$ is the global best position of colony and $Q_l = [q_{l1}, q_{l2}, \ldots, q_{lD}]^T$ is the individual best position of the ith particle. The inertia weight is ϕ and the number of hidden layer nodes is g. w_1 and w_2 are employed for representing the factors of learning. The range of the speed is denoted as $[v_{0min}, v_{0max}]$ and terms κ_1 and κ_2 are stochastically ascertained in range U(0,1).

2.4. ELM Optimization Learning Based on Data Driven

The installation of the ELM network structure has a non-negligible influence on the forecasting accuracy of the traffic flow model. In this article, we employ PSO instead of the original random method for generating the initial population of GSA, to improve its performance. Then, the hybrid evolutionary algorithm is employed for completing the data-driven optimization tasks, which are transformed from a selection of input weight and hidden layer threshold in ELM. Figure 2 demonstrates the workflow of the obtained data-driven traffic flow forecasting model, which is termed the PSOGSA-ELM model.

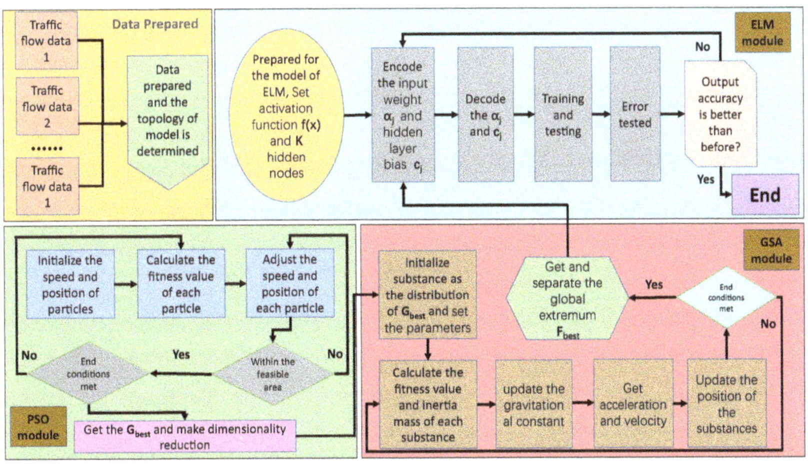

Figure 2. The network structure of the proposed PSOGSA-ELM.

3. Experiments

3.1. Data Description

In this section, four benchmark traffic datasets are employed for appraising the PSOGSA-ELM model. Wang et al. [42] collect these datasets from four freeways A1, A2, A4, and A8, which end at Amsterdam A10 Ring Road. MONICA loop detectors are employed for collecting these datasets from 20 May to 24 June 2010, and the detection location is demonstrated in Figure 3.

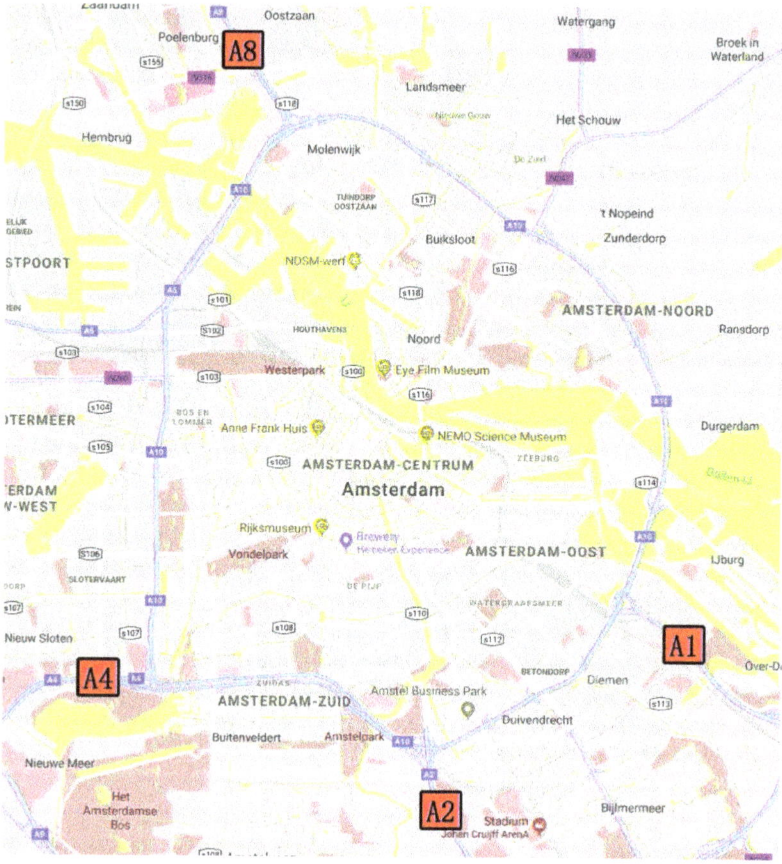

Figure 3. Base road conditions of A1, A2, A4, and A8 highways in Amsterdam.

The raw traffic flow data are summarized by rolling stocks every hour per minute, which consists of five weeks. The following is the fundamental message of the four motorways.

- The A1 freeway is an extremely significant route in Europe whose extraordinary position is the link between the German border and Amsterdam. The first 3+ barrier-separated lanes with high-occupancy vehicle (HOV) in Europe is located on the A1 freeway. Therefore, forecasting traffic flow accurately is thrown down the gauntlet because the flow on an HOV vehicle lane changes dramatically over time.
- The A2 expressway links the Belgian border and the city of Amsterdam, which is one of the expressways with the highest traffic flow in the Netherlands. The data collected before the road widening in 2010 could be employed for evaluating the performance of the proposed framework when the road falls into traffic congestion in our research.
- As a section of the Rijksweg 4, the A4 expressway in the Netherlands is another high priority, starting from Amsterdam and ending at the Belgian border.
- A8 is the shortest of the four freeways, starting from the A10 motorway at interchange Coenplein to the Zaandijk, and the total length is less than 10 km.

Li et al. [43] proposed a statistical learning method, which is applied for correcting and complementing the missing values in the original data collected by the detector.

3.2. Evaluation Criterion

In this article, two frequently used criteria are applied to test the forecasting performance. The root means square error (RMSE) demonstrates the average difference between the predictive value and the measured value. The mean absolute percentage error (MAPE) calculates the percentage of the differences. The mathematical definitions of the two criteria are shown in Equations (16) and (17), respectively.

$$\text{RMSE} = \sqrt{\frac{1}{P_0}\sum_{p_0=1}^{P_0}(\hat{u}(p_0) - u(p_0))^2}, \tag{16}$$

$$\text{MAPE} = \frac{1}{P_0}\sum_{p_0=1}^{P_0}\left|\frac{\hat{u}(p_0) - u(p_0)}{u(p_0)}\right| \times 100\%, \tag{17}$$

where $\hat{u}(p_0)$ and $u(p_0)$ denote the predictive value and the measured value of the p_0th sample.

3.3. Performance Evaluation

To assess the prediction performance of PSOGSA-ELM, we compare the proposed model with some traffic flow models which are commonly applied in the intelligent transportation system.

Historical average (HA): HA is employed for forecasting the average of the identical time on an identical day in the weeks before a given time in a day.

Exponential smoothing (ES): Exponential smoothing (ES) is a particular weighted moving average method (MA), which is an important category of time series analysis and prediction methods [44]. The forecasted values during the observation period are further affected by the recently observed values due to the unequal weights given by the observed values at various times. To mirror the flatness of the trend change, we employ the double exponential smoothing method for setting parameter α_0 in the model to 0.4.

Artificial neural network (ANN): ANN is a kind of nonparametric learning model with a single hidden layer neural network structure. According to the network parameters criteria in [45], we set the MSE target value as 0.001, the maximum number of neurons as 40, the number of hidden layers as 1, and the expansion speed of the radial basis function as 2000. Based on the default value, 25 neurons are set to add between displays.

Decision trees (DTs): The DT model, which is based on the classification and regression tree (CART), is employed for forecasting traffic flows in our experiment. In CART, the robustness against missing data and noise is strong, and the prior hypothesis is not necessary. The detailed knowledge about CART is in [46].

Autoregression (AR): The AR has been widely applied to forecasting traffic flow as a linear regression model. In AR, the linear combination of stochastic variables at a previous moment is employed for describing the random variables at a later moment, and then, the randomness of traffic flow could be handled effectively. We set the parameter $\hat{p}$ from 0 to 8 according to the suggestion in [20].

Seasonal autoregressive integrated moving average (SARIMA): In the data collected regularly, there are usually sequential lag relationships, whose correlation could be further excavated and applied by the SARIMA model for forecasting the traffic flow [35]. We set the parameters of the model as SARIMA$(1,0,1) \times (0,1,1)_{1008}$, $\phi_0 = 0.8$, $\theta_0 = 0.4$, $\Theta_0 = 0.8$.

Support vector machine regression (SVR): The detailed description of SVR is in [20]. In our experiment, the kernel function of the SVR model is selected as the radial basis function (RBF). The maximum difference between traffic flow determines the cost parameter $\hat{C}$, in which the regression horizon is set to 8.

To prove the optimized capability of the hybrid data-driven model, the ELM optimized by genetic algorithm (GA-ELM) and the standard extreme learning machine is compared with the proposed model. Since substances are randomly distributed in GA and hybrid

PSOGSA, each run will generate different results. Therefore, the outcomes of 100 runs are regarded as the outcomes on every benchmark dataset for the GA-ELM model and the PSOGSA-ELM model in this comparative experiment.

We can find in Tables 1 and 2 that the PSOGSA-ELM has remarkable advantages in forecasting the performance of all four benchmark datasets.

Table 1. The RMSE (vehs/h) of different forecasting models on datasets collected from A1, A2, A4, and A8, respectively.

Model	A1	A2	A4	A8
HA	404.84	348.96	357.85	218.72
ES	315.82	226.40	237.76	174.67
ANN	299.64	212.95	225.86	166.50
DT	316.57	224.79	243.19	238.35
AR	301.44	214.22	226.12	166.71
SARIMA	308.44	221.08	228.36	169.36
SVR	329.09	259.74	253.66	190.30
ELM	300.67	208.84	224.54	172.69
GA-ELM	291.42	211.43	228.57	169.25
PSOGSA-ELM	**288.03**	**204.09**	**220.52**	**163.92**

Table 2. The MAPE (%) of different forecasting models on datasets collected from A1, A2, A4, and A8, respectively.

Model	A1	A2	A4	A8
HA	16.87	15.53	16.72	16.24
ES	11.94	10.75	11.97	12.00
ANN	12.61	10.89	12.49	12.53
DT	12.08	10.86	12.34	13.62
AR	13.57	11.59	12.70	12.71
SARIMA	12.81	11.25	12.05	12.44
SVR	14.34	12.22	12.23	12.48
ELM	11.92	10.32	12.09	12.58
GA-ELM	11.86	10.30	11.87	12.26
PSOGSA-ELM	**11.53**	**10.16**	**11.67**	**12.02**

As shown in Table 1, the RMSEs of proposed model are 12.48%, 21.42%, 13.06%, and 13.86% lower than the RMSEs of SVR at A1, A2, A4, and A8, respectively. The RMSEs of the proposed model are 8.80%, 9.85%, 7.25%, and 6.15% lower than the RMSEs of ES at A1, A2, A4, and A8, respectively. The RMSEs of the proposed model are 3.87%, 4.16%, 2.36%, and 1.55% lower than the RMSEs of ANN, at A1, A2, A4, and A8, respectively. As shown in Table 2, the MAPEs of the proposed model are 8.82%, 8.89%, 3.15%, and 3.38% lower than the MAPEs of SARIMA at A1, A2, A4, and A8, respectively. The MAPEs of the proposed model are 3.27%, 1.55%, 3.47%, and 4.45% lower than the MAPEs of standard ELM at A1, A2, A4, and A8, respectively. The MAPEs of the proposed model are 2.78%, 1.36%, 1.68%, and 1.96% lower than the MAPEs of GA-ELM at A1, A2, A4, and A8, respectively.

Then, Akaike Information Criterion (AIC) is introduced into our experiment, as demonstrated in Table 3.

Table 3. Comparative experiment on AICc.

Model	A1	A2	A4	A8
ELM	15.429	15.544	15.168	14.267
GA-ELM	15.416	15.522	15.136	14.161
PSOGSA-ELM	**15.325**	**15.430**	**15.055**	**14.156**

AIC includes both simplicity and accuracy as references while evaluating the performance of different models [47,48]. In Table 3, we discover that the AIC of the PSOGSA-ELM model is the smallest of the three models related to ELM. That is to say, our proposed model performs better in terms of accuracy and simplicity.

In Figure 4a–d, the deviation between the short-term traffic flow predicted values of the model and the practical measured values are visualized intuitively. The purple lines demonstrate the measured values, whereas the green lines represent the predicted values. The errors between the predicted value and measured value divided by the ground truth, termed the relative error of the model, are plotted with a black line. In Figure 4, we can find the related errors calculated by experiments approached 0 most of the time, which proved the outstanding performance of the PSOGSA-ELM model in the scenes of A1, A2, A4, and A8.

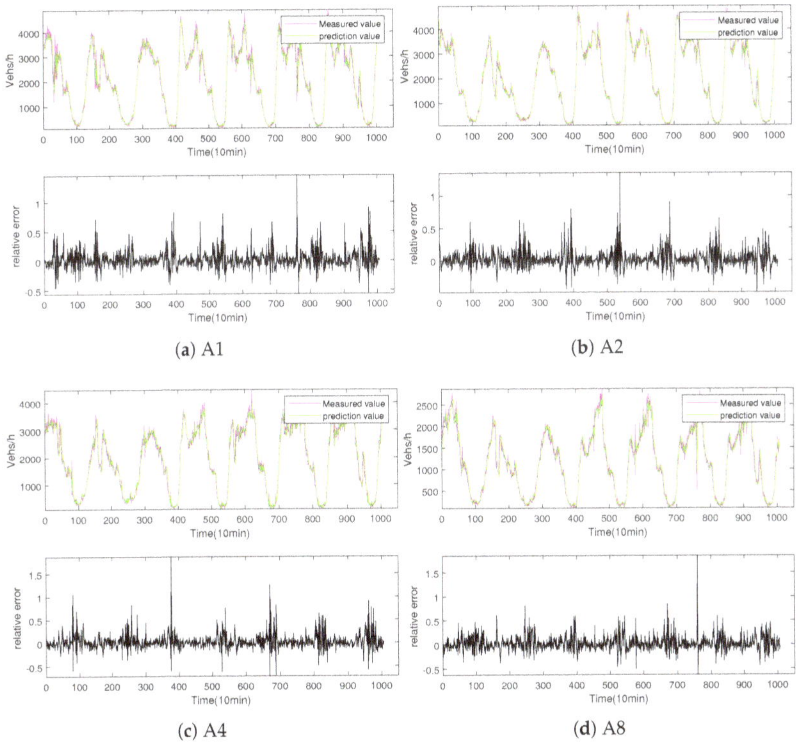

Figure 4. (**a–d**) show the predicted values of the PSOGSA-ELM model, the measured values in a week, and the forecasting related error, respectively.

In addition, an evaluation index dedicated to traffic flow forecasting, termed GEH statistics [49–51], is also employed for analyzing the results. Table 4 lists the GEH statistics value of the prediction outcomes of proposed models on four base datasets.

Table 4. GEH statistics of the GSA-ELM model.

Dataset	A1	A2	A4	A8
GEH	6.13	4.48	4.88	4.81

In Table 4, we can find that the GEH of the prediction results for most benchmark datasets is less than 5. On the A1 dataset, the value of GEH is 6.12, which is probably because the A1 dataset has stronger volatility than the other three datasets. The fitting performance of the model is in good accordance with the evaluation standard of GEH.

3.4. Ablation Study

The fluctuation of traffic flow over a continuous time rather than minute-to-minute fluctuation is the object of traffic flow forecasting study [21,42]. Consequently, we regard the traffic flow data aggregation of a 1-min average in the subsequent 10 min as the 10-min data and employ it for forecasting tasks. The original data made of 5 weeks of measurement is classified as a training set and testing set in our experiment. The training set includes the samples in the first four weeks and the testing set consists of the samples in the fifth week, whereas the number of samples measured every week is 1008. The time interval is stipulated as 8 and hidden layer nodes of ELM are set to 30. On this basis, we apply the classical sigmoid function as the activation function. The specific parameter settings of PSO and GSA are shown in Table 5. MAPE and RMSE are employed for evaluating the optimization performance of PSOGSA. The trend for the forecasting performance corresponding to the number of algorithm iterations is demonstrated in Figure 5. In Table 5, it obvious that the values of RMSE and MAPE both tend to smooth when the number of iterations is more than 80, which testifies to the rationality of setting the maximum number of iterations of the GSA module as 100.

Table 5. The parameters setting of GSA module and PSO.

Algorithm	Paramater	Value
PSO	Range of inertia weights	[0.4,0.9]
	Number of particles	40
	$c1$	1.7
	$c2$	1.3
	Maximum Iterations	150
GSA	Population size	300
	G_0	100
	v	20
	Maximum Iterations	100

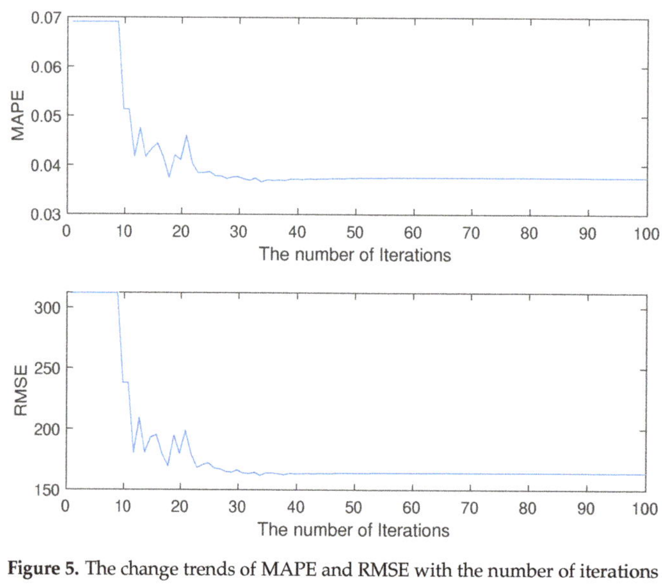

Figure 5. The change trends of MAPE and RMSE with the number of iterations of GSA.

For evaluating the ability of PSOGSA to optimize ELM network structure parameters based on data-driven methods, we introduce a genetic algorithm (GA), which is a popular optimization algorithm, to our comparative experiment. The non-specific parameters of GA are set to be the same as PSOGSA for a fair comparison. The number of iterations of GA is also stipulated as 100, whereas the variation probability is 0.03, the generation gap is 0.95 and the crossover probability is 0.85. Detailed information on the genetic algorithm optimized ELM (GA-ELM) is shown in [52]. As two characteristic periods, the morning peak and afternoon peak are chosen for evaluating the optimization performance of PSOGSA and GA in determining the parameter of ELM. Among them, the time interval from 7:30 to 9:30 represents the morning peak and that from 13:30 to 14:30 represents the afternoon peak. Tables 6 and 7 demonstrate the forecasting performances of three types of models during the morning and afternoon high peak periods, respectively.

Table 6. The forecasting performance during the morning peak period while optimizing ELM with different optimization algorithms.

The Morning Peak Period	Groundtruth	ELM	Prediction GA-ELM	PSOGSA-ELM
6/11/7:30	3546	3274.033	3270.369	3392.933
6/11/8:30	3792	3700.290	3724.208	3756.983
6/11/9:30	4184	3691.265	3734.778	3801.143
6/14/7:30	2670	2641.334	2662.170	2649.311
6/14/8:30	3116	2934.568	2957.073	2976.761
6/14/9:30	3094	3005.691	3023.728	3033.094
6/15/7:30	2817	2999.734	3012.434	2920.417
6/15/8:30	2893	2846.403	2808.657	2807.973
6/15/9:30	3154	3225.806	3200.339	3239.240
RMSE		217.03	206.39	**164.44**
MAPE		5.01	4.69	**3.76**

Table 7. The forecasting performance during the afternoon peak period while optimizing ELM with different optimization algorithms.

The Afternoon Peak Period	Groundtruth	ELM	Prediction GA-ELM	PSOGSA-ELM
6/11/13:30	3948	3957.867	3973.349	3956.204
6/11/14:00	4373	4179.630	4437.895	44,407.233
6/11/14:30	3542	3976.427	4030.626	3968.726
6/14/13:30	3817	3369.284	3346.841	3376.680
6/14/14:00	4135	3734.672	3744.345	3812.346
6/14/14:30	4197	4261.105	4384.840	4272.334
6/15/13:30	3732	3394.333	3430.046	3431.599
6/15/14:00	4032	3818.189	3842.358	3827.597
6/15/14:30	4549	3895.383	3947.706	3908.953
RMSE		361.78	356.10	**338.08**
MAPE		7.62	7.57	**6.82**

In Figures 6 and 7, the forecasting error, which is the absolute value of the measurement minus the forecasting, is shown in two categories: the morning and the afternoon rush hour, respectively. Tables 6 and 7 demonstrate that the RMSE and MAPE of the PSOGSA-ELM model are lower than the other comparable models in these periods. In Figures 6 and 7, the PSOGSA-ELM model realizes a lower forecasting error than other comparison models in different scenarios. Thus, the network structure of the ELM model could be optimized by hybrid PSOGSA better than GA during the high peak period in the morning and afternoon. Moreover, we also consider the traffic flow in a low traffic period. Midnight in the morning, covering the period from 23:30 to 00:30 is considered the low traffic period in our experiment. During this time, the violent fluctuation of RMSE could be caused by a small forecasting error.

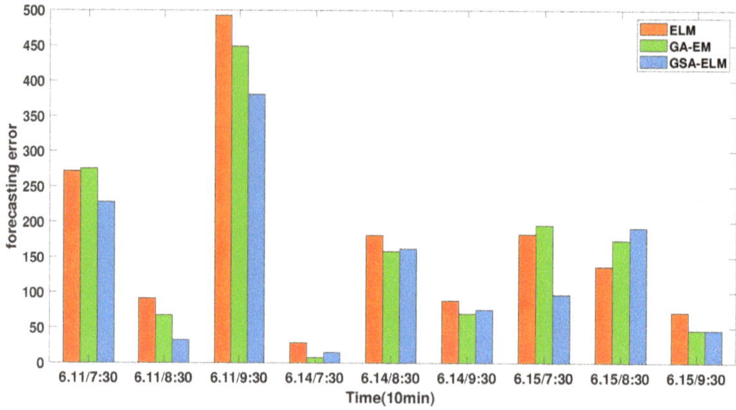

Figure 6. The forecasting errors during the morning peak period while optimizing ELM with different optimization algorithms.

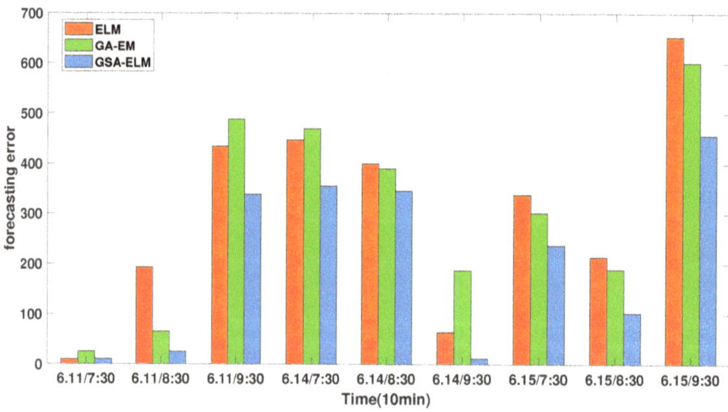

Figure 7. The forecasting errors during the afternoon peak period while optimizing ELM with different optimization algorithms.

When the traffic flow is low at midnight, the prediction results from ELM optimized by different algorithms are shown in Table 8. Figure 8 shows the forecasting errors of three models during this period, which illustrates that PSOGSA is better than the genetic algorithm in determining the network parameters of ELM. Consequently, the optimization performance for the ELM of hybrid PSOGSA is better than GA under different traffic flow situations. To further reduce the stochasticity of the prediction performances, the traffic flow in more diversified periods is employed for a comparative experiment of several models, as shown in Figure 9.

Table 8. The forecasting performance during the low traffic period at midnight while optimizing ELM with different optimization algorithms.

The Midnight Period	Ground Truth	ELM	Prediction GA-ELM	PSOGSA-ELM
6/11/23:30	297	235.481	238.125	238.980
6/12/00:00	243	236.766	233.857	241.629
6/12/00:30	229	337.797	313.061	309.774
6/12/23:30	297	264.544	247.249	259.573
6/13/00:00	192	232.681	243.316	212.192
6/13/00:30	426	402.075	342.899	374.851
6/13/23:30	241	246.560	236.844	236.777
6/14/00:00	187	336.153	323.598	261.377
6/14/00:30	284	368.125	335.396	316.246
RMSE		73.25	69.88	**48.20**
MAPE		24.47	24.02	**15.93**

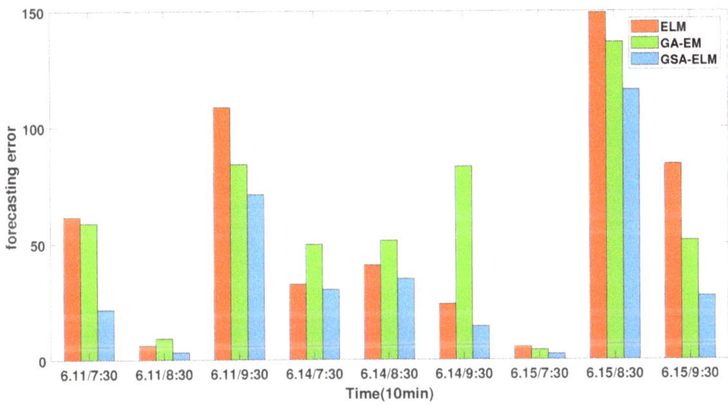

Figure 8. The forecasting errors during the low traffic period at midnight while optimizing ELM with different optimization algorithms.

To assess the comprehensive performance of the hybrid model proposed in this article, ELM, GA-ELM, and PSOGSA-ELM are selected for a comparative experiment about running time. In Table 9, we can find that the running time of ELM is the fastest of the three due to its random parameter generation process. Nevertheless, the target of the data-driven model, minimizing the forecasting error, could hardly be realized by randomly generated parameters. Meanwhile, on the basis of determining the parameters reasonably of the forecasting model, PSOGSA-ELM still maintains a low running time, which is lower than GA-ELM. The training of the proposed model costs about 83 seconds in our experiments on the benchmark dataset. Fortunately, we only need to train the model one time. The forecasting time of the proposed model is the same as the general extreme learning machine, i.e., less than 0.1 second. The parameters of the proposed model are automatically optimized in a data-driven fashion, and the only required input is traffic flow data. Therefore, the algorithm can be effectively applied to other traffic scenes at different locations without human interaction.

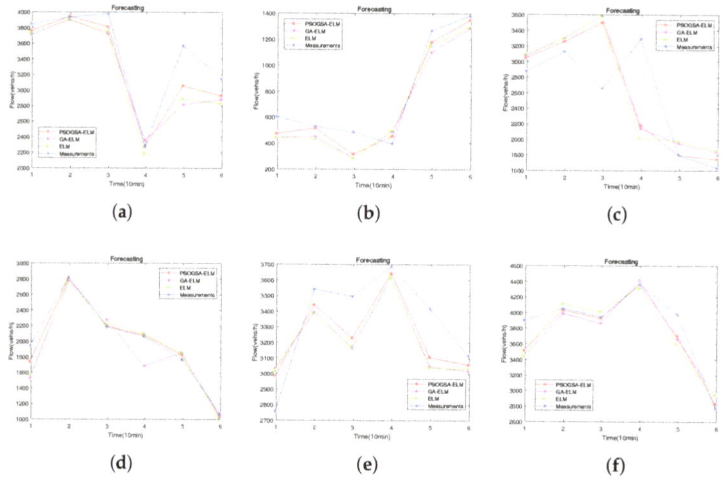

Figure 9. Under the conditions of large traffic flow fluctuations, the forecasting performance of different algorithms optimized ELM is shown as (**a**–**f**).

Table 9. The computational time of ELM, GA-ELM, and GSA-ELM.

Model	Computational Time (s)
ELM	0.0516
GA-ELM	100.2139
PSOGSA-ELM	83.8456

With accurate predicted future traffic flow, the policymakers can adjust the time slice of the traffic lights to make perspective traffic management based on the future traffic flow for effective leverage of the road resources. The policymakers can also adjust the driving rules to control the traffic on the road network to optimize the allocation and management of road resources. Moreover, the spreading of the future traffic flow by public media can also induce vehicles to choose alternative ways spontaneously to improve the traffic conditions.

4. Conclusions

In this paper, we develop a two-stage data-driven hybrid extreme learning model for short-term traffic flow forecasting. Comparative experiments on the trained model show that the RMSEs of the proposed model are 3.87%, 4.16%, 2.36%, and 1.55% lower than the RMSEs of the state-of-the-art model, at four benchmark datasets, respectively. The MAPEs of the proposed model are 2.78%, 1.36%, 1.68%, and 1.96% lower than the MAPEs of the state-of-the-art model at four benchmark datasets, respectively. Consequently, the experimental results demonstrate the model can automatically determine the optimal hyperparameters of the extreme learning machine in a data-driven fashion. Since the hyperparameters of the model are optimized automatically in a data-driven manner, the model can be conveniently deployed to different intelligent traffic systems without human intervention. In the future, we will improve forecasting accuracy by spatiotemporal learning on other models.

Author Contributions: Conceptualization, T.Z. and Z.C.; Data curation, Y.C.; Formal analysis, H.D. and J.G.; Funding acquisition, T.Z.; Investigation, J.G. and B.H.; Methodology, Z.C.; Project administration, T.Z. and J.G.; Supervision, Y.C.; Validation, B.H. and Y.C.; Visualization, H.D.; Writing—original draft, Z.C. and B.H.; Z.C., B.H. and H.D. contribute equally. All authors have read and agreed to the published version of the manuscript.

Funding: This work was supported by the National Natural Science Foundation of China (No. 61902232), the 2022 Guangdong Basic and Applied Basic Research Foundation (No. 2022A1515011590), the STU Incubation Project for the Research of Digital Humanities and New Liberal Arts (No. 2021DH-3), and the 2020 Li Ka Shing Foundation Cross-Disciplinary Research Grant (No. 2020LKSFG05D).

Institutional Review Board Statement: Not applicable.

Informed Consent Statement: Not applicable.

Data Availability Statement: The data that support the findings of this study are available from the corresponding author upon reasonable request.

Conflicts of Interest: The authors declare no conflict of interest.

References

1. Cai, L.; Lei, M.; Zhang, S.; Yu, Y.; Zhou, T.; Qin, J. A noise-immune lstm network for short-term traffic flow forecasting. *Chaos Interdiscip. J. Nonlinear Sci.* **2020**, *30*, 023135. [CrossRef] [PubMed]
2. Olayode, I.O.; Tartibu, L.K.; Okwu, M.O.; Ukaegbu, U.F. Development of a hybrid artificial neural network-particle swarm optimization model for the modelling of traffic flow of vehicles at signalized road intersections. *Appl. Sci.* **2021**, *11*, 8387. [CrossRef]
3. Li, Z.; Cao, Q.; Zhao, Y.; Zhuo, R. Signal cooperative control with traffic supply and demand on a single intersection. *IEEE Access* **2018**, *6*, 54407–54416.
4. Li, Z.; Cao, Q.; Zhao, Y.; Tao, P.; Zhuo, R. Krill herd algorithm for signal optimization of cooperative control with traffic supply and demand. *IEEE Access* **2019**, *7*, 10776–10786.
5. Chen, L.; Yang, D.; Zhang, D.; Wang, C.; Li, J. Deep mobile traffic forecast and complementary base station clustering for C-RAN optimization. *J. Netw. Comput. Appl.* **2018**, *121*, 59–69. [CrossRef]
6. Ahmed, M.S.; Cook, A.R. *Analysis of Freeway Traffic Time-Series Data by Using Box-Jenkins Techniques*; Number 722; 1979. Available online: https://trid.trb.org/view/148123 (accessed on 9 May 2022).
7. Yang, H.; Li, X.; Qiang, W.; Zhao, Y.; Zhang, W.; Tang, C. A network traffic forecasting method based on SA optimized ARIMA–BP neural network. *Comput. Netw.* **2021**, *193*, 108102. [CrossRef]
8. Cai, L.; Zhang, Z.; Yang, J.; Yu, Y.; Zhou, T.; Qin, J. A noise-immune Kalman filter for short-term traffic flow forecasting. *Phys. A Stat. Mech. Appl.* **2019**, *536*, 122601. [CrossRef]
9. Zhou, T.; Jiang, D.; Lin, Z.; Han, G.; Xu, X.; Qin, J. Hybrid dual Kalman filtering model for short-term traffic flow forecasting. *IET Intell. Transp. Syst.* **2019**, *13*, 1023–1032. [CrossRef]
10. Olayode, I.O.; Tartibu, L.K.; Okwu, M.O. Prediction and modeling of traffic flow of human-driven vehicles at a signalized road intersection using artificial neural network model: A South African road transportation system scenario. *Transp. Eng.* **2021**, *6*, 100095. [CrossRef]
11. Olayode, I.O.; Severino, A.; Campisi, T.; Tartibu, L.K. Prediction of Vehicular Traffic Flow using Levenberg-Marquardt Artificial Neural Network Model: Italy Road Transportation System. *Commun.-Sci. Lett. Univ. Zilina* **2022**, *24*, E74–E86. [CrossRef]
12. Cai, L.; Yu, Y.; Zhang, S.; Song, Y.; Xiong, Z.; Zhou, T. A sample-rebalanced outlier-rejected k-nearest neighbor regression model for short-term traffic flow forecasting. *IEEE Access* **2020**, *8*, 22686–22696. [CrossRef]
13. Cai, L.; Chen, Q.; Cai, W.; Xu, X.; Zhou, T.; Qin, J. SVRGSA: A hybrid learning based model for short-term traffic flow forecasting. *IET Intell. Transp. Syst.* **2019**, *13*, 1348–1355. [CrossRef]
14. Zheng, S.; Zhang, S.; Song, Y.; Lin, Z.; Jiang, D.; Zhou, T. A noise-immune boosting framework for short-term traffic flow forecasting. *Complexity* **2021**, *2021*, 5582974. [CrossRef]
15. Cai, W.; Yang, J.; Yu, Y.; Song, Y.; Zhou, T.; Qin, J. PSO-ELM: A hybrid learning model for short-term traffic flow forecasting. *IEEE Access* **2020**, *8*, 6505–6514. [CrossRef]
16. Cui, Z.; Huang, B.; Dou, H.; Tan, G.; Zheng, S.; Zhou, T. GSA-ELM: A hybrid learning model for short-term traffic flow forecasting. *IET Intell. Transp. Syst.* **2022**, *16*, 41–52. [CrossRef]
17. Hu, X.; Xu, X.; Xiao, Y.; Chen, H.; He, S.; Qin, J.; Heng, P.A. SINet: A scale-insensitive convolutional neural network for fast vehicle detection. *IEEE Trans. Intell. Transp. Syst.* **2018**, *20*, 1010–1019. [CrossRef]
18. Xu, X.; Yu, T.; Hu, X.; Ng, W.W.; Heng, P.A. SALMNet: A structure-aware lane marking detection network. *IEEE Trans. Intell. Transp. Syst.* **2020**, *22*, 4986–4997. [CrossRef]
19. Li, L.; Lin, Y.; Du, B.; Yang, F.; Ran, B. Real-time traffic incident detection based on a hybrid deep learning model. *Transp. A Transp. Sci.* **2022**, *18*, 78–98. [CrossRef]
20. Zhou, T.; Han, G.; Xu, X.; Lin, Z.; Han, C.; Huang, Y.; Qin, J. δ-agree AdaBoost stacked autoencoder for short-term traffic flow forecasting. *Neurocomputing* **2017**, *247*, 31–38. [CrossRef]
21. Zhou, T.; Han, G.; Xu, X.; Han, C.; Huang, Y.; Qin, J. A learning-based multimodel integrated framework for dynamic traffic flow forecasting. *Neural Process. Lett.* **2019**, *49*, 407–430. [CrossRef]
22. Li, L.; Qin, L.; Qu, X.; Zhang, J.; Wang, Y.; Ran, B. Day-ahead traffic flow forecasting based on a deep belief network optimized by the multi-objective particle swarm algorithm. *Knowl.-Based Syst.* **2019**, *172*, 1–14. [CrossRef]

23. Qu, Z.; Li, H.; Li, Z.; Zhong, T. Short-term traffic flow forecasting method with MB-LSTM hybrid network. *IEEE Trans. Intell. Transp. Syst.* **2020**, *23*, 225–235.
24. Lu, H.; Ge, Z.; Song, Y.; Jiang, D.; Zhou, T.; Qin, J. A temporal-aware lstm enhanced by loss-switch mechanism for traffic flow forecasting. *Neurocomputing* **2021**, *427*, 169–178. [CrossRef]
25. Fang, W.; Zhuo, W.; Yan, J.; Song, Y.; Jiang, D.; Zhou, T. Attention meets long short-term memory: A deep learning network for traffic flow forecasting. *Phys. A Stat. Mech. Appl.* **2022**, *587*, 126485. [CrossRef]
26. Luo, X.; Peng, J.; Liang, J. Directed hypergraph attention network for traffic forecasting. *IET Intell. Transp. Syst.* **2022**, *16*, 85–98. [CrossRef]
27. Li, L.; He, S.; Zhang, J.; Ran, B. Short-term highway traffic flow prediction based on a hybrid strategy considering temporal–spatial information. *J. Adv. Transp.* **2016**, *50*, 2029–2040. [CrossRef]
28. Lu, H.; Huang, D.; Song, Y.; Jiang, D.; Zhou, T.; Qin, J. St-trafficnet: A spatial-temporal deep learning network for traffic forecasting. *Electronics* **2020**, *9*, 1474. [CrossRef]
29. Li, S.; Zhuang, C.; Tan, Z.; Gao, F.; Lai, Z.; Wu, Z. Inferring the trip purposes and uncovering spatio-temporal activity patterns from dockless shared bike dataset in Shenzhen, China. *J. Transp. Geogr.* **2021**, *91*, 102974. [CrossRef]
30. Yang, S.; Li, H.; Luo, Y.; Li, J.; Song, Y.; Zhou, T. Spatiotemporal Adaptive Fusion Graph Network for Short-Term Traffic Flow Forecasting. *Mathematics* **2022**, *10*, 1594. [CrossRef]
31. Dou, H.; Tan, J.; Wei, H.; Wang, F.; Yang, J.; Ma, X.G.; Wang, J.; Zhou, T. Transfer inhibitory potency prediction to binary classification: A model only needs a small training set. *Comput. Methods Programs Biomed.* **2022**, *215*, 106633. [CrossRef]
32. Zhou, T.; Dou, H.; Tan, J.; Song, Y.; Wang, F.; Wang, J. Small dataset solves big problem: An outlier-insensitive binary classifier for inhibitory potency prediction. *Knowl.-Based Syst.* **2022**. [CrossRef]
33. Ahila, R.; Sadasivam, V.; Manimala, K. An integrated PSO for parameter determination and feature selection of ELM and its application in classification of power system disturbances. *Appl. Soft Comput.* **2015**, *32*, 23–37. [CrossRef]
34. Huang, G.B.; Zhu, Q.Y.; Siew, C.K. Extreme learning machine: Theory and applications. *Neurocomputing* **2006**, *70*, 489–501. [CrossRef]
35. Lippi, M.; Bertini, M.; Frasconi, P. Short-term traffic flow forecasting: An experimental comparison of time-series analysis and supervised learning. *IEEE Trans. Intell. Transp. Syst.* **2013**, *14*, 871–882. [CrossRef]
36. Hu, W.; Yan, L.; Liu, K.; Wang, H. A short-term traffic flow forecasting method based on the hybrid PSO-SVR. *Neural Process. Lett.* **2016**, *43*, 155–172. [CrossRef]
37. Lv, L.; Wang, W.; Zhang, Z.; Liu, X. A novel intrusion detection system based on an optimal hybrid kernel extreme learning machine. *Knowl.-Based Syst.* **2020**, *195*, 105648. [CrossRef]
38. Manoharan, J.S. Study of variants of Extreme Learning Machine (ELM) brands and its performance measure on classification algorithm. *J. Soft Comput. Paradig. (JSCP)* **2021**, *3*, 83–95.
39. Rashedi, E.; Nezamabadi-Pour, H.; Saryazdi, S. GSA: A gravitational search algorithm. *Inf. Sci.* **2009**, *179*, 2232–2248. [CrossRef]
40. Eappen, G.; Shankar, T. Hybrid PSO-GSA for energy efficient spectrum sensing in cognitive radio network. *Phys. Commun.* **2020**, *40*, 101091. [CrossRef]
41. Kennedy, J.; Eberhart, R. Particle swarm optimization. In Proceedings of the ICNN'95—International Conference on Neural Networks, Perth, WA, Australia, 27 November–1 December 1995; Volume 4, pp. 1942–1948.
42. Wang, Y.; Van Schuppen, J.H.; Vrancken, J. Prediction of traffic flow at the boundary of a motorway network. *IEEE Trans. Intell. Transp. Syst.* **2013**, *15*, 214–227. [CrossRef]
43. Li, Y.; Li, Z.; Li, L. Missing traffic data: Comparison of imputation methods. *IET Intell. Transp. Syst.* **2014**, *8*, 51–57. [CrossRef]
44. Chan, K.Y.; Dillon, T.S.; Singh, J.; Chang, E. Neural-network-based models for short-term traffic flow forecasting using a hybrid exponential smoothing and Levenberg–Marquardt algorithm. *IEEE Trans. Intell. Transp. Syst.* **2011**, *13*, 644–654. [CrossRef]
45. Zhu, J.Z.; Cao, J.X.; Zhu, Y. Traffic volume forecasting based on radial basis function neural network with the consideration of traffic flows at the adjacent intersections. *Transp. Res. Part C Emerg. Technol.* **2014**, *47*, 139–154. [CrossRef]
46. Li, Y.; Guo, Z.; Yang, J.; Fang, H.; Hu, Y. Prediction of ship collision risk based on CART. *IET Intell. Transp. Syst.* **2018**, *12*, 1345–1350. [CrossRef]
47. Moeeni, H.; Bonakdari, H.; Ebtehaj, I. Integrated SARIMA with neuro-fuzzy systems and neural networks for monthly inflow prediction. *Water Resour. Manag.* **2017**, *31*, 2141–2156. [CrossRef]
48. Altinisik, Y.; Van Lissa, C.J.; Hoijtink, H.; Oldehinkel, A.J.; Kuiper, R.M. Evaluation of inequality constrained hypotheses using a generalization of the AIC. *Psychol. Methods* **2021**, *26*, 599. [CrossRef] [PubMed]
49. Friedrich, M.; Pestel, E.; Schiller, C.; Simon, R. Scalable GEH: A Quality Measure for Comparing Observed and Modeled Single Values in a Travel Demand Model Validation. *Transp. Res. Rec.* **2019**, *2673*, 722–732. [CrossRef]
50. Sinha, A.; Bassil, D.; Chand, S.; Virdi, N.; Dixit, V. Impact of Connected Automated Buses in a Mixed Fleet Scenario With Connected Automated Cars. *IEEE Trans. Intell. Transp. Syst.* 2021, *early access*. [CrossRef]
51. Joseph, J.; Rao, A.M.; Velmuruganc, S.; Puwar, S.S. Analysis of Surrogate Safety Performance Parameters for an Interurban Corridor. *J. Sci. Ind. Res. (JSIR)* **2021**, *80*, 956–965.
52. Krishnan, G.S.; Kamath, S. A novel GA-ELM model for patient-specific mortality prediction over large-scale lab event data. *Appl. Soft Comput.* **2019**, *80*, 525–533. [CrossRef]

mathematics

Article

A Modified γ-Sutte Indicator for Air Quality Index Prediction

Dong-Her Shih [1], To Thi Hien [2,3], Ly Sy Phu Nguyen [2,3], Ting-Wei Wu [1,*] and Yen-Ting Lai [1]

1 Department of Information Management, National Yunlin University of Science and Technology, Douliu 64002, Taiwan
2 Faculty of Environment, University of Science, 227 Nguyen Van Cu Street, District 5, Ho Chi Minh City 700000, Vietnam
3 Vietnam National University, Linh Trung Ward, Thu Duc District, Ho Chi Minh City 700000, Vietnam
* Correspondence: wutingw@yuntech.edu.tw

Abstract: Air pollution has become an essential issue in environmental protection. The Air Quality Index (AQI) is often used to determine the severity of air pollution. When the AQI reaches the red level, the proportion of asthma patients seeking medical treatment will increase by 30% more than usual. If the AQI can be predicted in advance, the benefits of early warning can be achieved. In recent years, a scholar has proposed an α-Sutte indicator which shows its excellence in time series prediction. However, the calculation of α-Sutte indicators uses a fixed weight. Thus, a β-Sutte indicator, using a dynamic weight with a high computation cost, has appeared. However, the computational complexity and sliding window required of the β-Sutte indicator are still high compared to the α-Sutte indicator. In this study, a modified γ-Sutte indicator, using a dynamic weight with a lower computational cost than the β-Sutte indicator, is proposed. In order to prove that the proposed γ-Sutte indicator has good generalization ability and is transferable, this study uses data from different regions and periods to predict the AQI. The results showed that the prediction accuracy of the γ-Sutte indicator proposed was better than other methods.

Keywords: Air Quality Index; α-Sutte indicator; γ-Sutte indicator; ensemble model; prediction; time series

MSC: 37M10; 62M10

1. Introduction

In recent years, air pollution has become an essential issue of environmental protection. According to the World Health Organization (WHO), seven million deaths worldwide were linked to air pollution in 2012 [1]. The International Agency for Research on Cancer (IARC) also classified air pollution as a human carcinogen for the first time in 2013 [2]. In Taiwan, ambient air pollution is assessed using the Pollutant Standards Index (PSI), which is outdated and does not measure the impact of various pollutants. Therefore, in December 2016, the Environmental Protection Bureau of Taiwan, Executive Yuan changed into a single index, the Air Quality Index (AQI), conforming to the standards of the United States. The WHO Air Quality Guidelines (AQG) noted that "long-term exposure to the AQI rating of 'orange' increases lung cancer mortality by 15 percent". The first Global Conference on Air Pollution and Health also noted that "29% of lung cancer deaths, 24% of strokes, 25% of heart attacks, and 43% of lung disease deaths are due to air pollution injuries". When the AQI reaches the "red" level, the proportion of asthma patients seeking medical treatment increases by 30%, compared to safer conditions. It will cause eye discomfort, dry throat, itching, and skin allergies in the public.

There are many methods for air quality prediction [3–7], with most recent studies using deep learning. Compared with time series analysis, the deep learning method takes a long time to calculate. Therefore, most air quality prediction research uses various time series analysis methods to predict air quality quickly. In recent years, Ahmar et al. [8] proposed the α-Sutte indicator (based on time series analysis), which showed its excellence in time series prediction; however, the calculation of the α-Sutte indicator uses fixed weights, and predictive power may be limited. Shih et al. [9] proposed the more accurate β-Sutte indicator, which uses dynamic weight. The β-Sutte indicator uses the data of the first seven days for training, and adopts the error dynamic weight method. The results showed that the prediction accuracy of the β-Sutte indicator is slightly better than that of the α-Sutte indicator. However, the computational complexity of the α-Sutte indicator and the β-Sutte indicator are $O(1)$ and $O(2n)$, respectively. The computational complexity and sliding window required of the β-Sutte indicator are still too high compared with the α-Sutte indicator. Therefore, a modified γ-Sutte indicator, that reduces the computational time complexity of the β-Sutte indicator is proposed in this study. The γ -sutte indicator only uses the data of the previous five days to make the prediction, and the computational cost is less than the β-Sutte indicator.

One of Taiwan's most famous industrial zones is The No. 6 Naphtha Cracking Complex (Mailiao). According to the "Risk Assessment Plan for environmental and Health Impacts of Air Pollution on Coastal Areas" report, since the first phase of the operation was completed in August 2000, the air quality of Yunlin County has changed, increasing mortality and cancer rates. To verify the validity of the γ-Sutte indicator proposed in this study, we will conduct AQI predictions in the No. 6 Naphtha Cracking Complex regions of Taiwan. In order to prove the transferability and generalizability of the γ-Sutte indicator proposed in this study, this study also uses a data set of the Vientiane area to predict the AQI over the past two years in units per hour. Several time series analysis indicators will be included in the study and their performance will be compared.

2. Preliminary

2.1. Air Quality Index (AQI)

In recent years, due to the increasingly prosperous development of industrial areas, transportation, and other factors, air pollution has become increasingly serious. The original "PSI index" and "PM2.5 index" air quality evaluation indexes can no longer cover all air pollution sources. The Environmental Protection Bureau of Taiwan, Executive Yuan changed the air quality assessment index to the "AQI Index" on 1 December 2016. The AQI was implemented by the US Environmental Protection Agency in 1999 [10]. AQI calculation mainly uses the concentration values of SO2, NO2, CO, O3, PM10, PM2.5, and other pollutants for conversion; in the calculation process, the Individual Air Quality Index (IAQI) is calculated first, and the sub-index values of different pollutants are converted. Then, the maximum value of each sub-index on the day is used as the AQI of the station on that day [11].

2.2. Related Work on AQI

AQI may be affected by many factors, such as meteorological conditions and strong emission sources [11], fossil fuels such as coal and oil [12], the COVID-19 epidemic [13], weather variables (such as maximum temperature, minimum temperature, wind, and whether it rains or snows) [14], etc. Previous studies used univariate and multivariate techniques to compare air quality predictions, and the results showed that univariate techniques had better results in AQI prediction [15]. Therefore, this study will use univariate techniques for AQI prediction.

In recent years, there have also been many types of research on air quality prediction, most of which use deep learning methods. For example, AQI data transformed by empirical mode decomposition (EMD) can be inputted into SVR to obtain better predictions [3]. Wu & Lin [4] used LSTM combined with quadratic decomposition and optimization algorithms. Wang et al. [5] proposed a new CT-LSTM method, which combined the Chi-square test (CT) and long- and short-term memory (LSTM) network models into a prediction model. Phruksahiran [16] adopted the ensemble prediction method using the geographically weighted prediction method (GWP). Yan et al. [17] established multi-time and multi-place deep learning models (LSTM, CNN, CNN-LSTM). However, Liu et al. [18] explained in their study that SVR (Support Vector Regression) could solve the problem of input vector dimensions, but it is difficult to use large-scale data in training, and SVR is sensitive to the selection of parameters and kernel functions. Although deep learning has strengths, such as its adaptability to data and learning power, the correctness of the model needs to go through complex verification, and the training speed is often slow.

2.3. *Sutte Indicator*

In the stock market, the stock trends of are relatively unstable. Therefore, Ahmar [19] proposed using the Sutte indicator, which is a method used to analyze the trend of stock prices in the past and predict the trend of stock prices in the future. The Sutte indicator used the list of LQ45 stocks listed on the Indonesian Stock Exchange to predict future stock price movements. The results were compared with those of SMA and MACD. The results showed that the Sutte indicator had good accuracy in MSE, MAD, and MAPE.

2.4. *α-Sutte Indicator*

The α-Sutte indicator [8] is an improved version of the Sutte indicator method, which provides better accuracy. It can not only predict stock price trends, but also be used to predict various time series data. The α-Sutte indicator only uses the previous four pieces of data $\{d(t-1), d(\mathrm{t}-2), d(\mathrm{t}-3), d(t-4)\}$ for prediction, and the sliding window sizes are four. Due to the fixed weight in the calculation of the α-Sutte indicator being fast, the α-Sutte indicator has practicability in predicting any type of data [20].

2.5. *β-Sutte Indicator*

The β-Sutte indicator [9] is an improved version of the α-Sutte indicator, which has been used to predict the cumulative number of COVID-19 cases and the number of new cases in the US. Their results showed that the β-Sutte indicator was more accurate than the α -Sutte indicator. In the prediction process, the sliding window size of the β-Sutte indicator was seven, and the dynamic weight was calculated according to the error function of passed days.

2.6. *Autoregressive Integrated Moving Average (ARIMA)*

The autoregressive integrated moving average (ARIMA) is a common time series data prediction model which can predict future data from previous and present time series data. The ARIMA has the advantages of a simple structure, typical, fast modeling speed, and high accuracy of prediction compared to other time series models [21]. The ARIMA has also been shown to achieve good results regarding the prediction of air quality data [22–24]. Ahmar [8] has also combined the ARIMA with many other methods (regression, Holt-Winters, etc.) to establish and evaluate his proposed α-Sutte indicator. In order to compare the prediction accuracy of the proposed γ-Sutte indicator, a typical ARIMA was selected for comparison in this study.

2.7. *Ensemble Model*

Previous studies have pointed out that the performance of an ensemble model is generally better than that of a single model, and the integration of single models can be used to solve different problems in various fields [25]. In recent years, most ensemble models have been used for time series prediction. Ahmar & Del Val [26] proposed a method named SutteARIMA, which uses an α-Sutte indicator and ARIMA in combination to establish an ensemble model for short-term the prediction of COVID-19 cases, as well as the Spanish stock market. The results showed that the performance of the proposed ensemble model was better than that of a single model. The βSA ensemble model proposed by Shih et al. [9] was used to predict the cumulative number of COVID-19 cases and the number of new cases in the United States; they found that the βSA ensemble model had the best predictive performance. Ejohwomu et al. [27] also used the ensemble model to predict PM2.5 concentrations, and the proposed ensemble model was found to produce the best prediction results. Therefore, this study also wanted to know whether the ensemble model would be better than the single model of the γ-Sutte indicator proposed in this study; thus, the results of the ensemble model were also included for comparison.

3. Materials and Methods

3.1. Data Collection

Data for this study were collected from the Daily Air Quality Index (AQI) data from the Environmental Information Open Platform of the Environmental Protection Department, Executive Yuan (https://data.epa.gov.tw/dataset/detail/AQX_P_434, accessed on 8 January 2022) [28]; the data were collected from January 2017 to December 2021, and the original data contained 11 variables, as shown in Table 1. Kumar & Goyal [29] pointed out that the change in air pollutant concentration emitted in the past can provide a reference for future air quality predictions. Therefore, the three variables"station name," "monitoring date," and AQI in the data set were used in this study.

Table 1. Dataset variable description.

Variable	Definition
siteid	station number
sitename	station name
monitordate	monitoring date
aqi	AQI Value
so2subindex	Sulfur dioxide sub-index
cosubindex	Carbon monoxide sub-index
o3subindex	Ozone sub-index
pm10subindex	suspended particulates sub-index
no2subindex	Nitrogen dioxide sub-index
o38subindex	Ozone 8-h sub-index
pm25subindex	fine suspended particulates sub-index

3.2. The α-Sutte and Proposed γ-Sutte Indicator

Definitions and descriptions of notations in this study are shown in Table 2.

Table 2. Notation of symbols.

Notation	Definition
$d(t)$	Observations at day t
$d(t-k)$	Observations at day $t-k$
D_i	The predicted value of day i
$\theta(t)$, θ	Observations on day $d(t-5)$
$\delta(t)$, δ	Observations on day $d(t-4)$
$\alpha(t)$, α	Observations on day $d(t-3)$
$\beta(t)$, β	Observations on day $d(t-2)$
$\gamma(t)$, γ	Observations on day $d(t-1)$
$\Delta p(t)$, Δp	$\delta(t)-\theta(t)$
$\Delta x(t)$, Δx	$\alpha(t)-\delta(t)$
$\Delta y(t)$, Δy	$\beta(t)-\alpha(t)$
$\Delta z(t)$, Δz	$\gamma(t)-\beta(t)$
$\varepsilon_a(t)$, $\varepsilon_b(t)$, $\varepsilon_g(t)$	Error function
$w_a(t)$, $w_b(t)$, $w_g(t)$	Dynamic weighting function

The α-Sutte indicator was proposed in 2017, and can be used to predict a variety of different time series data [8]. During the forecasting process, the α-Sutte indicator only uses the previous four data points (γ, β, α, δ) to make a next-point forecast. It is therefore flexible when using any type of data [8]. The equation of the α-Sutte indicator is shown in Equation (1):

$$D_i = \frac{\alpha\left[\frac{\Delta x}{\frac{\alpha+\delta}{2}}\right] + \beta\left[\frac{\Delta y}{\frac{\beta+\alpha}{2}}\right] + \gamma\left[\frac{\Delta z}{\frac{\gamma+\beta}{2}}\right]}{3} \quad (1)$$

As can be seen in Equation (1), the α-Sutte indicator divides static weight, which is 1/3, into three different error items to make the final forecast. Although the β-Sutte indicator [9] uses dynamic weight to achieve a better result than the α-Sutte indicator, the sliding window size of β-Sutte indicator is 7 in calculating the dynamic weight. To reduce the computational cost further, the sliding window size of our new proposed γ-Sutte indicator is set to 5 in calculating dynamic weights. The equations of the proposed γ-Sutte indicator are shown in Equation (2).

$$D_i = w_a(t)\cdot a(t) + w_b(t)\cdot b(t) + w_g(t)\cdot g(t) \quad (2)$$

where

$$a(t) = \left|\frac{\alpha(t)-\delta(t)}{\delta(t)}\right|,\ b(t) = \left|\frac{\beta(t)-\alpha(t)}{\alpha(t)}\right|,\ g(t) = \left|\frac{\gamma(t)-\beta(t)}{\beta(t)}\right|,\ c(t) = \left|\frac{\delta(t)-\theta(t)}{\theta(t)}\right| \quad (3)$$

and

$$w_a(t) = \frac{\frac{1}{\varepsilon_a(t)}}{\sum_{j=1}^{3}\frac{1}{\varepsilon_j(t)}},\ w_b(t) = \frac{\frac{1}{\varepsilon_b(t)}}{\sum_{j=1}^{3}\frac{1}{\varepsilon_j(t)}},\ w_g(t) = \frac{\frac{1}{\varepsilon_g(t)}}{\sum_{j=1}^{3}\frac{1}{\varepsilon_j(t)}} \quad (4)$$

where

$$\varepsilon_a(t) = |\alpha(t) - c(t)|,\ \varepsilon_b(t) = |\alpha(t) - a(t)|,\ \varepsilon_g(t) = |\alpha(t) - b(t)| \quad (5)$$

3.3. Overall Experimental Process

This section will introduce the overall experimental process of the single model and the ensemble model in detail. The overall experimental scenario is shown in Figure 1. The proposed γ-Sutte indicator was evaluated and compared with other single models and ensemble models. This study first carried out the prediction of a single time series model through the evaluation stage to compare different evaluation metrics to find the best prediction method. The ensemble model was also carried out according to a similar process. This study aims to establish whether a single time series model is sufficient to meet the prediction results in the prediction of AQI, or whether an ensemble model is needed to achieve a better prediction.

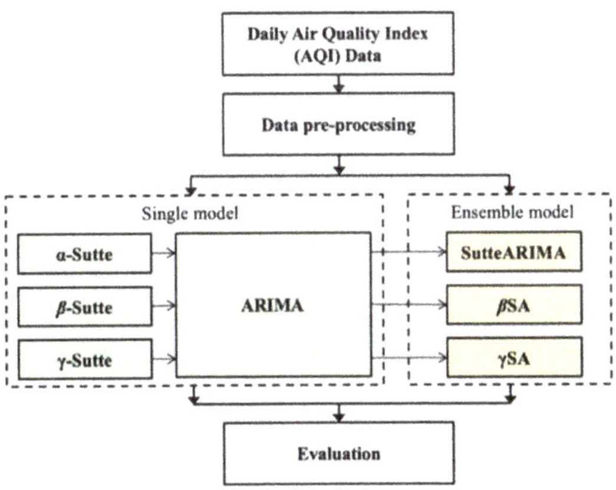

Figure 1. The overall experimental scenario.

The experiment was divided into two stages. The first stage was the evaluation of a single time series model. The γ-Sutte indicator proposed in this study was compared with other methods (α-Sutte, β-Sutte, and ARIMA) using various evaluation metrics. Next was the evaluation stage of the ensemble model. Similar to the previous step, various evaluation metrics of the ensemble model (SutteARIMA, βSA, γSA) were compared.

3.3.1. Evaluation Process of Time Series Single Models

The evaluation process of the time series single models included data pre-processing, weight training, prediction of the α-Sutte indicator, the β-Sutte indicator, the γ-Sutte indicator, and ARIMA.

The detailed research process was as follows:

1. Data pre-processing: To ensure the authenticity of the data, the negative value and outliers were removed during the preprocessing;
2. The γ-Sutte indicator used a sliding window size of 5 to make the prediction as shown in Figure 2. For example, the γ-Sutte indicator used $d(1), d(2), d(3), d(4)$, and $d(5)$ to predict D_6, then used $d(2), d(3), d(4), d(5)$, and $d(6)$ to predict D_7, and so on;
3. The sliding window size of the γ -Sutte indicator proposed in this study was set to 5, and took $d(1)$, $d(2)$, $d(3)$, $d(4)$, and $d(5)$, and used Equation (3) to calculate the variation of $\{c(t), a(t), b(t), g(t)\}$;
4. After the calculation, three error values $\{\varepsilon_a(t),\ \varepsilon_b(t),\ \varepsilon_g(t)\}$ of $c(t), a(t)$, and $b(t)$ were calculated using Equation (5);
5. The results from Step 4: $\varepsilon_a(t),\ \varepsilon_b(t),\ \varepsilon_g(t)$ were adopted to Equation (4) to calculate the dynamic weights $\{w_a(t),\ w_b(t),\ w_g(t)\}$;
6. The weight obtained in Step 5 was put into Equation (2) to calculate the predicted value D_6;
7. The four methods (α-Sutte indicator, β-Sutte indicator, γ-Sutte indicator, and ARIMA) of the time series single model were all evaluated using evaluation metrics.

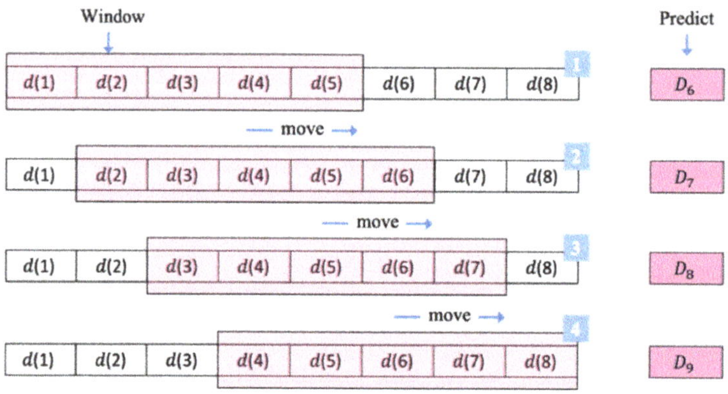

Figure 2. Sliding window of the γ-Sutte indicator.

3.3.2. The Evaluation Process of the Ensemble Models

The ensemble model evaluation process was divided into data preprocessing, weight training, SutteARIMA ensemble model prediction, βSA ensemble model prediction, γSA ensemble model prediction, and were evaluated by the chosen metrics.

The detailed evaluation process is described as follows:

1. Data pre-processing: To ensure the authenticity of the data, the negative value and outliers were removed during the preprocessing;
2. The ARIMA method used the same dataset, then averaged the results of the α-Sutte indicator and ARIMA, to become the final result of the SutteARIMA;

3. The results of the other two methods, the β-Sutte indicator, and the γ-Sutte indicator, were averaged with the ARIMA results to form the results of the βSA, and the γSA ensemble models;
4. The results of the three ensemble models were evaluated using the evaluation metrics.

3.4. Evaluation Metrics

This study applied four general metrics in the evaluation, including mean absolute percentage error (MAPE), mean absolute error (MAE), root mean square error (RMSE), and coefficient of determination (R^2). The smaller, the better for the first three indicators, and the bigger, the better for the last one.

The range of MAE and MAPE is from 0 to infinity. When the predicted value is completely consistent with the real value, MAE will be equal to 0; that is a perfect model. The greater the error, the greater the value of MAE. When MAPE is 0%, it means a perfect model; when MAPE is greater than 100%, it means an inferior model. The smaller the MAPE value is, the better accuracy the prediction model has. RMSE can measure the average difference between the predicted value and the actual value, and estimate the accuracy of the prediction model to predict the target value. The lower the RMSE value, the more accurate the prediction model [3]. R^2 ranges from 0 to 1. If $R^2 = 0$, it indicates that the model fit is poor; on the contrary, if $R^2 = 1$, the model fit is perfect. The larger the value is, the better the model fit is [30]. The forecast results of this study were obtained by using R, with the SutteForecastR package. Ahmar et al. [8] established the first α-Sutte indicator, using the stock price prediction of Turkish stocks as an experiment, and employed multiple forecasting methods (ARIMA, Regression, etc.) with MSE and RMSE as the evaluation metrics, and showed that the results of the α-Sutte indicator were the best. Therefore, this study also adopted the same methodology by using a different dynamic weighting function to evaluate the prediction results of the γ-Sutte indicator proposed.

4. Results

4.1. Time Series Single Model Evaluation

Four time series methods (the α-Sutte indicator, the β-Sutte indicator, the γ-Sutte indicator, and ARIMA) were evaluated for the prediction of the daily AQI for the No. 6 Naphtha Cracking Complex regions. The sliding window size of each method was different. The α-Sutte indicator was used to show the predicted values by the alpha.sutte() function of the sutteForecastR package in R. The β-Sutte indicator had the sliding window size set to 7, and the γ-Sutte indicator was set to 5. The ARIMA used the auto.arima() function in the FORECAST package in R to present the predicted value. Figure 3a shows the five-year prediction trend chart of the Naphtha Cracking Complex regions, both for the single time series and Figure 3b shows the five-year prediction trend chart for the ensemble model for comparison, where the X-axis is the year, and the Y-axis is the AQI value. According to the trend of the predicted value and the actual value in Figure 3, the rise and fall were very similar. However, and the pros and cons of the method could not be evaluated immediately. The time series model results predicting AQI daily over five years with the evaluation metrics are shown in Table 3.

Table 3 shows the comparisons of AQI prediction results (including ARIMA, the α-Sutte, the β-Sutte, and the γ-Sutte) daily in the No. 6 Naphtha Cracking Complex region in the past five years, as well as a variety of evaluation metrics (MAPE, MAE, RMSE, and R^2); bold font represents the best evaluation result. The results showed that the γ-Sutte ranked at the top in all evaluation metrics.

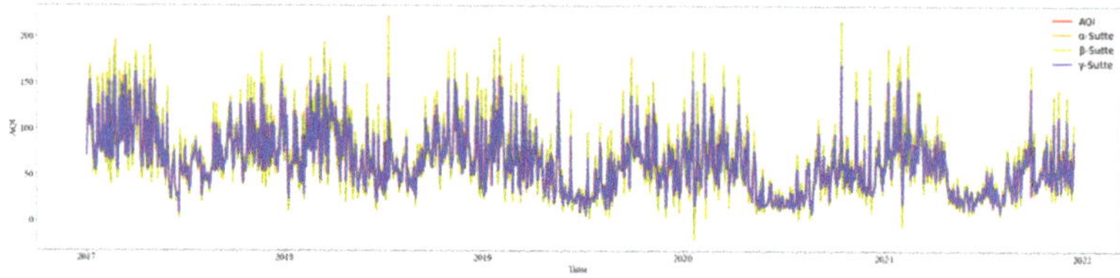

(**a**)

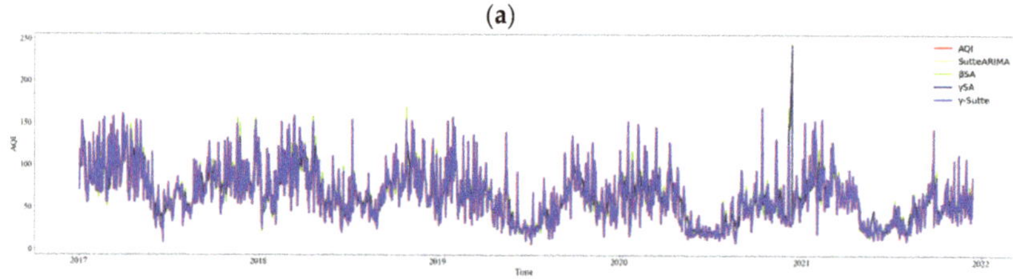

(**b**)

Figure 3. Five-year prediction chart of No. 6 Naphtha Cracking Complex regions. (**a**) Time series model; (**b**) Ensemble model.

Table 3. Prediction results of the time series model in No. 6 Naphtha Cracking Complex region.

Evaluation Metrics	α-Sutte	β-Sutte	γ-Sutte	ARIMA
MAPE	35.52503	35.33326	**28.15433**	44.45941
MAE	20.40166	20.35359	**16.3663**	**16.3663**
RMSE	28.86724	28.69002	**23.18071**	34.22783
R^2	0.4682005	0.4660149	**0.5347211**	0.1757319

4.2. Ensemble Model Evaluation

This study evaluated the prediction results of the three ensemble model methods (SutteARIMA, βSA, γSA) for the daily AQI of the No. 6 Naphtha Cracking Complex region. All methods used sliding windows, but the sliding window size of each method was different. The SutteARIMA first used the Auto.arima () function in the Forecast package of R to present ARIMA's predicted value, then took the average value of the α-Sutte indicator and obtained the results of SutteARIMA. The βSA ensemble model was based on a sliding window size of 7, and the final result was the average of the β-Sutte indicator and ARIMA results. The sliding window size for the the γSA ensemble model was 5, and the final result was averaged by the γ-Sutte indicator and ARIMA results. Figure 4a shows the prediction trend chart of the ensemble models in 2021, for example; the single time series, in Figure 4b, is also shown for comparison. As it is difficult to see the difference from each trend chart, the prediction results of ensemble model in after the daily AQI in No. 6 Naphtha Cracking Complex region was evaluated using MAPE, MAE, RMSE, and R^2, which are shown in Table 4.

Table 4 compares the ensemble model forecast results of the No. 6 Naphtha Cracking Complex regions over five years. This study has compared the proposed γ-Sutte indicator with other ensemble models (SutteARIMA, the βSA, the γSA) using specific evaluation metrics (MAPE, MAE, RMSE, R^2). In Table 4, the bold font represents the best evaluation result. The proposed γ-Sutte had the best evaluation results in both the single time series model and the ensemble model.

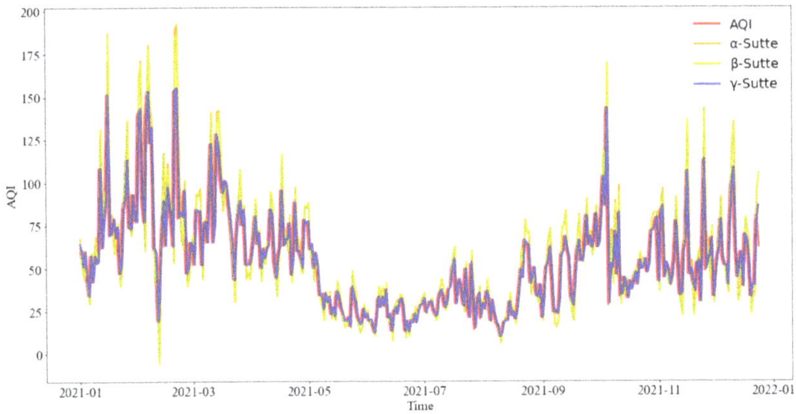

(a)

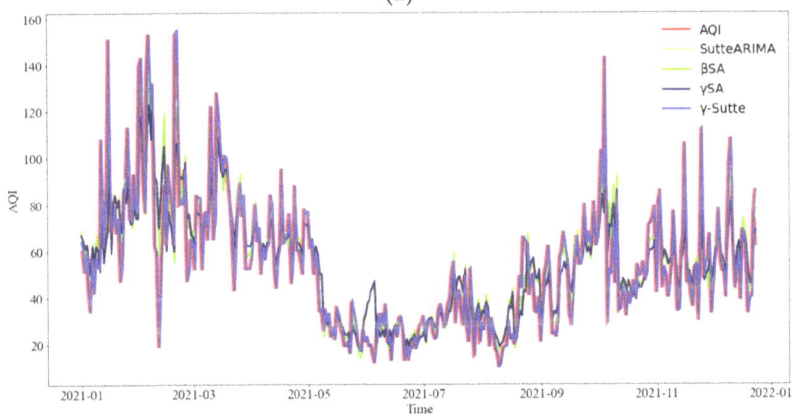

(b)

Figure 4. 2021 prediction chart of No. 6 Naphtha Cracking Complex regions. (**a**) Ensemble model; (**b**) Single time series.

Table 4. Results of the ensemble model in No. 6 Naphtha Cracking Complex regions.

Evaluation Metrics	SutteARIMA	βSA	γSA	γ-Sutte
MAPE	32.60922	32.29693	32.1901	**28.15433**
MAE	17.25304	17.18177	17.10884	**16.3663**
RMSE	24.52663	24.45834	24.21541	**23.18071**
R^2	0.4643722	0.4633891	0.4499986	**0.5347211**

5. Discussion

5.1. Transferable

"Transferable" refers to the fact that findings can be applied to objects or occasions other than the research context to understand people's feelings about the same experience [31]. In order to verify that the method proposed for short-term AQI prediction can be applied to different datasets, Zhang et al. [7] showed in their study that the accuracy of the proposed method was the highest in any dataset, which also demonstrated its transferability. In order to verify the transferability of the proposed γ -Sutte indicator, four time series model methods (the α-Sutte indicator, the β-Sutte indicator, the γ-Sutte indicator, and ARIMA) and three ensemble model methods (SutteARIMA, the βSA, and the γSA) were applied to the AQI data of the Vientiane district, the capital city of Laos. The hourly AQI dataset for Vientiane is from the Air Quality data of the United States Consulate in Laos (https://www.airnow.gov/, accessed on 8 January 2022) [32] from January 2019 to December 2020; there are six variables in the original data. Three variables, "name of the station," "date of monitoring," and "air quality index," are used in this study; the variables and definitions of the dataset are shown in Table 5.

Table 5. Variables and definitions for the Vientiane area.

Variables	Definitions
Site	name of the station
Date.LT.	date of monitoring
AQI	air quality index
AQI.Category	Categories of air quality index
Raw.Conc.	-
QC.Name	-

Figure 5 shows the prediction trend of the two-year time series model and ensemble model in the Vientiane area of this study. The trend chart for 2020 is shown in Figure 6. The data preprocessing method and research process in the Vientiane area were the same as in the No. 6 Naphtha Cracking Complex region. The difference between the two is that the former predicts the AQI in days, while the latter predicts the AQI in hours. The comparison between the evaluation metrics of the other method is shown in Table 6.

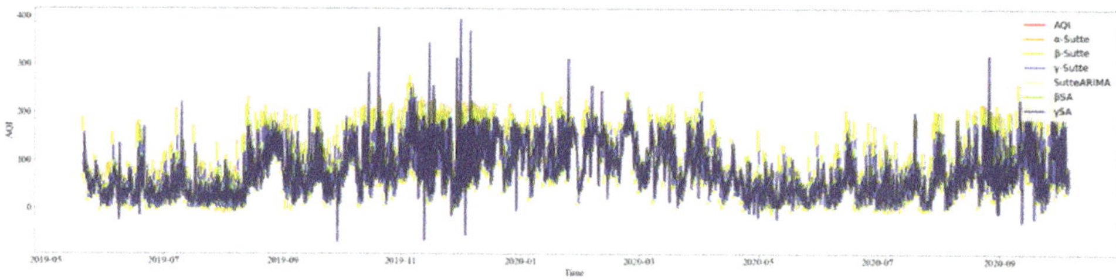

Figure 5. Two-year trend chart of the time series model and ensemble model in the Vientiane area.

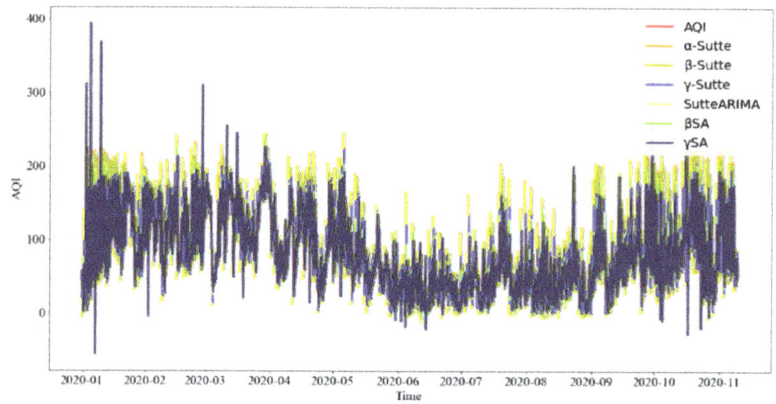

Figure 6. Time series model and ensemble model trend chart of the Vientiane area in 2020.

Table 6. Prediction results of time series model and ensemble model in the Vientiane area.

Evaluation Metrics	α-Sutte	β-Sutte	γ-Sutte	ARIMA	SutteARIMA	βSA	γSA
MAPE	22.78845	22.61683	**19.79801**	63.85786	35.03214	34.90172	38.71741
MAE	10.90479	10.77376	**9.059488**	29.66419	15.5703	15.54959	17.72079
RMSE	16.08355	15.8108	**13.76311**	45.62253	23.58507	23.58148	26.33336
R^2	0.9175967	0.9200563	**0.9286815**	0.4358475	0.7988707	0.7991491	0.7499707

Table 6 shows the evaluation results of predicting the AQI in the Vientiane area by hours in the past 2 years; The table shows the comparison of different evaluation metrics (MAPE, MAE, RMSE, and R^2) in the single time series model (the α-SUtte, the β-Sutte, the γ-Sutte, and ARIMA) and the ensemble model (SutteARIMA, the βSA, and the γSA). The bold font represents the best evaluation result. The γ-Sutte was still the top method among all models. This study also found that the γ-Sutte indicator had good results for both day and hour predictions.

5.2. Discussion

In this study, the previous time series models (the α-Sutte indicator, the β-Sutte indicator, the γ-Sutte indicator, and ARIMA) and ensemble models (SutteARIMA, the βSA, and the γSA) were compared in their ability to predict the daily AQI of No. 6 Naphtha Cracking Complex region in Taiwan, and the hourly AQI of the Vientiane area in Laos. The results of these two different regions are shown in Table 7 with the evaluation metrics (MAPE, MAE, RMSE, and R^2). Bold font represents the best result across evaluations. The γ-Sutte indicator proposed in this study has the best prediction results compared to all others. It can be seen that the γ-Sutte indicator proposed in this study has good prediction performance in different regional datasets and different time segments. The results are discussed as follows:

1. The α-Sutte indicator [8] uses fixed weight, while the γ-Sutte indicator proposed in this study used dynamic weight to make predictions. The effect of dynamic weight on prediction was better than fixed weight because the weight was adjusted at all times according to the sliding window. Therefore, the prediction results of the β-Sutte indicator [9] in another study was also better than the α-Sutte indicator; this was verified in this study. Figures 7 and 8 show the operation of the sliding window of the α-Sutte indicator and the β-Sutte indicator. Although the prediction results of the β-Sutte indicator were slightly better than that of the α-Sutte indicator, the required time window size was much larger than that of the α-Sutte indicator.
2. The β-Sutte indicator [9] used the dynamic error weight and the sliding window size of 7 (in Figure 8), while the γ-Sutte indicator proposed in this study also used a different error dynamic weight to make predictions, with a sliding window size of only 5 (in Figure 3). In addition, the computational complexity of the α-Sutte indicator, the β-Sutte indicator, and the γ-Sutte indicator were $O(1)$, $O(2n)$, and $O(n)$, respectively. The computational cost of the γ-Sutte indicator was relatively low compared to the β-sutte indicator. Nevertheless, the prediction results of the γ-Sutte indicator were better than the β-sutte indicator, indicating that the prediction results may be better if an appropriate error function and sliding window size are selected.
3. Although the prediction results of the ARIMA model, which had a relatively high calculation time, was not better than that of the γ-Sutte indicator proposed in this study, the prediction results of ARIMA were still better than that of other time series models, indicating that the ARIMA prediction model is still feasible to use in time series analysis.
4. Traditionally, the prediction results of the ensemble model were better than those of the single model. However, if the prediction results of the single model selected are

not very good, then they will weaken the advantages of the ensemble model; this was verified in the experiment of this study.

Table 7. The prediction results of the time series and ensemble models in two regions.

Area	Metrics	α-Sutte	β-Sutte	γ-Sutte	ARIMA	SutteARIMA	βSA	γSA
Mailiao	MAPE	35.52503	35.33326	**28.15433**	44.45941	32.60922	32.29693	32.1901
	MAE	20.40166	20.35359	**16.3663**	**16.3663**	17.25304	17.18177	17.10884
	RMSE	28.86724	28.69002	**23.18071**	34.22783	24.52663	24.45834	24.21541
	R^2	0.4682005	0.4660149	**0.5347211**	0.1757319	0.4643722	0.4633891	0.4499986
Vientiane	MAPE	22.78845	22.61683	**19.79801**	63.85786	35.03214	34.90172	38.71741
	MAE	10.90479	10.77376	**9.059488**	29.66419	15.5703	15.54959	17.72079
	RMSE	16.08355	15.8108	**13.76311**	45.62253	23.58507	23.58148	26.33336
	R^2	0.9175967	0.9200563	**0.9286815**	0.4358475	0.7988707	0.7991491	0.7499707

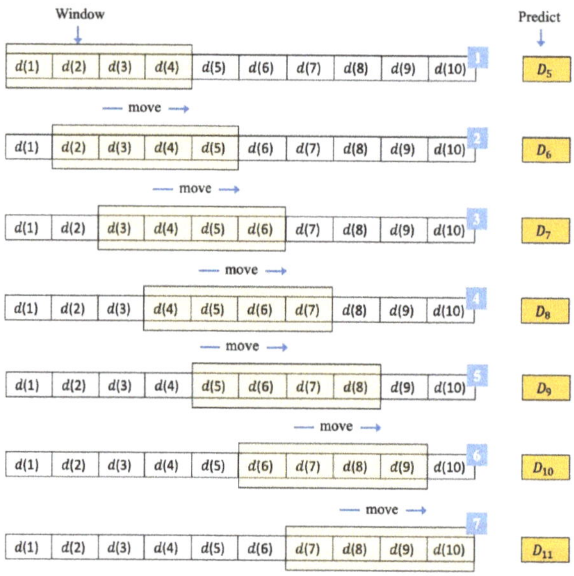

Figure 7. Sliding window of the α-Sutte indicator.

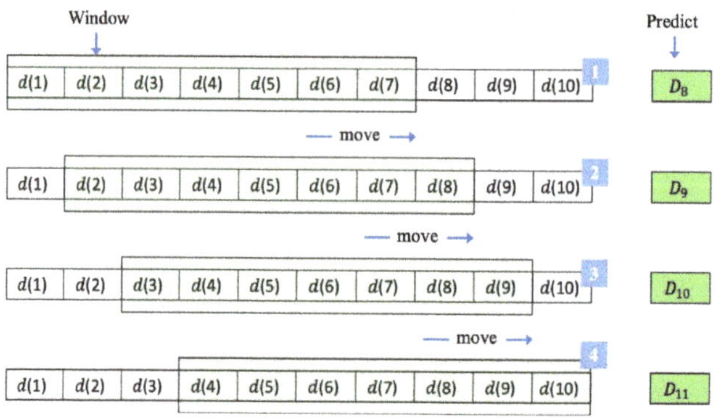

Figure 8. Sliding window of the β-Sutte indicator.

6. Conclusions

Ahmar et al. [8] proposed the α-Sutte indicator based on time series analysis, which was shown to be excellent in time series prediction; however, the calculation of the α-Sutte indicator uses fixed weights. Shih et al. [9] proposed another more accurate β-Sutte indicator which used dynamic weight. However, the computational complexity and sliding window required of the β-Sutte indicator were still too high when compared with the α-Sutte indicator. Therefore, a modified γ-Sutte indicator to reduce the computational time and complexity of the β-Sutte indicator was proposed in this study. The computational complexity of the α-Sutte indicator, the β-Sutte indicator, and the γ-Sutte indicator were $O(1)$, $O(2n)$, and $O(n)$, respectively. The computational cost of the γ-Sutte indicator was relatively low compared to the β-sutte indicator. Nevertheless, the prediction results of the γ-Sutte indicator were better than both the α-Sutte indicator and the β-sutte indicator. The γ-Sutte indicator only used the data of the previous five days to make predictions, and the computational cost was less than the β-Sutte indicator. The final results showed that the evaluation metrics of the γ -Sutte indicator (MAPE, MAE, RMSE, and R^2) were better than those of the other six methods (the α-Sutte indicator, the β-Sutte indicator, ARIMA, SutteARIMA, the βSA, and the γSA) in all areas. In addition, this study also proved the transferability of the γ-Sutte indicator as an air quality predictor in the Vientiane area. Therefore, the γ-Sutte indicator is an effective air quality prediction indicator.

This study has the following limitations and recommendations for the future:

1. To calculate dynamic weight, the training calculation time of the γ-Sutte indicator proposed in this study was higher than that of the α-Sutte indicator which uses a fixed weight. The calculation cost was lower than that of the β-Sutte indicator with dynamic weight. However, the prediction results of the γ-Sutte indicator was among the best. Nevertheless, if the prediction results are arbitrary and with acceptable accuracy, the α-Sutte indicators may be the best option.
2. In addition to the daily AQI prediction in the Mailiao district, this study also conducted the hourly AQI prediction experiment in the Vientiane district. The results showed that the γ-Sutte Indicator also had good prediction ability in different periods, representing this method's transferability and generalization.
3. The main reason why the modified γ-Sutte indicator was proposed is that although the prediction abilities of the β-Sutte indicator established by Shih [9] were slightly better than those of the α-Sutte indicator, the calculation cost was higher than that of α-Sutte. Therefore, this study proposed a more efficient modified γ-Sutte indicator.
4. In the prediction of AQI, other variables should be considered in the future, such as wind direction, nearby stations, climate, etc.
5. For the ensemble model, combinations of the γ-Sutte indicator with other time series methods in the future to form a better model should be explored, such as the Holt-Winters Model.
6. In addition, perhaps deep learning and artificial neural networks can be compared together in the future. Wang [33] proposed an optimized echo state network for effective time series prediction. Compared with other artificial neural networks, the most apparent advantage of echo state network (ESN) is its more straightforward network structure and lower computational cost. Two real-time series datasets were used for prediction experiments, and the experimental results of the optimized ESN were also quite excellent. Xu [34] proposed multi-variable LSTM (MV-LSTM) to better capture the different temporal dynamics of multivariate sequences in an interpretable form. This model dramatically improves the prediction model's performance and has a good effect on the housing load prediction. By evaluating each variable's contribution to the prediction, the multi-quantile prediction of multiple time steps in the future can be generated.

Author Contributions: Conceptualization, D.-H.S.; data curation, L.S.P.N., T.-W.W. and Y.-T.L.; formal analysis, T.-W.W. and Y.-T.L.; funding acquisition, T.T.H.; investigation, T.T.H.; methodology, D.-H.S., L.S.P.N., T.-W.W. and Y.-T.L.; project administration, D.-H.S. and T.T.H.; software, Y.-T.L.; validation, L.S.P.N.; writing—original draft, T.-W.W. and Y.-T.L.; writing—review & editing, D.-H.S. All authors have read and agreed to the published version of the manuscript.

Funding: This work was partially supported by the Taiwan Ministry of Science and Technology (grants MOST 110-2927-I-224-001). The funder had no role in study design, data collection and analysis, decision to publish, or preparation of the manuscript.

Conflicts of Interest: The authors declare no conflict of interest.

References

1. World Health Organization. Ambient (Outdoor) Air Quality and Health, Fact Sheet No. 313. Available online: http://www.who.int/mediacentre/factsheets/fs313/en/ (accessed on 1 August 2022).
2. International Agency for Research on Cancer (IARC). Outdoor Air Pollution. In *IARC Monographs on the Evaluation of Carcinogenic Risks to Humans*; International Agency for Research on Cancer: Lyon, France, 2013; Volume 109.
3. Zhu, S.; Lian, X.; Liu, H.; Hu, J.; Wang, Y.; Che, J. Daily air quality index forecasting with hybrid models: A case in China. *Environ. Pollut.* **2017**, *231*, 1232–1244. [CrossRef]
4. Wu, Q.; Lin, H. A novel optimal-hybrid model for daily air quality index prediction considering air pollutant factors. *Sci. Total Environ.* **2019**, *683*, 808–821. [CrossRef]
5. Wang, J.; Li, J.; Wang, X.; Wang, J.; Huang, M. Air quality prediction using CT-LSTM. *Neural Comput. Appl.* **2021**, *33*, 4779–4792. [CrossRef]
6. Han, Y.; Li, V.O.; Lam, J.C.; Pollitt, M. How BLUE is the sky? Estimating air qualities in Beijing during the Blue-Sky Day period (2008–2012) by Bayesian multi-task LSTM. *Environ. Sci. Policy* **2021**, *116*, 69–77. [CrossRef]
7. Zhang, L.; Na, J.; Zhu, J.; Shi, Z.; Zou, C.; Yang, L. Spatiotemporal causal convolutional network for forecasting hourly PM2.5 concentrations in Beijing, China. *Comput. Geosci.* **2021**, *155*, 104869. [CrossRef]
8. Ahmar, A.S.; Rahman, A.; Mulbar, U. Implementation of α-Sutte Indicator to Forecasting Consumer Price Index in Turkey. In Proceedings of the International Conference On Mathematics and Natural Sciences, Bali, Indonesia, 6–7 September 2017; pp. 1–4.
9. Shih, D.-H.; Wu, T.-W.; Shih, M.-H.; Yang, M.-J.; Yen, D.C. A Novel βSA Ensemble Model for Forecasting the Number of Confirmed COVID-19 Cases in the US. *Mathematics* **2022**, *10*, 824. [CrossRef]
10. Cheng, W.-L.; Chen, Y.-S.; Zhang, J.; Lyons, T.; Pai, J.-L.; Chang, S.-H. Comparison of the revised air quality index with the PSI and AQI indices. *Sci. Total Environ.* **2007**, *382*, 191–198. [CrossRef]
11. Benchrif, A.; Wheida, A.; Tahri, M.; Shubbar, R.M.; Biswas, B. Air quality during three covid-19 lockdown phases: AQI, PM2.5 and NO_2 assessment in cities with more than 1 million inhabitants. *Sustain. Cities Soc.* **2021**, *74*, 103170. [CrossRef]
12. Li, Y.; Chiu, Y.-h.; Lu, L.C. Energy and AQI performance of 31 cities in China. *Energy Policy* **2018**, *122*, 194–202. [CrossRef]
13. Ren, Y.-S.; Narayan, S.; Ma, C.-q. Air quality, COVID-19, and the oil market: Evidence from China's provinces. *Econ. Anal. Policy* **2021**, *72*, 58–72. [CrossRef]
14. Li, X.; Hu, Z.; Cao, J.; Xu, X. The impact of environmental accountability on air pollution: A public attention perspective. *Energy Policy* **2022**, *161*, 112733. [CrossRef]
15. Sethi, J.K.; Mittal, M. Analysis of air quality using univariate and multivariate time series models. In Proceedings of the 2020 10th International Conference on Cloud Computing, Data Science & Engineering (Confluence), Noida, India, 29–31 January 2020.
16. Phruksahiran, N. Improvement of air quality index prediction using geographically weighted predictor methodology. *Urban Clim.* **2021**, *38*, 100890. [CrossRef]
17. Yan, R.; Liao, J.; Yang, J.; Sun, W.; Nong, M.; Li, F. Multi-hour and multi-site air quality index forecasting in Beijing using CNN, LSTM, CNN-LSTM, and spatiotemporal clustering. *Expert Syst. Appl.* **2021**, *169*, 114513. [CrossRef]
18. Liu, H.; Yan, G.; Duan, Z.; Chen, C. Intelligent modeling strategies for forecasting air quality time series: A review. *Appl. Soft Comput.* **2021**, *102*, 106957. [CrossRef]
19. Ahmar, A.S. Sutte Indicator: A technical indicator in stock market. *Int. J. Econ. Financ. Issues* **2017**, *7*, 223–226.
20. Ahmar, A.S. A comparison of α-Sutte Indicator and ARIMA methods in renewable energy forecasting in Indonesia. *Int. J. Eng. Technol.* **2018**, *7*, 20–22. [CrossRef]
21. Lippi, M.; Bertini, M.; Frasconi, P. Short-term traffic flow forecasting: An experimental comparison of time-series analysis and supervised learning. *IEEE Trans. Intell. Transp. Syst.* **2013**, *14*, 871–882. [CrossRef]
22. Rekhi, J.K.; Nagrath, P.; Jain, R. Forecasting Air Quality of Delhi Using ARIMA Model. In *Advances in Data Sciences, Security and Applications*; Springer: Berlin/Heidelberg, Germany, 2020; pp. 315–325.
23. Aladağ, E. Forecasting of particulate matter with a hybrid ARIMA model based on wavelet transformation and seasonal adjustment. *Urban Clim.* **2021**, *39*, 100930. [CrossRef]
24. Gopu, P.; Panda, R.R.; Nagwani, N.K. Time Series Analysis Using ARIMA Model for Air Pollution Prediction in Hyderabad City of India. In *Soft Computing and Signal Processing*; Springer: Berlin/Heidelberg, Germany, 2021; pp. 47–56.

25. Li, Y.; Pan, Y. A novel ensemble deep learning model for stock prediction based on stock prices and news. *Int. J. Data Sci. Anal.* **2022**, *13*, 139–149. [CrossRef]
26. Ahmar, A.S.; Del Val, E.B. SutteARIMA: Short-term forecasting method, a case: COVID-19 and stock market in Spain. *Sci. Total Environ.* **2020**, *729*, 138883. [CrossRef]
27. Ejohwomu, O.A.; Shamsideen Oshodi, O.; Oladokun, M.; Bukoye, O.T.; Emekwuru, N.; Sotunbo, A.; Adenuga, O. Modelling and Forecasting Temporal PM2.5 Concentration Using Ensemble Machine Learning Methods. *Buildings* **2022**, *12*, 46. [CrossRef]
28. Executive Yuan. Environmental Information Open Platform of the Environmental Protection Department. Available online: https://data.epa.gov.tw/dataset/detail/AQX_P_434 (accessed on 8 January 2022).
29. Kumar, A.; Goyal, P. Forecasting of daily air quality index in Delhi. *Sci. Total Environ.* **2011**, *409*, 5517–5523. [CrossRef] [PubMed]
30. Shahid, N.; Shah, M.A.; Khan, A.; Maple, C.; Jeon, G. Towards Greener Smart Cities and Road Traffic Forecasting Using Air Pollution Data. *Sustain. Cities Soc.* **2021**, *72*, 103062. [CrossRef]
31. Korstjens, I.; Moser, A. Series: Practical guidance to qualitative research. Part 4: Trustworthiness and publishing. *Eur. J. Gen. Pract.* **2018**, *24*, 120–124. [CrossRef]
32. Air Quality Data of the United States Consulate in Laos. Available online: https://www.airnow.gov/ (accessed on 8 January 2022).
33. Wang, Z.; Zeng, Y.R.; Wang, S.; Wang, L. Optimizing echo state network with backtracking search optimization algorithm for time series forecasting. *Eng. Appl. Artif. Intell.* **2019**, *81*, 117–132. [CrossRef]
34. Xu, C.; Li, C.; Zhou, X. Interpretable LSTM Based on Mixture Attention Mechanism for Multi-Step Residential Load Forecasting. *Electronics* **2022**, *11*, 2189. [CrossRef]

mathematics

MDPI

Article

Column-Type Prediction for Web Tables Powered by Knowledge Base and Text

Junyi Wu [1], Chen Ye [1,2,3,*], Haoshi Zhi [1] and Shihao Jiang [1]

1 College of Computer Science and Technology, Hangzhou Dianzi University, Hangzhou 310018, China
2 College of Computer Science and Technology, Nanjing University of Aeronautics and Astronautics, Nanjing 210016, China
3 Jubang Group Co., Ltd., Yueqing 325600, China
* Correspondence: chenye@hdu.edu.cn

Abstract: Web tables are essential for applications such as data analysis. However, web tables are often incomplete and short of some critical information, which makes it challenging to understand the web table content. Automatically predicting column types for tables without metadata is significant for dealing with various tables from the Internet. This paper proposes a CNN-Text method to deal with this task, which fuses CNN prediction and voting processes. We present data augmentation and synthetic column generation approaches to improve the CNN's performance and use extracted text to get better predictions. The experimental result shows that CNN-Text outperforms the baseline methods, demonstrating that CNN-Text is well qualified for the table column type prediction.

Keywords: column type prediction; knowledge base; convolutional neural network (CNN); text data

MSC: 68P20; 68T07

1. Introduction

In recent years, the information contained in the vast data ocean has been mixed with the exponential growth of web data. Thus, the way by which to extract useful information from web data and put it into practice has become a hotspot. In data analytics, understanding web table content's semantic structure and meaning are invaluable in popular areas such as data integration, data cleaning, machine learning, and knowledge discovery. Tables on the web page are high-value data because they are often used to present important information in an organized and easily readable way. Thus, the organization and structure of tables on a web page make them a valuable source of data for many applications. However, web tables may lack essential information, making information collection difficult.

Example 1. *Figure 1 shows a web table example crawled on the Internet, which doesn't have a column header, column schema, and table title. It is unclear what the data in each column represents, making it difficult to understand the table content.*

	Column1	Column2
1	Windermere	5.69 sq mi(14.7 km^2)
2	Kielder Reservoir	3.86 sq mi(10.0 km^2)
3	Ullswater	3.44 sq mi(8.9 km^2)
4	Bassenthwaite Lake	2.06 sq mi(5.3 km^2)
5	Derwent Water	2.06 sq mi(5.3 km^2)

Figure 1. A web table example.

To reasonably use the table's contents without column name information, it is possible to understand the semantic information in the table with the help of additional and sufficient relevant information, such as tabular master data [1], domain experts [2], and crowdsourcing [3]. However, these resources may be scarce and are usually costly to employ. Fortunately, there exists an increasing availability of knowledge bases (KBs) such as Yago [4], DBpedia [5], and Freebase [6], which are well-curated and cover a large portion of web data. Thus, we can annotate table elements with entity or type information in the KBs to understand the semantics of each column in the web table.

Challenges. However, dealing with the column-type prediction task with the help of KBs suffers from several issues. First, because the web tables often come from complex semistructured webpages, metadata (such as table names and column names) are often missing, incomplete, or ambiguous. The lack of such semantically rich information poses a vast challenge to existing column-type prediction approaches [7–9]. Secondly, the performance of a model varies with the specific architecture and hyperparameters used, as well as the quality and amount of training data. Existing methods [10,11] that use a single model to complete column-type prediction tasks are not compelling enough. Thirdly, the metadata and the cells in the table lack contextual information; thus, it is difficult to predict correct column names.

In this paper, we propose a CNN-Text model for tackling these challenges. First, we use the lookup method to provide more semantic information related to tabular contents and propose a data augmentation approach to generate additional data for robustness. For the second challenge, we introduce the method of combining CNN with voting to obtain more accurate results. For the third challenge, we rationally use the text extracted from the knowledge base to provide contextual information of entities to help improve prediction accuracy.

Contributions. We summarize our contributions as follows.

- We propose a novel model CNN-Text, which contains the CNN and voting modules, which makes the column-type prediction results more accurate.
- We propose a data augmentation method for column-type prediction, which enables the CNN model to have better generalization ability.
- We conducted a series of experiments to demonstrate that CNN-Text is effective and the performance has been significantly improved compared with the baseline methods.

2. Related Work

The tabular data-prediction task aims to match table elements with semantic types, including cell-entity and column-type predictions. Recent methods mainly focus on column-type prediction [7–9,11–13], except that PGM [10], TabGCN [14], and Meimei [15] simultaneously finish these two tasks. However, TabGCN requires a complex algorithm to transform data into graphs and is sensitive to dirty data. Furthermore, PGM and Meimei use the Markov random field framework for prediction, which uses costly handcrafted features. Tabbie [8] averages embedding of rows and columns for obtaining embedding of cells. TURL [7] and Doduo [11] utilize the transformer to build features with respective pretraining methods. The above techniques need large quantities of artificially labeled corpora for training. Colnet [12] and TCN [9] capture features by convolutional networks. Note that the idea of Colnet is close to ours, but our methods construct a novel framework combined with a keyword coverage voting mechanism and get better performance on real-world datasets.

Representation learning. Nowadays, the representation learning approaches can be divided into three categories: discrete methods [16,17], distributed methods [18,19], and deep learning methods [7,8,11,12,14]. The discrete representation methods use discrete vectors for representation, which cannot express the semantic information of words and will encounter the problem of sparse data and loss of information. The distributed representation methods model the relationship between the context and the target word by considering the contextual information. However, such methods are mainly based on statistical computing, and the feature representation effect depends on the corpus size. The representation methods based on deep learning use deep neural networks to extract features and represent them as embeddings for various downstream tasks. Based on Word2vec [20], we use CNNs to capture deeper semantic information of tables.

Collective approaches. The collective approaches accomplish the objective by combining multiple learning tasks. Current ensemble methods for table annotation tasks are mainly divided into joint inference methods [10,15,21,22] and iterative methods [7,8,11,12]. The joint inference method combines the prediction results of multiple learners to obtain the final goal. The iterative method updates the model parameters through multiple epochs using optimizers to obtain better scores on the evaluation dataset. Both methods achieve good results with metadata (such as column names and table names) but perform poorly on tabular data consisting only of cells. We combine the strengths of these two methods while using the CNN model to iteratively update the parameters to obtain better results. We also use the joint inference method to combine the CNN prediction results and the text classifier prediction results on the two datasets.

3. Problem Definition

In this section, we first define the table and text and then define the problem of column-type prediction.

Table definition. Given a table set T, table $t \in T$ contains at least one unlabeled column K, composed of the attribute descriptions of various entities $E = \{e_1, e_2, \ldots\}$.

Table dataset details. The T2Dv2 [12] includes common table entries on the Internet, with 237 labeled primary key (PK) columns and 174 labeled nonprimary key (NPK) columns, where each label corresponds to a fine-grained DBpedia class. Limaye has various tables collected from Wikipedia. We use the version derived from the literature [23], which contains 84 PK columns with labels.

Text definition. Suppose a text set S is obtained from KBs, wherein each piece of text $s \in S$ describes an entity e in the table $t \in T$, and its content may contain multiple entities e and classes c that contribute to the column-type prediction.

Column-type prediction. The tabular data prediction task includes the cell entity prediction, the column-type prediction, and the column pair relation prediction tasks. Following [12], we focus on the column-type prediction task, which aims to predict a possible class $c \in C$ for an unlabeled column K in strict mode or a set $C_K = \{c_1, c_2, \ldots\} \in C$ of possible classes in tolerant mode.

4. Methodology

This section introduces the overall structure of CNN-Text, as shown in Figure 2. CNN-Text includes four essential parts: lookup, data augmentation, CNN training, and column-type prediction. The lookup module is designed to obtain tabular semantic information from the KB. Then, the data augmentation module enriches the dataset based on the abovementioned information for CNN training. Finally, we fuse the prediction of CNN and voting to obtain the final prediction results, where voting utilizes the explanatory text extracted from the KB. We elaborate on each part in detail in the following sections.

4.1. Lookup

Looking up the KBs for external tabular information is the crucial step of our CNN-Text framework. As seen from Figure 3, the structured data in the KBs includes classes and entities with many-to-many logic relationships. A class can contain multiple entities, while an entity can also belong to various classes. Thus, we can easily find the relationship between entities and entities, entities and classes, or classes and classes by looking up the KBs.

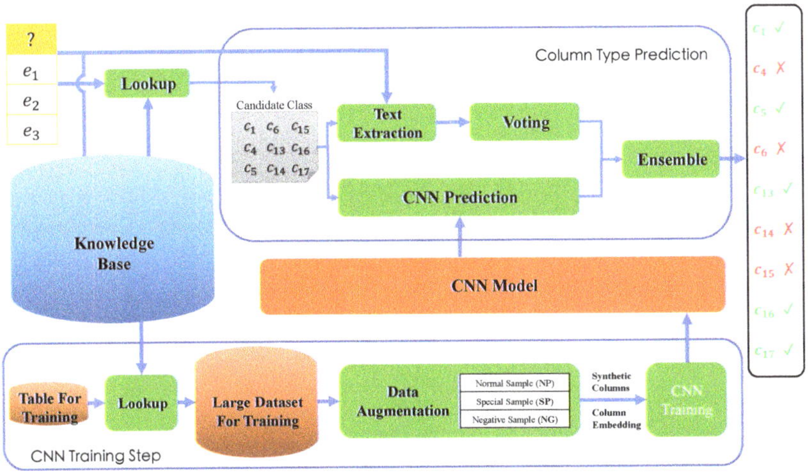

Figure 2. The architecture of CNN-Text.

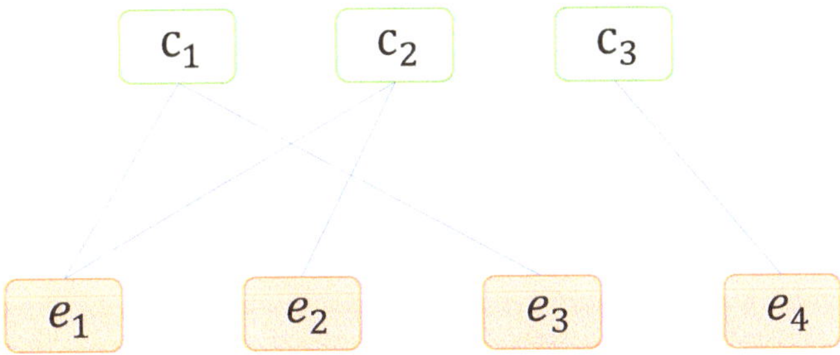

Figure 3. The relationships between the classes and the entities in a KB.

We propose expanding the training set based on the original dataset through a KB. Figure 4a shows an example of a table structure. The entities in the same column belong to a specific class shown in the table header, e.g., $\{e_1, e_2, e_3\}$ belongs to c_1. Considering an entity may belong to multiple classes in a KB, we expand the training set in three steps. First, we extend classes by querying the KB based on the class name, finding similar classes for each class in the original table. As shown in Figure 4b, the classes $\{c_4, c_5, c_6\}$, $\{c_7, c_8, c_9\}$, $\{c_{10}, c_{11}, c_{12}\}$ represent the similar classes queried by class c_1, c_2, c_3, respectively. The second step is to find other possible classes from the KB which contain entities in the table based on the entity names, e.g., the class c_{13} is queried by the entity e_1. Finally, we query the KB to get more entities corresponding to each known class, where the retrieved entities will be supplementally added to the training set of the corresponding class. For instance, $\{e_{10}, \ldots, e_{22}\}$ are the retrieved entities queried by classes $\{c_4, c_5, \ldots, c_{17}\}$ from the KB.

When expanding the training set for different columns, there may be cases in which different columns have the same class, and we merge all of them to be the extra training set. After finishing the above operations for every class and entity in table $t \in T$, we get a larger dataset for the following data augmentation, training, and voting process.

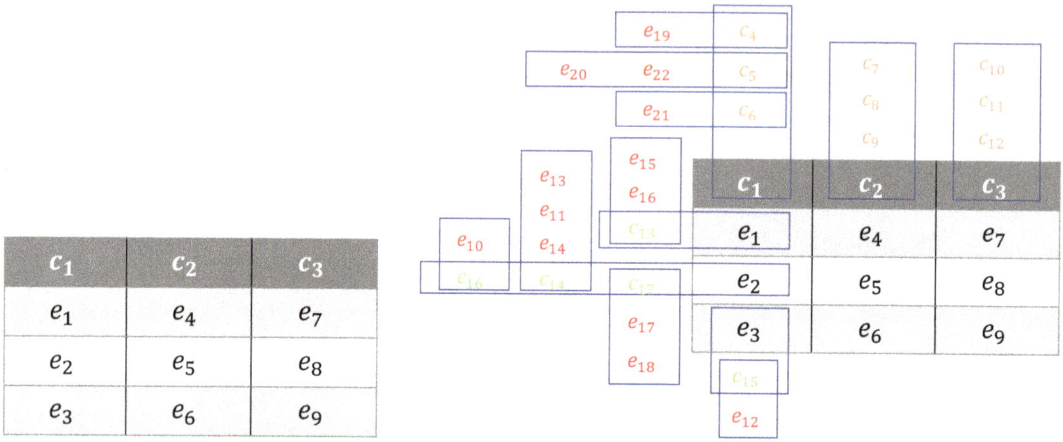

(a) (b)

Figure 4. (**a**) An example of table t. (**b**) Entity and class expansion for table t.

4.2. Data Augmentation

To capture intrinsic relationships among entities, alleviate overfitting, and enrich the dataset, we propose generating three types of synthetic column samples. Before this, we divide entities into corresponding categories.

Entity categorization. After expanding the training set with more classes and entities during lookup, we propose a data augmentation approach to generate three types of entities for synthetic column generation, i.e., negative entity, special positive entity, and normal positive entity. Then we use them to generate synthetic columns for CNN training. Specifically, for a specific class c, if an entity e belongs to c and is contained in table t, then e is defined as a special positive entity of c. Similarly, we define the entity belonging to the class but derived from the KB instead of table t as the normal positive entity. Last but not least, suppose the entities e_1 and e_2 come from different classes c_1 and c_2. We define e_1 as the negative entity of c_1 and e_2 as the negative entity of c_2.

Synthetic column samples. Based on three types of entities, we augment synthetic column samples for training. Specifically, to generate a j-length special positive sample SP for class c, each special positive entity is combined with $(j-1)$ randomly selected special positive entities. Similarly, a j-length normal positive sample NP for class c includes j randomly selected normal positive entities. While for the generation of the negative sample NG for class c, the special/normal positive and negative entities are mixed, where the number of positive and negative entities must be greater than 1.

Example 2. *As shown in Figure 5, we have a training set of class "Fish": "Spotted bass", "Crappie", "European perch", "Rainbow darter", etc. Suppose $j = 3$, we combine each entity with other two entities as one synthetic column, such as ["Spotted bass", "Rainbow darter", "Golden edhorse"], ["Crappie", "Cottus carolinae", "Flathead catfish"], etc.*

Remark 1. *The synonyms for the class name can augment the training set through the KB search. Thus, we also enrich the dataset by replacing some entities with their synonyms to improve CNN-Text's robustness.*

Entity of class "Fish"	Spotted bass	Crappie	European perch	Rainbow darter	Common carp	Roanoke logperch	Cottus carolinae	Semotilus	Golden Redhorse	Flathead catfish
Synthetic column 1	Spotted bass			Rainbow darter					Golden edhorse	
Synthetic column 2		Crappie					Cottus carolinae			Flathead catfish
Synthetic column 3			European perch		Common carp	Roanoke logperch				
Synthetic column 4	Spotted bass			Rainbow darter				Semotilus		
Synthetic column 5		Crappie			Common carp		Cottus carolinae			
Synthetic column 6						Roanoke logperch	Cottus carolinae			Flathead catfish
Synthetic column 7	Spotted bass		European perch				Cottus carolinae			
Synthetic column 8				Rainbow darter		Roanoke logperch		Semotilus		
Synthetic column 9		Crappie							Golden Redhorse	Flathead catfish
Synthetic column 10	Spotted bass				Common carp					Flathead catfish

Figure 5. An illustration of synthetic columns.

4.3. The CNN Training

This section describes the CNN model, where we elaborate on column embedding generation and CNN training.

Column embedding. We transform columns into vectors as CNN inputs for training. Specifically, for each column K, we split all the entities and integrate them into a word sequence $w_1, w_2, \ldots, w_n$, where n is the length of each word sequence and w_n refer to the n-th word in the word sequence. To simplify computation, we guarantee that all word sequences are of the same length n. If the word sequence length is greater than n, we discard redundant parts of word sequences. If the word sequence length is less than n, we use NaN to fill in the missing pieces of sequences of insufficient length.

Then, we convert column K into the embedding features $\mathbf{x}(K) \in \mathbb{R}^{n \times d}$ via word vectorization and vector superposition, as follows:

$$\mathbf{x}(K) = \mathbf{v}(w_1) \otimes \mathbf{v}(w_2) \otimes \cdots \otimes \mathbf{v}(w_n), \tag{1}$$

where $\mathbf{v}(\cdot)$ represents the d-dimensional vector representation of w with a shape of $1 \times d$, and $\otimes$ represents a vector dimension superposition. $\mathbf{v}(\cdot)$ can be obtained by Word2vec methods [20], where similar words get vectors with close distances. Therefore, we obtain the column embedding $\mathbf{x}(K) \in \mathbb{R}^n \times d$ for column K, which will be transmitted to CNN as inputs.

Example 3. *Consider there exists a column containing entities "Trivial. Pursuit", "Shadowrun", "Go (game)", and "Bakugan Battle Brawlers". To generate word embedding, we removed trivial symbols, converted all words to lowercase, and concatenated all words into a sequence: "trivial pursuit shadowrun go game bakugan battle". If n is 5, the word sequence will be truncated to "trivial, pursuit, shadowrun, go, game" and then converted to column embedding according to* Equation (1)*. Although if n is 10, the sequence will be supplemented to "trivial, pursuit, shadowrun, go, game, bakugan, battle, NaN, NaN, NaN", and then converted to column embedding.*

Convolution neural network. Considering that the CNNs are effective at exploring the regional syntax of words [12], we use the CNN model to extract the features of a synthetic column composed of multiple words. The architecture of the entire CNN model is shown in Figure 6, including a convolution layer, a pooling layer, a fully connected layer, and a sigmoid activation layer. The convolution base layer is responsible for extracting features, the pooling layer is used to reduce the dimension for alleviating huge parameters and preventing overfitting, the fully connected layer is used to change the feature dimension, and the sigmoid activation layer is to output the prediction result. Considering feature vectors belonging to different classes have various significant partial features to focus on, we train an individual binary classifier in the CNN model for each candidate class for much more proper attention over specific partial features. Thus, the output dimension after the fully connected layer is 1.

The CNN input is the embedding $\mathbf{x}(K)$ of a column K. We use a convolutional layer that includes m multiple filters to extract features, the kernel size of each filter w is $l \times d$, and the height l has various choices (e.g., 2,3,4). We obtain the feature vector $\mathbf{f}$ via convolution layer,

$$\mathbf{f} = h(\mathbf{x}(K) \otimes W + b), \tag{2}$$

where W, b is the weight matrix and bias matrix, respectively. $\otimes$ denotes the convolution operation, and $h(\cdot)$ is an activation function. The feature vector $\mathbf{f}_i$ output by the i-th filter has a size of $d \times (n - j + 1)$,

$$\mathbf{f}_i = h(w \bullet \mathbf{x}(K)_{i:i+j-1} + b_i), \tag{3}$$

where $\bullet$ represents the matrix dot product operation. We process these feature vectors by using a max pooling layer that stacks the maximum value of each feature vector together, and then we get a vector $\mathbf{f}'$ with size $m \times 1$,

$$\mathbf{f}' = [max(\mathbf{f}_1), max(\mathbf{f}_2), \ldots, max(\mathbf{f}_m)]. \tag{4}$$

Then we use a fully connected (FC) layer and sigmoid function to predict the label of a column for a specific candidate class from the learned distributed feature representation as follows,

$$p = sigmoid(h(W \bullet \mathbf{f}' + b)), \tag{5}$$

where $W \in \mathbb{R}^{m \times 1}$ is the weight matrix, $b \in \mathbb{R}^{1 \times 1}$ is the bias matrix.

Finally, CNN-Text uses the cross-entropy loss function to calculate the loss based on the predicted label of each column and its true label and reversely updates the parameters after derivation. The computation formula is shown in Equation (6):

$$Loss = -\sum_{i=1}^{n} p(x_i) log(q(x_i)), \tag{6}$$

where p, q, and n represent the predicted label, the true label, and the number of class types, respectively.

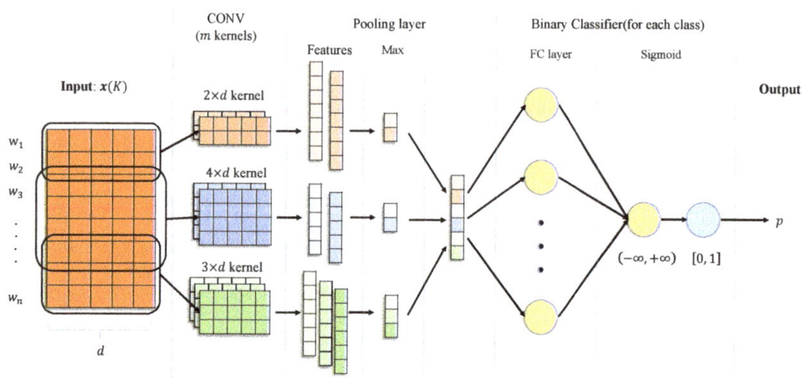

Figure 6. The CNN architecture (for one specific candidate class prediciton).

4.4. Column-Type Prediction

Introducing and utilizing additional information is very effective for annotating tabular data that often lack metadata. In addition to CNN prediction, CNN-Text designs a voting module to provide different prediction results based on KB's textual information. Then, an ensemble approach is proposed to fuse the prediction results of the CNN model and voting.

Candidate Class. To find the possible classes a column belongs to, CNN-Text uses the lookup method in the KB. For entity e_1, we get c_1, c_2 that e_1 belongs to from the KB, and for e_2, we get c_3 that e_2 belongs to. We defined the classes of each entity in a column as the candidate classes of the column. If a column K contains e_1, e_2, the candidate class for this column will be c_1, c_2, c_3.

Text extraction. For an entity e, besides looking up its class c in the KBs, CNN-Text extracts its unstructured, explanatory description text s to obtain more attribute information. For example, for the entity "Arduino", looking up the KB for its classes, we get the keywords "Device" and "Information Appliance". While searching for its text description, we get an entire paragraph of sentences, as shown in Figure 7. Then, we adopt part-of-speech tagging tools [24–26] to extract keywords which may be the entities or classes, such as "open-source hardware", "software company", "digital devices", "microcontrollers", and "kits". From the example, we can infer that an in-depth description of an entity can be obtained by extracting unstructured text from the KB. This description has a higher probability of including multiple possible classes to which it belongs.

Entity	Text
Cold Pike	Cold Pike is a fell in the English Lake District. It is a satellite of Crinkle Crags and stands above the Upper Duddon Valley.
High Hartsop Dodd	High Hartsop Dodd is a fell in the English Lake District, an outlier of the Fairfield group in the Eastern Fells. It stands above Kirkstone Pass on the road from Ullswater to Ambleside.
Arduino	Arduino is an open-source hardware and software company, project, and user community that designs and manufactures single-board microcontrollers and microcontroller kits for building digital devices. Arduino board designs use a variety of microprocessors and controllers. The boards are equipped with sets of digital and analog input/output (I/O) pins that may be interfaced to various expansion boards or breadboards and other circuits. The boards feature serial communications interfaces, including Universal Serial Bus (USB) on some models, which are also used for loading programs. The microcontrollers can be programmed using the C and C++ programming languages, using a standard API which is also known as the Arduino language, inspired by the Processing language and used with a modified version of the Processing IDE. In addition to using traditional compiler toolchains, the Arduino project provides an integrated development environment (IDE) and a command line tool developed in Go....

Figure 7. Explanatory text for entities.

Voting. With the extracted text, we vote on all candidate classes for a given column, and the voting result determines whether it belongs to the corresponding class. Specifically, we gather all defining words (e.g., entities and types related to the class) into a keyword vocabulary and calculate the keyword coverage in all extracted text corresponding to entities under that given column. The coverage is defined as v^c, i.e., the probability of the column belonging to each candidate class c.

CNN Prediction. For a column, the trained CNN model predicts the probability $\{p^{c_1}, \ldots, p^{c_n}\}$ for all candidate classes $\{c_1, \ldots, c_n\}$. As the time complexity of permuting and combining all entities as input is exponential, we adopt two methods to build multiple subcolumns: (1) the sliding window method to select a continuous part of entities or (2) random selection. The number of subcolumns for each column sample is defined as η, and we evaluate the model performance under different η in the experiments. The CNN model predicts the probability for each subcolumn, and finally, these results are averaged to get the CNN prediction result,

$$p^c = \frac{1}{\eta} \sum_{i=1}^{\eta} p_i^c, \tag{7}$$

where p_i^c represents the probability of the i-th subcolumn belonging to candidate class c.

Ensemble. Voting utilizes keyword features through the statistical method, and CNN captures the context information among the entities. To take advantage of both methods, we use an ensemble approach [12] to calculate the final probability s^c of each candidate class c by fusing the CNN and voting results,

$$s^c = \begin{cases} v^c, & v^c < \varphi_2 \text{ or } v^c \geq \varphi_1; \\ p^c, & \text{otherwise,} \end{cases} \tag{8}$$

where φ_1 and φ_2 are hyperparameters ($0 \leq \varphi_2 \leq \varphi_1 \leq 1$). The formula illustrates that we accept the voting result when it is greater than or equal to φ_1 or less than φ_2. Otherwise, we reject it and adopt the predicted result from CNN. Last but not least, we create a prediction threshold ϵ for judging whether the final result can provide sufficient evidence for column-type prediction; that is, we accept column K to be predicted as class c if $s^c \geq \epsilon$.

5. Experiments

5.1. Experiment Setup

Datasets. We use two datasets to demonstrate CNN-Text's performance. The statistics of datasets are summarized in Table 1, where # Cell(Avg.) represents the average number of cells in the table. Considering the few labeled samples in datasets, we adopt the synthetic columns generated by the data augmentation as the training data while keeping the original labeled part of the dataset as the test set for evaluation. The random subcolumn generation will construct η subcolumn training sample for each synthetic column sample. Specifically, we use $\eta \times 84$ training samples and 84 validation (or testing) samples for Limaye, and we use $\eta \times 411$ training samples and 411 validation (or testing) samples for T2Dv2.

Table 1. Dataset statistics.

Dataset	# Column (Labeled)	# Cell (Avg.)
T2Dv2	411	124
Limaye	84	23

Compared methods. To verify the effectiveness of CNN-Text, we compare our model with the SOTA methods ColNet and T2K Match. We summarize these methods below.

- T2K Match [13] is an iterative matching method that combines schema matching and instance matching, the major process of which includes candidate selection, value-based matching, property-based matching, and iterative matching.
- ColNet [12] is a framework that utilizes a KB, word representations, and machine learning to automatically train prediction models for annotating types of entity columns.

Implementation details. We implement the proposed CNN-Text method in Tensorflow and Word2Vec [20] Library. For Word2Vec, we use GoogleNews pretrained corpus [27], which contains 300-dimensional vectors for three million words and phrases. We use Spacy as the part-of-speech tagging tool. For external information, we use Wikipedia to extend the entity and the class in lookup process, and we use DBpedia to query unstructured text. All the experiments are performed on an R9-3900X server with 32G RAM and 1080Ti GPU. The training epoch is set to 50. The average training time per epoch for CNN module in CNN-Text ranges from 0.5556 s for Limaye to 8.5657 s for T2Dv2, and the training time of ColNet is similar. But for the prediction process, CNN-Text takes 19.98 s for T2Dv2 and 2.95 s for Limaye whereas ColNet takes 12.6 s for T2Dv2 and 2.34 s for Limaye. We adopt precision, recall, and F1-score metrics to compare our method's performance with other baseline methods. To ensure the repeatability and validity of the model, all experiments were repeated five times, and the scores were averaged to obtain the final results. To verify the model's performance on both single-label and multilabel classification, we use the "tolerant" mode and the "strict" mode for evaluation, which involve different truth datasets.

Generally, we got only one or two truth values in strict mode, while tolerant typically has more (up to five) truth values for each label of column. Therefore, we compute metrics' scores for strict mode based on a single-label classification problem, but scores for tolerant mode are based on a multilabel classification problem. The length of subcolumn for ColNet and CNN-Text is set to 2 and 4 (subsequent experiments will demonstrate). For CNN-Text, we manually optimize φ_1 and φ_2 to 0.5 and 0.08, respectively.

5.2. Experimental Results

Tables 2 and 3 illustrate the performance of various methods on the Limaye dataset and T2Dv2 dataset respectively, where we only use the augmented data derived from the whole original dataset as the training set and use original labeled columns as the test set. Limaye does not have labeled NPK columns, so we can only accomplish the type prediction for PK columns. First, T2K Match only adopts the candidate matching method, which cannot fully utilize the semantic features buried in columns. Therefore, T2K Match achieves the worst results on all datasets and in all evaluation modes. On the Limaye dataset, CNN-Text outperforms other methods in both modes, which can contribute to the impact of combining the CNN prediction with the voting mechanism. CNN module focuses on capturing the critical entity information in the column, and its prediction results are more inclined to the types labeled in the original dataset. At the same time, the voting mechanism adopts a method similar to knowledge base matching, which can efficiently complete the prediction for those types from the knowledge base. Therefore, the combination of this method and CNN can make up for the defect that CNN cannot predict the type from the knowledge base well. In the strict mode, the recall of CNN-Text can be improved by nearly 6%, and the F1-score can be improved by 2.9% and the precision is generally improved. While in the tolerant mode, the F1-score of CNN-Text has a 4.7% improvement compared with ColNet, with significantly increased precision and naturally enhanced recall. On the T2Dv2 dataset, CNN-Text achieves comparable performance with Colnet, while both are still much higher than T2K Match. These results indicate that the extracted text of T2Dv2 is dirty to describe the corresponding entity, bringing about poor voting results.

Table 2. Performance comparison on T2Dv2.

Evaluation Mode	Method	All Columns			PK Columns		
		Precision	Recall	F1	Precision	Recall	F1
Tolerant	T2K Match	0.664	0.773	0.715	0.738	0.895	0.809
	ColNet	0.886	0.807	0.847	0.942	0.906	0.924
	CNN-Text	0.868	0.829	0.848	0.923	0.912	0.918
Strict	T2K Match	0.624	0.727	0.671	0.729	0.884	0.799
	ColNet	0.749	0.757	0.753	0.853	0.874	0.864
	CNN-Text	0.743	0.767	0.754	0.843	0.883	0.863

Table 3. Performance comparison on Limaye.

Evaluation Mode	Method	PK Columns		
		Precision	Recall	F1
Tolerant	T2K Match	0.560	0.408	0.472
	ColNet	0.796	0.799	0.798
	CNN-Text	0.811	0.791	0.801
Strict	T2K Match	0.453	0.330	0.382
	ColNet	0.603	0.639	0.620
	CNN-Text	0.607	0.697	0.649

Data augmentation validation. To show the effect of data augmentation, we added a comparative experiment on whether to use the data generated by data augmentation to train the model. For Limaye, the average number of original samples and augmented samples per class are 42 and 2492 respectively. For T2Dv2, the average number of original samples and augmented samples per class are 320 and 17,493 respectively. We divided the original dataset into 70% of the training set and 30% of the test set, and the data augmentation was only conducted on 70% of the training set. We train three variants of models: (A) using only 70% of the original dataset, (B) using only the augmented dataset from 70% of the training set, (C) using both 70% of the original dataset and the dataset generated by data augmentation. The results are shown in Tables 4 and 5. We can find that variants (B) and (C) using the augmented dataset outperform variant (A), which only uses the original dataset in both restrict and tolerant mode, and the greatest improvement is achieved for the Limaye dataset in tolerant mode, close to 42%. Therefore, it demonstrates the effectiveness of data augmentation. Across all experiments, variant (B) performs best in most cases. It achieves the highest precision and F1-score in all tolerant modes and most strict modes. Variant (B) achieves better scores than variant (C), showing that only using the dataset generated by data augmentation as the training set can alleviate the overfitting problem of using a mixed dataset used by variant (C). Therefore, using the different dataset from data augmentation as the training set is worthwhile. It is also worth considering why the model performs differently on different datasets. The experiment results on the Limaye dataset have better results because the Limaye dataset has relatively straightforward and tidy data fields, and we can get better results when querying the KB and voting. But T2Dv2 contains many special or dirty characters, and the text extracted from KB contains less valuable keywords. These two problems make it difficult for CNN prediction and precise voting.

Table 4. Validation experiment results (precision, recall, F1-score) on T2Dv2.

Mode	Strict (All Columns)			Tolerant (All Columns)			Strict (PK Columns)			Tolerant (PK Columns)		
Metric	Precision	Recall	F1	Precision	Recall	F1	Precision	Recall	F1	Precision	Recall	F1
(A)	0.5679	0.0335	0.0632	0.4610	0.1130	0.1810	0.7931	0.0587	0.1094	1.0000	0.0270	0.0520
(B)	0.5097	0.1142	0.1866	0.4851	0.2495	0.3295	0.7931	0.0587	0.1094	1.0000	0.0270	0.0520
(C)	0.4952	0.1135	0.1846	0.4908	0.2516	0.3327	0.6555	0.1992	0.3056	1.0000	0.1230	0.2180

Table 5. Validation experiment results (precision, recall, F1-score) on Limaye.

Mode	Strict			Tolerant		
Metric	Precision	Recall	F1	Precision	Recall	F1
(A)	0.1459	0.5533	0.2310	0.1980	0.8074	0.3180
(B)	0.6186	0.4918	0.5479	0.7004	0.7664	0.7319
(C)	0.5644	0.5205	0.5416	0.4561	0.7869	0.5774

Ablation study. We conduct the ablation experiment to verify the effect of CNN-Text, which ensembles the voting and CNN modules. Table 6 shows the experiment results of CNN, Voting, and CNN-Text, from which we can see that CNN-Text utilizes the advantages of CNN and Voting, therefore achieving the best performance.

Table 6. Ablation experiment results (precision, recall, and F1-score) on Limaye.

Evaluation Mode	Method	PK Columns		
		Precision	Recall	F1
Tolerant	CNN	0.763	0.820	0.791
	Voting	0.732	0.660	0.694
	CNN-Text	0.811	0.791	0.801
Strict	CNN	0.576	0.619	0.597
	Voting	0.571	0.447	0.501
	CNN-Text	0.607	0.697	0.649

Effect of the number of subcolumns. We investigated the effect of subcolumn number η on the experimental results (precision, recall, F1-score). Figure 8 shows the results of ColNet and CNN-Text, which indicates that the performance of CNN-Text is better than ColNet under the same number of subcolumns. What is more, the scores of ColNet achieve the highest when η is set to 4, whereas CNN-Text performs best when it comes to 2. To maximize their performance, we set η of ColNet and CNN-Text to 2 and 4, respectively.

Case study. To prove the performance of CNN-Text, we select several examples from the Limaye dataset to analyze why text can improve the performance of CNN-Text. In the strict mode, there is only one truth value of the dataset, and there can only be one strict class "Book" in "file151614_2_cols_rows105.csv". For Colnet, the highest predicted probability is "Work" (probability is 0.91), while the probability of the actual class "Book" is only 0.80, so Colnet will incorrectly predict the type as "Work". While for CNN-Text, after introducing text features, the predicted probability of "Book" will increase from 0.80 to 1.00, which leads the detection model to output the correct classification result "Book". The same goes for another file "file223755_0_cols1_rows27.csv". Therefore, in the strict evaluation mode, the recall can be improved a lot, so as to the F1-score, and from the prediction probability of other classes, the text features we used do not affect the expression of the original model too much.

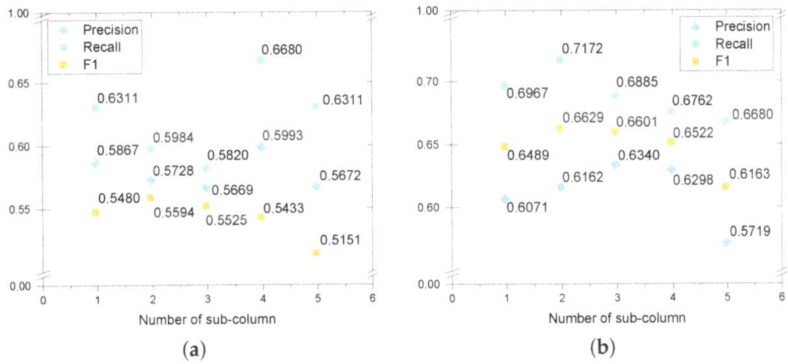

Figure 8. (**a**) The performance of ColNet in different η of sub-columns. (**b**) The performance of CNN-Text in different η of subcolumns.

For Limaye, when evaluating CNN-Text, the prediction threshold ϵ is set to 0.5. As a result, in the two files in Table 7, although CNN-Text improves the prediction probability of the truth value under the strict mode, CNN-Text and ColNet can predict all the truth values, so the model prediction effect of the two models is similar under the tolerant mode. Similarly, to verify this phenomenon's universality, we select other data for further analysis. In Table 8, we use bold text to indicate that the prediction value is accepted by exceeding the threshold ϵ of 0.5. Intuitively, CNN-Text and ColNet can classify almost all classes correctly under tolerant mode. But CNN-Text can identify the class "College" that ColNet cannot predict in "file101640_0_cols1_rows31.csv", which also verifies that CNN-Text has a certain degree of improvement in tolerant mode.

Table 7. Partial example prediction probability table for Limaye in strict mode.

Filename(.csv)	Truth Value	Predicte Result		
		Target	ColNet	CNN-Text
file151614_2_cols1_rows105	Book	Place	0.09	0.09
		Architectural Structure	0.09	0.09
		Work	**0.91**	0.91
		Location	0.10	0.10
		Sport Facility	0.08	0.08
		Book	0.8	**1.00**
		Television Show	0.31	0.31
		Person	0.16	0.16
		Agent	0.19	0.19
		Film	0.32	0.32
		Organisation	0.13	0.13
		Written Work	0.81	0.81
file223755_0_cols1_rows27	Film	File	0.76	**1.00**
		Musical Work	0.28	0.28
		Work	**0.99**	0.99
		Album	0.18	0.18

Table 8. Partial example prediction probability table for Limaye in tolerant mode.

Filename(.csv)	Truth Value	Predicte Result		
		Target	ColNet	CNN-Text
file101640_0_cols1_rows31	University, EducationalInstitution, Agent, Collage, Organisation	Location	0.15	0.15
		College	0.31	**1.00**
		Agent	**0.92**	**0.92**
		Place	0.14	0.14
		Soccer Club	0.03	0.03
		City	0.05	0.05
		Populated Place	0.03	0.03
		Educational Institution	**0.95**	**0.95**
		Person	0.05	0.05
		Architectural Structure	0.14	0.14
		Building	0.16	0.16
		University	**0.94**	**1.00**
		Organisation	**0.92**	**0.92**
file227142_1_cols1_rows7	Work, Software	Software	**0.97**	**0.97**
		Work	**0.96**	**0.96**
		Device	**0.41**	**0.41**

6. Conclusions

We propose CNN-Text, a novel column-type prediction model based on CNN and voting. Compared with baseline methods, with little difference in time cost, however, CNN-Text can extract more meaningful textual information from the knowledge base as a piece of solid evidence for prediction, eliminating the prediction failure caused by insufficient information in the web table data. We evaluate CNN-Text on T2Dv2 and Limaye datasets in strict and tolerant modes. The evaluation results demonstrate that CNN-Text is well qualified for the column-type prediction task. Note that current dataset for column-type prediction is scarce, small and precious. We do not adopt the pretraining method as it will require a huge cost. In the future, we aim to find more valuable datasets to develop our model with the pretraining method.

Author Contributions: Conceptualization, C.Y.; data curation, H.Z. and S.J.; formal analysis, J.W.; funding acquisition, C.Y.; methodology, J.W.; project administration, C.Y.; resources, C.Y.; software, J.W., H.Z., and S.J.; supervision, C.Y.; validation, J.W., H.Z., and S.J.; writing—original draft, J.W.; writing—review & editing, C.Y. All authors have read and agreed to the published version of the manuscript.

Funding: This paper was partially supported by Natural Science Foundation of Zhejiang Province (No. LQ22F020032), National Natural Science Foundation of China (No. 62202132), and National Key Research and Development Program of Chi na (No. 2022YFE0199300).

Data Availability Statement: Not applicable.

Conflicts of Interest: The authors declare no conflict of interest.

References

1. Haneem, F.; Ali, R.; Kama, N.; Basri, S. Descriptive analysis and text analysis in systematic literature review: A review of master data management. In Proceedings of the 2017 International Conference on Research and Innovation in Information Systems (ICRIIS), Langkawi, Malaysia, 16–17 July 2017; pp. 1–6.
2. White, R.W.; Dumais, S.T.; Teevan, J. Characterizing the influence of domain expertise on web search behavior. In Proceedings of the Second ACM International Conference on Web Search and Data Mining, Barcelona, Spain, 9–11 February 2009; pp. 132–141. . [CrossRef]
3. Fan, J.; Lu, M.; Ooi, B.C.; Tan, W.C.; Zhang, M. A hybrid machine-crowdsourcing system for matching web tables. In Proceedings of the 2014 IEEE 30th International Conference on Data Engineering, Chicago, IL, USA, 31 March–4 April 2014; pp. 976–987. [CrossRef]
4. Tanon, T.P.; Weikum, G.; Suchanek, F.M. YAGO 4: A Reason-able Knowledge Base. In Proceedings of the ESWC, Crete, Greece, 31 May–4 June 2020; pp. 583–596. [CrossRef]
5. Auer, S.; Bizer, C.; Kobilarov, G.; Lehmann, J.; Cyganiak, R.; Ives, Z. DBpedia: A Nucleus for a Web of Open Data. In Proceedings of the ISWC, Busan, Korea, 11–15 November 2007; pp. 722–735. [CrossRef]
6. Bollacker, K.; Evans, C.; Paritosh, P.; Sturge, T.; Taylor, J. Freebase: A collaboratively created graph database for structuring human knowledge. In Proceedings of the 2008 ACM SIGMOD International Conference on Management of Data, Vancouver, BC, Canada, 10–12 June 2008; pp. 1247–1250. [CrossRef]
7. Deng, X.; Sun, H.; Lees, A.; Wu, Y.; Yu, C. TURL: Table Understanding through Representation Learning. *SIGMOD Rec.* **2022**, *51*, 33–40. [CrossRef]
8. Iida, H.; Thai, D.; Manjunatha, V.; Iyyer, M. TABBIE: Pretrained Representations of Tabular Data. In Proceedings of the 2021 Conference of the North American Chapter of the Association for Computational Linguistics: Human Language Technologies, Online, 6–11 June 2021; pp. 3446–3456. [CrossRef]
9. Wang, D.; Shiralkar, P.; Lockard, C.; Huang, B.; Dong, X.L.; Jiang, M. TCN: Table Convolutional Network for Web Table Interpretation. In Proceedings of the Web Conference 2021, Virtual Event, Ljubljana, Slovenia, 19–23 April 2021; pp. 4020–4032. [CrossRef]
10. Limaye, G.; Sarawagi, S.; Chakrabarti, S. Annotating and Searching Web Tables Using Entities, Types and Relationships. In Proceedings of the VLDB Endow, Singapore, 13–17 September 2010; Volume 3, pp. 1338–1347. [CrossRef]
11. Suhara, Y.; Li, J.; Li, Y.; Zhang, D.; Demiralp, Ç.; Chen, C.; Tan, W.C. Annotating Columns with Pre-trained Language Models. In Proceedings of the 2022 International Conference on Management of Data, Charleston, SC, USA, 7–9 November 2022; pp. 1493–1503. [CrossRef]
12. Chen, J.; Jiménez-Ruiz, E.; Horrocks, I.; Sutton, C. ColNet: Embedding the Semantics of Web Tables for Column Type Prediction. In Proceedings of the AAAI Conference on Artificial Intelligence, Honolulu, HI, USA, 27 January–1 February 2019; pp. 29–36. [CrossRef]
13. Ritze, D.; Lehmberg, O.; Bizer, C. Matching HTML Tables to DBpedia. In Proceedings of the 5th International Conference on Web Intelligence, Mining and Semantics, Larnaca Cyprus, 13–15 July 2015; pp. 10:1–10:6. [CrossRef]
14. Pramanick, A.; Bhattacharya, I. Joint Learning of Representations for Web-tables, Entities and Types using Graph Convolutional Network. In Proceedings of the 16th Conference of the European Chapter of the Association for Computational Linguistics: Main Volume, Online, 19–23 April 2021; pp. 1197–1206. [CrossRef]
15. Takeoka, K.; Oyamada, M.; Nakadai, S.; Okadome, T. Meimei: An Efficient Probabilistic Approach for Semantically Annotating Tables. In Proceedings of the AAAI Conference on Artificial Intelligence, Honolulu, HI, USA, 27 January–1 February 2019; pp. 281–288. [CrossRef]
16. Broder, A.Z.; Glassman, S.C.; Manasse, M.S.; Zweig, G. Syntactic Clustering of the Web. *Comput. Netw.* **1997**, *29*, 1157–1166. [CrossRef]
17. Grauman, K.; Darrell, T. The Pyramid Match Kernel: Discriminative Classification with Sets of Image Features. In Proceedings of the Tenth IEEE International Conference on Computer Vision (ICCV'05), Beijing, China, 17–21 October 2005; pp. 1458–1465. [CrossRef]
18. Blei, D.M.; Ng, A.Y.; Jordan, M.I. Latent Dirichlet Allocation. In Proceedings of the Advances in Neural Information Processing Systems 14, Vancouver, BC, Canada, 3–8 December 2001; pp. 601–608.
19. Dumais, S.T.; Furnas, G.W.; Landauer, T.K.; Deerwester, S. Using latent semantic analysis to improve access to textual information. In Proceedings of the SIGCHI Conference on Human Factors in Computing Systems, Washington, DC, USA, 15–19 May 1988; pp. 281–285. [CrossRef]

20. Adewumi, T.P.; Liwicki, F.; Liwicki, M. Word2Vec: Optimal hyperparameters and their impact on natural language processing downstream tasks. *Open Comput. Sci.* **2022**, *12*, 134–141. [CrossRef]
21. Bhagavatula, C.S.; Noraset, T.; Downey, D. TabEL: Entity Linking in Web Tables. In Proceedings of the International Semantic Web Conference, Bethlehem, PA, USA, 11–15 October 2015; pp. 425–441. [CrossRef]
22. Chu, X.; Morcos, J.; Ilyas, I.F.; Ouzzani, M.; Papotti, P.; Tang, N.; Ye, Y. KATARA: A Data Cleaning System Powered by Knowledge Bases and Crowdsourcing. In Proceedings of the 2015 ACM SIGMOD International Conference on Management of Data, Melbourne, VIC, Australia, 31 May–4 June 2015; pp. 1247–1261. [CrossRef]
23. Efthymiou, V.; Hassanzadeh, O.; Rodriguez-Muro, M.; Christophides, V. Matching Web Tables with Knowledge Base Entities: From Entity Lookups to Entity Embeddings. In Proceedings of the International Semantic Web Conference, Vienna, Austria, 21–25 October 2017; pp. 260–277. [CrossRef]
24. Chiche, A.; Yitagesu, B. Part of speech tagging: A systematic review of deep learning and machine learning approaches. *J. Big Data* **2022**, *9*, 10. [CrossRef]
25. Samohi, A.; Mitelman, D.W.; Bar, K. Using Cross-Lingual Part of Speech Tagging for Partially Reconstructing the Classic Language Family Tree Model. In Proceedings of the 3rd Workshop on Computational Approaches to Historical Language Change, Dublin, Ireland, 26–27 May 2022; pp. 78–88. [CrossRef]
26. Schmitt, X.; Kubler, S.; Robert, J.; Papadakis, M.; LeTraon, Y. A Replicable Comparison Study of NER Software: StanfordNLP, NLTK, OpenNLP, SpaCy, Gate. In Proceedings of the 2019 Sixth International Conference on Social Networks Analysis, Management and Security (SNAMS), Granada, Spain, 22–25 October 2019; pp. 338–343. [CrossRef]
27. Mikolov, T.; Chen, K.; Corrado, G.; Dean, J. Efficient Estimation of Word Representations in Vector Space. *arXiv* **2013**, arXiv:1301.3781.

mathematics

MDPI

Article

The Classification of Application Users Supporting and Facilitating Travel Mobility Using Two-Step Cluster Analysis

Jaroslav Mašek [1], Vladimíra Štefancová [1,*], Jaroslav Mazanec [2] and Petra Juránková [3]

1 Department of Railway Transport, Faculty of Operation and Economics of Transport and Communications, University of Zilina, Univerzitna 1, 01026 Zilina, Slovakia
2 Department of Quantitative Methods and Economic Informatics, Faculty of Operation and Economics of Transport and Communications, University of Zilina, Univerzitna 1, 01026 Zilina, Slovakia
3 OLTIS Group a. s., Dr. Milady Horákové 1200/27a, 779 00 Olomouc, Czech Republic
* Correspondence: vladimira.stefancova@fpedas.uniza.sk

Abstract: There is a significant and supported trend toward the achievement of ensuring continuous door-to-door travel in the pan-European transport network. Many innovative programs are dedicated to this topic through assigned projects. This paper is based on the concrete partial results of the H2020 project Shift2Rail IP4 to support the deployment of mobility as a service (IP4MaaS). Attitudes towards travel for demonstration sites were assessed based on the outputs of a sample of respondents from two countries. Cooperation in working on the IP4MaaS project was also provided by a partner from Slovakia (UNIZA) and the Czech Republic (OLTIS). Mathematical statistical tools were used to evaluate the available data to find a connection with promoting mobility as a service. This paper aims to identify differences in travelers' needs with a focus on using applications using two-step cluster analysis. The research resulted in the identification of differences in traffic behavior within MaaS activities when comparing different clusters reflecting preferences for using a website or mobile application.

Keywords: mobility; cluster analysis; MaaS activities; H2020

MSC: 37N40; 62H30; 91C20

1. Introduction

The door-to-door strategy is gradually coming to the fore, even with the idea of providing continuous transport services connecting several operators within one digital platform. Promoting door-to-door mobility is a very current topic that is being studied in numerous studies. Research in Dresden focused on identifying the needs and preferences of public transport users for mobile applications to support mobility [1]. As part of transport planning, the decision of transport routes and the inclusion of private door-to-door services to ensure transport service is taken as a key element [2]. In Singapore, a public transport routing approach was assessed, including door-to-door shared services [3]. The option of continuous traffic service also applies to the reduced-mobility population. Research in Barcelona highlighted the importance of door-to-door transportation services even for disadvantaged road users, emphasizing the influence of road characteristics and the need for priority-based trip allocation [4]. Research in Turkey examined the impact of the availability of transport infrastructure and the attractiveness of the region on regional mobility [5].

Digitization in general provides a wide range of available data, which makes it possible to understand and link user behavior. Processing data from multiple communication systems and interconnected subsystems helps in the development of smart cities [6]. In the context of the design of a smart city, the interaction between mobile applications and transport itself is especially important. When setting up a functional system, a process consisting of a sufficient amount of traffic data, map documents, and outputs from real-time sensors or transport operators is considered [7]. The identification of factors influencing urban tourists' receptivity as well as citizens traveling for work or school is an important input when assessing mobility [8]. The effective operation of public transport systems is closely related to a detailed understanding of the behavior of its participants. In Hong Kong, research focused on evaluating spatial, temporal, modal, and targeted user group parameters based on data from smart cards [9]. Knowing the social demographics of passengers is the basis for the future design of transport services. This topic was addressed by a study that used data extracted from traffic cards to understand and assess the travel habits of different population groups [10]. A study in Canada focused on assessing the impact of transport mobility benefits on older non-working citizens [11]. Business trips have a significant impact on the increased demand for transport services. A Swedish study tested the interaction of the application of mobility services with the reservation and implementation of business trips in the context of public transport as well [12]. Part of the provision of transport is also the offer of shared mobility services in urban areas. Understanding the decision-making process when choosing public transport or alternative shared means plays a significant role in setting up a mobility plan [13]. A French study evaluated mobility with lower density, and the results showed that it is in such cases that carpooling and walking in conjunction with mobile apps are most applied [14]. Shifting traffic in cities to public transport services ensuring mobility is also closely related to a properly set parking policy, especially in city centers [15]. The choice of transport mode is also connected with the assessment of safety. Travel users perceive the provision of safe driving very sensitively and have high expectations for intelligent transport systems [16,17].

Cluster analysis is widely used in various areas, including the transport sector. In a Portuguese urban area, cluster analysis was used to investigate the segmentation of public transport users and their perception of satisfaction with transport services, revealing four user segments [18]. London's public transport network was an area of research that considered the heterogeneity of commuters and assessed the diversity of urban residents as well as temporal attributes within days and sequences of activities [19]. Another English study focused on the approach to the analysis of travel workflows based on geodemographic classification [20]. The recognition of the important predictor was identified through cluster analysis in traffic congestion, while the factors influencing the management, flow, and functioning of traffic were outlined [21]. The impact of transport on carbon dioxide emissions in Chinese cities was also examined using a two-stage cluster analysis, which was divided into various categories based on the degree of impact of each driver [22]. Another study focused on traffic from the point of view of motorcyclists, and segmented motorcycle crashes into homogeneous clusters through cluster analysis [23].

Mobility as a service (MaaS) can be expressed as a tool to achieve sustainable mobility and increase the share of trips by public transport [24]. It is based on the idea of access to a centralized platform for planning, payment, and travel management along with the combination of several types of transport [25]. From another point of view, MaaS emphasizes the need to focus on finding the most acceptable way of moving and deciding to make that move [26]. The term MaaS represents a tool to support mobility. Numerous studies are devoted to this topic. The London study pointed to the potential of the mobility as a service package from the point of view of supporting shared modes. More than half of the respondents confirmed that they would be interested in trying new modes of transport and, thus, supporting travel by shared modes [27]. MaaS is defined as a user-oriented service concept providing people with door-to-door mobility solutions. The importance of future planned bus transport in the context of MaaS appears to be an essential element in strengthening public transport [28]. The possibility of unified search, reservation, and payment through a digital platform helps to promote mobility. Even though it focuses more on passenger transport, the idea of integration of freight transport was also investigated, as the means of freight transport affects the capacity of road traffic and, thus, affects mobility [29]. The MaaS scheme operates in various industries, and it is described in many studies. Another London study focused on examining newly existing mobility services such as car sharing or bike sharing and their impact on urban mobility [30]. The legislative framework within the digital market in the context of Maas is addressed by research that pointed to the need to harmonize the legal framework for personal multimodal transport [31]. A Dutch study also addressed the topic of MaaS implementation and its impact on passengers' transportation, in which five different clusters were identified concerning individuals' inclinations [32]. An Australian study assessed consumer preferences, where willingness to use MaaS was shown to be dependent on age and life stage [33]. A German study addressed MaaS from the perspective of identifying key motivational determinants and their interrelationships [34].

The Maas initiative provides a comprehensive approach to solving urban mobility through a single interface, with technical support and a journey planner as desirable elements [35]. From the results of research on the use of MaaS in Metro Manila, it was concluded that the respondents highlighted the reliability and cost savings, and about 80% of them would use the MaaS application [36]. A Belgian pilot study looked at the possibilities of replacing the car with the effects of MaaS, with findings indicating the impact of MaaS on car ownership and use [37]. Another study on MaaS focused on mobility as a service preferences in the context of understanding potential demand from the perspective of different subscription options [38]. The international Delphi study gathered the opinions of experts on the future implementation of MaaS, in which their attitudes and reactions to vulnerabilities as well as opportunities were considered [39]. The impact of shared mobility on MaaS was addressed in a case study in Madrid, where emerging shared mobility operators and their provided transport services were investigated [40]. Travel behavior and the connection to MaaS were addressed in another study, where the preference for public transport from the perspective of passengers with a motor vehicle was compared [41]. The need for innovation and the provision of public benefits to the traveling public was highlighted as a significant prerequisite for the future preference for MaaS [42].

Solving key social trends such as reducing greenhouse gas emissions or solving problems with congested roads are positive effects that are expected. Shift2Rail IP4 supports MaaS routing to offer transport services and specific route settings directly with individual operators through a digital platform. The IP4MaaS project aimed to support the deployment of MaaS schemes by testing technologies developed under IP4 within Shift2Rail through complementary IP4MaaS projects through demonstration implementation. This project involved 26 participants from eight countries (Belgium, Spain, Greece, Italy, Poland, Croatia, the Czech Republic, and Slovakia) to achieve jointly set goals. Project activities between partners were strengthened by mutual co-creation such as brainstorming, workshops, and imaginative activities with the aim of harmonizing opinions and achieving set goals through project demonstrations [43].

2. Materials and Methods

The data from our questionnaire survey led to us obtaining the needs and expectations of potential users within MaaS activities. We used a conversational survey using the Coney tool, while the questions were asked via chat. It was easy to answer the list of questions in the form of an online interview through this platform. The original English version was translated into several languages, while our partial survey used the Czech language. The survey was anonymous and took place from 1 March 2022 to the end of April [43]. The questionnaire was answered by respondents over the age of 18. The questionnaire was divided into two sections: a socio-demographic section (age, gender, social status) and an application section focusing on functionality and user-friendliness. We segmented users using two-step cluster analysis in the statistical analytical program SPSS 26. This program was used to calculate the relative importance of the predictor (see Figure 1) based on the formula below.

$$\mathrm{VI_i} = \frac{-\log_{10}(\mathrm{sig_i})}{\max_{j\in\Omega}\left(-\log_{10}\left(\mathrm{sig_j}\right)\right)} \tag{1}$$

where:

Ω is a set of predictor and evaluation fields;
sig_i is a p-value computed by applying a certain test. If sig_i equals 0, set $sig_i = MinDouble$, where MinDouble is the minimal double value [44].

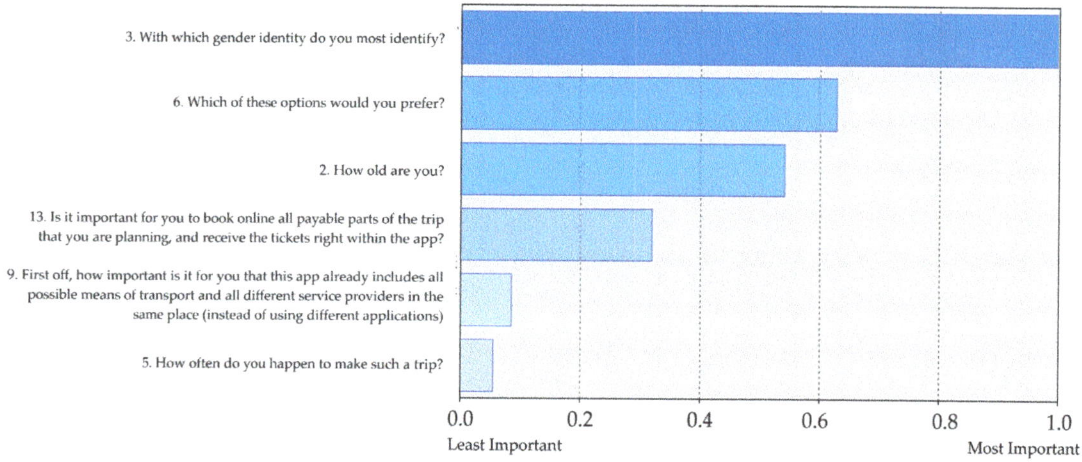

Figure 1. Predictor importance of all inputs.

Clustering is a known way of segmentation in many areas, including k-means, hierarchical clusters, and two-step clusters. Two-step cluster analysis is a different algorithm from traditional clustering techniques for handling categorical and continuous variables, determining the automatic selection of the number of clusters, and scalability. In other words, the method uses categorical and continuous variables [45]. Two-step cluster analysis is useful when the dataset has a complex structure or when there is no clear prior knowledge about the number of clusters. This approach provides a flexible and effective way to uncover the underlying structure in the data and generate meaningful insights.

Distance measures explain how the similarity between two clusters is computed using log-likelihood and Euclidean distance. Euclidean measures only use continuous variables, in contrast to log-likelihood distance. This method assumes that all variables are independent. Moreover, continuous variables should be normally distributed, and categorical variables should be multinomial.

2.1. Log-Likelihood Distance

The log-likelihood distance (also known as the log-likelihood ratio) is a measure of the difference between two probability distributions. It is commonly used in information theory and machine learning to compare the fit of two models to a given set of data. The log-likelihood distance is defined as the difference between the log-likelihood of the observed data using one model and the log-likelihood of the same data using a second model. A smaller log-likelihood distance between two models indicates that the two models are more similar in their predictions for the observed data, while a larger log-likelihood distance indicates that the models are less similar. In other words, a model with a higher log-likelihood is considered to be a better fit for the data, and the log-likelihood distance can be used to compare the goodness-of-fit of different models. Finally, using log-likelihood distance in two-step cluster analysis can provide a more robust clustering method compared to methods that only use Euclidean distance or other measures of similarity. The distance between clusters i and j is defined as

$$d_{(i)(j)} = \xi_i + \xi_j - \xi_{(i,j)} \quad (2)$$

$$\xi_s = -N_s\left(\left(\sum_{k=1}^{K^A}\frac{1}{2}\log\left(\hat{\sigma}_k^2+\hat{\sigma}_{sk}^2\right)\right)+\left(\sum_{k=1}^{K^B}\hat{E}_{sk}\right)\right) \tag{3}$$

$$\hat{E}_{sk} = -\sum_{l=1}^{L_k}\left(\frac{N_{skl}}{N_s} * \log\left(\frac{N_{skl}}{N_s}\right)\right) \tag{4}$$

where:

K^A is the total number of continuous variables;
K^B is the total number of categorical variables;
L_k is the number of categories for the kth categorical variable;
N_s is the total number of data records in cluster s;
N_{skl} is the number of records in cluster s whose categorical variable k takes the l category;
$\hat{\sigma}_k^2$ is the estimated variance of the continuous variable k;
$\hat{\sigma}_{sk}^2$ is the estimated variance of the continuous variables k in cluster j;
$d_{(i)(j)}$ is the distance between the i and the j;
(i, j) is the index representing cluster formed by combining clusters i and j [45].

2.2. Optimal Cluster Number

The optimal number of clusters is identified by the maximum value of the ratio of distance measures according to [46,47] in the statistical analytical program IBM SPSS 26. BIC and AIC are calculated for each number of clusters within a specific range. These indicators identify the optimal number of clusters. AIC (Akaike information criterion) and BIC (Bayesian information criterion) are both measures of the goodness-of-fit of a statistical model used to compare different models and select the best one. Both AIC and BIC balance the model's goodness-of-fit with its complexity, as a model with too many parameters can easily fit the data too well, but at the cost of overfitting. In general, AIC and BIC provide similar information, but BIC tends to favor simpler models, while AIC is more balanced between fit and complexity. The choice of which measure to use depends on the specific problem and the trade-off between model fit and complexity that is desired. BIC statistics for a partition with R clusters are calculated as:

$$BIC_R = -2\sum_{r=1}^{R}\xi_r + m_r\log(N) \tag{5}$$

with

$$m_r = R\left\{2K^A + \sum_{k=1}^{K^B}(L_k - 1)\right\} \tag{6}$$

where:

BIC_R is the Bayesian information criterion;
m_r is the ratio in the r-cluster developed during the hierarchical clustering stage;
L_k is the number of groups in k categorical variables [47,48].

In addition, we also monitored the ratio of BIC changes and the ratio of distance measures. However, the statistical analytical program automatically determines the optimal number of clusters without the author's decision [49].

2.3. Cluster Quality

The silhouette coefficient is a measure of the quality of a clustering solution in unsupervised machine learning. It provides a way to assess the similarity of the data points within a cluster and the dissimilarity between different clusters. The silhouette coefficient ranges from −1 to 1, where a value close to 1 indicates that the data points in a cluster are well separated and similar to each other, while a value close to −1 indicates that the data points in a cluster are dissimilar and assigned to the wrong cluster. A value close to 0 indicates that the data points are indifferently similar to their cluster and the neighboring clusters. In other words, the silhouette value identifies poor classification (from −1.0 to 0.2), fair classification (from 0.2 to 0.5), and good classification (from 0.5 to 1.0) [50]. This coefficient is computed for each data point, and the average silhouette score for all data points provides an overall measure of the quality of the clustering solution. The silhouette score can be used to compare different clustering solutions and to determine the optimal number of clusters for a given dataset. The silhouette value is calculated as

$$SW_i = \frac{b_i - a_i}{\max(a_i, b_i)} \tag{7}$$

$$a_i = \frac{\sum_{j \in C_g (j \neq i)} D_{ij}}{n_q - 1} \tag{8}$$

$$b_i = \frac{\sum_{j \in C_h} D_{ij}}{n_h} \tag{9}$$

$$SC = \frac{\sum_{i=1}^{n} SW_i}{n} \tag{10}$$

where:

SW_i is the silhouette coefficient for the ith object;
SC is the average silhouette coefficient;
a_i is the average of the minimum distance between the ith objects in the same cluster (average intra-cluster distance);
b_i is the average of the minimum distance between the ith objects in a different cluster (average inter-cluster distance);
C_g, C_h are cluster elements;
D_{ij} is the distance;
n_q, n_h are the number of objects in the gth (hth) cluster;
n is the total number of observations [50,51].

It is a widely used metric for evaluating clustering solutions and is particularly useful for datasets with defined clusters or for datasets with a large number of clusters.

3. Results

Optimal cluster number. Table 1 reveals important metrics such as BIC, BIC change, ratio of BIC, and ratio of distance measures determining the optimal number of clusters. The maximum value of the ratio of distance measures identifies four clusters as the optimal number.

Cluster quality. The silhouette measure is higher than 0.2. This metric represents the fair zone. These results demonstrate that the behaviors are significantly different from each other, but respondents in individual groups have similar features and preferences.

Cluster structure. Table 2 shows that the total number of respondents is 350, but all four clusters consist of 261 respondents. Other respondents are excluded due to missing data. As can be seen, clusters consist of different numbers of respondents. We find that the third cluster consists of more than 80 respondents (31.40%). On the other hand, the first cluster includes fewer than 50 respondents (18.00%).

Moreover, Figure 1 shows that the most significant predictors are gender (100%), user preference focusing on using a website, mobile application, or both (63%), and age category (54%). Other predictors are less significant. Predictor importance explains the relative importance of each predictor.

Table 1. Optimal cluster number based on ratio of distance measures.

Number of Clusters	Schwarz's Bayesian Criterion (BIC)	BIC Change [a]	Ratio of BIC Changes [b]	Ratio of Distance Measures [c]
1	2794.695			
2	2603.075	−191.62	1.000	1.220
3	2459.052	−144.023	0.752	1.127
4	2339.487	−119.565	0.624	1.648
5	2295.396	−44.091	0.230	1.058
6	2257.667	−37.728	0.197	1.066
7	2226.747	−30.92	0.161	1.061
8	2201.740	−25.007	0.131	1.325
9	2200.588	−1.152	0.006	1.027
10	2201.336	0.749	−0.004	1.088
11	2207.889	6.552	−0.034	1.052
12	2217.721	9.832	−0.051	1.031
13	2229.430	11.709	−0.061	1.020
14	2242.326	12.896	−0.067	1.201
15	2265.164	22.838	−0.119	1.042

[a] The changes are from the previous number of clusters in the table. [b] The ratios of changes are relative to the change for the two-cluster solution. [c] The ratios of distance measures are based on the current number of clusters against the previous number of clusters.

Table 2. The total sample divided into four clusters.

		N	% of Combined	% of Total
Cluster	1	47	18.00%	13.40
	2	70	26.80%	20.00
	3	82	31.40%	23.40
	4	62	23.80%	17.170
	Combined	261	100.00%	74.60
Excluded Cases		89		25.40
Total		350		100.00%

Figure 2 shows that the respondents are divided into four clusters. These clusters are made up of respondents with similar demographic characteristics and preferences for using applications. As can be seen, these clusters are created using six input categorical variables such as gender, age category, trip frequency, and user preferences. The color scale distinguishes predictors by within-cluster importance (see the legend).

Table 3 demonstrates that the first cluster consists exclusively of respondents aged 18 to 24. Other age groups are not represented in this cluster. On the other hand, the fourth cluster consists of respondents from 25 to 64 years old; both age categories from 25 to 44 and 45 to 64 have equal representation. Finally, the second and third clusters have diverse representations in all age categories. We find that the second cluster consists primarily of respondents from 18 to 24 years old, unlike the third cluster. This cluster consists of respondents from 25 to 44 years old (44.80% of this age group).

Table 3. The age of the respondents and their division into clusters.

		18–24 Years		25–44 Years		45–64 Years	
		Frequency	%	Frequency	%	Frequency	%
Cluster	1	47	42.70	0	0.00	0	0.00
	2	32	29.10	17	19.50	21	32.80
	3	31	28.20	39	44.80	12	18.80
	4	0	0.00	31	35.60	31	48.40
Combined		110	100.00	87	100.00	64	100.00

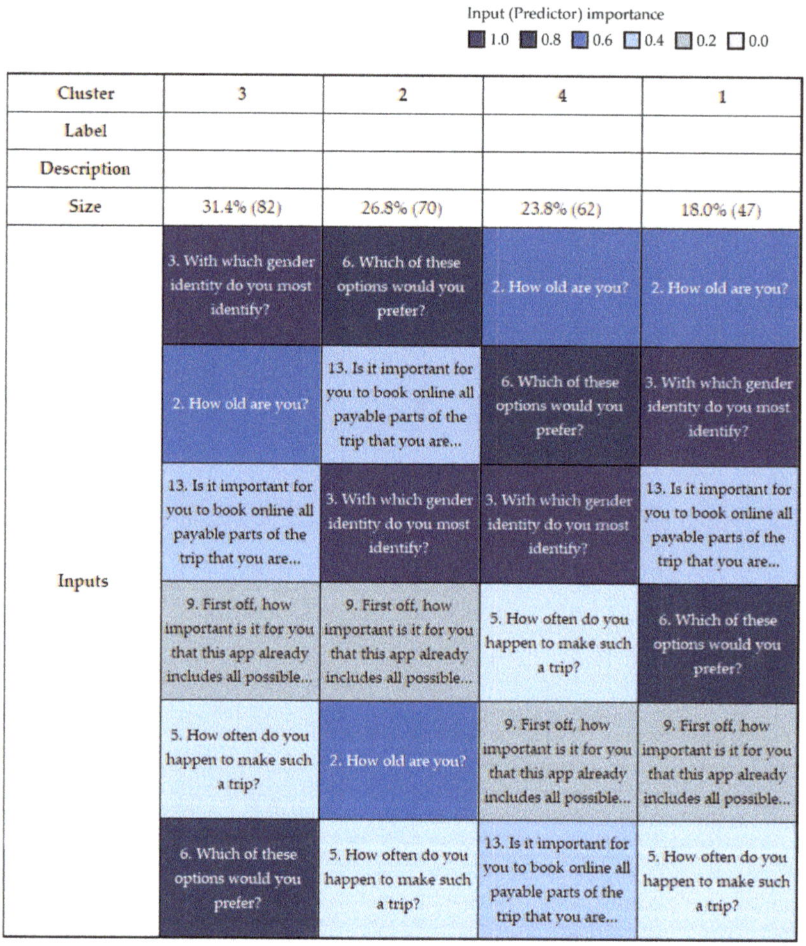

Cluster	3	2	4	1
Label				
Description				
Size	31.4% (82)	26.8% (70)	23.8% (62)	18.0% (47)
Inputs	3. With which gender identity do you most identify?	6. Which of these options would you prefer?	2. How old are you?	2. How old are you?
	2. How old are you?	13. Is it important for you to book online all payable parts of the trip that you are...	6. Which of these options would you prefer?	3. With which gender identity do you most identify?
	13. Is it important for you to book online all payable parts of the trip that you are...	3. With which gender identity do you most identify?	3. With which gender identity do you most identify?	13. Is it important for you to book online all payable parts of the trip that you are...
	9. First off, how important is it for you that this app already includes all possible...	9. First off, how important is it for you that this app already includes all possible...	5. How often do you happen to make such a trip?	6. Which of these options would you prefer?
	5. How often do you happen to make such a trip?	2. How old are you?	9. First off, how important is it for you that this app already includes all possible...	9. First off, how important is it for you that this app already includes all possible...
	6. Which of these options would you prefer?	5. How often do you happen to make such a trip?	13. Is it important for you to book online all payable parts of the trip that you are...	5. How often do you happen to make such a trip?

Figure 2. The four user clusters (inputs sorted by within-cluster importance).

Table 4 reveals that the first cluster consists only of men, unlike the third group. On the other hand, the second and fourth groups are made up of both sexes, but the majority are men.

Table 4. The gender of the respondents and their division into clusters.

		Female		Male	
		Frequency	**%**	**Frequency**	**%**
Cluster	1	0	0.00	47	28.80
	2	3	3.10	67	41.10
	3	82	83.70	0	0.00
	4	13	13.30	49	30.10
Combined		98	100.00	163	100.00

Table 5 demonstrates that respondents in the second and third clusters often go on trips, unlike the other groups.

Table 5. The frequency of trips and their division into clusters.

		Very Often		Frequently		Rarely		Sometimes		Never	
		Frequency	%	Frequency	%	Frequency	%	Frequency	%	Frequency	%
Cluster	1	6	10.70	13	18.30	11	21.60	16	23.20	1	7.10
	2	20	35.70	21	29.60	7	13.70	18	26.10	4	28.60
	3	16	28.60	27	38.00	21	41.20	18	26.10	0	0.00
	4	14	25.00	10	14.10	12	23.50	17	24.60	9	64.30
Combined		56	100.00	71	100.00	51	100.00	69	100.00	14	100.00

Table 6 shows that mobile applications are popular for three of the four clusters; the exception is the second cluster. This cluster prefers a web application as opposed to a mobile application.

Table 6. The user preferences and their division into clusters.

		Web App		Mobile App		I Do Not Care	
		Frequency	%	Frequency	%	Frequency	%
Cluster	1	0	0.00	47	24.50	0	0.00
	2	29	76.30	15	7.80	26	83.90
	3	9	23.70	68	35.40	5	16.10
	4	0	0.00	62	32.30	0	0.00
Combined		38	100.00	192	100.00	31	100.00

Table 7 demonstrates that access to information about all possible means of transport in the same place is extremely and very important for most users.

Table 7. The degrees of importance of having traffic schedules and services in one place and their distribution into clusters.

		Extremely Important/Very Important		Moderately Important		Not Important at All/Slightly Important	
		Frequency	%	Frequency	%	Frequency	%
Cluster	1	45	19.40	1	5.60	1	9.10
	2	55	23.70	6	33.30	9	81.80
	3	72	31.00	10	55.60	0	0.00
	4	60	25.90	1	5.60	1	9.10
Combined		232	100.00	18	100.00	11	100.00

Table 8 reveals that respondents substantially prefer online booking and quick access to tickets in the app in all clusters except the second cluster.

Table 8. The degrees of importance of having access to all tickets in one app and their distribution into clusters.

		Extremely Important/Very Important		Moderately Important		Not Important at All/Slightly Important	
		Frequency	%	Frequency	%	Frequency	%
Cluster	1	47	25.10	0	0.00	0	0.00
	2	24	12.80	27	58.70	19	67.90
	3	70	37.40	6	13.00	6	21.40
	4	46	24.60	13	28.30	3	10.70
Combined		187	100.00	46	100.00	28	100.00

Moreover, Appendix A contains the tables dividing respondents into clusters according to selected variables.

Cluster comparison. Figure 3 compares all four clusters. We find that the third (red) cluster consists only of women who prefer mobile applications to web applications (almost 83%). Most women are between 25 and 45 years old (47.6%). These women often go on trips, and online booking of all parts of the trip and quick access to transport information in one application is very or extremely important. The other groups include mainly men. Moreover, the first (green) cluster comprises only men. Men prefer the mobile app in all clusters except the second cluster. The results show that most of the men are between 18 and 24 years old. Finally, frequent travel is typical for the second (light blue) cluster, with a lower preference for online booking of all parts of the trip as the only cluster. However, information about all possible means of transport is very or extremely important. Even though the first (green) and fourth (dark blue) clusters travel less often than the other groups, both groups prefer one mobile application with all important information about means of transport and online booking with easy access to tickets.

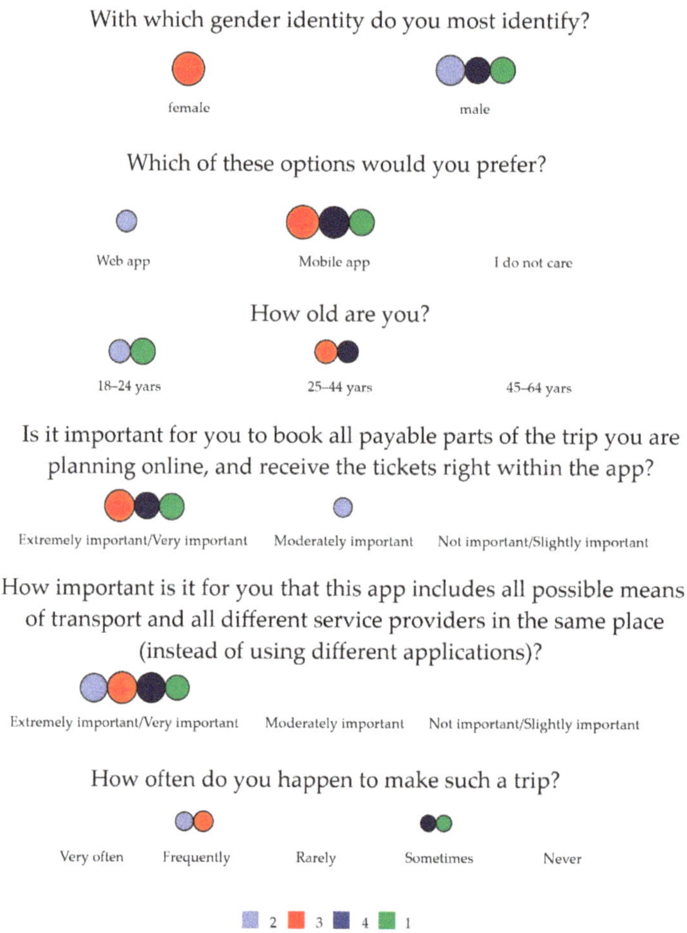

Figure 3. Cluster comparison.

4. Discussion

The field of transport offers a lot of data, which with proper analysis and interpretation can bring a lot of benefits. The following studies performed cluster analysis for sequencing enormous amounts of traffic data to categorize them according to related characteristics and understand mutual associations [52,53]. The cluster segmentation technique made it possible to sort travel attendees based on travel distance and frequency of attendance to present a proposal for market applications [54]. In our case, the respondents were divided according to similar demographic characteristics as well as preferences for using a web or mobile application. Two-step cluster analysis was used in the selection of transport simulation model parameter values for the rapid processing of enormous amounts of data with both continuous and categorical variables [55]. Our dataset was also redistributed using a two-step clustering method based on the significance of the variables. Cluster analysis was applied to create homogeneous transport markets, where markets of comparable sizes were combined into one group [56]. The assignment of our sample resulted from grouping into homogeneous groups according to travel behavior. In another study, passenger demand for public transport services was predicted through the spatial clustering of applications [57]. Our research focused on comparing the preferences of users using a web or a mobile application. A study in the United States assessed the interaction between travelers and online travel systems using cluster analysis [58]. Support for spatial planning of transport in cities is related to the efficient processing of traffic data. Cluster analysis evaluated travel data in terms of the interaction of travel flows and spatial structure [59]. The impact of fares on the status of public transport was investigated by a study in Italy that used cluster analysis to segment passengers [60]. In our article, we examined the preference for online reservations with easy access to tickets. The prediction of the flow of passenger transport was conducted using cluster analysis, which divided the stations into six categories concerning their patterns of passenger transport [61].

Our paper focused on identifying differences in passenger needs through a statistical analytical tool. Two-step cluster analysis was applied to a wide range of available data from a survey reflecting traffic behavior within MaaS activities. The sample consisted of approximately 300 respondents divided into four clusters. The most influential predictors were gender, user preferences for using a website or mobile application, and age composition. The third cluster was made up of working-age women who prefer mobile applications to web applications, for whom quick access to online booking information is essential. The other groups were dominated by men, while the first cluster was composed exclusively of men. Even though the second cluster in terms of frequent travel was not extremely interested in online booking, the opposite was true in the other clusters. In the first, third, and fourth clusters, respondents preferred reservations through a mobile application, while they rated the availability of traffic information as extremely important.

The limited sample that was available for analytical purposes can be considered a limitation of our research. As part of further research activities, we would be interested in expanding awareness of MaaS activities among the public as well.

5. Conclusions

Traffic movement prediction is determined by the demand for transport services. Identifying real demand is an essential aspect that is facilitated by constantly advancing and improving intelligent transport systems with designed mobility applications. Profiling public transport users is an important prerequisite for understanding the perception and behavior of passengers using public transport services. Achieving the segmentation of public transport participants with the same or at least related features is possible through cluster analysis.

In recent years, the MaaS initiative has been developed, which focuses on understanding travel behavior and combines the offer of transport services of operators on one global platform. The intention of this direction is the possibility of providing online reservations, payments, and the availability of travel information for business but also private trips by supporting all modes of transport within the framework of public transport.

In this paper, the partial results of the demonstration activities of Shift2Rail IP4 for the Slovak and Czech sides were evaluated. Data reflecting travel attitudes were obtained from the online conversational inquiry tool. Cluster analysis was used to evaluate the sample, in which an optimal number of four clusters was identified. Individual clusters consisted of different numbers of respondents with similar characteristics.

This article aimed to identify the differences in the needs of passengers to determine the direction of the use of the application with a focus on the future development of mobility as a service. The importance of individual predictors was determined based on the attitudes towards the input variables. The three most important predictors were considered in descending order, namely gender, web or mobile application preference, and age category. The results of our research indicated that respondents are interested in timely traffic information and prefer a mobile application for online booking. The benefit of this paper was to highlight the partial demographic results affecting travel activities within MaaS for the Czech and Slovak sides. The results of this research for the Czech and Slovak participation are useful for supplementing the overall evaluation of the perception of MaaS in the world.

Author Contributions: Conceptualization, J.M. (Jaroslav Mašek), V.Š., J.M. (Jaroslav Mazanec) and P.J.; methodology, J.M. (Jaroslav Mazanec) and V.Š.; software, J.M. (Jaroslav Mazanec); validation, J.M. (Jaroslav Mašek) and P.J.; formal analysis, J.M. (Jaroslav Mazanec) and V.Š.; investigation, V.Š. and J.M. (Jaroslav Mazanec); resources, J.M. (Jaroslav Mašek); data curation, J.M. (Jaroslav Mašek) and P.J.; writing—original draft preparation, V.Š. and J.M. (Jaroslav Mazanec); writing—review and editing, J.M. (Jaroslav Mašek), V.Š., J.M. (Jaroslav Mazanec) and P.J.; visualization, J.M. (Jaroslav Mazanec) and V.Š.; supervision, J.M. (Jaroslav Mašek) and P.J.; project administration, J.M. (Jaroslav Mašek), V.Š. and J.M. (Jaroslav Mazanec); funding acquisition, J.M. (Jaroslav Mašek). All authors have read and agreed to the published version of the manuscript.

Funding: This paper was supported by the Shift2Rail Joint Undertaking under the European Union's Horizon 2020 research and innovation program under grant agreement no. 101015492, Shift2Rail IP4 to support the deployment of Mobility as a Service (IP4MaaS).

Data Availability Statement: All data used here are available on request from the authors.

Conflicts of Interest: The authors declare no conflict of interest.

Appendix A

Table A1. Age structure.

Age	Cluster							
	1	2	3	4	1	2	3	4
	abs.				%			
18–24 years	47	32	31	0	100.00	45.71	37.80	0.00
25–44 years	0	17	39	31	0.00	24.29	47.56	50.00
45–64 years	0	21	12	31	0.00	30.00	14.63	50.00
Total	47	70	82	62	100.00	100.00	100.00	100.00

Table A2. Gender structure.

Gender	Cluster							
	1	2	3	4	1	2	3	4
	abs.				%			
Female	0	3	82	13	0.00	4.29	100.00	20.97
Male	47	67	0	49	100.00	95.71	0.00	79.03
Total	47	70	82	62	100.00	100.00	100.00	100.00

Table A3. Frequency of trip.

Frequency of Trip	Cluster							
	1	2	3	4	1	2	3	4
	abs.				%			
Very often	6	20	16	14	12.77	28.57	19.51	22.58
Frequently	13	21	27	10	27.66	30.00	32.93	16.13
Rarely	11	7	21	12	23.40	10.00	25.61	19.35
Sometimes	16	18	18	17	34.04	25.71	21.95	27.42
Never	1	4	0	9	2.13	5.71	0.00	14.52
Total	47	70	82	62	100.00	100.00	100.00	100.00

Table A4. User preference.

Preference	Cluster							
	1	2	3	4	1	2	3	4
	abs.				%			
Web app	0	29	9	0	0.00	41.43	10.98	0.00
Mobile app	47	15	68	62	100.00	21.43	82.93	100.00
I do not care	0	26	5	0	0.00	37.14	6.10	0.00
Total	47	70	82	62	100.00	100.00	100.00	100.00

Table A5. Degree of importance of having access to all possible means of transport and all different service providers in the same place.

Importance	Cluster							
	1	2	3	4	1	2	3	4
	abs.				%			
Extremely important/Very important	45	55	72	60	95.74	78.57	87.80	96.77
Moderately important	1	6	10	1	2.13	8.57	12.20	1.61
Not important at all/Slightly important	1	9	0	1	2.13	12.86	0.00	1.61
Total	47	70	82	62	100.00	100.00	100.00	100.00

Table A6. Degree of importance of all payable parts of the trip.

Importance	Cluster							
	1	2	3	4	1	2	3	4
	abs.				%			
Extremely important/Very important	47	24	70	46	100.00	34.29	85.37	74.19
Moderately important	0	27	6	13	0.00	38.57	7.32	20.97
Not important at all/Slightly important	0	19	6	3	0.00	27.14	7.32	4.84
Total	47	70	82	62	100.00	100.00	100.00	100.00

References

1. Stopka, U. Identification of User Requirements for Mobile Applications to Support Door-to-Door Mobility in Public Transport. In *Human-Computer Interaction. Applications and Services, Proceedings of the 16th International Conference, HCI International 2014 Heraklion, Crete, Greece, 22–27 June 2014*; Springer: Berlin/Heidelberg, Germany, 2014; pp. 513–524. [CrossRef]
2. Ceder, A. Urban mobility and public transport: Future perspectives and review. *Int. J. Urban Sci.* **2021**, *25*, 455–479. [CrossRef]
3. Medina, S.A.O.; Wang, B. Public transport routing including fixed schedule, shared on-demand and door-to-door services. *Procedia Comput. Sci.* **2019**, *151*, 846–851. [CrossRef]
4. Portell, L.; Morera, S.; Ramalhinho, H. Door-to-Door Transportation Services for Reduced Mobility Population: A Descriptive Analytics of the City of Barcelona. *Int. J. Environ. Res. Public Health* **2022**, *19*, 4536. [CrossRef]
5. Mraihi, R.; Anis, R. Impact of transport infrastructure on regional mobility: Application of social equity approach. In Proceedings of the 2013 International Conference on Advanced Logistics and Transport, Sousse, Tunisia, 29–31 May 2013; pp. 284–289. [CrossRef]
6. Zou, X.; Cao, J.; Sun, W.; Guo, Q.; Wen, T. Flow data processing paradigm and its application in smart city using a cluster analysis approach. *Clust. Comput.* **2019**, *22*, 435–444. [CrossRef]
7. Bellini, P.; Bilotta, S.; Cenni, D.; Nesi, P.; Paolucci, M.; Soderi, M. Knowledge Modeling and Management for Mobility and Transport Applications. In Proceedings of the IEEE 4th International Conference on Collaboration and Internet Computing (CIC), Philadelphia, PA, USA, 18–20 October 2018; pp. 364–371. [CrossRef]
8. Souza, V.S.; Marques, S.R.B.D.V. Factors influencing urban tourists' receptivity to ecogamified applications: A study on transports and mobility. *Int. J. Tour. Cities* **2022**, *8*, 820–843. [CrossRef]
9. Halvorsen, A.; Koutsopoulos, H.N.; Ma, Z.; Zhao, J. Demand management of congested public transport systems: A conceptual framework and application using smart card data. *Transportation* **2020**, *47*, 2337–2365. [CrossRef]
10. Abbasi, S.; Ko, J.; Min, J. Measuring destination-based segregation through mobility patterns: Application of transport card data. *J. Transp. Geogr.* **2021**, *92*, 103025. [CrossRef]
11. Spinney, J.E.; Scott, D.; Newbold, B. Transport mobility benefits and quality of life: A time-use perspective of elderly Canadians. *Transp. Policy* **2009**, *16*, 1–11. [CrossRef]
12. Andersson, A.; Hiselius, L.W.; Berg, J.; Forward, S.; Arnfalk, P. Evaluating a Mobility Service Application for Business Travel: Lessons Learnt from a Demonstration Project. *Sustainability* **2020**, *12*, 783. [CrossRef]
13. Vinayak, P.; Dias, F.F.; Astroza, S.; Bhat, C.R.; Pendyala, R.M.; Garikapati, V.M. Accounting for multi-dimensional dependencies among decision-makers within a generalized model framework: An application to understanding shared mobility service usage levels. *Transp. Policy* **2018**, *72*, 129–137. [CrossRef]
14. Le Boennec, R.; Nicolaï, I.; Da Costa, P. Assessing 50 innovative mobility offers in low-density areas: A French application using a two-step decision-aid method. *Transp. Policy* **2019**, *83*, 13–25. [CrossRef]
15. Cirianni, F.M.M.; Leonardi, G. Analysis of transport modes in the urban environment: An application for a sustainable mobility system. *Sustain. City IV Urban Regen. Sustain.* **2006**, *93*, 637–645. [CrossRef]
16. Malone, K.; Silla, A.; Johanssen, C.; Bell, D. Safety, mobility and comfort assessment methodologies of intelligent transport systems for vulnerable road users. *Eur. Transp. Res. Rev.* **2017**, *9*, 1–16. [CrossRef]
17. Manasseh, C.; Sengupta, R. Middleware to enhance mobile communications for road safety and traffic mobility applications. *IET Intell. Transp. Syst.* **2010**, *4*, 24–36. [CrossRef]
18. Vicente, P.; Reis, E. Profiling public transport users through perceptions about public transport providers and satisfaction with the public transport service. *Public Transp.* **2016**, *8*, 387–403. [CrossRef]
19. Goulet-Langlois, G.; Koutsopoulos, H.N.; Zhao, J. Inferring patterns in the multi-week activity sequences of public transport users. *Transp. Res. Part C Emerg. Technol.* **2016**, *64*, 1–16. [CrossRef]
20. Martin, D.; Gale, C.; Cockings, S.; Harfoot, A. Origin-destination geodemographics for analysis of travel to work flows. *Comput. Environ. Urban Syst.* **2018**, *67*, 68–79. [CrossRef]
21. Yaduvanshi, R.; Bansal, S.; Kumar, A. Factors Affecting Traffic Management using Two Step Cluster. *Int. J. Eng. Adv. Technol.* **2019**, *9*, 1184–1189. [CrossRef]
22. Qin, H.; Huang, Q.; Zhang, Z.; Lu, Y.; Li, M.; Xu, L.; Chen, Z. Carbon dioxide emission driving factors analysis and policy implications of Chinese cities: Combining geographically weighted regression with two-step cluster. *Sci. Total Environ.* **2019**, *684*, 413–424. [CrossRef]
23. Chang, F.; Xu, P.; Zhou, H.; Chan, A.H.; Huang, H. Investigating injury severities of motorcycle riders: A two-step method integrating latent class cluster analysis and random parameters logit model. *Accid. Anal. Prev.* **2019**, *131*, 316–326. [CrossRef]
24. Santos, G.; Nikolaev, N. Mobility as a Service and Public Transport: A Rapid Literature Review and the Case of Moovit. *Sustainability* **2021**, *13*, 3666. [CrossRef]
25. Tomaino, G.; Teow, J.; Carmon, Z.; Lee, L.; Ben-Akiva, M.; Chen, C.; Leong, W.Y.; Li, S.; Yang, N.; Zhao, J. Mobility as a service (MaaS): The importance of transportation psychology. *Mark. Lett.* **2020**, *31*, 419–428. [CrossRef]
26. Hensher, D.A.; Xi, H. Mobility as a service (MaaS): Are effort and seamlessness the keys to MaaS uptake? *Transp. Rev.* **2022**, *42*, 269–272. [CrossRef]
27. Matyas, M.; Kamargianni, M. The potential of mobility as a service bundles as a mobility management tool. *Transportation* **2019**, *46*, 1951–1968. [CrossRef]

28. Hensher, D.A. Future bus transport contracts under a mobility as a service (MaaS) regime in the digital age: Are they likely to change? *Transp. Res. Part A Policy Pract.* **2017**, *98*, 86–96. [CrossRef]
29. Le Pira, M.; Tavasszy, L.A.; Correia, G.H.D.A.; Ignaccolo, M.; Inturri, G. Opportunities for integration between Mobility as a Service (MaaS) and freight transport: A conceptual model. *Sustain. Cities Soc.* **2021**, *74*, 103212. [CrossRef]
30. Kamargianni, M.; Li, W.; Matyas, M.; Schäfer, A. A Critical Review of New Mobility Services for Urban Transport. *Transp. Res. Procedia* **2016**, *14*, 3294–3303. [CrossRef]
31. Murati, E. Mobility-as-a-service (MaaS) digital marketplace impact on EU passengers' rights. *Eur. Transp. Res. Rev.* **2020**, *12*, 62. [CrossRef]
32. Alonso-González, M.J.; Hoogendoorn-Lanser, S.; van Oort, N.; Cats, O.; Hoogendoorn, S. Drivers and barriers in adopting Mobility as a Service (MaaS)—A latent class cluster analysis of attitudes. *Transp. Res. Part A Policy Pract.* **2020**, *132*, 378–401. [CrossRef]
33. Vij, A.; Ryan, S.; Sampson, S.; Harris, S. Consumer preferences for Mobility-as-a-Service (MaaS) in Australia. *Transp. Res. Part C Emerg. Technol.* **2020**, *117*, 102699. [CrossRef]
34. Schikofsky, J.; Dannewald, T.; Kowald, M. Exploring motivational mechanisms behind the intention to adopt mobility as a service (MaaS): Insights from Germany. *Transp. Res. Part A Policy Pract.* **2020**, *131*, 296–312. [CrossRef]
35. Georgakis, P.; Almohammad, A.; Bothos, E.; Magoutas, B.; Arnaoutaki, K.; Mentzas, G. Heuristic-Based Journey Planner for Mobility as a Service (MaaS). *Sustainability* **2020**, *12*, 10140. [CrossRef]
36. Hasselwander, M.; Bigotte, J.F.; Antunes, A.P.; Sigua, R.G. Towards sustainable transport in developing countries: Preliminary findings on the demand for mobility-as-a-service (MaaS) in Metro Manila. *Transp. Res. Part A Policy Pract.* **2022**, *155*, 501–518. [CrossRef]
37. Storme, T.; De Vos, J.; De Paepe, L.; Witlox, F. Limitations to the car-substitution effect of MaaS. Findings from a Belgian pilot study. *Transp. Res. Part A Policy Pract.* **2020**, *131*, 196–205. [CrossRef]
38. Ho, C.Q.; Mulley, C.; Hensher, D.A. Public preferences for mobility as a service: Insights from stated preference surveys. *Transp. Res. Part A Policy Pract.* **2020**, *131*, 70–90. [CrossRef]
39. Jittrapirom, P.; Marchau, V.; van der Heijden, R.; Meurs, H. Future implementation of mobility as a service (MaaS): Results of an international Delphi study. *Travel Behav. Soc.* **2020**, *21*, 281–294. [CrossRef]
40. Arias-Molinares, D.; García-Palomares, J.C. Shared mobility development as key for prompting mobility as a service (MaaS) in urban areas: The case of Madrid. *Case Stud. Transp. Policy* **2020**, *8*, 846–859. [CrossRef]
41. Alyavina, E.; Nikitas, A.; Njoya, E.T. Mobility as a service and sustainable travel behaviour: A thematic analysis study. *Transp. Res. Part F Traffic Psychol. Behav.* **2020**, *73*, 362–381. [CrossRef]
42. Smith, G.; Sochor, J.; Karlsson, I.M. Mobility as a Service: Development scenarios and implications for public transport. *Res. Transp. Econ.* **2018**, *69*, 592–599. [CrossRef]
43. Project Description-IP4MaaS D2.3 Demonstration Requirements and Scenarios F-REL_Final. Available online: https://www.ip4maas.eu/wp-content/uploads/2022/07/IP4M-D2.3-Demonstration-requirements-and-scenarios-F-REL_final.pdf (accessed on 15 January 2023).
44. IBM SPSS Statistics 22 Algorithms. Available online: https://www.sussex.ac.uk/its/pdfs/SPSS_Statistics_Algorithms_22.pdf (accessed on 15 January 2023).
45. IBM SPSS Statistics Base 28. Available online: https://www.ibm.com/docs/en/SSLVMB_28.0.0/pdf/IBM_SPSS_Statistics_Base.pdf (accessed on 15 January 2023).
46. Şchiopu, D. Applying TwoStep cluster analysis for identifying bank customers' profile. *Buletinul* **2010**, *62*, 66–75.
47. Tevdovski, D. Twostep cluster analysis: Segmentation of the largest companies in Macedonia. In Proceedings of the International Scientific Conference: Challenges for Analysis of the Economy, the Businesses and Social Progress, Szeged, Hungary, 19–21 November 2009.
48. Astuti, A.B.; Fernandes, A.A.R.; Amaliana, L.; Yanti, I.; Isaskar, R. Step Cluster Analysis for Tourist Segmentation Coastal Object for Green Marketing Strategy. *IOP Conf. Ser. Earth Environ. Sci.* **2019**, *239*, 012019. [CrossRef]
49. Rađenović, Ž.; Boshkov, T. Economic Effects of Congress Tourism: Two-Step Cluster Approach. *Chall. Tour. Bus. Logist. 21st Century* **2022**, *5*, 185–192. [CrossRef]
50. Supandi, A.; Saefuddin, A.; Sulvianti, I.D. Two step Cluster Application to Classify Villages in Kabupaten Madiun Based on Village Potential Data. *Xplore J. Stat.* **2021**, *10*, 12–26. [CrossRef]
51. Goyal, N.; Gupta, K.; Kumar, N. Clustering-based hierarchical framework for multiclass classification of leaf images. *IEEE Trans. Ind. Appl.* **2022**, *58*, 4076–4085. [CrossRef]
52. Řezanková, H. Different approaches to the silhouette coefficient calculation in cluster evaluation. In Proceedings of the 21st International Scientific Conference AMSE Applications of Mathematics and Statistics in Economics, Kutná Hora, Czech Republic, 29 August–2 September 2018; pp. 1–10.
53. Arongna, A.; Sulonggaowa, S. Application of travel service recommendation algorithm based on cloud computing. *J. Phys. Conf. Ser.* **2021**, *1852*, 42090. [CrossRef]
54. Warnick, R.B.; Bojanic, D.C.; Mathur, A.; Ninan, D. Segmenting Event Attendees Based on Travel Distance, Frequency of Attendance, and Involvement Measures: A Cluster Segmentation Technique. *Event Manag.* **2011**, *15*, 77–90. [CrossRef]
55. Zenina, N.; Romanovs, A.; Merkuryev, Y. Transport Simulation Model Calibration with Two-Step Cluster Analysis Procedure. *Inf. Technol. Manag. Sci.* **2015**, *18*, 49–56. [CrossRef]
56. Gremm, C. The effect of intermodal competition on the pricing behaviour of a railway company: Evidence from the German case. *Res. Transp. Econ.* **2018**, *72*, 49–64. [CrossRef]

57. Thiagarajan, R.; Prakashkumar, S. Identification of Passenger Demand in Public Transport Using Machine Learning. *Webology* **2021**, *18*, 223–236. [CrossRef]
58. Park, S.; Kim, D.-Y. Assessing language discrepancies between travelers and online travel recommendation systems: Application of the Jaccard distance score to web data mining. *Technol. Forecast. Soc. Chang.* **2017**, *123*, 381–388. [CrossRef]
59. Akin, D.; Alasalvar, S. Estimate Urban Growth and Expansion by Modeling Urban Spatial Structure Using Hierarchical Cluster Analyses of Interzonal Travel Data. *Int. J. Syst. Dyn. Appl.* **2016**, *5*, 16–41. [CrossRef]
60. Salis, S.; Barabino, B.; Useli, B. Segmenting Fare Evader Groups by Factor and Cluster Analysis. *WIT Trans. Built Environ.* **2017**, *176*, 503–515. [CrossRef]
61. Park, Y.; Choi, Y.; Kim, K.; Yoo, J.K. Machine learning approach for study on subway passenger flow. *Sci. Rep.* **2022**, *12*, 2754. [CrossRef] [PubMed]

mathematics

Article

High-Dimensional Variable Selection for Quantile Regression Based on Variational Bayesian Method

Dengluan Dai, Anmin Tang * and Jinli Ye

Yunnan Key Laboratory of Statistical Modeling and Data Analysis, Yunnan University, Kunming 650091, China; ddl12021213126@mail.ynu.edu.cn (D.D.); jinliye@mail.ynu.edu.cn (J.Y.)
* Correspondence: tam1973as@ynu.edu.cn; Tel.: +86-187-87121838

Abstract: The quantile regression model is widely used in variable relationship research of moderate sized data, due to its strong robustness and more comprehensive description of response variable characteristics. With the increase of data size and data dimensions, there have been some studies on high-dimensional quantile regression under the classical statistical framework, including a high-efficiency frequency perspective; however, this comes at the cost of randomness quantification, or the use of a lower efficiency Bayesian method based on MCMC sampling. To overcome these problems, we propose high-dimensional quantile regression with a spike-and-slab lasso penalty based on variational Bayesian (VBSSLQR), which can, not only improve the computational efficiency, but also measure the randomness via variational distributions. Simulation studies and real data analysis illustrated that the proposed VBSSLQR method was superior or equivalent to other quantile and nonquantile regression methods (including Bayesian and non-Bayesian methods), and its efficiency was higher than any other method.

Keywords: quantile regression; spike-and-slab prior; variational Bayesian; high-dimensional data

MSC: 62-08

1. Introduction

Quantile regression, as introduced by Koenker and Bassett (1978) [1], is an important statistical inference about the relationship between quantiles of the response distribution and available covariates, and can offer a practically significant alternative to the traditional mean regression, because it provides a more comprehensive description of the response distribution than the mean. Moreover, quantile regression can capture the heterogeneous impact of regressors on different parts of the distribution [2], has excellent computational properties [3], exhibits robustness to outliers, and has a wide applicability [4]. For these reasons, quantile regression has attracted extensive attention in the literature. For example, see [5] for a Bayesian quantile regression with asymmetric Laplace distribution used to specify the likelihood, [6] for a Bayesian nonparametric approach to inference for quantile regression, ref. [7] for a mechanism of Bayesian inference of quantile regression models, and [8] for model selection in quantile regression, among others.

Although there is a growing literature on quantile regression, to the best of our knowledge, little of the existing quantile regression models have focused on high-dimensional data with variable numbers and larger sample sizes. In practice, a large number of variables may be collected and some of these will be insignificant and should be excluded from the final model. In the past two decades, there has been active methodological research on penalized methods for significant variable selection in linear parametric models. For example, see [9] for ridge regression, ref. [10] for a least absolute shrinkage and selection operator (Lasso), ref. [11] for smoothly clipped absolute deviation penalty (SCAD), ref. [12] for elastic net penalty, and ref. [13] for adaptive lasso methods. These methods have been extended to quantile regression; for example, see [14] for a L_1-regularization method for quantile regression, and ref. [15] for variable selection of quantile regression using SCAD and adaptive-Lasso penalties. Nevertheless, the aforementioned regularization methods discussed are both computationally complex and unstable. Additionally, they fail to account for prior information about parameters, which can lead to an unsatisfactory parametric estimation accuracy. In recent decades, Bayesian approaches to variable selection and parameter estimation have garnered significant attention. This is because they can substantially enhance the accuracy and efficiency of parametric estimation, by imposing various priors on model parameters, consistently selecting crucial variables, and providing more information for variable selection than penalization methods for highly nonconvex optimization problems. For example, see [16] for a Bayesian Lasso where the L_1 penalty is involved in Laplace prior, [17] for a Bayesian form of adaptive Lasso, ref. [18] for Bayesian Lasso quantile regression (BLQR), and [19] for Bayesian adaptive Lsso quantile regression (BALQR). The literature mentioned above implemented the standard Gibbs sampler for posterior computation, which is not easily scalable for high-dimensional data, where the number of variables is large compared with the sample size [20].

To address this issue, the Bayesian variable selection method with a spike-and-slab prior [20] has been favored by researchers, and this can be applied to high-dimensional data at the cost of a heavy computation burden. As a computationally efficient alternative to Markov chain Monte Carlo (MCMC) simulation, variational Bayes (VB) methods are gaining traction in machine learning and statistics for approximating posterior distributions in Bayesian inference. High-efficiency variational Bayesian spike-and-slab lasso(VBSSL) has been explored for certain high-dimensional models. Ray and Szabo (2022) [21] used a VBSSL method in a high-dimensional linear model, with regression coefficient's prior specified as a mixture of Laplace distribution and Dirac mass. Yi and Tang (2022) [22] used VBSSL technology in high-dimensional linear mixed models, with a interesting prior parameter as a mixture of two Laplace distributions. However, to the best of our knowledge, there has been little work done on a VBSSL method for quantile regression. Xi et al. (2016) [23] considered Bayesian variable selection for nonparametric quantile regression with a small variable dimension, in which a spike-and-slab prior was chosen as a mixture of the point mass at zero and normal distribution. In this paper, to reduce the computational burden and quantify the parametric uncertainty, we propose quantile regression with spike-and-slab lasso penalty based on variational Bayesian (VBSSLQR), in which the prior is a mixture of two Laplace distributions, with a smaller or larger variance, respectively.

The main contributions of this paper are as follows: First, our proposed VBSSLQR method can perform variable selection for high-dimensional quantile regression at a relatively low computational cost, and without the need for nonconvex optimization, while also avoiding the curse of dimensionality problem. Second, in contrast to mean regressions, our proposed quantile approach offers a more systematic strategy for analyzing how covariates impact the various quantiles of the response distribution. Third, in ultra-high-dimensional regression, the mean regression errors are frequently presumed to be subGaussian, which is not required in our setting.

The rest of the paper is organized as follows: In Section 2, for high-dimensional data, we propose an efficient quantile regression with a spike-and-slab lasso penalty based on variational Bayes (VBSSLQR). In Section 3, we randomly generate high-dimensional data with $n = 200$ and $p = 500$ (excluding intercept items), and perform 500 simulation experiments, to explore the performance of our algorithm and compare it with other quantile regression methods (Bayesian and non-Bayesian) and nonquantile regression methods. The results show that our method is superior to other approaches in the case of high-dimensional data. We applied VBSSLQR to a real dataset that contained information about crime in various cities in the United States, and compared it with other quantile regression methods. The results showed that our method also had a good performance and excellent efficiency with real data, and the relevant results are shown in Section 4.

Some concluding remarks are given in Section 5. Technical details are presented in the Appendices A–D.

2. Models and Methods

2.1. Quantile Regression

Consider a dataset of n independent subjects. For the ith subject, let y_i be the response, while $\boldsymbol{x}_i = (1, x_{i1}, ..., x_{ir})^\top$ is an $(r+1) \times 1$ predictor vector, a simple linear regression model is defined as follows:

$$y_i = \boldsymbol{x}_i^\top \boldsymbol{\beta} + \varepsilon_i, i = 1, 2, \cdots, n, \tag{1}$$

where $\boldsymbol{\beta} = (\beta_0, \beta_1, \cdots, \beta_r)^\top$ is the regression coefficient vector with β_0 corresponding to the intercept terms, and ε_i represents the error term with unknown distribution. It is usual to assume that the τth quantile of the random error term is 0; that is, $Q_\tau(\varepsilon_i) = 0$ for $0 < \tau < 1$. According to this assumption, the form of τth quantile regression of model (1) is specified as follows:

$$Q_{y_i}(\tau|\boldsymbol{x}_i) = \boldsymbol{x}_i^\top \boldsymbol{\beta}, \tag{2}$$

where $Q_{y_i}(\tau|\boldsymbol{x}_i)$ is the inverse cumulative distribution function of y_i, given $\boldsymbol{x}_i$ evaluated at τ. The estimate of the regression coefficient vector $\boldsymbol{\beta}$ in Equation (2) is

$$\begin{aligned} \hat{\boldsymbol{\beta}} &= \underset{\boldsymbol{\beta} \in \boldsymbol{R}^{r+1}}{\operatorname{argmin}} \left[\sum_{i: y_i \geq \boldsymbol{x}_i \boldsymbol{\beta}} \tau |y_i - \boldsymbol{x}_i^\top \boldsymbol{\beta}| + \sum_{i: y_i < \boldsymbol{x}_i \boldsymbol{\beta}} (1-\tau) |y_i - \boldsymbol{x}_i^\top \boldsymbol{\beta}| \right] \\ &= \underset{\boldsymbol{\beta} \in \boldsymbol{R}^{r+1}}{\operatorname{argmin}} \sum_{i=1}^{n} \rho_\tau (y_i - \boldsymbol{x}_i^\top \boldsymbol{\beta}), \end{aligned} \tag{3}$$

where the loss function $\rho_\tau(\mu) = \mu \times (\tau - \mathrm{I}(\mu < 0))$ with the indicator function $\mathrm{I}(\cdot)$.

In light of [5,24], minimizing Equation (3) is equivalent to maximizing the likelihood of n independent individuals with the ith one distributed as an asymmetric Laplace distribution (ALD) specified as

$$p(y_i|\boldsymbol{x}_i, \boldsymbol{\beta}, \sigma, \tau) = \frac{\tau(1-\tau)}{\sigma} \exp\left\{ -\rho_\tau \left(\frac{y_i - \mu_i}{\sigma} \right) \right\}, \tag{4}$$

where the local parameter $\mu_i = \boldsymbol{x}_i^\top \boldsymbol{\beta}$, the scale parameter $\sigma > 0$, and the skewness parameter τ is between 0 and 1; obviously, ALD is a Laplace distribution when $\tau = 0.5$ and $\mu_i = 0$. However, it is computationally infeasible to carry out statistical inference based directly on Equation (4) involving the nondifferentiable point μ_i. Following [25], Equation (4) can be rewritten in the following hierarchical fashion:

$$\begin{cases} y_i = \boldsymbol{x}_i^\top \boldsymbol{\beta} + k_1 z_i + \sqrt{k_2 \sigma z_i} \xi_i, \\ z_i | \sigma \overset{\text{i.i.d.}}{\sim} \operatorname{Exp}\left(\frac{1}{\sigma}\right), \\ \xi_i \overset{\text{i.i.d.}}{\sim} N(0,1), \\ z_i \text{ is independent of } \xi_i, \end{cases} \tag{5}$$

where $k_1 = \frac{1-2\tau}{\tau(1-\tau)}$, $k_2 = \frac{2}{\tau(1-\tau)}$ and $\operatorname{Exp}\left(\frac{1}{\sigma}\right)$ denotes the exponential distribution with mean σ, whose specific density function is $p(z_i|\sigma) = \frac{1}{\sigma} \exp\left(-\frac{1}{\sigma} z_i\right) \mathrm{I}(z_i > 0)$. Equation (5) illustrates that an asymmetric Laplace distribution can also be represented as a mixture of exponential and standard normal distributions, which allows us to express a quantile regression model as a normal regression model, in which the response has the following conditional distribution:

$$y_i | \boldsymbol{x}_i, \boldsymbol{\beta}, z_i, \sigma \overset{\text{ind}}{\sim} N\left(\boldsymbol{x}_i^\top \boldsymbol{\beta} + k_1 z_i, k_2 \sigma z_i\right).$$

For the above-defined quantile regression model with high-dimensional covariate vector (r is large enough), it is of interest to estimate the parameter vector $\boldsymbol{\beta}$ and to identify the critical covariates. To this end, we considered Bayesian quantile regression based on spike-and-slab lasso, as follows:

2.2. Bayesian Quantile Regression Based on a Spike-and-Slab Lasso

As early as 2016, Xi et al. [23] applied a spike-and-slab prior to Bayesian quantile regression, but their proposed prior was a mixture of zero particle and normal distribution with large variance, and the estimate of posterior density was obtained using a Gibbs sampler. To offer novel theoretical insights into a class of continuous spike-and-slab priors, Rockova (2018) [26] introduced a novel family of spike-and-slab priors, which are a mixture of two density functions with spike or slab probability. In this paper, we adopt a spike-and-slab lasso prior with a mixture of two Laplace distributions with large or small variance, respectively [26], which facilitates the variational Bayesian technique for approximating the posterior density of parameters and for improving the efficiency of the algorithm. In light of ref. [26], given the indicator $\gamma_j = 0$ or 1, the prior of $\boldsymbol{\beta}$ in the Bayesian quantile regression model (5) can be written as

$$\pi(\boldsymbol{\beta}|\gamma) = \prod_{j=0}^{r} \pi(\beta_j|\gamma_j) = \prod_{j=0}^{r} [\gamma_j \Psi_0(\beta_j|\lambda_0) + (1-\gamma_j)\Psi_1(\beta_j|\lambda_1)], \tag{6}$$

where the Laplace density $\Psi_0(\beta_j|\lambda_0) = \frac{\lambda_0}{2}\exp(-\lambda_0|\beta_j|)$ and $\Psi_1(\beta_j|\lambda_1) = \frac{\lambda_1}{2}\exp(-\lambda_1|\beta_j|)$ with precision parameters λ_0 and λ_1 satisfying that $\lambda_0 \gg \lambda_1$, the indicator variable set $\gamma = \{\gamma_j | j = 0, 1, \cdots, r\}$, the jth variable is active when $\gamma_j = 0$, and inactive otherwise. Similarly to [27], the Laplace distribution for the regression coefficient β_j can be represented as a mixture of a normal distribution and an exponential distribution, specifically the distribution of β_j can be expressed as a hierarchical structure, as follows:

$$\begin{aligned} \beta_j \mid h_{0j}^2, h_{1j}^2, \gamma_j &\overset{\text{ind.}}{\sim} \gamma_j N\left(0, h_{0j}^2\right) + (1-\gamma_j) N\left(0, h_{1j}^2\right), \\ h_{0j}^2 \mid \lambda_0^2 &\overset{\text{i.i.d.}}{\sim} \text{Exp}\left(\frac{\lambda_0^2}{2}\right), \\ h_{1j}^2 \mid \lambda_1^2 &\overset{\text{i.i.d.}}{\sim} \text{Exp}\left(\frac{\lambda_1^2}{2}\right), \\ \gamma_j &\overset{\text{i.i.d.}}{\sim} B(\pi_\gamma), \end{aligned} \tag{7}$$

where $B(\pi_\gamma)$ denotes the Bernoulli distribution, with π_γ being the probability that indicator variable γ_j equals one for $j = 0, 1, \cdots, r$, and specifies the prior of π_γ as a Beta distribution $\text{Be}(a_{\pi_\gamma}, b_{\pi_\gamma})$, where hyperparameters a_{π_γ} and b_{π_γ}, λ_0^2, and λ_1^2 are regularization parameters to identify important variables, for which we consider the following conjugate priors:

$$\lambda_0^2 \sim \text{Ga}(\nu_{\lambda_0}, 1), \lambda_1^2 \sim \text{Ga}(\nu_{\lambda_1}, 1),$$

where $\text{Ga}(a, b)$ denotes the gamma distribution with shape parameter a and scale parameter b. As mentioned above, λ_0 and λ_1 should satisfy that $\lambda_0 \gg \lambda_1$, to this end, we select hyperparmeters ν_{λ_0} and ν_{λ_1} to satisfy that $\nu_{\lambda_0} \gg \nu_{\lambda_1}$. The prior of scale parameter σ in (5) is an inverse gamma distribution $\text{IG}(a_\sigma, b_\sigma)$ of the hyperparameters $a_\sigma = 1$ and $b_\sigma = 0.01$ in the paper leading to almost non-informative prior.

Under a Bayesian statistical paradise, based on the above priors and likelihood of quantile regression, it is required to induce the following posterior distribution $\pi(\boldsymbol{\theta}|\boldsymbol{D}) \propto p(\boldsymbol{\theta}, \boldsymbol{D})$, where $\boldsymbol{\theta} = \{\boldsymbol{\beta}, \boldsymbol{z}, \sigma, \gamma, \boldsymbol{h}_0^2, \boldsymbol{h}_1^2, \lambda_0^2, \lambda_1^2, \pi_\gamma\}$, the latent variable set $\boldsymbol{z} = \{z_i | i = 1, \cdots, n\}$, $\boldsymbol{h}_0^2 = \{h_{0j}^2 | j = 0, 1, \cdots, r\}$, $\boldsymbol{h}_1^2 = \{h_{1j}^2 | j = 0, 1, \cdots, r\}$, observing set $\boldsymbol{D} = \{\boldsymbol{y}, \boldsymbol{x}\}$ with the response set $\boldsymbol{y} = \{y_i | i = 1, \cdots, n\}$ and covariate set $\boldsymbol{x} = \{x_i | i = 1, \cdots, n\}$. Based on the hierarchical structure (5) of the quantile regression likelihood $p(y_i|x_i, \beta)$ and the hierarchical structure (7) of the spike-and-slab prior to regression coefficient vector β, we derive the joint density

$$\begin{aligned}
p(\theta, D) &= \prod_{i=1}^{n} N(y_i \mid x_i^\top \beta + k_1 z_i, k_2 \sigma z_i) \mathrm{Exp}(z_i \mid \sigma^{-1}) \mathrm{Ga}(\lambda_0^2 | v_{\lambda_0}, 1) \mathrm{Ga}(\lambda_1^2 | v_{\lambda_1}, 1) \\
&\times \prod_{j=0}^{r} \left[N(\beta_j \mid 0, h_{0j}^2)\right]^{\gamma_j} \left[N(\beta_j \mid 0, h_{1j}^2)\right]^{(1-\gamma_j)} \mathrm{Exp}(h_{0j}^2 \mid \frac{\lambda_0^2}{2}) \mathrm{Exp}(h_{1j}^2 \mid \frac{\lambda_1^2}{2}) \\
&\times \prod_{j=0}^{r} B(\gamma_j \mid 1, \pi_\gamma) \mathrm{Be}(\pi_\gamma | a_{\pi_\gamma}, b_{\pi_\gamma}) \mathrm{IG}(\sigma | a_\sigma, b_\sigma) \\
&\propto \prod_{i=1}^{n} (k_2 \sigma z_i)^{-\frac{1}{2}} \exp\left(-\frac{(y_i - x_i^\top \beta - k_1 z_i)^2}{2 k_2 \sigma z_i} \right) \frac{1}{\sigma} \exp\left(-\frac{z_i}{\sigma} \right) (\lambda_0^2)^{v_{\lambda_0} - 1} \exp(-\lambda_0^2) \\
&\times (\lambda_1^2)^{(v_{\lambda_1} - 1)} \exp(-\lambda_1^2) \prod_{j=0}^{r} \left[\frac{1}{\sqrt{h_{0j}^2}} \exp\left(-\frac{\beta_j^2}{2 h_{0j}^2} \right) \right]^{\gamma_j} \left[\frac{1}{\sqrt{h_{1j}^2}} \exp\left(-\frac{\beta_j^2}{2 h_{1j}^2} \right) \right]^{(1-\gamma_j)} \\
&\times \frac{\lambda_0^2}{2} \exp\left(-\frac{\lambda_0^2}{2} h_{0j}^2 \right) \frac{\lambda_1^2}{2} \exp\left(-\frac{\lambda_1^2}{2} h_{1j}^2 \right) \prod_{j=0}^{r} \pi_\gamma^{\gamma_j} (1 - \pi_\gamma)^{1-\gamma_j} \pi_\gamma^{a_{\pi_\gamma} - 1} (1 - \pi_\gamma)^{b_{\pi_\gamma} - 1} \\
&\times \frac{b_\sigma^{a_\sigma}}{\Gamma(a_\sigma)} \sigma^{-a_\sigma - 1} \exp\left(-\frac{b_\sigma}{\sigma} \right).
\end{aligned} \tag{8}$$

Although sampling from the aforementioned posterior is simple, it becomes increasingly time-consuming for higher dimension quantile models. To tackle this issue, we developed a faster and more efficient alternative method based on variational Bayesian.

2.3. *Quantile Regression with a Spike-and-Slab Lasso Penalty Based on Variational BAYESIAN*

At present, the most commonly variational Bayesian approximation posterior distribution methods use mean field approximation theory [28], which has the highest efficiency among variational methods, especially for those parameters or parameter block with conjugate priors. Bayesian quantile regression needs to take into account that the variance of each observation value is different, and each y_i corresponds to a potential variable z_i, which will result in the algorithm efficiency of quantile regression being lower than that of general mean regression. Therefore, in this paper, we use the variational Bayesian algorithm of the mean field approximation, which is the most efficient algorithm, to derive the quantile regression model with the spike-and-slab lasso penalty.

Based on variational theory, we choose a densities for random variables θ from variational family $\mathcal{F}$, which having the same support Θ as the posterior density $\pi(\theta \mid D)$. We approximate the posterior density $\pi(\theta \mid D)$ by any variational density $q(\theta) \in \mathcal{F}$. The variational Bayesian method is to seek the optimal approximation to $\pi(\theta \mid D)$ by minimizing the Kullback-Leibler divergence between $q(\theta)$ and $\pi(\theta \mid D)$, which is an optimization problem that can be expressed as:

$$q^*(\theta) = \underset{q(\theta) \in \mathcal{F}}{\operatorname{argmin}} \, \mathrm{KL}[q(\theta) \parallel \pi(\theta \mid D)],$$

where $\mathrm{KL}[q(\theta) \parallel \pi(\theta \mid D)] = \int_\Theta q(\theta) \log \frac{q(\theta)}{\pi(\theta \mid D)} d\theta$, which is not less than zero and equal to zero if, and only if, $q(\theta) \equiv \pi(\theta \mid D)$. The posterior density $\pi(\theta \mid D) = \frac{p(\theta, D)}{p(D)}$ with the joint distribution $p(\theta, D)$ of parameter θ and data D and the marginal distribution $p(D)$ data D. Since $p(D) = \int_\Theta p(\theta, D) d\theta$, which does not have an analytic expression for our considered model, it is rather difficult to implement the optimization problem presented above. It is easy to induce that

$$\log p(D) = \mathrm{KL}[q(\theta) \parallel \pi(\theta \mid D)] + \mathcal{L}\{q(\theta)\} \geq \mathcal{L}\{q(\theta)\},$$

in which the evidence lower bound (ELOB) $\mathcal{L}\{\mathrm{q}(\boldsymbol{\theta})\} = \mathrm{E}_{\mathrm{q}(\boldsymbol{\theta})}[\log p(\boldsymbol{\theta}, \boldsymbol{D})] - \mathrm{E}_{\mathrm{q}(\boldsymbol{\theta})}[\log \mathrm{q}(\boldsymbol{\theta})]$ with $\mathrm{E}_{\mathrm{q}(\boldsymbol{\theta})}[\cdot]$ representing the expectation taken with respect to the variational density $\mathrm{q}(\boldsymbol{\theta})$. Thus, minimizing $\mathrm{KL}[\mathrm{q}(\boldsymbol{\theta}) \parallel \pi(\boldsymbol{\theta} \mid \boldsymbol{D})]$ is equivalent to maximizing $\mathcal{L}\{\mathrm{q}(\boldsymbol{\theta})\}$ because $\log p(\boldsymbol{D})$ does not depend on $\boldsymbol{\theta}$. That is,

$$\mathrm{q}^*(\boldsymbol{\theta}) = \operatorname*{argmin}_{\mathrm{q}(\boldsymbol{\theta}) \in \mathcal{F}} \mathrm{KL}[\mathrm{q}(\boldsymbol{\theta}) \parallel \pi(\boldsymbol{\theta} \mid \boldsymbol{D})] = \operatorname*{argmax}_{\mathrm{q}(\boldsymbol{\theta}) \in \mathcal{F}} \mathcal{L}\{\mathrm{q}(\boldsymbol{\theta})\},$$

which indicates that seeking the optimal approximation problem of $\pi(\boldsymbol{\theta} \mid \boldsymbol{D})$ becomes maximizing $\mathcal{L}\{\mathrm{q}(\boldsymbol{\theta})\}$ under the variational family $\mathcal{F}$. The complexity of the approximation problem heavily is related to the variational family $\mathcal{F}$. Therefore, choosing a comparatively simple variational family $\mathcal{F}$ to optimize the objective function $\mathcal{L}\{\mathrm{q}(\boldsymbol{\theta})\}$ with respect to $q(\boldsymbol{\theta})$ is fascinating.

Following the commonly used approach to choosing a tractable variational family $\mathcal{F}$ in the variational studies, we consider the frequently-used mean-field theory, which assumes that blocks of $\boldsymbol{\theta}$ are mutually independent and each is measured by the parameters of the variational density. Obviously, the variational density $\mathrm{q}(\boldsymbol{\theta})$ is assumed to be factorized across the blocks of $\boldsymbol{\theta}$:

$$\mathrm{q}(\boldsymbol{\theta}) = \prod_{j=0}^{r} \mathrm{q}_1(\beta_j, \gamma_j)\mathrm{q}_2(h_{0j}^2)\mathrm{q}_3(h_{1j}^2) \prod_{i=1}^{n} \mathrm{q}_4(z_i)\mathrm{q}_5(\lambda_0^2)\mathrm{q}_6(\lambda_1^2)\mathrm{q}_7(\pi_\gamma)\mathrm{q}_8(\sigma) \equiv \prod_{s}^{8} \mathrm{q}_s(\boldsymbol{\theta}_s),$$

in which form of each variational densities $\mathrm{q}_s(\boldsymbol{\theta}_s)$'s is unknown, but the above assumed factorization across components is predetermined. Moreover, the best solutions for $\mathrm{q}_s(\boldsymbol{\theta}_s)$'s are to be achieved by maximizing $\mathcal{L}\{\mathrm{q}(\boldsymbol{\theta}_1, \cdots, \boldsymbol{\theta}_8)\}$ with respect to variational densities $\mathrm{q}_1(\boldsymbol{\theta}_1), \cdots, \mathrm{q}_8(\boldsymbol{\theta}_8)$ by the coordinate ascent method, where $\boldsymbol{\theta} = \{\boldsymbol{\theta}_1, \cdots, \boldsymbol{\theta}_8\}$ where $\boldsymbol{\theta}_s$ can be either a scalar or a vector. This means that when the correlation between several unknown parameters or potential variables cannot be ignored, they should be put in the same block and merged into $\boldsymbol{\theta}_s$. Following the idea of the coordinate ascent method given in ref. [29], when fixing other variational factors $\mathrm{q}_k(\boldsymbol{\theta}_k)$ for $k \neq s$, i.e., the optimal density $\mathrm{q}_s^*(\boldsymbol{\theta}_s)$, which maximizes $\mathcal{L}\{\mathrm{q}(\boldsymbol{\theta})\}$ with respect to $\mathrm{q}_s(\boldsymbol{\theta}_s)$, is shown to take the form

$$\mathrm{q}_s^*(\boldsymbol{\theta}_s) \propto \exp\{\mathrm{E}_{-\boldsymbol{\theta}_s}[\log p(\boldsymbol{\theta}, \boldsymbol{D})]\}, \tag{9}$$

where $\log p(\boldsymbol{\theta}, \boldsymbol{D})$ is the logarithm of the joint density function and $\mathrm{E}_{-s}[\cdot]$ is the expectation taken with respect to the density $\prod_{k \neq s} \mathrm{q}_k(\boldsymbol{\theta}_k)$ for $s = 1, \cdots, 8$.

According to Equations (8) and (9), we can derive the variational posterior for each parameter as follows (see Appendix A for the details):

$$\begin{aligned}
&\beta_j \overset{\text{i.i.d.}}{\sim} \mu_{\gamma_j} N\left(\mu_{0j}, \sigma_{0j}^2\right) + (1 - \mu_{\gamma_j}) N\left(\mu_{1j}, \sigma_{1j}^2\right), \text{ for } j = 1, \cdots, r, \\
&h_{0j}^2 \overset{\text{i.i.d.}}{\sim} \mu_{\gamma_j} \mathrm{GIG}\left(\frac{1}{2}, \mathrm{E}_{\lambda_0^2}(\lambda_0^2), \sigma_{0j}^2 + \mu_{0j}^2\right) + (1 - \mu_{\gamma_j}) \mathrm{Exp}\left(\frac{1}{2}\mathrm{E}_{\lambda_0^2}(\lambda_0^2)\right), \\
&h_{1j}^2 \overset{\text{i.i.d.}}{\sim} (1 - \mu_{\gamma_j}) \mathrm{GIG}\left(\frac{1}{2}, \mathrm{E}_{\lambda_1^2}(\lambda_1^2), \sigma_{1j}^2 + \mu_{1j}^2\right) + \mu_{\gamma_j} \mathrm{Exp}\left(\frac{1}{2}\mathrm{E}_{\lambda_1^2}(\lambda_1^2)\right), \\
&\lambda_0^2 \sim \mathrm{Ga}\left(r + 1 + \nu_{\lambda_0}, 1 + \frac{1}{2}\sum_{j=1}^{r} \mathrm{E}_{h_{0j}^2}(h_{0j}^2)\right), \\
&\lambda_1^2 \sim \mathrm{Ga}\left(r + 1 + \nu_{\lambda_1}, 1 + \frac{1}{2}\sum_{j=1}^{r} \mathrm{E}_{h_{1j}^2}(h_{1j}^2)\right), \\
&\gamma_j \overset{\text{i.i.d.}}{\sim} B\left(1, (1 + \mathrm{e}^{\zeta_i})^{-1}\right), \text{ for } j = 0, 1, \cdots, r, \\
&\pi_\gamma \sim \mathrm{Be}\left(a + \sum_{j=0}^{r} \mu_{\gamma_j}, r + 1 + b - \sum_{j=0}^{r} \mu_{\gamma_j}\right),
\end{aligned}$$

$$z_i \overset{\text{i.i.d.}}{\sim} \text{GIG}\left(\frac{1}{2}, a_{z_i}, b_{z_i}\right), \quad \text{for } i = 1, 2, \cdots, n,$$
$$\sigma \sim \text{IG}\left(\frac{3}{2}n + a_\sigma, c_\sigma\right),$$

where $\text{GIG}(\cdot,\cdot,\cdot)$ denotes generalized inverse Gaussian distribution,

$$\begin{aligned}
\mu_{0j} &= \sigma_{0j}^2 \frac{\text{E}_\sigma(\sigma^{-1})}{k_2} \sum_{i=1}^{n} \left[\text{E}_{z_i}\left(z_i^{-1}\right)\left(y_i - \boldsymbol{x}_{i,(-j)}^\top \boldsymbol{\mu}_{\boldsymbol{\beta}_{(-j)}}\right) - k_1\right] x_{ij}, \\
\sigma_{0j}^2 &= \left[\text{E}_{h_{0j}^2|\gamma_j=1}\left(h_{0j}^{-2}\right) + \frac{\text{E}_\sigma(\sigma^{-1})}{k_2} \sum_{i=1}^{n} x_{ij}^2 \text{E}_{z_i}\left(z_i^{-1}\right)\right]^{-1}, \\
\mu_{1j} &= \sigma_{1j}^2 \frac{\text{E}_\sigma(\sigma^{-1})}{k_2} \sum_{i=1}^{n} \left[\text{E}_{z_i}\left(z_i^{-1}\right)\left(y_i - \boldsymbol{x}_{i,(-j)}^\top \boldsymbol{\mu}_{\boldsymbol{\beta}_{(-j)}}\right) - k_1\right] x_{ij}, \\
\sigma_{1j}^2 &= \left[\text{E}_{h_{1j}^2|\gamma_j=0}(h_{1j}^{-2}) + \frac{\text{E}_\sigma(\sigma^{-1})}{k_2} \sum_{i=1}^{n} x_{ij}^2 \text{E}_{z_i}\left(z_i^{-1}\right)\right]^{-1},
\end{aligned} \tag{10}$$

and

$$\begin{aligned}
\zeta_j &= \text{E}_{\pi_\gamma}(\log(1-\pi_\gamma)) - \text{E}_{\pi_\gamma}(\log \pi_\gamma) + \frac{1}{2}\text{E}_{h_{0j}^2|\gamma_j=1}(\log h_{0j}^2) - \frac{1}{2}\text{E}_{h_{1j}^2|\gamma_j=0}(\log h_{1j}^2) \\
&\quad + \frac{1}{2}\{\log \sigma_{1j}^2 - \log \sigma_{0j}^2\} + \frac{1}{2}(\log\sigma_{1j}^2 - \log\sigma_{0j}^2) + \frac{1}{2}(\mu_{1j}^2(\sigma_{1j}^2)^{-1} - \mu_{0j}^2(\sigma_{0j}^2)^{-1}), \\
a_{z_i} &= \frac{\text{E}_\sigma(\sigma^{-1})}{k_2}\left(k_1^2 + 2k_2\right), \\
b_{z_i} &= \frac{\text{E}_\sigma(\sigma^{-1})}{k_2}[(y_i - \boldsymbol{x}_i^\top \boldsymbol{\mu}_{\boldsymbol{\beta}})^2 + \boldsymbol{x}_i^\top \boldsymbol{\Sigma}_{\boldsymbol{\beta}} \boldsymbol{x}_i], \\
c_\sigma &= \frac{1}{2k_2} \sum_{i=1}^{n} \{k_1^2 \mu_{z_i} + \text{E}_{z_i}(z_i^{-1})[(y_i - \boldsymbol{x}_i^\top \boldsymbol{\mu}_{\boldsymbol{\beta}})^2 + \boldsymbol{x}_i^\top \boldsymbol{\Sigma}_{\boldsymbol{\beta}} \boldsymbol{x}_i] \\
&\quad - 2k_1(y_i - \boldsymbol{x}_i^\top \boldsymbol{\mu}_{\boldsymbol{\beta}})\} + \sum_{i=1}^{n} \mu_{z_i} + b_\sigma.
\end{aligned}$$

In the above equation, $\mu_{\lambda_0^2} = \text{E}_{\lambda_0^2}(\lambda_0^2)$, and $\mu_{\lambda_1^2}, \mu_{\beta_j}, \mu_{\gamma_j}, \mu_{z_i}$ are similar to $\mu_{\lambda_0^2}$, $\boldsymbol{\mu}_{\boldsymbol{\beta}} = (\mu_{\beta_0}, \mu_{\beta_1}, \cdots, \mu_{\beta_p})^\top$ with $\mu_{\beta_j} = \mu_{\gamma_j}\mu_{0j} + (1-\mu_{\gamma_j})\mu_{1j}$, and $\boldsymbol{\mu}_{\boldsymbol{\beta}_{(-j)}}$ is a $p \times 1$ vector with the jth component of vector $\boldsymbol{\mu}_{\boldsymbol{\beta}}$ deleted, $\boldsymbol{\Sigma}_{\boldsymbol{\beta}} = \text{diag}\left(\sigma_{\beta_0}^2 \sigma_{\beta_1}^2, \cdots \sigma_{\beta_p}^2\right)$ with $\sigma_{\beta_j}^2 = \mu_{\gamma_j}\sigma_{0j}^2 + (1-\mu_{\gamma_j})\sigma_{1j}^2 + \mu_{\gamma_j}(1-\mu_{\gamma_j})(\mu_{0j} - \mu_{1j})^2$.

In the section above, we derived the variational posterior of each parameter. Using the idea of coordinate axis optimization, we can update each variational distribution iteratively until it converges.

For this reason, we list the variational Bayesian spike-and-slab lasso quantile regression (VBSSLQR) algorithm as shown in Algorithm 1:

Algorithm 1 Variational Bayesian spike-and-slab lasso quantile regression (VBSSLQR).

Input:

Data $\boldsymbol{y}$, predictors $\boldsymbol{x}$, prior parameters $\nu_{\lambda_0} = 10^4, \nu_{\lambda_1} = 1, a_\sigma = 1, b_\sigma = 0.01, a = b = 1$, precision $\epsilon = 0.01$ and quantile τ;

Output:

Optimized variational parameters $\mathrm{E}_{\beta_j}(\beta_j)$, $\mathrm{Var}_{\beta_j}(\beta_j)$ for $j = 0, 1, \cdots, r$ and the corresponding Bayesian confidence interval.

Initialize: $\boldsymbol{\mu}_{\boldsymbol{\beta}}^{(0)}$; $\mathrm{E}^{(0)}_{h^2_{0j}|\gamma_j=1}(\frac{1}{h^2_{0j}}) = 0.01$; $\mathrm{E}^{(0)}_{h^2_{1j}|\gamma_j=0}(\frac{1}{h^2_{1j}}) = 1$;$\boldsymbol{\mu}_{\boldsymbol{\gamma}}^{(0)} = \mathbf{0.5}$;

$\mathrm{E}^{(0)}_{\lambda_0^2}(\lambda_0^2) = 100$; $\mathrm{E}^{(0)}_{\lambda_1^2}(\lambda_1^2) = 1$; $\mathrm{E}^{(0)}_{\pi_\gamma}(\log \pi_\gamma) = 0$;$\mathrm{E}^{(0)}_{\sigma}(\sigma^{-1}) = 1$;

$\mathrm{E}^{(0)}_{\pi_\gamma}(\log(1-\pi_\gamma)) = -1$;$\boldsymbol{\gamma}^{(0)} = \mathbf{0}$; $\mathrm{E}^{(0)}_{z_i}(z_i) = \mathrm{E}^{(0)}_{z_i}(z_i^{-1})$;

while $|d^{(t)}| > \varepsilon$ **do**

for $j = 0$ to r **do**

Update ${\sigma^2}^{(t+1)}_{0j}$, $\mu^{(t+1)}_{0j}$, ${\sigma^2}^{(t+1)}_{1j}$ and $\mu^{(t+1)}_{1j}$ according to Equation (10).

Update $\mathrm{E}^{(t+1)}_{h^2_{0j}|\gamma_j=1}(h^2_{0j})$, $\mathrm{E}^{(t+1)}_{h^2_{0j}}(h^2_{0j})$, $\mathrm{E}^{(t+1)}_{h^2_{0j}|\gamma_j=1}(h^{-2}_{0j})$, $\mathrm{E}^{(t+1)}_{h^2_{0j}|\gamma_j=1}(\log h^2_{0j})$ according to $\mathrm{q}(h^2_{0j})$,

Update $\mathrm{E}^{(t+1)}_{h^2_{1j}|\gamma_j=0}(h^2_{1j})$, $\mathrm{E}^{(t+1)}_{h^2_{1j}}(h^2_{1j})$, $\mathrm{E}^{(t+1)}_{h^2_{1j}|\gamma_j=0}(h^{-2}_{1j})$, $\mathrm{E}^{(t+1)}_{h^2_{1j}|\gamma_j=0}(\log h^2_{1j})$ according to $\mathrm{q}(h^2_{1j})$,

Update $\mathrm{E}^{(t+1)}_{\gamma_j}(\gamma_j)$ according to the variational posterior $\mathrm{q}(\gamma_j)$,

Update $\mathrm{E}^{(t+1)}_{\beta_j}(\beta_j)$ and $\mathrm{Var}^{(t+1)}_{\beta_j}(\beta_j)$,

end for

Update $\mathrm{E}^{(t+1)}_{\lambda_0^2}(\lambda_0^2)$ according to the variational posterior $\mathrm{q}(\lambda_0^2)$,

Update $\mathrm{E}^{(t+1)}_{\lambda_0^2 1}(\lambda_1^2)$ according to the variational posterior $\mathrm{q}(\lambda_1^2)$,

Update $\mathrm{E}^{(t+1)}_{\pi_\gamma}(\pi_\gamma)$, $\mathrm{E}^{(t+1)}_{\pi_\gamma}(\log \pi_\gamma)$ and $\mathrm{E}^{(t+1)}_{\pi_\gamma}(\log(1-\pi_\gamma))$ according to $\mathrm{q}(\pi_\gamma)$,

for $i = 1$ to n **do**

Update $\mathrm{E}^{(t+1)}_{z_i}(z_i)$ and $\mathrm{E}^{(t+1)}_{z_i}(z_i^{-1})$ according to the variational posterior $\mathrm{q}(z_i)$,

end for

Update $\mathrm{E}^{(t+1)}_{\sigma}(\sigma)$ and $\mathrm{E}^{(t+1)}_{\sigma}(\sigma^{-1})$ according to the variational posterior $\mathrm{q}(\sigma)$,

$|d^{(t+1)}| = \max\Big\{|\boldsymbol{\theta}^{(t+1)}_{q_1} - \boldsymbol{\theta}^{(t)}_{q_1}|, \ldots, |\boldsymbol{\theta}^{(t+1)}_{q_m} - \boldsymbol{\theta}^{(t)}_{q_m}|\Big\}$,

end while

In Algorithm 1 above, $\Psi(\cdot)$ is the digamma function and the expectation $\mathrm{E}^{(t+1)}_{h^2_{0j}|\gamma_j=1}(\log h^2_{0j})$ of $\log h^2_{0j}$ with respect to generalized inverse Gaussian distribution. Thus, we assume that $x \sim \mathrm{GIG}(p, a, b)$, then:

$$\mathrm{E}_x(\log x) = \frac{\frac{\mathrm{dK}_p(\sqrt{ab})}{\mathrm{d}p}}{\mathrm{K}_p(\sqrt{ab})} - \frac{1}{2}\ln(\frac{a}{b}), \tag{11}$$

where $\mathrm{K}_p(\cdot)$ represents the Bessel function of the second kind. Note that there is no analytic solution or function to the differential of the modified Bessel function. Therefore, we approximate $\mathrm{E}_x(\log x)$ using the second-order Taylor expansion of $\log x$. This paper lists the expectations of some parameter functions about variational posteriors involved in Algorithm 1; see Appendix B for details. Based on our proposed VBSSLQR algorithm, in the next section, we randomly generate high-dimensional data, conduct simulation research, and compare the performance with other methods. Notably, the asymptotic variance of the quantile regression is reciprocal proportional to the density of the errors at the quantile point. In cases where n is small and we estimate extreme quantiles, the correlating asymptotic variance will be large, resulting in less precise estimates [23]. Therefore, the regression coefficient is difficult to estimate at an extreme quantile and this is feasible when the sample sizes needs to be increased appropriately.

3. Simulation Studies

In this section, we used simulated high-dimensional data with a sample size $n = 200$ and variable number $r = 500$, in order to study the performance of VBSSLQR and compare it with existing methods, including linear regression with a lasso penalty (Lasso), linear regression with an adaptive lasso penalty (ALasso), quantile regression with a lasso penalty (QRL), quantile regression with an adaptive lasso penalty (QRAL), Bayesian regularized quantile regression with a lasso penalty (BLQR), and Bayesian regularized quantile regression with an adaptive lasso penalty (BALQR). The data in the simulation studies were generated using Equation (1), in which the covariate vector $\boldsymbol{x}_i$ was randomly generated from the multivariate normal distribution $N(\mathbf{0}, \boldsymbol{\Sigma})$ with the (k,l)th of $\boldsymbol{\Sigma}$ being $0.5^{|k-l|}$. Among these covariates, we only considered the ten important explanatory variables that have significant impact on the dependent variable. We set the 1, 51, 101, 151, 201, 251, 301, 351, 401, and 451 predictors to be active, and their regression coefficients are −3, −2.5, −2, −1.5, −1, 1, 1.5, 2, 2.5, 3, and the rest are zero. In addition, we discuss the performance of various approaches in the case of two types of random error; namely, independent and identically distributed (i.i.d.) random errors and heterogeneous random errors.

3.1. Independent and Identically Distributed Random Errors Random

In this subsection, with reference to [19,23], we set the random errors ε_i's in Equation (1) to be independently and identically distributed and consider the following five different distributions with τ quantile being zero:

- The error $\varepsilon_i \overset{\text{i.i.d.}}{\sim} N(-\mu, 1)$ with μ being the τ quantile of $N(0,1)$, for $i = 1, \cdots, n$;
- The error $\varepsilon_i \overset{\text{i.i.d.}}{\sim} \text{Laplace}(-\mu, 1)$ with μ being the τ quantile of Laplace$(0,1)$, where Laplace(a,b) denotes the Laplace distribution with location parameter a and scale parameter b;
- The error $\varepsilon_i \overset{\text{i.i.d.}}{\sim} 0.1N(-\mu_1, 9) + 0.9N(-\mu_2, 1)$ with μ_1 and μ_2 respectively being the τ quantile of $N(0,9)$ and $N(0,1)$;
- The error $\varepsilon_i \overset{\text{i.i.d.}}{\sim} 0.1\text{Laplace}\,(-\mu_1, 9) + 0.9\text{Laplace}(-\mu_2, 1)$ with μ_1 and μ_2 respectively being the τ quantile of Laplace$(0,9)$ and Laplace$(0,1)$;
- The error $\varepsilon_i \overset{\text{i.i.d.}}{\sim} \text{Cauchy}(-\mu, 0.2)$ with μ being the τ quantile of Cauchy$(0, 0.2)$, where Cauchy(a,b) denotes the Cauchy distribution with location parameter a and scale parameter b;

For all of the above error distributions with any $\tau \in (0.3, 0.5, 0.7)$, we ran 500 replications for each method, and evaluated the performance using two criteria. The first criterion was the median of mean absolute deviations (MMAD), which quantifies the general distance between the estimated conditional quantile and the true conditional quantile. Specifically, the mean absolute deviation (MAD) in any replication is defined as $\frac{1}{n}\sum_{i=1}^{n} |\boldsymbol{x}_i\boldsymbol{\beta} - \boldsymbol{x}_i\hat{\boldsymbol{\beta}}_\tau)|$, where $\hat{\boldsymbol{\beta}}_\tau$ is the estimate of regression coefficient $\boldsymbol{\beta}$ given τ. The second criterion of the mean of true positives (TP) and false positives (FP) was selected for each method.

Table 1 shows the median and standard deviation (SD) of MADs estimated using each method for simulations with homogeneous errors. It is clear that our method was either optimal (bold) in all cases, especially in quantile $\tau = 0.3, 0.7$, or that our approach was significantly superior to the other six methods. When the error distribution was normal, a Laplace and normal mixture, the MMAD of the BALQR method was suboptimal. When the error distribution was Cauchy, the MMAD of the QRL approach was suboptimal, but Table 2 shows that this sacrificed the complexity of the model. When the error distribution was a Laplace mixture, the MMAD of the lasso approach was suboptimal; however, it selected an overfitting quantile regression model with about 30 FP variables, as can be seen from Table 2. It is particularly important to note that, in the case of high dimensional data, the MMAD for the quantile regression model with the lasso penalty or adaptive lasso penalty is not less than the MMAD for general linear models with a lasso penalty. Therefore, it is inappropriate to use a lasso penalty or adaptive lasso in this case.

Table 1. The median and standard deviation of 500 MADs estimated using various methods in simulations with i.i.d. errors.

Quantile	Error Distribution	Method						
		Lasso	ALasso	QRL	QRAL	BLQR	BALQR	VBSSLQR
$\tau = 0.3$	normal	0.60 (0.06)	0.89 (0.14)	0.88 (0.07)	3.90 (0.20)	1.28 (0.17)	0.55 (0.09)	**0.21** (0.05)
	Laplace	0.72 (0.08)	0.97 (0.15)	1.06 (0.15)	3.95 (0.20)	1.44 (0.21)	0.68 (0.20)	**0.24** (0.06)
	normal mixture	0.76 (0.09)	1.04 (0.14)	1.02 (0.15)	3.95 (0.21)	1.42 (0.19)	0.71 (0.16)	**0.23** (0.05)
	Laplace mixture	0.89 (0.13)	1.13 (0.18)	1.24 (0.33)	4.06 (0.23)	1.69 (0.32)	1.07 (0.31)	**0.26** (0.07)
	Cauchy	1.23 (4.59)	1.46 (12.07)	0.59 (0.62)	4.24 (12.40)	1.92 (1.07)	1.98 (4.95)	**0.11** (0.60)
$\tau = 0.5$	normal	0.40 (0.05)	0.81 (0.16)	0.80 (0.07)	3.90 (0.21)	1.21 (0.19)	0.29 (0.07)	**0.20** (0.05)
	Laplace	0.56 (0.08)	0.90 (0.17)	1.01 (0.16)	3.96 (0.21)	1.35 (0.22)	0.46 (0.23)	**0.20** (0.05)
	normal mixture	0.53 (0.07)	0.89 (0.17)	0.96 (0.13)	3.95 (0.20)	1.36 (0.25)	0.41 (0.21)	**0.21** (0.05)
	Laplace mixture	0.74 (0.13)	1.02 (0.20)	1.20 (0.22)	4.01 (0.23)	1.72 (0.32)	0.83 (0.32)	**0.21** (0.06)
	Cauchy	1.31 (28.87)	1.44 (10.15)	0.48 (0.16)	4.40 (32.20)	2.026 (1.16)	4.28 (4.47)	**0.07** (0.71)
$\tau = 0.7$	normal	0.61 (0.06)	0.93 (0.16)	0.88 (0.07)	3.88 (0.21)	1.22 (0.19)	0.56 (0.11)	**0.20** (0.05)
	Laplace	0.71 (0.08)	1.02 (0.16)	1.06 (0.16)	3.97 (0.20)	1.36 (0.27)	0.67 (0.20)	**0.25** (0.07)
	normal mixture	0.75 (0.09)	1.06 (0.17)	1.01 (0.14)	3.94 (0.21)	1.32 (0.23)	0.75 (0.19)	**0.22** (0.05)
	Laplace mixture	0.89 (0.13)	1.20 (0.21)	1.24 (0.32)	4.01 (0.22)	1.65 (0.33)	0.99 (0.36)	**0.26** (0.09)
	Cauchy	1.22 (8.78)	1.60 (8.43)	0.60 (0.60)	4.27 (13.65)	2.28 (1.25)	3.02 (2.91)	**0.12** (1.14)

The bold represents the optimal result in each scenario.

In order to show the results of variable selection more intuitively, we introduced TP (true positives) and FP (false positives), to calculate the mean of TP and FP of 500 repeated simulations, respectively. Detailed results are shown in Table 2 below:

Table 2. Mean TP/FP of various methods for simulation with i.i.d. errors.

Quantile	Error Distribution	Method						
		Lasso TP/FP	ALasso TP/FP	QRL TP/FP	QRAL TP/FP	BLQR TP/FP	BALQR TP/FP	VBSSLQR TP/FP
$\tau = 0.3$	normal	10.00/38.24	9.80/0.20	10.00/175.01	5.00/95.33	8.48/0.00	10.00/0.02	**10.00/0.02**
	Laplace	10.00/40.43	9.75/0.34	9.99/169.28	5.00/94.88	8.06/0.00	9.86/0.13	**10.00/0.01**
	normal mixture	10.00/38.84	9.73/0.31	9.99/163.96	5.00/95.39	8.19/0.00	9.90/0.10	**10.00/0.00**
	Laplace mixture	10.00/37.99	9.62/0.71	9.87/146.31	5.00/95.25	7.43/0.00	9.50/0.70	**10.00/0.01**
	Cauchy	8.21/29.05	7.95/7.09	9.87/97.34	4.66/94.49	6.11/0.00	7.35/13.24	**9.83/0.00**
$\tau = 0.5$	normal	10.00/39.00	9.75/0.29	10.00/156.04	5.00/94.73	8.37/0.00	10.00/0.01	**10.00/0.01**
	Laplace	10.00/38.06	9.69/0.47	9.99/107.53	5.00/95.30	7.97/0.00	9.81/0.09	**10.00/0.00**
	normal mixture	10.00/39.03	9.69/0.57	10.00/112.74	5.00/95.33	8.10/0.00	9.86/0.06	**10.00/0.00**
	Laplace mixture	10.00/39.71	9.55/0.83	9.94/71.54	5.00/94.77	7.40/0.00	9.53/0.47	**10.00/0.00**
	Cauchy	8.19/29.31	8.04/7.06	10.00/8.50	4.55/95.67	5.53/0.00	6.03/22.94	**9.77/0.00**
$\tau = 0.7$	normal	10.00/38.85	9.70/0.41	10.00/174.87	5.00/95.40	8.41/0.00	9.99/0.03	**10.00/0.01**
	Laplace	10.00/37.68	9.64/0.67	9.99/168.15	5.00/95.05	7.91/0.00	9.77/0.13	**10.00/0.01**
	normal mixture	10.00/38.38	9.63/0.63	9.99/165.65	5.00/95.76	8.11/0.00	9.88/0.08	**10.00/0.01**
	Laplace mixture	10.00/39.64	9.41/1.22	9.88/150.33	5.00/95.56	7.32/0.00	9.50/1.03	**9.99/0.01**
	Cauchy	8.35/30.24	7.54/8.17	9.89/97.85	4.65/95.19	5.73/0.00	6.81/17.95	**9.36/0.00**

The bold represents the optimal result in each scenario.

It is possible to conclude from the results in Table 2 that the lasso method can generally select all true active variables, but it fits many false active variables; and when the random error is a Cauchy distribution, it cannot select all true active variables; A lasso approach can identify true active variables, but there are also some misjudged behaviors, especially when the random error distribution is a Cauchy distribution; Although the QRL approach can identify real active variables, it still contains many false active variables, and the model it identifies has a high complexity; the QRAL method cannot identify all true active variables, and incorrectly identifies some inactive variables; In the case of high-dimensional data, the BLQR approach cannot select all the true active variables, but it also does not incorrectly select inactive variables. The true active variable selected using the BALQR method is better than using the BLQR method, but some inactive variables are incorrectly selected, especially when the random error distribution is the Cauchy distribution. Our VBSSLQR method not only had the smallest MMAD, but also could select true active variables and eliminate most false active variables. As a whole, our method was superior to the other six methods for variable selection, especially in quantile $\tau = 0.3, 0.7$, performing significantly better than BLQR, BALQR, and QRL.

3.2. Heterogeneous Random Errors

Now we consider the case of heterogeneous random errors, to demonstrate the performance of our method. In this subsection, the data were generated from the following model:

$$y_i = x_i^\top \beta + (1 + u_i)\varepsilon_i, \tag{12}$$

where $u_i \overset{i.i.d.}{\sim} U(0,1)$, in which $U(a,b)$ represents the uniform distribution with support set (a,b). The design matrix x_i was generated in the same way as above, and the regression coefficient β was set as before. Furthermore, in the simulation study, we combined x_i and u_i; that is, u_i was also a covariate. Finally, random error ε_i was also generated from the five different distributions defined in Section 3.1.

We also studied the performance of the quantile $\tau \in (0.3, 0.5, 0.7)$ under the different methods and simulated 500 times, to calculate the MMAD and mean of TP/FP. We list the experimental results in Tables 3 and 4.

Table 3. The median and standard deviation of 500 MADs were estimated via various methods for simulations with heterogeneous random errors.

Quantile	Error Distribution	Method						
		Lasso	ALasso	QRL	QRAL	BLQR	BALQR	VBSSLQR
$\tau = 0.3$	normal	0.91 (0.10)	1.13 (0.15)	1.31 (0.14)	3.96 (0.22)	1.57 (0.22)	0.90 (0.20)	**0.30** (0.07)
	Laplace	1.08 (0.13)	1.24 (0.17)	1.61 (0.39)	4.09 (0.23)	1.93 (0.29)	1.23 (0.35)	**0.36** (0.13)
	normal mixture	1.14 (0.14)	1.32 (0.17)	1.55 (0.35)	4.06 (0.24)	1.92 (0.31)	1.31 (0.35)	**0.33** (0.11)
	Laplace mixture	1.36 (0.21)	1.51 (0.23)	2.34 (0.60)	4.27 (0.26)	2.30 (0.42)	2.05 (0.52)	**0.39** (0.24)
	Cauchy	1.91 (102.51)	1.94 (33.45)	1.17 (0.80)	4.80 (19.32)	2.49 (1.11)	3.90 (3.39)	**0.15** (0.98)
$\tau = 0.5$	normal	0.61 (0.08)	0.93 (0.17)	1.21 (0.12)	3.96/0.21	1.39 (0.27)	0.50 (0.22)	**0.30** (0.07)
	Laplace	0.87 (0.13)	1.12 (0.20)	1.53 (0.25)	4.09 (0.23)	1.84 (0.33)	1.06 (0.35)	**0.29** (0.08)
	normal mixture	0.81 (0.12)	1.08 (0.19)	1.44 (0.21)	4.05 (0.23)	1.77 (0.31)	1.08 (0.37)	**0.31** (0.08)
	Laplace mixture	1.12 (0.21)	1.31 (0.25)	1.84 (0.32)	4.28 (0.29)	2.25 (0.41)	1.65 (0.56)	**0.32** (0.12)
	Cauchy	1.93 (2.23)	1.93 (107.59)	0.74 (0.27)	4.93 (15.90)	2.88 (1.23)	3.72 (4.80)	**0.09** (0.88)
$\tau = 0.7$	normal	0.92 (0.09)	1.20 (0.17)	1.32 (0.14)	3.97/0.20	1.38 (0.26)	0.86 (0.21)	**0.31** (0.09)
	Laplace	1.07 (0.13)	1.31 (0.18)	1.61 (0.37)	4.09 (0.22)	1.95 (0.33)	1.29 (0.31)	**0.37** (0.15)
	normal mixture	1.14 (0.14)	1.40 (0.19)	1.53 (0.33)	4.08 (0.23)	1.85 (0.36)	1.31 (0.29)	**0.34** (0.10)
	Laplace mixture	1.38 (0.20)	1.58 (0.23)	2.16 (0.61)	4.32 (0.28)	2.37 (0.52)	1.86 (0.50)	**0.40** (0.25)
	Cauchy	1.76 (3.76)	2.01 (17.31)	1.24 (0.76)	4.65 (31.22)	4.01 (1.30)	4.31 (18.21)	**0.16** (1.04)

The bold represents the optimal result in each scenario.

For heterogeneous random errors, our approach was still the best, similarly to for i.i.d. random errors. It is noteworthy that the VBSSLQR method was more robust than the other methods, and our method had the smallest MMAD change compared to the case of i.i.d. random errors. We can see that the MMAD of our method remained basically unchanged, while the MMAD of the other six methods differed by more than 0.5 compared to the i.i.d. random errors in some states.

We also investigated the mean of TP and FP for heterogeneous random errors under different quantiles τ. The results are listed in Table 4, which shows that the effect of variable selection of heterogeneous random errors was slightly lower than the effect of variable selection of i.i.d. random errors under the same sample size, but our method still provided the best selection results.

Table 4. Mean TP/FP of the various methods for simulations with heterogeneous random errors.

Quantile	Error Distribution	Method						
		Lasso TP/FP	ALasso TP/FP	QRL TP/FP	QRAL TP/FP	BLQR TP/FP	BALQR TP/FP	VBSSLQR TP/FP
$\tau = 0.3$	normal	10.00/40.76	9.72/0.35	9.98/170.29	5.00/95.23	7.97/0.00	9.75/0.13	**10.00/0.03**
	Laplace	10.00/38.80	9.54/0.83	9.73/140.09	4.99/94.59	7.23/0.00	9.31/1.20	**9.97/0.05**
	normal mixture	10.00/38.79	9.59/0.74	9.74/136.63	5.00/95.82	7.29/0.00	9.35/1.23	**9.98/0.04**
	Laplace mixture	9.95/37.96	9.17/2.07	8.82/76.98	4.96/95.42	6.53/0.00	8.51/4.48	**9.83/0.05**
	Cauchy	7.46/26.86	7.15/10.23	9.56/66.04	4.43/95.56	4.86/0.00	5.73/24.57	**9.52/0.00**
$\tau = 0.5$	normal	10.00/39.21	9.67/0.44	9.99/142.56	5.00/95.56	7.93/0.00	9.86/0.16	**10.00/0.05**
	Laplace	10.00/39.03	9.49/0.93	9.81/89.76	5.00/95.33	7.07/0.00	9.32/1.09	**9.99/0.01**
	normal mixture	10.00/38.44	9.51/0.86	9.83/85.73	4.99/95.27	7.41/0.00	9.28/0.96	**9.99/0.02**
	Laplace mixture	9.96/38.91	9.26/2.08	9.33/31.13	4.95/95.76	6.23/0.00	8.75/4.13	**9.97/0.02**
	Cauchy	7.24/25.47	7.23/9.37	9.99/4.30	4.26/95.95	4.54/0.00	5.92/24.88	**9.60/0.00**
$\tau = 0.7$	normal	10.00/40.58	9.59/0.52	9.98/171.43	5.00/95.53	7.88/0.00	9.76/0.16	**10.00/0.07**
	Laplace	10.00/39.20	9.44/1.14	9.74/144.66	4.99/95.20	6.87/0.00	9.26/0.97	**9.95/0.06**
	normal mixture	10.00/38.29	9.38/1.14	9.76/138.14	5.00/95.49	7.04/0.00	9.30/1.30	**9.99/0.02**
	Laplace mixture	9.96/38.88	9.08/2.37	8.93/85.78	4.96/95.02	5.95/0.00	8.69/3.50	**9.81/0.05**
	Cauchy	7.64/27.34	7.16/10.19	9.61/68.75	4.52/96.36	3.59/0.00	5.79/24.92	**9.46/0.00**

The bold represents the optimal result in each scenario.

We also calculated the mean execution times of various Bayesian quantile regressions under different quantile τ for different distributions of random errors, and list the results in Table A1 of Appendix C, which illustrates that our proposed VBSSLQR approach was a lot more efficient than BLQR and BALQR, for which we sampled MCMC 1000 times and discarded the first 500 times, and made a statistical inference based on 500 samples (the experimental study shows that the algorithm converged after 500 samples). In order to illustrate the feasibility of applying our proposed VBSSLQR to cases with smaller effect sizes, we changed the above active predictors to 1, while the other settings remained unchanged. The performance of our proposed method is shown in Table A2, which illustrates that the results were not significantly different from those of Tables 1 and 2 when random errors had an independent identical distribution, and slightly worse than those of Tables 3 and 4 when the random errors were heterogeneous.

4. Examples

In this section, we analyzed a real dataset containing information about crime in various cities across the United States. This dataset is accessible from the University of Irvine machine learning repository (http://archive.ics.uci.edu/ml/datasets/communities+and+crime, accessed on 1 May 2023). We calculated the per capital rate of violent crimes by dividing the total number of violent crimes by the population of each city. The violent crimes considered in our analysis were those classified as murder, rape, robbery, and assault, as per United States law. The observed individuals were communities. The dataset has 116 variables, where the first four columns are response, name of the community, code of county, and code of community; the middle features are demographic information about each community, such as population, age, race, and income; and the final columns are regions. According to the source: "the data combines socio-economic data from the 1990 US Census, law enforcement data from the 1990 US LEMAS survey, and crime data from the 1995 FBI UCR". This dataset has been applied for quantile regression [30]. The dataset is available at

- train set: https://academics.hamilton.edu/mathematics/ckuruwit/Data/Crime/train.csv (accessed on 1 May 2023).
- test set: https://academics.hamilton.edu/mathematics/ckuruwit/Data/Crime/test.csv (accessed on 1 May 2023).

Our dependent variable of interest was the murder rate of each city, denoted as y_i for the ith city. As the murder rate denotes the most dangerous violent crimes, we choose this variable. Studying factors correlated with the response dependent variable is of significant importance for the public and law enforcement agencies.

To adapt the data to our model, we preprocessed the data as follows:

- Delete columns from the data set that contain missing data.
- Delete the data when the response variable y_i equals 0, because this is not an issue of interest to us.
- Transform y_i: $y_i' = \log \frac{y_i}{1-y_i}$ and let y_i' be the new response variable.
- Convert some qualitative variables into quantitative variables.
- Standardized covariates.

After the above data preprocessing, we obtained 1060 observation objects and 95 covariates in the training set, and we obtained 122 observation objects and 95 covariates in the testing set. We implemented a quantile regression model between the 96 predictors (including intercept) and the response y_i' with different quantiles.

In this section, we compare QRL, QRAL, BLQR, and BALQR with our method VBSSLQR for real datasets, all with quantile penalty regression. Under different quantiles $\tau \in (0.1, 0.3, 0.5, 0.7, 0.9)$, we compared the performance of the different approaches. We counted the root mean squared error (RMSE) of each method under each quantile τ and the number of selected active variables, to evaluate the performance of each approach on the test set, where the RMSE was evaluated using RMSE $= \sqrt{\frac{1}{n}\sum_{i=1}^{n}(y_i - \hat{y}_{\tau i})^2}$ with $\hat{y}_{\tau i}$ being the fitted value of response y_i under quantile τ. Finally, the results are listed in Table 5 below.

Table 5. RMSE of fitting test dataset and the number of active variables for the various methods for the real dataset.

Method	RMSE/Number of Active Variables				
	$\tau = 0.1$	$\tau = 0.3$	$\tau = 0.5$	$\tau = 0.7$	$\tau = 0.9$
QRL	1.36/64	0.94/65	1.09/66	0.93/57	1.21/53
QRAL	3.11/37	3.05/40	3.08/37	2.84/36	3.10/32
BLQR	1.34/1	1.08/1	1.03/1	1.08/1	1.30/1
BALQR	1.67/2	1.08/1	1.02/1	1.08/1	1.30/1
VBSSLQR	**1.34**/12	**0.94**/9	**0.78**/12	**0.83**/7	**1.14**/9

The bold represents the optimal result in each scenario.

To visually show the results listed in Table 4, the best results are in bold under each quantile τ. Clearly, our method performed better than the other methods for all quantiles, and the active variables selected by our method were suitable, which means that our method was very competitive compared with the other methods. The BLQR and BALQR approaches could only identify the intercept, and they could not identify the variables that really affected the response quantile. The QRL and QRAL methods were prone to overfitting, because they recognized too many active variables. Finally, the efficiency of our method with real data was also significantly higher than that of the other approaches. Although BLQR, QRL, and our proposed method had the same RMSE performance at $\tau = 0.1, 0.3$, BLQR showed underfitting and QRL showed overfitting. Thus, we believe there is sufficient evidence to show that our method was very competitive with the other approaches.

Similarly to [30], we list the active variables selected under each quantile in Table 6. Thus, Table 6 shows the variable selection of our proposed method with real data.

Table 6. Crime data analysis: variable selection.

Quantile Level (τ)	Quantile Specific Variables			
0.1	racepctblack	pctUrban	PctLess9thGrade	TotalPctDiv
	PctNotHSGrad	PctOccupMgmtProf	FemalePctDiv	PctPersDenseHous
	NumInShelters	PctHousOccup	PctBornSameState	
0.3	racepctblack	NumInShelters	FemalePctDiv	PctPersDenseHous
	TotalPctDiv	PctHousOwnOcc	RentLowQ	MedRent
0.5	racePctWhite	racePctHisp	FemalePctDiv	TotalPctDiv
	PctWorkMom	PctSpeakEnglOnly	HousVacant	PctVacantBoarded
	RentLowQ	MedRent	NumInShelters	
0.7	racePctWhite	racePctAsian	FemalePctDiv	TotalPctDiv
	PctVacantBoarded		NumInShelters	
0.9	racePctWhite	racePctAsian	indianPerCap	PctOccupManu
	MalePctDivorce	PctHousOccup	PctVacantBoarded	NumInShelters

In the above table, our method selected only a small number of predictors at each quantile level. Notably, only the variable "NumInShelters" had an impact on the response at all quantiles; the variables "FemalePctDiv" and "TotalPctDiv" had an impact on the response at $\tau = 0.1, 0.3, 0.5, 0.7$; the variable "PctVacantBoarded" had an impact on the response at $\tau = 0.5, 0.7, 0.9$; the variable "racePctWhite" had an impact on the response at $\tau = 0.5, 0.7, 0.9$; and the other variables affected a few quantiles of response. Therefore, the five variables selected from the quantile regression model were

- PctVacantBoarded: percentage of households that are vacant and boarded up to prevent vandalism.
- NumInShelters: number of shelters in the community.
- FemalePctDiv: percentage of females who are divorced.
- TotalPctDiv: percentage of people who are divorced.
- racePctWhite: percentage of people of white race.

In order to obtain a better understanding of these five common variables, we plot their correlation to the response.

Figure 1 depicts the relationship between the five common variables and the murder rate. Only the correlation between the NumInShelters and murder rate is not obvious, with MalePctDivorce, RentLowQ, racePctWhite, and PctVacantBoarded significantly affecting the murder rate. The variable racePctWhite and murder rate are negatively correlated, while FemalePctDiv, TotalPctDiv, PctVacantBoarded, and murder rate are positively correlated. This result was in accordance with the practical situation, and it can be seen that our results were basically consistent with that of [30]. Our method could more comprehensively select important variables under the same quantile. Therefore, the percentage of females who are divorced, percentage of persons who are divorced, the percentage of households that are vacant and boarded up to prevent from vandalism, and the percentage of people with white race affect the murder rate.

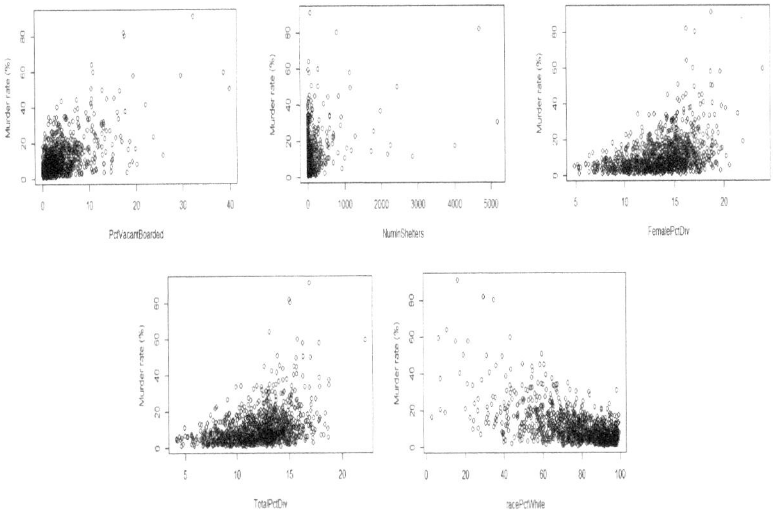

Figure 1. Correlation between murder rate and common variables.

5. Conclusions

In this paper, we propose variational Bayesian spike-and-slab lasso quantile regression variable selection and estimation. This method applies spike-and-slab lasso prior to each regression coefficient β, thus punishing the regression coefficient β. The spike prior distribution we choose is a small variance Laplace distribution, while the slab prior distribution is a large variance Laplace distribution [26]. It is precisely because it punishes each regression coefficient β that it has a powerful variable selection function, but this also brings a problem of low efficiency, especially when introducing a spike-and-slab prior into quantile regression (note, the algorithm efficiency of quantile regression is inherently lower than that of general regression approaches). In order to solve the problem of inefficiency (influenced by both the quantile regression and spike-and-slab lasso prior) and to make the algorithm feasible. We introduced a variational Bayesian method, to approximate the posterior distribution of each parameter. The simulation studies and real data analyses illustrated that the quantile regression with the spike-and-slab lasso penalty based on variational Bayesian method performed effectively and exhibited a robust competitiveness compared with other approaches (Bayesian method or non-Bayesian method, quantile regression, or nonquantile regression), especially in the case of high-dimensional data. In future research work, it would be significant to improve the interpretability and computational efficiency of ultra-high-dimensional quantile regression based on VB and dimension reduction techniques.

Author Contributions: Conceptualization, D.D. and A.T.; methodology, A.T. and D.D.; software, D.D. and J.Y.; validation, A.T., D.D. and J.Y. ; formal analysis, D.D. and A.T; investigation, D.D., J.Y. and A.T.; Preparation of the original work draft, A.T. and D.D.; visualization, D.D. and J.Y.; supervision, funding acquisition, D.D., A.T. and J.Y. All authors have read and agreed to the published version of the manuscript.

Funding: This work was supported by the National Natural Science Foundation of China (No. 11961079), Yunnan Univeristy Multidisciplinary Team Construction Projects in 2021, and Yunnan University Quality Improvement Plan for Graduate Course Textbook Construction (CZ22622202).

Institutional Review Board Statement: Not applicable.

Informed Consent Statement: Not applicable.

Data Availability Statement: The research data are available on the website http://archive.ics.uci.edu/ml/datasets/communities+and+crime, accessed on 1 May 2023.

Conflicts of Interest: The authors declare no conflict of interest.

Appendix A. Deduction

Based on the mean-field variational Formula (9), from the joint density (8), it is required to induce the following variational distributions.

$$
\begin{aligned}
q_1(\beta_j,\gamma_j) \propto & \exp\Bigg\{ \mathrm{E}_{-\beta_j,-\gamma_j}\Bigg[\sum_{i=1}^{n} \log N(y_i \mid \boldsymbol{x}_i^{\top}\boldsymbol{\beta}+k_1 z_i, k_2\sigma z_i) + \gamma_j \log N(\beta_j \mid 0, h_{0j}^2) \\
& +(1-\gamma_j)\log N(\beta_j \mid 0, h_{0j}^2) + \log B(\gamma_j \mid 1, \pi_\gamma)\Bigg]\Bigg\} \\
\propto & \exp\Bigg\{ -\frac{1}{2k_2}\mathrm{E}_\sigma(\sigma^{-1})\Bigg[\sum_{i=1}^{n} \mathrm{E}_{z_i}(z_i^{-1})x_{ij}^2\beta_j^2 + 2\sum_{i=1}^{n} x_{ij}(\mathrm{E}_{z_i}(z_i^{-1}) \\
& (y_i - \boldsymbol{x}_{i,(-j)}^{\top}\boldsymbol{\mu}_{\boldsymbol{\beta}_{(-j)}}) - k_1)\beta_j\Bigg] - \frac{\gamma_j}{2}\mathrm{E}_{h_{0j}^2}(\log 2\pi h_{0j}^2) - \frac{\gamma_j}{2}\mathrm{E}_{h_{0j}^2}(\frac{1}{h_{0j}^2})\beta_j^2 \\
& - \frac{(1-\gamma_j)}{2}\mathrm{E}_{h_{1j}^2}(\log 2\pi h_{1j}^2) - \frac{(1-\gamma_j)}{2}\mathrm{E}_{h_{0j}^2}(\frac{1}{h_{1j}^2})\beta_j^2 + \gamma_j \mathrm{E}_{\pi_\gamma}(\log \pi_\gamma) \\
& +(1-\gamma_j)\mathrm{E}_{\pi_\gamma}(\log(1-\pi_\gamma))\Bigg\} \\
\propto & \exp\Bigg\{ \Bigg[-\frac{1}{2k_2}\mathrm{E}_\sigma(\sigma^{-1})\sum_{i=1}^{n} \mathrm{E}_{z_i}(z_i^{-1})x_{ij}^2 - \frac{\gamma_j}{2}\mathrm{E}_{h_{0j}^2}(\frac{1}{h_{0j}^2}) - \frac{(1-\gamma_j)}{2}\mathrm{E}_{h_{0j}^2}(\frac{1}{h_{1j}^2})\Bigg]\beta_j^2 \\
& - \frac{1}{k_2}\sum_{i=1}^{n} x_{ij}(\mathrm{E}_{z_i}(z_i^{-1})(y_i - \boldsymbol{x}_{i,(-j)}^{\top}\boldsymbol{\mu}_{\boldsymbol{\beta}_{(-j)}}) - k_1)\beta_j + \gamma_j \mathrm{E}_{\pi_\gamma}(\log \pi_\gamma) \\
& +(1-\gamma_j)\mathrm{E}_{\pi_\gamma}(\log(1-\pi_\gamma)) - \frac{\gamma_j}{2}\mathrm{E}_{h_{0j}^2}(\log 2\pi h_{0j}^2) - \frac{(1-\gamma_j)}{2}\mathrm{E}_{h_{1j}^2}(\log 2\pi h_{1j}^2)\Bigg\},
\end{aligned}
$$

where $\boldsymbol{\mu}_{\boldsymbol{\beta}_{(-j)}} = \mathrm{E}_{\boldsymbol{\beta}_{(-j)}}(\boldsymbol{\beta}_{(-j)})$. therefore, given $\gamma_j = k$, for $k = 0$ and 1, then

$$
\begin{aligned}
q_1(\beta_j \mid \gamma_j = k) \propto \exp\Bigg\{ \mathrm{E}_{-\beta_j|\gamma_j=k}\Bigg[& \sum_{i=1}^{n} \log N(y_i \mid \boldsymbol{x}_i^{\top}\boldsymbol{\beta}+k_1 z_i, k_2\sigma z_i) + k\log N(\beta_j \mid 0, h_{0j}^2) \\
& +(1-k)\log N(\beta_j \mid 0, h_{0j}^2)\Bigg]\Bigg\},
\end{aligned}
$$

if $\gamma_j = 0$ then

$$
\begin{aligned}
q_1(\beta_j \mid \gamma_j = 0) \propto & \exp\Bigg\{ \Bigg[-\frac{1}{2k_2}\mathrm{E}_\sigma(\sigma^{-1})\sum_{i=1}^{n} \mathrm{E}_{z_i}(z_i^{-1})x_{ij}^2 - \frac{1}{2}\mathrm{E}_{h_{1j}^2|\gamma_j=0}(\frac{1}{h_{1j}^2})\Bigg]\beta_j^2 \\
& -\frac{1}{k_2}\sum_{i=1}^{n} x_{ij}(\mathrm{E}_{z_i}(z_i^{-1})(y_i - \boldsymbol{x}_{i,(-j)}^{\top}\boldsymbol{\mu}_{\boldsymbol{\beta}_{(-j)}}) - k_1)\beta_j\Bigg\}, \\
\beta_j \mid \gamma_j = 0 & \overset{\text{i.i.d.}}{\sim} N(\mu_{1j}, \sigma_{1j}^2),
\end{aligned}
$$

if $\gamma_j = 1$ then

$$
q_1(\beta_j \mid \gamma_j = 1) \propto \exp\Bigg\{ \Bigg[-\frac{1}{2k_2}\mathrm{E}_\sigma(\sigma^{-1})\sum_{i=1}^{n} \mathrm{E}_{z_i}(z_i^{-1})x_{ij}^2 - \frac{1}{2}\mathrm{E}_{h_{0j}^2|\gamma_j=1}(\frac{1}{h_{0j}^2})\Bigg]\beta_j^2
$$

$$-\frac{1}{k_2}\sum_{i=1}^{n} x_{ij}(\mathrm{E}_{z_i}(z_i^{-1})(y_i - \boldsymbol{x}_{i,(-j)}^{\top}\boldsymbol{\mu}_{\beta_{(-j)}}) - k_1)\beta_j\Bigg\},$$

$$\beta_j \mid \gamma_j = 1 \overset{\text{i.i.d.}}{\sim} N(\mu_{0j}, \sigma_{0j}^2),$$

therefore $\beta_j \overset{\text{i.i.d.}}{\sim} \sum_{k=0}^{1} \mathrm{p}(\gamma_j = k)N(\mu_{kj}, \sigma_{kj}^2)$, for $j = 0, 1, \cdots, r$, where

$$\mu_{kj} = \sigma_{kj}^2 \frac{\mathrm{E}_{\sigma}(\sigma^{-1})}{k_2}\sum_{i=1}^{n}\Big[\mathrm{E}_{z_i}(z_i^{-1})(y_i - \boldsymbol{x}_{i,(-j)}^{\top}\boldsymbol{\mu}_{\beta_{(-j)}}) - k_1\Big]x_{ij},$$

$$\sigma_{kj}^2 = \left[\mathrm{E}_{h_{kj}^2|\gamma_j=1-k}(h_{kj}^{-2}) + \frac{\mathrm{E}_{\sigma}(\sigma^{-1})}{k_2}\sum_{i=1}^{n} x_{ij}^2 \mathrm{E}_{z_i}(z_i^{-1})\right]^{-1},$$

for $k = 1$ and 2. similarly, if $\gamma_j = 1$ then

$$\mathrm{q}_2(h_{0j}^2 \mid \gamma_j = 1) \propto \exp\left\{\mathrm{E}_{-h_{0j}^2|\gamma_j=1}\left[\log N(\beta_j \mid 0, h_{0j}^2) + \log \mathrm{Exp}(h_{0j}^2 \mid \frac{\lambda_0^2}{2})\right]\right\}$$

$$\propto (h_{0j}^2)^{-\frac{1}{2}}\exp\left\{-\frac{\mathrm{E}_{\beta_j|\gamma_j=1}(\beta_j^2)}{2h_{0j}^2} - \frac{\mathrm{E}_{\lambda_0^2}(\lambda_0^2)}{2}h_{0j}^2\right\}$$

$$= (h_{0j}^2)^{-\frac{1}{2}}\exp\left\{-\frac{1}{2}\left[\frac{\mu_{0j}^2 + \sigma_{0j}^2}{h_{0j}^2} + \mathrm{E}_{\lambda_0^2}(\lambda_0^2)h_{0j}^2\right]\right\},$$

$$h_{0j}^2 \mid \gamma_j = 1 \overset{\text{i.i.d.}}{\sim} \mathrm{GIG}(\frac{1}{2}, \mathrm{E}_{\lambda_0^2}(\lambda_0^2), \mu_{0j}^2 + \sigma_{0j}^2),$$

if $\gamma_j = 0$ then

$$\mathrm{q}_3(h_{0j}^2 \mid \gamma_j = 0) \propto (h_{0j}^2)^{-\frac{1}{2}}\exp\left\{-\frac{1}{2}\mathrm{E}_{\lambda_0^2}(\lambda_0^2)h_{0j}^2\right\},$$

$$h_{0j}^2 \mid \gamma_j = 0 \overset{\text{i.i.d.}}{\sim} \mathrm{Exp}(\frac{1}{2}\mathrm{E}_{\lambda_0^2}(\lambda_0^2)),$$

therefore

$$\mathrm{q}_2(h_{0j}^2) = \mathrm{p}(\gamma_j = 1)\mathrm{GIG}(\frac{1}{2}, \mathrm{E}_{\lambda_0^2}(\lambda_0^2), \sigma_{0j}^2 + \mu_{0j}^2) + \mathrm{p}(\gamma_j = 0)\mathrm{Exp}(\frac{1}{2}\mathrm{E}_{\lambda_0^2}(\lambda_0^2)).$$

similarly,

$$\mathrm{q}_3(h_{1j}^2) = \mathrm{p}(\gamma_j = 0)\mathrm{GIG}(\frac{1}{2}, \mathrm{E}_{\lambda_1^2}(\lambda_1^2), \sigma_{1j}^2 + \mu_{1j}^2) + \mathrm{p}(\gamma_j = 1)\mathrm{Exp}(\frac{1}{2}\mathrm{E}_{\lambda_1^2}(\lambda_1^2)),$$

where μ_{kj} and σ_{kj}^2 are the same as above, for $k = 1$ and 0, from $\mathrm{q}(\beta_j, \gamma_j)$ then

$$\mathrm{q}_1(\beta_j, \gamma_j = 1) = \mathrm{C}\exp\left\{-\frac{1}{2}\sigma_{0j}^{-2}\beta_j^2 + \frac{\mu_{0j}}{\sigma_{0j}^2}\beta_j + \mathrm{E}_{\pi_\gamma}(\log \pi_\gamma) - \frac{1}{2}\mathrm{E}_{h_{0j}^2|\gamma_j=1}(\log h_{0j}^2)\right\},$$

integral out β_j obtain

$$\mathrm{p}(\gamma_j = 1) = \int \mathrm{q}(\beta_j, \gamma_j = 1)d\beta_j$$

$$= \mathrm{C}\sqrt{\sigma_{0j}^2}\exp\left\{\mu_{0j}^2(2\sigma_{0j}^2)^{-1} + \mathrm{E}_{\pi_\gamma}(\log \pi_\gamma) - \frac{1}{2}\mathrm{E}_{h_{0j}^2|\gamma_j=1}(\log h_{0j}^2)\right\}.$$

similarly,

$$\begin{aligned}\mathrm{p}(\gamma_j=0)&=\int \mathrm{q}(\beta_j,\gamma_j=0)d\beta_j\\&=C\sqrt{\sigma_{1j}^2}\exp\left\{\mu_{1j}^2(2\sigma_{1j}^2)^{-1}+\mathrm{E}_{\pi_\gamma}(\log(1-\pi_\gamma))-\frac{1}{2}\mathrm{E}_{h_{1j}^2|\gamma_j=0}(\log h_{1j}^2)\right\}.\end{aligned}$$

letting

$$\begin{aligned}\zeta_j=&\log\mathrm{p}(\gamma_j=0)-\log\mathrm{p}(\gamma_j=1)\\=&\mathrm{E}_{\pi_\gamma}(\log(1-\pi_\gamma))-\mathrm{E}_{\pi_\gamma}(\log\pi_\gamma)+\frac{1}{2}\mathrm{E}_{h_{0j}^2|\gamma_j=1}(\log h_{0j}^2)\\&-\frac{1}{2}\mathrm{E}_{h_{1j}^2|\gamma_j=0}(\log h_{1j}^2)+\frac{1}{2}(\log\sigma_{1j}^2-\log\sigma_{0j}^2)+\frac{1}{2}(\mu_{1j}^2(\sigma_{1j}^2)^{-1}-\mu_{0j}^2(\sigma_{0j}^2)^{-1}),\end{aligned}$$

then

$$\mathrm{p}(\gamma_j=1)=\frac{1}{1+\mathrm{e}^{\zeta_i}},\ \mathrm{p}(\gamma_j=0)=\frac{\mathrm{e}^{\zeta_i}}{1+\mathrm{e}^{\zeta_i}},$$

therefore $\gamma_j \overset{\text{i.i.d.}}{\sim} B(1,(1+\mathrm{e}^{\zeta_i})^{-1})$, for $j=0,1,\cdots,r$, where μ_{kj} and σ_{kj}^2 are the same as above, for $k=1$ and 2.

$$\begin{aligned}\mathrm{q}_5(\lambda_0^2)\propto&\exp\left\{\mathrm{E}_{-\lambda_0^2}\left[\sum_{j=0}^{r}\log\mathrm{Exp}(h_{0j}^2\,|\,\frac{\lambda_0^2}{2})+\log\pi(\lambda_0^2)\right]\right\}\\\propto&(\lambda_0^2)^{\nu_{\lambda_0}+r+1-1}\exp\left\{-\frac{\sum_{j=0}^{r}\mathrm{E}_{h_{0j}^2}(h_{0j}^2)}{2}\lambda_0^2-\lambda_0^2\right\}\\\lambda_0^2\sim&\mathrm{Ga}(\nu_{\lambda_0}+r+1,\frac{\sum_{j=0}^{r}\mathrm{E}_{h_{0j}^2}(h_{0j}^2)}{2}+1),\end{aligned}$$

similarly,

$$\lambda_1^2\sim\mathrm{Ga}(\nu_{\lambda_1}+r+1,\frac{\sum_{j=0}^{r}\mathrm{E}_{h_{1j}^2}(h_{1j}^2)}{2}+1),$$

where ν_{λ_0} and ν_{λ_1} are hyperparameters.

$$\begin{aligned}\mathrm{q}_7(\pi_\gamma)\propto&\exp\left\{\mathrm{E}_{-\pi_\gamma}\left[\sum_{j=0}^{r}\log B(\gamma_j\,|\,1,\pi_\gamma)+\log\pi(\pi_\gamma)\right]\right\}\\=&\exp\left\{\sum_{j=0}^{r}\mathrm{E}_{\gamma_j}(\gamma_j)\log\pi_\gamma+(r+1-\sum_{j=0}^{r}\mathrm{E}_{\gamma_j}(\gamma_j))\log(1-\pi_\gamma)\right.\\&\left.+(a-1)\log\pi_\gamma+(b-1)\log(1-\pi_\gamma)\right\}\\=&(\pi_\gamma)^{a-1+\sum_{j=0}^{r}\mathrm{E}_{\gamma_j}(\gamma_j)}(1-\pi_\gamma)^{r+b+1-1-\sum_{j=0}^{r}\mathrm{E}_{\gamma_j}(\gamma_j)},\end{aligned}$$

therefore $\pi_\gamma\sim\mathrm{Be}(a+\sum_{j=0}^{r}\mathrm{E}_{\gamma_j}(\gamma_j),r+b+1-\sum_{j=0}^{r}\mathrm{E}_{\gamma_j}(\gamma_j))$ where a,b are hyperparameters.

$$\begin{aligned}\mathrm{q}_4(z_i)\propto&\exp\left\{\mathrm{E}_{-z_i}\left[\log N(y_i\,|\,\boldsymbol{x}_i^\top\boldsymbol{\beta}+k_1z_i,k_2\sigma z_i)+\log\mathrm{E}(z_i\,|\,\sigma^{-1})\right]\right\}\\\propto&z_i^{\frac{1}{2}-1}\exp\left\{-\frac{1}{2}\left[\frac{\mathrm{E}_\sigma(\sigma^{-1})}{k_2}((k_1^2+2k_2)z_i+\frac{(y_i-\boldsymbol{x}_i^\top\boldsymbol{\mu}_\beta)^2+\boldsymbol{x}_i^\top\boldsymbol{\Sigma}_\beta\boldsymbol{x}_i}{z_i})\right]\right\},\end{aligned}$$

therefore $z_i \overset{\text{i.i.d.}}{\sim} \text{GIG}(\frac{1}{2}, a_{z_i}, b_{z_i})$, for $i = 1, \cdots, n$, where

$$a_{z_i} = \frac{\text{E}_\sigma(\sigma^{-1})}{k_2}(k_1^2 + 2k_2), b_{z_i} = \frac{\text{E}_\sigma(\sigma^{-1})}{k_2}[(y_i - \boldsymbol{x}_i^\top \boldsymbol{\mu}_\beta)^2 + \boldsymbol{x}_i^\top \boldsymbol{\Sigma}_\beta \boldsymbol{x}_i],$$

with k_1 and k_2 being constants and $\boldsymbol{\Sigma}_\beta$ is a $(p+1) \times (p+1)$ diagonal matrix with jth entry being $\text{Var}(\beta_j)$.

$$\begin{aligned} q_8(\sigma) \propto & \exp\left\{\text{E}_{-\sigma}\left[\sum_{i=1}^n \log N(y_i \mid \boldsymbol{x}_i^\top \boldsymbol{\beta} + k_1 z_i, k_2 \sigma z_i) + \log \text{E}(z_i \mid \sigma^{-1}) + \log \pi(\sigma)\right]\right\} \\ \propto & (\frac{1}{\sigma})^{\frac{n}{2}+n+a_\sigma-1} \exp\left\{-\frac{1}{2k_2}\left[k_1^2 \text{E}_{z_i}(z_i) + \text{E}_{z_i}(z_i^{-1})((y_i - \boldsymbol{x}_i^\top \boldsymbol{\mu}_\beta)^2 + \boldsymbol{x}_i^\top \boldsymbol{\Sigma}_\beta \boldsymbol{x}_i)\right.\right. \\ & \left.\left. -2k_1(y_i - \boldsymbol{x}_i^\top \boldsymbol{\mu}_\beta)\right]\sigma^{-1} - \sum_{i=1}^n \text{E}_{z_i}(z_i)\sigma^{-1} - b_\sigma \sigma^{-1}\right\}, \end{aligned}$$

therefore $\sigma \sim \text{IG}(\frac{3}{2}n + a_\sigma, c_\sigma)$, where a_σ, b_σ are hyperparameters and

$$\begin{aligned} c_\sigma = & \frac{1}{2k_2} \sum_{i=1}^n \{k_1^2 \text{E}_{z_i}(z_i) + \text{E}_{z_i}(z_i^{-1})[(y_i - \boldsymbol{x}_i^\top \boldsymbol{\mu}_\beta)^2 + \boldsymbol{x}_i^\top \boldsymbol{\Sigma}_\beta \boldsymbol{x}_i] \\ & - 2k_1(y_i - \boldsymbol{x}_i^\top \boldsymbol{\mu}_\beta)\} + \sum_{i=1}^n \text{E}_{z_i}(z_i) + b_\sigma. \end{aligned}$$

Appendix B. Expectation

The expectation of some parameter functions about variational posteriors:

Since $\beta_j \overset{\text{i.i.d.}}{\sim} \sum_{k=0}^1 \text{p}(\gamma_j = k) N(\mu_{kj}, \sigma_{kj}^2)$, therefore

$$\text{E}_{\beta_j}(\beta_j) = \sum_{k=0}^1 \text{p}(\gamma_j = k) \text{E}_{\beta_j|\gamma_j=k}(\beta_j) = \sum_{k=0}^1 \text{p}(\gamma_j = k) \mu_{kj},$$

$$\text{Var}_{\beta_j}(\beta_j) = \text{p}(\gamma_j = 1)\sigma_{0j}^2 + \text{p}(\gamma_j = 0)\sigma_{1j}^2 + \text{p}(\gamma_j = 1)\text{p}(\gamma_j = 0)(\mu_{0j} - \mu_{1j})^2,$$

$$\text{E}_{\beta_j|\gamma_j=k}(\beta_j^2) = \mu_{kj}^2 + \sigma_{kj}^2, k = 0, 1.$$

Since $h_{0j}^2 \overset{\text{i.i.d.}}{\sim} \text{p}(\gamma_j = 1)\text{GIG}(\frac{1}{2}, \text{E}_{\lambda_0^2}(\lambda_0^2), \sigma_{0j}^2 + \mu_{0j}^2) + \text{p}(\gamma_j = 0)\text{Exp}(\frac{1}{2}\text{E}_{\lambda_0^2}(\lambda_0^2))$, therefore

$$\text{E}_{h_{0j}^2}(\frac{1}{h_{0j}^2}) = \sum_{k=0}^1 \text{p}(\gamma_j = k) \text{E}_{h_{0j}^2|\gamma_j=k}(\frac{1}{h_{0j}^2}),$$

where $\text{E}_{h_{0j}^2|\gamma_j=1}(\frac{1}{h_{0j}^2}) = \sqrt{\text{E}_{\lambda_0^2}(\lambda_0^2)(\text{E}_{\beta_j|\gamma_j=1}(\beta_j^2))^{-1}}$ and $\text{E}_{h_{0j}^2|\gamma_j=0}(\frac{1}{h_{0j}^2}) = 2[\text{E}_{\lambda_0^2}(\lambda_0^2)]^{-1}$,

$$\text{E}_{h_{0j}^2|\gamma_j=1}(h_{0j}^2) = \sqrt{\text{E}_{\beta_j|\gamma_j=1}(\beta_j^2)(\text{E}_{\lambda_0^2}(\lambda_0^2))^{-1}} + (\text{E}_{\lambda_0^2}(\lambda_0^2))^{-1}.$$

Since $h_{1j}^2 \overset{\text{i.i.d.}}{\sim} \text{p}(\gamma_j = 0)\text{GIG}(\frac{1}{2}, \text{E}_{\lambda_1^2}(\lambda_1^2), \sigma_{1j}^2 + \mu_{1j}^2) + \text{p}(\gamma_j = 1)\text{Exp}(\frac{1}{2}\text{E}_{\lambda_1^2}(\lambda_1^2))$, therefore

$$\text{E}_{h_{1j}^2}(\frac{1}{h_{1j}^2}) = \sum_{k=0}^1 \text{p}(\gamma_j = k) \text{E}_{h_{1j}^2|\gamma_j=k}(\frac{1}{h_{1j}^2}),$$

where $\text{E}_{h_{1j}^2|\gamma_j=1}(\frac{1}{h_{1j}^2}) = 2[\text{E}_{\lambda_1^2}(\lambda_1^2)]^{-1}$ and $\text{E}_{h_{1j}^2|\gamma_j=0}(\frac{1}{h_{1j}^2}) = \sqrt{\text{E}_{\lambda_1^2}(\lambda_1^2)(\text{E}_{\beta_j|\gamma_j=0}(\beta_j^2))^{-1}}$,

$$\text{E}_{h_{1j}^2|\gamma_j=0}(h_{1j}^2) = \sqrt{\text{E}_{\beta_j|\gamma_j=0}(\beta_j^2)(\text{E}_{\lambda_1^2}(\lambda_1^2))^{-1}} + (\text{E}_{\lambda_1^2}(\lambda_1^2))^{-1}.$$

Since $\sigma \sim \mathrm{IG}(\frac{3}{2}n + a_\sigma, c_\sigma)$, therefore

$$\mathrm{E}_\sigma(\sigma^{-1}) = (\frac{3}{2}n + a_\sigma)\frac{1}{c_\sigma},\ \mathrm{E}_\sigma(\sigma) = (\frac{3}{2}n + a_\sigma - 1)^{-1}c_\sigma,$$

Since $z_i \overset{\text{i.i.d.}}{\sim} \mathrm{GIG}(\frac{1}{2}, a_{z_i}, b_{z_i})$, therefore

$$\mathrm{E}_{z_i}(z_i^{-1}) = \sqrt{a_{z_i}(b_{z_i})^{-1}},\ \mathrm{E}_{z_i}(z_i) = \sqrt{b_{z_i}(a_{z_i})^{-1}} + (a_{z_i})^{-1}.$$

Since $\lambda_k^2 \sim \mathrm{Ga}(\nu_{\lambda_k} + r + 1, \frac{\sum_{j=0}^r \mathrm{E}_{h_{kj}^2}(h_{kj}^2)}{2} + 1)$, for $k = 0$ and 1, therefore

$$\mathrm{E}_{\lambda_k^2}(\lambda_k^2) = (r + 1 + \nu_{\lambda_k})(1 + \frac{1}{2}\sum_{j=0}^{r}\mathrm{E}_{h_{kj}^2}(h_{kj}^2))^{-1}.$$

Since $\pi_\gamma \sim \mathrm{Be}(a + \sum_{j=0}^r \mathrm{E}_{\gamma_j}(\gamma_j), r + b + 1 - \sum_{j=0}^r \mathrm{E}_{\gamma_j}(\gamma_j))$, therefore

$$\mathrm{E}_{\pi_\gamma}(\log \pi_\gamma) = \Psi(a + \sum_{j=0}^{r}\mathrm{E}_{\gamma_j}(\gamma_j)) - \Psi(a + b + r + 1),$$

$$\mathrm{E}_{\pi_\gamma}(\log(1 - \pi_\gamma)) = \Psi(r + b + 1 - \sum_{j=0}^{r}\mathrm{E}_{\gamma_j}(\gamma_j)) - \Psi(a + b + r + 1),$$

$$\mathrm{E}_{\pi_\gamma}(\pi_\gamma) = (a + \sum_{j=0}^{r}\mathrm{E}_{\gamma_j}(\gamma_j))(a + r + b + 1)^{-1}.$$

Since $\gamma_j \overset{\text{i.i.d.}}{\sim} B\big(1, (1 + e^{\zeta_i})^{-1}\big)$, therefore

$$\mathrm{E}_{\gamma_j}(\gamma_j) = \mathrm{p}(\gamma_j = 1) = (1 + e^{\zeta_i})^{-1}.$$

Appendix C. Efficiency Comparison between Bayesian Quantile Regression Methods

Table A1. Mean execution times of the various Bayesian quantile regression methods in the simulation.

Quantile	Error Distribution	Method					
		i.i.d. Random Errors			Heterogenous Random Errorss		
		BLQR	BALQR	VBSSLQR	BLQR	BALQR	VBSSLQR
$\tau = 0.3$	normal	146.45 s	144.56 s	**18.06** s	146.48 s	174.88 s	**28.77** s
	Laplace	145.26 s	144.62 s	**18.82** s	145.86 s	173.44 s	**30.08** s
	normal mixture	144.52 s	145.27 s	**18.11** s	143.48 s	147.63 s	**28.99** s
	Laplace mixture	145.86 s	146.28 s	**19.07** s	145.82 s	171.69 s	**30.38** s
	Cauchy	145.24 s	144.63 s	**16.06** s	145.89 s	174.68 s	**25.64** s
$\tau = 0.5$	normal	144.62 s	144.52 s	**15.30** s	144.67 s	174.39 s	**25.23** s
	Laplace	144.54 s	145.26 s	**15.00** s	144.57 s	172.84 s	**24.51** s
	normal mixture	144.62 s	145.26 s	**15.39** s	144.63 s	173.62 s	**25.21** s
	Laplace mixture	147.68 s	145.83 s	**15.14** s	147.62 s	172.25 s	**25.13** s
	Cauchy	145.21 s	144.53 s	**12.38** s	145.86 s	173.42 s	**20.72** s
$\tau = 0.7$	normal	147.29 s	144.37 s	**18.74** s	146.48 s	173.46 s	**31.05** s
	Laplace	144.62 s	145.27 s	**19.89** s	144.64 s	174.61 s	**33.86** s
	normal mixture	145.84 s	145.24 s	**19.00** s	145.27 s	172.84 s	**31.60** s
	Laplace mixture	147.57 s	147.98 s	**19.88** s	147.68 s	173.42 s	**34.31** s
	Cauchy	145.87 s	142.86 s	**16.87** s	146.28 s	173.45 s	**28.12** s

The bold represents the optimal result in each scenario and "s" denotes seconds.

Appendix D. Simulation Studies for Cases with Smaller Effect Sizes

Table A2. The performance of our proposed method for cases with smaller effect sizes.

Quantile	Distribution	Errors					
		i.i.d. Random Errors			Heterogenous Random Errorss		
		MMAD(sd)	TP	FP	MMAD(sd)	TP	FP
$\tau = 0.3$	normal	0.21(0.05)	10.00	0.13	0.33(0.10)	10.00	0.25
	Laplace	0.25(0.08)	10.00	0.15	0.42(0.34)	9.56	0.37
	normal mixture	0.23(0.06)	10.00	0.07	0.36(0.16)	9.93	0.23
	Laplace mixture	0.29(0.10)	9.99	0.16	0.98(0.50)	8.32	0.38
	Cauchy	0.12(0.55)	9.43	0.00	0.16(0.76)	8.73	0.01
$\tau = 0.5$	normal	0.20(0.06)	10.00	0.16	0.32(0.09)	10.00	0.29
	Laplace	0.20(0.06)	10.00	0.06	0.32(0.11)	9.99	0.20
	normal mixture	0.22(0.06)	10.00	0.10	0.34(0.10)	10.00	0.21
	Laplace mixture	0.22(0.07)	10.00	0.06	0.33(0.26)	9.76	0.17
	Cauchy	0.07(0.50)	9.55	0.00	0.10(0.69)	9.00	0.00
$\tau = 0.7$	normal	0.21(0.06)	10.00	0.13	0.34(0.10)	10.00	0.37
	Laplace	0.25(0.08)	10.00	0.15	0.40(0.18)	9.91	0.38
	normal mixture	0.23(0.06)	10.00	0.16	0.36(0.12)	9.99	0.31
	Laplace mixture	0.27(0.09)	10.00	0.17	0.43(0.30)	9.66	0.33
	Cauchy	0.11(0.61)	9.38	0.00	0.15(0.67)	9.13	0.00

References

1. Koenker, R.; Bassett, G. Regression quantile. *Econometrica* **1978**, *46*, 33–50. [CrossRef]
2. Buchinsky, M. Changes in the united-states wage structure 1963–1987—Application of quantile regression. *Econometrica* **1994**, *62*, 405–458. [CrossRef]
3. Thisted, R.; Osborne, M.; Portnoy, S.; Koenker, R. The gaussian hare and the laplacian tortoise: Computability of squared-error versus absolute-error estimators—Comments and rejoinders. *Stat. Sci.* **1997**, *12*, 296–300.
4. Koenker, R.; Hallock, K. Quantile regression. *J. Econ. Perspect.* **2001**, *15*, 143–156.
5. Yu, K.; Moyeed, R. Bayesian quantile regression. *Stat. Probab. Lett.* **2001**, *54*, 437–447. [CrossRef]
6. Taddy, M.A.; Kottas, A. A bayesian nonparametric approach to inference for quantile regression. *J. Bus. Econ. Stat.* **2010**, *28*, 357–369. [CrossRef]
7. Hu, Y.; Gramacy, R.B.; Lian, H. Bayesian quantile regression for single-index models. *Stat. Comput.* **2013**, *23*, 437–454. [CrossRef]
8. Lee, E.R.; Noh, H.; Park, B.U. Model selection via bayesian information criterion for quantile regression models. *J. Am. Stat. Assoc.* **2014**, *109*, 216–229. [CrossRef]
9. Frank, I.; Friedman, J. A statistical view of some chemometrics regression tools. *Technometrics* **1993**, *35*, 109–135. [CrossRef]
10. Tibshirani, R. Regression shrinkage and selection via the lasso. *J. R. Stat. Soc. Ser. B* **1996**, *58*, 267–288. [CrossRef]
11. Fan, J.; Li, R. Variable selection via nonconcave penalized likelihood and its oracle properties. *J. Am. Stat. Assoc.* **2001**, *96*, 1348–1360.
12. Zou, H.; Hastie, T. Regularization and variable selection via the elastic net. *J. R. Stat. Soc. Ser.-Stat. Methodol.* **2005**, *67*, 301–320. [CrossRef]
13. Zou, H. The adaptive lasso and its oracle properties. *J. Am. Stat. Assoc.* **2006**, *101*, 1418–1429. [CrossRef]
14. Koenker, R. Quantile regression for longitudinal data. *J. Multivar. Anal.* **2004**, *91*, 74–89. [CrossRef]
15. Wu, Y.; Liu, Y. Variable selection in quantile regession. *Stat. Sin.* **2009**, *19*, 801–817.
16. Park, T.; Casella, G. The bayesian lasso. *J. Am. Stat. Assoc.* **2008**, *103*, 681–686. [CrossRef]
17. Leng, C.; Tran, M.N.; Nott, D. Bayesian adaptive Lasso. *Ann. Inst. Stat. Math.* **2014**, *66*, 221–244. [CrossRef]
18. Li, Q.; Xi, R.; Lin, N. Bayesian regularized quantile regression. *Bayesian Anal.* **2010**, *5*, 533–556. [CrossRef]
19. Alhamzawi, R.; Yu, K.; Benoit, D.F. Bayesian adaptive Lasso quantile regression. *Stat. Model.* **2012**, *12*, 279–297. [CrossRef]
20. Ishwaran, H.; Rao, J. Spike and slab variable selection: Frequentist and bayesian strategies. *Ann. Stat.* **2005**, *33*, 730–773. [CrossRef]
21. Ray, K.; Szabo, B. Variational bayes for high-dimensional linear regression with sparse priors. *J. Am. Stat. Assoc.* **2022**, *117*, 1270–1281. [CrossRef]
22. Yi, J.; Tang, N. Variational bayesian inference in high-dimensional linear mixed models. *Mathematics* **2022**, *10*, 463. [CrossRef]
23. Xi, R.; Li, Y.; Hu, Y. Bayesian quantile regression based on the empirical likelihood with spike and slab priors. *Bayesian Anal.* **2016**, *11*, 821–855. [CrossRef]
24. Koenker, R.; Machado, J. Goodness of fit and related inference processes for quantile regression. *J. Am. Stat. Assoc.* **1999**, *94*, 1296–1310. [CrossRef]

25. Tsionas, E. Bayesian quantile inference. *J. Stat. Comput. Simul.* **2003**, *73*, 659–674. [CrossRef]
26. Rockova, V. Bayesian estimation of sparse signals with a continuous spike-and-slab prior. *Ann. Stat.* **2018**, *46*, 401–437. [CrossRef]
27. Alhamzawi, R.; Ali, H.T.M. The bayesian adaptive lasso regression. *Math. Biosci.* **2018**, *303*, 75–82. [CrossRef]
28. Parisi, G.; Shankar, R. Statistical field theory. *Phys. Today* **1988**, *41*, 110. [CrossRef]
29. Beal, M.J. Variational Algorithms for Approximate Bayesian Inference. Ph.D Thesis, University of London, London, UK, 2003.
30. Kuruwita, C.N. Variable selection in the single-index quantile regression model with high-dimensional covariates. *Commun. Stat.-Simul. Comput.* **2021**, *52*, 1120–1132. [CrossRef]

mathematics MDPI

Review

Multi-Source Data Repairing: A Comprehensive Survey

Chen Ye [1,2,3], Haoyang Duan [1], Hengtong Zhang [4], Hua Zhang [1,*], Hongzhi Wang [5] and Guojun Dai [1,*]

1 Hangzhou Dianzi University, Hangzhou 310018, China
2 Nanjing University of Aeronautics and Astronautics, Nanjing 210016, China
3 Jubang Group Co., Ltd., Yueqing 325600, China
4 Tencent AI Lab, Shenzhen 518054, China
5 Harbin Institute of Technology, Harbin 150001, China
* Correspondence: zhangh@hdu.edu.cn (H.Z.); daigj@hdu.edu.cn (G.D.)

Abstract: In the era of Big Data, integrating information from multiple sources has proven valuable in various fields. To ensure a high-quality supply of multi-source data, repairing different types of errors in the multi-source data becomes critical. This paper categorizes errors in multi-source data into entity information overlapping, attribute value conflicts, and attribute value inconsistencies. We first summarize existing repairing methods for these errors and then examine and review the study of the detection and repair of compound-type errors in multi-source data. Finally, we indicate further research directions in multi-source data repair.

Keywords: multiple sources; data quality; data repairing; entity resolution; truth discovery; data dependencies

MSC: 68P20; 68T07

1. Introduction

In recent years, extensive data sources, including social media, crowdsourcing platforms, and ubiquitous sensor networks, continuously generate vast amounts of data. Conducting data analytics on such massive amounts of data can benefit decision-making and knowledge discovery. Often, data points describing the same object or event originate from multiple sources, resulting in multi-source data. For example, descriptions of a particular item may vary across different commercial platforms. Consequently, multi-source data inevitably have different forms of representation and various errors, which can impact their overall value. To ensure the provision of high-quality multi-source data, it is essential to detect and rectify inconsistencies and mistakes.

Traditional data quality problems are identified according to five dimensions [1]: data consistency [2], information completeness [3,4], data deduplication [5,6], data currency [7,8], and data accuracy [9]. The existing data repairing literature has been mostly focused on data deduplication in multi-source data while addressing other dimensions for the single source/database. Although methods for single-source data can be applied to multi-source data by resolving data quality issues within each source separately, the task of repairing multi-source data differs from that of single-source data. Single-source repairing aims to achieve complete and consistent data through error detection and repair according to the dimensions above. In contrast, multi-source repairing seeks reliable integrated information by repairing conflicts and inconsistencies among data sources, presenting new challenges. Compared to data repairing methods for single sources, techniques for multi-source data face the following data quality problems:

(1) Due to varying representations and formats of entities among multiple data sources, the primary challenge of multi-source repair is to identify overlapping data, particularly by matching records that refer to the same real-world entity. This task involves purging

duplicate information and consolidating and merging complementary information to achieve a consistent view of real-world entities.

(2) For a given entity, each attribute value may have observations provided by a certain number of data sources. However, multi-source conflicts may arise due to recording errors, intentional errors, conflicts, and outdated data across different data sources. To address this issue, it is crucial to determine the correct attribute values for each entity among the conflicted observations.

(3) In addition to multi-source conflicts, inconsistencies may occur among multi-source observations of different entities. Here, data consistency refers to the validity and integrity of attribute values for these entities. To ensure the quality of integrated data, it is necessary to design robust integrity constraints and practical algorithms for detecting and repairing inconsistencies within multi-source data.

To summarize, besides the single-source problems in the multi-source case, the specific data quality issues in multi-source data come from three major categories: entity information overlapping, attribute value conflicts, and attribute value inconsistency [10]. As shown in Figure 1, the existing work usually resolves the entity information overlapping by entity resolution over the multi-source instances. The detection strategy is blocking, and the repair strategy is matching. For multi-source attribute value conflicts, the general solution is truth discovery, which detects inter-source conflicts and resolves them by evaluating the reliability of the data sources. For attribute information inconsistencies among different entities, existing approaches use various integrity constraints to detect and find the "least costly" consistent repair.

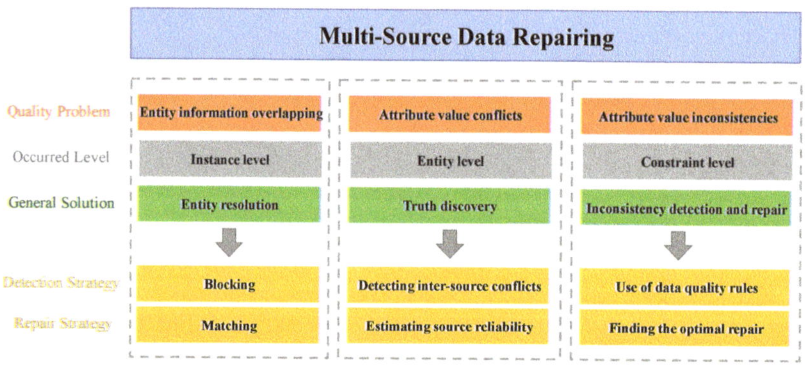

Figure 1. Multi-source data repairing methods.

This paper comprehensively reviews recent research in entity resolution (Section 2), truth discovery (Section 3), and inconsistency detection and repair (Section 4). As the types of errors mentioned above may exist simultaneously and influence each other, we also examine and review the study of compound error detection and repair (Section 5). Finally, we indicate further research directions in multi-source data repairing (Section 6).

2. Entity Resolution

Different data providers may have different descriptions of the same thing (including data formats and representations), and each description of an entity is called a reference to that entity. Entity resolution (ER) is the process of resolving and mapping real-world entities from a "collection of references" [11]. ER is also known as record linkage, object identification, individual identification, and duplicate detection. Intuitively, it is computationally expensive to directly match each pair of records in two data sources by calculating the similarity pair by pair. To avoid the excessive complexity generated by direct matching, the existing work typically divides ER into two steps [12]: (1) blocking and (2) matching.

Specifically, the blocking step divides records that do not represent the same entity into different blocks so that only records within the same block need to be matched, avoiding comparing many records between blocks. Matching refers to determining whether two representations refer to the same real-world entity. For example, whether two records (**Name**: *Kristen Smith*, **Street**: *2 Hurley Pl*, **City**: *South Fork, MN 48503*, **Sex**: *Female*) and (**LastName**: *Smith*, **FirstName**: *Kristen L.*, **Gender**: *F*, **Address**: *2 Hurley Place, South Fork MN, 48503-5998*) refer to the same person *Kristen Smith*. Next, we review recent ER approaches and discuss them in two types: learning-based methods and non-learning-based methods.

2.1. Non-Learning-Based Methods

Most of the non-learning approaches were proposed before artificial intelligence (AI) became widespread. The methods in this category are summarized in Table 1. For a better understanding, we organize them into a novel taxonomy that consists of *Schema-type*, *Step*, and *Knowledge-based*, and detail the related papers according to *Schema-type*.

- *Schema-type*: distinguishes between *schema-aware* or *schema-agnostic* methods. The former indicates that the method selects some specific attribute values for blocking and matching, and these selected attributes are discriminative or contain less noisy data. The latter does not consider pattern information and extracts information from all attribute values.
- *Step*: divides the methods into three categories based on the steps included. *Blocking* means that the method contains only blocking steps, *matching* means that the process consists of only matching, *blocking–matching* implies that the method proposes a complete framework for ER, including both blocking and matching.
- *Knowledge-based*: classifies the methods into *yes*, which means that external knowledge, such as knowledge bases, rules, constraints, etc., are introduced into the techniques, and *no*, which means that they are not.

Table 1. Non-learning-based methods.

Method	Schema Type	Step	Knowledge-Based
Standard blocking [5]	Schema-aware	Blocking	No
Sorted blocking [13]	Schema-aware	Blocking	No
CrowdER [14]	Schema-aware	Blocking-matching	No
Swoosh [15]	Schema-aware	Matching	No
SEMR [16]	Schema-aware	Matching	Yes
Rule-based ER [17]	Schema-aware	Blocking–matching	Yes
DMCE [18]	Schema-aware	Matching	Yes
Token blocking [19]	Schema-agnostic	Blocking	No
Attribute clustering blocking [20]	Schema-agnostic	Blocking	No
SiGMa [21]	Schema-agnostic	Matching	No
MinoanER [22]	Schema-agnostic	Blocking–matching	No

Schema-aware. Methods of this type assume that the input entity profiles adhere to a known schema. Based on this schema and respective domain knowledge, one can select the attributes most suitable for blocking and matching. We then discuss precisely what methods are available in this category [5,13–18].

In terms of blocking, standard blocking [5] is the basis of the blocking algorithm, which represents each entity with one or more key values. Each block corresponds to a specific key value and contains all the entities represented by that key value. It involves the most straightforward functionality: an expert selects the most suitable attributes, and a transformation function concatenates (parts of) their values to form blocking keys. For every distinct key, a block is created containing all corresponding entities. Comparing records in the same block can reduce the number of record comparisons in the original ER.

Through combining the standard blocking and sort technologies, ref. [13] proposes an entity resolution blocking technology called sorted blocking. Sorted blocking sorts all blocking key values according to dictionary order. The ordered entities are then divided into blocks based on the prefixes of the blocking keys, and the records within one block are compared. In addition, the algorithm uses a windowing technique to avoid losing any matches. Records from different blocks in the window are also involved in the comparison calculation. The sorted blocking algorithm does not limit the block size, which can lead to large blocks taking up a significant amount of processing time.

In terms of matching, swoosh [15] focuses on "pairwise ER", which matches and merges records operating on two records at a time. Swoosh defines two functions, match and merge, where match identifies duplicates and merge combines two duplicate records into one. There are also methods [14,16–18] for obtaining matching results for record pairs by introducing knowledge of manual annotation information, knowledge bases, rule constraints, etc., through knowledge-based approaches.

SEMR [16] studies how to synthesize matching rules from positive–negative matching examples. It presents a system that introduces real-world associated constraints to improve the accuracy of the synthesized matching rules. This system matches the performance of machine learning (ML) methods and produces concise rules. Rule-based ER [17] considers that records referring to the same entity observed in different periods may be different. The authors use data quality rules, such as matching dependency and data currency, to derive temporal records' information in the time order and the trend of their attributes' evolutionwith time elapsing. Based on the obtained information, a temporal-based clustering method is proposed to improve the accuracy of matching on datasets containing hidden temporal information.

DMCE [18] focuses on entity classification, which is relevant but not identical to matching. They propose a rule-based framework using positive and negative rules to discover miscategorized entities. Positive rules are conservatively used to find disjoint partitions, so the entities within the same partition should be categorized together. The partition with the largest size is called the pivot partition under the realistic assumption that the largest partition is correct. Negative rules are used to compare other partitions with the pivot partition to discover dissimilar entities as miscategorized entities.

In addition to the above work, a more specific type of crowdsourced blocking uses machine-based techniques to remove evident non-repetitive entities while using valuable human resources to examine situations that require human insight. Following this idea, CrowdER [14] proposes a hybrid human–machine ER approach, which first uses machine-based techniques to label the non-similar record pairs and asks the crowd to verify only the remaining pairs.

Schema-agnostic. Methods of this type make no assumptions about schema knowledge, disregarding complete attribute names. We discuss several representatives [19–22] in this category.

In essence, token blocking (TB) [19] is based on the idea that profiles of duplicate entities have at least one value in common, independently of the corresponding attribute names. Therefore, all entities that contain the same token in any attribute of their profile are placed in one block, resulting in redundancy that each entity is contained in multiple blocks. To improve TB, attribute clustering blocking [20] requires the common tokens of two entities to appear in syntactically similar attributes. These attribute names correspond to similar values but are not necessarily semantically matching (unlike schema matching). First, it clusters attributes based on the similarities of their aggregate values. Each attribute is connected to its most similar one, and the transitive closure of the connected attributes forms disjoint clusters. A $block_{k,t}$ is then defined for every token t in the values of the attributes belonging to cluster k.

Next, we introduce two schema-agnostic methods for matching. SiGMa [21] selects as seed matches the pairs with identical entity names. Then, it propagates the matching decisions on the compatible neighbors of existing matches. Unique mapping clustering is applied for detecting duplicates. That is, for every newly matched pair, the similarities of the neighbors are recomputed, and their position in the priority queue is updated. SiGMa is an iterative propagation algorithm that leverages structural information from the relationship graph and flexible similarity measures between entity properties in a greedy local search, making it scalable. MinoanER [22] also employs unique mapping clustering. However, it differs from SiGMa. MinoanER leverages a token-based similarity of entities to define a new metric that derives the similarity of neighboring entities from the most important relations. A composite blocking method is employed to capture different sources of matching evidence from entities' content, neighbors, or names. The search space of candidate pairs for comparison is compactly abstracted by a novel disjunctive blocking graph and processed by a non-iterative, massively parallel matching algorithm that consists of four generic, schema-agnostic matching rules.

2.2. Learning-Based Methods

With the development of AI, learning methods are used to solve ER problems. We summarize these methods in Table 2, classified according to *step*, *knowledge-based*, *learning type*, and *pre-trained LM*. As *step* and *knowledge-based* are introduced in Section 2.1, we detail *learning type* and *pre-trained LM* as follows:

- *Learning type*: distinguishes these methods into *supervised*, *unsupervised*, *semi-supervised*, and *deep learning*, where we uniform all the learning-based methods belonging to the field of deep learning (DL) to *deep learning*.
- *Pre-trained LM*: Identifying and distinguishing entities requires capturing their semantic similarities, which requires significant language understanding and domain knowledge. Pre-trained transformer-based language models (LMs) perform well on the ER task due to their ability to understand language and their ability to learn where to pay attention. This dimension divides methods into *yes* and *no*. The former indicates introducing a pre-trained LM, while the latter does not.

Table 2. Learning-based methods.

Method	Step	Knowledge-Based	Learning Type	Pre-Trained LM
ApproxDNF [23]	Blocking	No	Supervised	No
BSL [24]	Blocking	No	Supervised	No
BGP [25]	Blocking	No	Supervised	No
CBLOCK [26]	Blocking	No	Supervised	No
KBPearl [27]	Matching	Yes	Supervised	No
CEA [28]	Matching	Yes	Supervised	No
AL-EM [29]	Matching	No	Supervised	No
Semi-supervised de-dup [30]	Matching	No	Semi-supervised	No
Map-Reduce-Based EI [31]	Matching	No	Unsupervised	No
ULEC [32]	Matching	No	Unsupervised	No

Table 2. *Cont.*

Method	Step	Knowledge-Based	Learning Type	Pre-Trained LM
ZeroER [33]	Matching	No	Unsupervised	No
RER [34]	Matching	Yes	Unsupervised	No
PERC [35]	Matching	Yes	Unsupervised	No
DeepER [36]	Blocking–matching	No	Deep learning	No
DeepMatcher [37]	Matching	No	Deep learning	No
DeepBlocking [38]	Blocking	No	Deep learning	No
DITTO [39]	Blocking–matching	Yes	Deep learning	Yes
Machop [40]	Matching	Yes	Deep learning	Yes
JointMatcher [41]	Matching	No	Deep learning	Yes

Supervised learning methods. Supervised learning is a type of machine learning where the training data usually contain features and labels. A function is then learned by mapping a feature vector to a label. Supervised learning in ER is generally conducted by obtaining feature vectors from matched/unmatched entity pairs and then understanding the mapping relationship between the vector pairs and the matched/unmatched labels. We next describe several representatives [23–29] of supervised learning.

Regarding blocking, ApproxDNF [23] uses small record clusters as samples to train an algorithm. The algorithm learns specific features from the data based on these samples, producing higher-quality results. The training instances for the learning process are pairs of records. These instances are used in the rule selection training analysis, which produces the best record sets in blocking. Then, these selected rules are combined to form expressions in a disjunctive normal form (DNF), which defines how records are blocked.

BSL blocking [24] is similar to ApproxDNF in its use of blocking rules. The main difference is how the training samples are used and how predicates are combined to produce the blocking strategy during the learning process. In practice, BSL blocking is usually used for samples containing a small number of positive training record pairs. As a result, the execution time may be less than the time taken to perform ApproxDNF.

Different from the above methods, BGP [25] uses genetic programming (GP) as the basis for solving adaptive blocking problems. BGP uses a tree representation of supervised blocking schemes, where each leaf node corresponds to a blocking predicate. In each round, a set of genetic programming operators, such as replication, mutation, and crossover, are applied to an initial, random block scheme set. Then, a fitness function infers the performance of the new schemes from the harmonic mean of genuine coverage of pairs (PC) and reduction ratio in the number of candidate pairs (RR), and the best ones are returned as output.

Another tree-based approach is CBLOCK [26], which automatically learns hash functions from attribute domains and a labeled dataset of duplicates. Subsequently, CBLOCK expresses blocking functions using a hierarchical tree structure composed of atomic hash functions. It guides the automated blocking process based on architectural constraints, such as by specifying the maximum size of each block. Each node that exceeds the maximum limit is split into smaller, disjoint blocks.

In terms of matching, KBPearl [27] and CEA [28] are proposed based on knowledge bases. KBPearl [27] constructs a semantic graph based on the knowledge extracted from the canonicalized facts and the side information. Then, KBPearl matches various entities for disambiguating the noun phrases and relation phrases in the facts by determining a dense subgraph from the semantic graph efficiently and effectively. CEA [28] identifies entities that refer to the same real-world object but locate in different knowledge graphs (KGs). It uses structural, semantic, and string signals to capture similarities between entities in heterogeneous knowledge graphs.

AL-EM [29] builds a unified active learning framework containing four essential components: feature extractor, learner, example selector, and evaluator. The feature extractor generates feature vectors for pairs of entities, and the learner learns from a limited amount of initial labeled pairs of entities to develop the initial model. The example selector chooses ambiguous, unlabeled examples that the model finds hard to predict the labels for any queries an Oracle (human or ground truth) for those labels. The newly labeled data is added to the cumulative training data to learn a refined model. The evaluator evaluates the learned model during each active learning iteration.

Unsupervised learning methods. Compared with supervised learning, unsupervised learning does not need labeled training examples and automatically classifies or clusters the input data. We introduce the following unsupervised learning methods [31–35].

In the process of matching, Map-reduce-based EI [31] proposes setting different weights for each attribute to effectively distinguish the effect of each attribute on the degree of entity description. After setting the weights, the similarity between records is calculated from the attribute values and weights, and then entity matching is carried out based on the graph clustering method. Different from Map-reduce-based EI [31], ULEC [32] proposes an unsupervised method to generate groups of value pairs that can be transformed in the same way, i.e., values that are logically the same with different formats share a transformation. Then, the groups are presented to a human for verification and the approved ones are used to standardize the data.

In ZeroER [33], similarity measures are used to create the feature matrix for the two input tables, and a blocking function is selected by the users. ZeroER clusters entity pairs based on the assumption that the similarity values for matched/unmatched entity pairs follow two different distributions. The authors propose a powerful generative model based on Gaussian mixture models for learning the match and unmatch distributions. All parameters can be learned by maximizing the data likelihood via an expectation-maximization algorithm without any labeled data.

Incorporating annotated information into matching is a good idea because humans can naturally recognize information about real-world entities represented in different ways. Considering the fact that workers' answers may not be accurate due to a lack of domain expertise, fatigue, malicious behavior, etc., RER [34] corrects the responses of an oracle through indirect "control queries" and finally obtains the correct annotated information. PERC [35] adopts an uncertain graph model to address the entity matching problem with noisy crowd answers. This model sets the problem of ER equivalent to finding the maximum-likelihood clustering.

Semi-supervised learning methods. Semi-supervised learning involves a small number of labeled samples and a large number of unlabeled samples, which is not commonly used in ER. Semi-supervised de-dup [30] regards matching as a clustering task, where the goal is to put records corresponding to the same physical entity in the same cluster while separating the records corresponding to different entities into different clusters. Based on restricted correlation clustering (RCC) [42], the authors develop a semi-supervised approach that leverages a small labeled dataset, which is carefully selected via an efficient sampling procedure based on locality-sensitive hashing (LSH).

Deep Learning. As seen from the above approaches, structured data are usually featured on entity attributes and compared for similarity to determine whether they match. However, with the increasing need for matching textual data, for example, matching the information on a company homepage with a Wikipedia page describing the company, traditional learning-based ER solutions (e.g., SVMs) may have difficulty matching text instances by featuring the attribute values of textual descriptions. Considering the fact that DL-based models are sensitive to each word in a textual description, they can automatically extract the semantic features of the entire record or the corresponding attributes for matching.

DeepER [36] proposes an LSH-based blocking approach that considers all attributes of a tuple and produces smaller blocks, compared with traditional methods that consider only a few attributes. For matching, it adopts an LSTM-based RNN with the Siamese architecture [43], a neural network architecture that has a pair of neural networks with the same architecture and shared parameters. DeepER first tokenizes each pair of entities, which are converted into distributed representations using a word embedding model. The model then aggregates token-level distributed representations into an entity representation for each entity. Next, the two entity representations are fed into a dense layer that calculates the similarity between the entities, followed by an output layer that predicts the matching.

DeepMatcher [37] extends DeepER by introducing an architecture template for deep learning ER methods with three main modules: (1) attribute embedding, which converts sequences of words used in the attribute values of an entity description to word embedding vectors; (2) attribute similarity representation, which applies a similarity function on the attribute embeddings of two descriptions to obtain a final similarity value of those descriptions (i.e., it learns the similarity function); and (3) a classifier, which uses the similarities between descriptions as features for a classifier that decides whether a pair of descriptions is a match (i.e., it learns the match function).

After DeepMatcher was proposed, the authors proposed DeepBlocking [38] to apply deep learning to blocking. Specifically, each tuple in two input tables is converted into a string by concatenating all the attribute values. The resulting strings are fed into word embedding, tuple embedding, and vector pairing. Word embedding converts the words in each string into a high-dimensional vector. Tuple embedding then combines these vectors into a single-valued vector representing the entire string (the original tuple). Finally, the vector-pairing module looks for similar vector pairs.

With the development of pre-trained LMs, DITTO [39] proposes an ER method, which serializes two records in a record pair and inputs them into a BERT (bidirectional encoder representation from transformers) model [44], while features are extracted by the BERT model. In this way, records with different structures can be uniformly processed as input to a classification model that determines whether to match. Based on modeling matching as a sentence pair classification problem and introducing pre-trained language models for fine-tuning, DITTO also proposes three optimization techniques: injecting domain knowledge, summarizing long texts so that their length meets the input requirements of the pre-trained models, and data augmentation of the training data. Machop [40] extends the work of Ditto by allowing for matching between data entries in different data formats (structured, semi-structured, and unstructured). JointMatcher [41] extends the work of Ditto by adding a relevance-aware segments encoder and a numerically aware segments encoder. Consequently, JointMatcher focuses more on similar and number-contained segments to capture more high-contextualized and fine-grained features, resulting in better performance than DITTO on small datasets with the same pre-trained LMs.

3. Truth Discovery

As different types of errors can exist in various data sources, the attribute values of an entity from multiple sources often contradict each other. To ensure data quality, we need to resolve such conflicts. An intuitive idea for eliminating conflicts is majority voting, which assumes that all sources are equally reliable. However, this assumption may not hold in most cases. To compensate for the lack of majority voting, the concept of truth discovery [45] has been introduced. Truth discovery, also known as data integration, aims to find the truths from multi-source conflicting data by simultaneously estimating the reliability of the data sources and inferring the true information.

Truth discovery was first proposed in the literature [46], and the basic idea is that the more reliable the data source, the more likely it is to provide correct data. The more correct data are provided, the more reliable the data source is. Since the reliability of a data source is usually not known in advance, truth discovery methods [46–49] mostly use iterative algorithms to perform reliability assessment of data sources and inference of truth in an alternating update mode. Usually, the algorithm starts with an initialization of source weights and then iteratively conducts the truth computation step and source weight estimation step. Some stopping criteria are adopted in practice to control the number of iterations. One commonly adopted criterion is verifying the change of identified truths or source weights and terminating the algorithm when the change is smaller than a pre-defined threshold.

We compare recent truth discovery approaches in Table 3. Here, we summarize them under different features, i.e., *labeled truths, entity dependency, source dependency, non-single truth,* and *truth discovery in crowdsourcing.*

Table 3. Truth discovery methods.

Method	Labeled Truths	Entity Dependency	Source Dependency	Non-Single Truth	Crowdsourcing
SSTF [50]	✓				
SLiMFast [51]	✓				
OpSTD [52]	✓				
Investment [53]		✓		✓	
GFFTD [54]		✓			
MTM [55]		✓			
DynaTD [56]		✓			
TD-corr [57]		✓			
OTD [58]		✓			
CRDI [59]		✓			
CTD [60]		✓			
ACCU [61]			✓		
MSS [62]			✓		✓
TDCD [63]			✓		
PrecRecCorr [64]			✓	✓	
LTM [65]				✓	
DART [66]				✓	
TEM(15) [67]				✓	
FairTD [68]					✓
TDSSA [69]					✓
MTD-CC [70]			✓	✓	✓
IMCC [71]			✓		✓

3.1. Labeled Truths

Most truth discovery methods are unsupervised due to the difficulty of collecting data with truth labels, while in [50–52,72], the authors argue that a small set of truths is available and thus the proposed algorithms which work in semi-supervised settings.

SSTF [50] focuses on the problem of truth discovery with semi-supervised graph learning by using a small set of ground truth data to help distinguish true facts from false ones and identify trustworthy data sources. SSTF requires that the ground truths be among the observations sources provided. This setting is impractical for many real-world applications, especially when ground truth and observations are real numbers. Thus, it performs poorly on datasets when object truths are continuous data.

To compensate for the above shortcomings, SLiMFast [51] uses a small amount of ground truth to obtain an initial estimate of the source accuracy and then uses an iterative process to obtain a final estimate of the source accuracy and the potential true value of the object. The work in [52] studies the semi-supervised truth discovery problem for continuous object truths. They propose an optimization-based semi-supervised truth discovery (OpSTD) method for discovering continuous object truths, in which the truth discovery problem is formulated as an optimization task where both object truths and source reliabilities are modeled as variables, and the ground truth is modeled as a regularization term to propagate its trustworthiness to the estimated truths.

3.2. Entity Dependency

In the general truth discovery framework, it is assumed that entities are independent and uncorrelated from each other. However, in real-world applications, different entities and attributes usually have certain relationships with each other and may influence each other. For example, there is a strong connection between the "city" and "province" where the same person lives, and in the same region, "A pays more than B" may mean "A pays more taxes than B". This dependency relationship between entities and attributes provides more clues, which can improve the accuracy of truth discovery.

In Investment [53] and GFFTD [54], the authors represent the relationships between entities as a priori knowledge or common sense. This external knowledge is translated into propositional constraints integrated into each round of truth discovery. Specifically, each truth (an entity and its corresponding attribute values) is represented as a [0, 1] variable, and then the associated truths are combined into propositional constraints based on external knowledge. The cost function is the distance between initial results based on truth discovery and new results satisfying the propositional constraints. By minimizing the cost function, the probability of each candidate truth being true is "corrected" during each iteration based on external knowledge. To ensure that this optimization problem is solvable, the truth of each entity is allowed to be "unknown" in order to lower the constraints and avoid possible constraint conflicts.

In comparison, refs. [53–55] combines information extraction and truth discovery to address the slot-filling validation task, to determine the trustworthiness of the output information extracted from different systems in the diverse corpus. The authors construct a multidimensional truth discovery model (MTM), a heterogeneous method comprising the system, the corpus, the extracted information, and the weight matrix between them. Similar to the iterative truth discovery process, the reliability of the information propagated is used to infer the reliability of the system and the corpus. In turn, the system's reliability and the corpus's reliability reassess the trustworthiness of the information it extracts. The authors construct knowledge graphs to establish dependencies between different time slots (entities) as a clue to initialize the trustworthiness of the information.

In another line of research, the works in [56,57] propose to exploit the temporal and spatial relationships between entities to improve the performance of the truth discovery algorithm. For example, today's maximum temperature is correlated with yesterday's; neighboring several streets may have similar traffic conditions. This correlation is measured as similarity is added to the optimization model, leading to better results. DynaTD [56] constructs a model of temporal relationships between entities on continuous data. TD-corr [57] can address both temporal and spatial relationships on continuous data, and their experiments show that capturing the relationships between entities can improve the performance of truth discovery since, in many practical applications, entity relationships can be viewed in large numbers by sensor-observation results. Building on [56,57], OTD [58] further models and integrates temporal trends in the evolution of truth guides the truth discovery.

Unlike all the above methods, ref. [59] proposes an approach, CRDI, to enhance the accuracy of truth discovery. CRDI uses the information in the relationships between entities to find more evidence for the correctness or incorrectness of the values generated by different data sources. The authors then propose an alternative approach [73], which uses relational machine learning methods to estimate the relations between entities and then uses these relations to estimate the true value using some fusion functions.

CTD [60] introduces denial constraints into the truth discovery problem and formulates it as a constrained optimization problem. To address the problem, they propose algorithms to partition the entities into disjoint groups and generate arithmetic constraints for each disjoint group separately. The true attribute values of the entities in each disjoint group are then derived by minimizing the objective function under the corresponding arithmetic constraints.

3.3. Source Dependency

Since copying sometimes occurs between multiple data sources (e.g., different websites on the Internet), detecting copying between data sources is essential to prevent erroneous information from being copied continuously, leading to a high proportion of error messages when discovering the truth. The main principle behind copy detection is that, if some sources make many common mistakes, they are not likely to be independent of each other. However, this principle becomes ineffective when some sources copy information from a good source.

In ACCU [61], the authors use a Bayesian model to infer the existence of copy relationships between data sources and confirm their dependence. This copy-detection process is combined with the truth discovery for iterative updates. MSS [62] mitigates the source relationship dependency problem by revealing the underlying group structure among data sources and performing truth discovery at the group level. This solution reduces the risk of overusing information from dependent data sources, especially when these data sources are unreliable.

In contrast to [61,62], which detect copy relationships between data sources from static data, TDCD [63] detects copy relationships between data sources from dynamic data sources, where the information provided by the data sources is changing. Given the historical update records of the data sources, the authors apply a hidden Markov model (HMM) to detect the copy relationships. The model iteratively evaluates source quality and updated information simultaneously, outputting changing copy relationships and truth.

In a separate line of research, PrecRecCorr [64] considers different correlations between data sources that are more general than copying. Sources may have positive correlations, such as copying information from each other, or negative correlations, such as providing data from complementary domains or focusing on different information domains. In general, observations from positively correlated sources should not increase the confidence that they are true values, and observations supported by only a few negatively correlated sources should not decrease the confidence that they are true values. The method models inter-source correlation with joint precision and joint recall and employs Bayesian analysis to infer whether an observation is true.

3.4. Non-Single Truth

Most methods usually assume that each entity has only one correct value for each entity. Based on this assumption, these methods aim to select the information with the highest confidence as the correct value. However, this "single truth" assumption does not always hold. For example, there are multiple authors for a book and also multiple actors/actresses for a movie.

In the literature [64,65], the authors propose the probabilistic graphical model to find multiple truths for each entity. In this case, considering only the credibility of the source does not distinguish between sources with low precision and those with low recall. Therefore, in [64], the authors calculate the precision and recall of the data source for finding multiple truths. Similarly, LTM [65] considers both false positive and negative aspects to find multiple truths for the same entity. DART [66] proposes an integrated Bayesian approach that exploits the unique features of the multi-truth problem to assign more reasonable confidence scores to candidate truth sets, combining data source domain knowledge and confidence scores to achieve unsupervised multiple truth discovery.

In addition to the above case of multiple true values, there is a particular case of no correct value [53,67]. For example, it is suitable to give an output of "unknown" for the questions (objects) about the death date of someone still alive. Investment [53] uses "unknown" to augment their data and provides an "unknown" answer when there is insufficient information or conflicting constraint. TEM [67] considers the has-truth questions, i.e., when the truth of an entity is not provided by any data source, the truth returned by truth discovery for that entity should be non-existent. The study evaluated three quality indicators of the data source in the search for truth, silent rate, false spoken rate, and true spoken rate, thus effectively filtering out information about entities for which there is no truth.

3.5. Truth Discovery in Crowdsourcing

In the past decade, crowdsourcing has emerged as a popular internet-based collaborative computing paradigm. In crowdsourcing systems, requesters can ask workers ("sources") for true values ("truths") of objects or events. Generally, sources could provide inconsistent or conflicting answers ("candidates") about the object. Researchers have studied truth discovery in crowdsourcing from different perspectives.

Crowdsourcing collects shared information from a large number of people and is often negatively impacted by unreliable sources with low-quality data. To address this problem, MSS [62] proposes a probabilistic model to jointly assess the reliability of sources and find true data. It also explicitly reveals the reliability of groups and minimizes the negative impacts of unreliable groups.

FairTD [68] argues from a fairness perspective that simply aggregating feedback from all crowdsourced workers will inevitably lead to race, gender, and political interference in the outcome. Thus, FairTD proposes a notion of difference in truth discovery, three theories of fairness enhancement, and an iterative method of estimating bias and truth to address the fairness problem in truth discovery. TDSSA [69] considers the truth discovery problem under Sybil attack and proposes a method to defend against strategic Sybil attack. The method assigns the same standard set of tasks to each worker in the cluster. It filters malicious worker feedback out by classifying each cluster as normal or malicious based on worker feedback.

FairTD and TDSSA ignore the correlation between candidates, so the inferred truth may differ from the ground truth. To solve this problem, ref. [70] proposes MTD-CC, multi-truth discovery with candidate correlations. Specifically, the authors first design a metric of potential function to measure the correlation between each pair of candidates based on the sources' votes and reliabilities. Then, they construct a Markov random field (MRF) to represent these correlations. Finally, they transform the MRF into a directed graph and cut it based on the Min-cut theorem to infer which candidates are truths.

Unlike the copy detection in Section 3.3, IMCC [71] considers the copying of workers in crowdsourcing. Some workers copy some (or all) of the data from other workers, making truth discovery more complicated if the wrong answer is copied. IMCC aims to design a crowdsourcing incentive mechanism for the truth discovery of textual answers with copiers. They formulate the problem of maximizing social welfare such that all tasks can be completed with the least confidence for truth discovery and design a three-stage incentive mechanism. In the contextual embedding and clustering stage, they construct and cluster the content vector representations of crowdsourced textual answers at the semantic level. In the truth discovery stage, they estimate the truth for each task based on the dependence and accuracy of workers. In the reverse auction stage, they design a greedy algorithm to select the winners and determine the payment.

4. Inconsistency Detection and Repair

Data consistency refers to data collection that does not contain semantically incorrect or conflicting data. For data consistency detection, existing studies [74–76] usually establish a set of data quality rules such that once inconsistent data appear in the database, the corresponding rules are violated so that the tuple violating the rules is discovered and repaired. Data quality rules describing consistency include function dependencies (FDs), conditional functional dependencies (CFDs), denial constraints (DCs), etc. The followings are brief descriptions of these three common data rules, respectively.

Consider a relational schema R with attributes $attr(R)$. An FD φ is defined as $X \rightarrow Y$, where $X \subseteq attr(R)$ and $Y \subseteq attr(R)$. An instance I of R satisfies FD φ, denoted as $I \models \varphi$ if for any two tuples t_α, t_β in I, such that $t_\alpha[X] = t_\beta[X]$, then $t_\alpha[Y] = t_\beta[Y]$. For example, an FD $[Country\ Code, Area\ Code] \rightarrow City$ is presented in Table 4, stating that the values of *Country Code* and the *Area Code* can determine the value of *City*.

A CFD φ on R is a pair $(R : X \rightarrow Y, T_p)$, where (1) X, Y are sets of attributes from $attr(R)$, (2) $R : X \rightarrow Y$ is a standard FD, referred to as the FD *embedded in* φ; and (3) T_p is a tableau with all attributes in X and Y, referred to as the *pattern tableau* of φ, where for each A in X or Y and each tuple $t \in T_p$, $t[A]$ is either a constant 'a' in the domain $dom(A)$ of A, or an unnamed variable '_'. If A appears in both X and Y, we use $t[A_L]$ and $t[A_R]$ to indicate the A field of t corresponding to A in X and Y, respectively [77]. For instance, given a CFD: $([Country\ Code, Zip] \rightarrow Street, (44, \_, \_))$, $[Country\ Code, Zip] \rightarrow Street$ refers to an FD and $(44, \_, \_)$ specifies the condition, i.e., when *Country Code* is 44, *Zip* uniquely determines *Street*.

A DC φ on R is defined as: $\forall t_\alpha, t_\beta, t_\gamma, \cdots \in R, \neg(P_1 \wedge P_2 \cdots \wedge P_m)$, where each predicate P_i is of the form $v_1 \theta v_2$ or $v_1 \theta c$ with $v_1, v_2 \in t_x[A], x \in \{\alpha, \beta, \gamma, \dots\}, A \in R$, c is a constant in the domain of A, and $\theta \in \{=, <, >, \neq, \leq, \geq\}$. For example, $\forall t_\alpha \in R, \neg(t_\alpha[Country\ Code] =$ '01' $\wedge\ t_\alpha[Area\ Code] =$ '908' $\wedge\ t_\alpha[City] \neq$ 'MH'), i.e., there is no tuple where *Country Code* is '01', *Area Code* is '08', and *City* is not 'MH'.

Table 4. An example of database information.

Tid	Country Code	Area Code	Phone	Name	Street	City	Zip
t_1	01	908	5219527	Mike	Tree Ave.	MH	07974
t_2	01	908	5219527	Rick	Tree Ave.	MH	07974
t_3	01	212	2018967	Joe	5th Ave	NYC	01202
t_4	01	908	2018967	Jim	Elm Str.	MH	07974
t_5	44	131	3314823	Ben	High St.	EDI	EH4 1DI
t_6	44	131	4675378	Ian	High St.	EDI	EH4 1DT
t_7	44	908	4675378	Ian	Port PI	MH	W1B 1JH
t_8	01	131	2018967	Sean	3rd Str.	UN	01202

The problem of repairing inconsistent data is making "minimal" changes to data collection that do not satisfy a given set of rules. In Table 5, we summarize the inconsistency detection and repair methods in two dimensions, *Data* and *Constraints*. *Data* divides the methods into *Table Data* and *Graph Data*, which represent the type of data handled by the method. *Constraints* refers to *FDs*, *CFDs*, *DCs*, and *Other Constraints*, which represent the data quality rules used in the method. Next, we discuss these papers according to *Data*.

Table 5. Inconsistency detection and repair methods.

	Data		Constraints			
	Table Data	**Graph Data**	**FDs**	**CFDs**	**DCs**	**Other Constraints**
FD-based value modification [78]	✓		✓			✓
FindVRepair [79]	✓		✓	✓		

Table 5. *Cont.*

	Data		Constraints			
	Table Data	Graph Data	FDs	CFDs	DCs	Other Constraints
CFD-based Detection [77]	✓			✓		
CFD-based value modification [80]	✓			✓		
Distributed Detection [81]	✓			✓		
Incremental Detection [82]	✓			✓		
C-Repair [83]	✓					✓
Holistic Repair [84]	✓				✓	
HoloClean [85]	✓				✓	✓
GFD-based Detection [86]		✓				✓
IncDect [87]		✓				✓
StarRepair [88]		✓				✓
Logic-based Graph Repair [89]		✓				✓

4.1. *Table Data*

Traditional repairing methods [2,90,91] directly delete the non-compliant records from the database so that the remaining records can comply with all the given universal integrity constraints (ICs). Since the errors in the remaining dataset are not increased when the records are deleted, it is always possible to iterate through the data repair, i.e., first finding the set of records that violate the constraint, then deleting a random record, and then testing the remaining dataset. This strategy is relatively simple, but a significant amount of information is lost. To address this issue, an alternative strategy [92] is proposed. Instead of adding or deleting any records, only certain fields are modified so that the entire collection can meet the pre-defined consistency requirements. This strategy allows for maximum preservation of the original information of the data collection.

In [78], the authors propose a repair model which detects tuples that violate FDs and inclusion dependencies (INDs) and modifies attribute values to ensure consistency in the database. The model describes the cost-based minimum repair measured by the tuple weights and the similarity of the values for each modification, which was not considered by any previous work. The tuple weights represent the confidence of each tuple placed by the users. The similarity of the values is defined as the minimum number of individual character insertions, deletions, and substitutions required to convert the original value to the repaired value.

In [77], the authors argue that FDs have been developed primarily for schema design and are often insufficient to capture the semantics of the data. They introduce CFDs, an extension of traditional FDs, which can capture data consistency by enforcing bindings of semantically related values. They provide an inference system analogous to Armstrong's axioms for FDs and consistency analysis. Since CFDs allow for data bindings, many individual constraints may hold on a table, complicating the detection of constraint violations. They first provide an SQL technique for finding violations of a single CFD, e.g., using group by statements and then extend it to validate multiple CFDs.

Following [78], FindVRepair [79] proposes a method for repairing the inconsistency errors in the database that violate FDs by minimizing the distance metric. The distance metric depends on the number of value modifications and the weight/confidence associated with the modified tuples. In addition, the authors show how to use CFDs for data repair. In [80], the authors propose two algorithms: one for automatically computing the repaired database that satisfies a given CFD set and the other for incrementally finding repairs in response to updates to a clean database. The former extends the FD-based cost model of [78] to ensure quality repairs are found when processing CFDs. The latter is an effective heuristic algorithm for finding fixes that respond to updates, i.e., the deletion or insertion of a set of tuples, and can also be used to find fixes for dirty databases.

In another line of research, ref. [81] describes the detection problem in various distributed environments. The authors formulate CFD violation detection for data partitioned horizontally or vertically as optimization problems measured by either response time or data shipment (i.e., the amount of data shipped from one site to another). They study CFD violation detection in horizontal partitioning but consider neither incremental detection nor algorithms for detecting errors in vertical partitions. The works in [81,82] provide such incremental algorithms for vertically partitioned and horizontally partitioned data and further propose optimization techniques for the incremental algorithm over vertical partitions.

Compared with the above CFD-based repairing methods, ref. [83] no longer focuses solely on databases containing CFDs but specifically on data containing conditional functional dependencies (CFDPs) with built-in predicates. The authors propose a heuristic algorithm for inconsistent data detection and repairing, which can repair inconsistent data violating the CFDPs in datasets under unsupervised circumstances. For data detection, the maximum dependency set is used to detect them. For data repairing, they use unsupervised machine learning to learn the correlation among attributes in datasets and integrate the minimum cost idea and information theory to repair, which makes the repair results most relevant to the initial values with minimum repair times.

The above techniques do not consider the interaction among different class constraint violations. Therefore, the researchers introduce the DCs for repairing [84,85], which subsumes several types of DCs, such as FDs and CFDs. The authors in [84] let users specify quality rules using DCs with ad hoc predicates. They introduce two data structures: the Conflict Hypergraph, which encodes all violations into a common graph structure, and the Repair Context, which encodes all necessary information on how to fix violations holistically.

The authors also introduce HoloClean [85], a framework for holistic data repairing driven by probabilistic inference. HoloClean unifies existing qualitative data repairing approaches, which rely on DCs or external data sources, with quantitative data repairing methods, which leverage statistical properties of the input data. With an inconsistent dataset as input, HoloClean automatically generates a probabilistic program to fix data.

Data quality rules by themselves are not sufficient to correctly resolve conflicts, or worse, may even introduce new errors when attempting to repair data. Thus, some studies [76,93] use master data or users to guide the repair process. In [76], the authors propose a method to find certain fixes based on master data, the concept of certain regions, and a class of editing rules. A certain region is a set of attributes for which the user is guaranteed to be correct. Given a certain region and master data, edit rules tell which attributes to fix and how to update them. Techniques for reasoning about edit rules are then developed to determine whether they lead to unique fixes and whether they can fix all attributes in the tuple relative to the master data and a certain region. A framework and algorithms are also proposed to find certain fixes by interacting with the user to ensure that a region is correct.

In [93], the authors introduce GDR, a guided data repair framework that incorporates user feedback in the repairing process to enhance and accelerate existing automated repair techniques while minimizing user involvement. Specifically, GDR consults the user on the updates that are most likely to be beneficial in improving data quality. Then, GDR uses existing machine learning methods to identify and apply the correct updates directly to the database without the actual involvement of the user on these specific updates.

4.2. Graph Data

Graph data inconsistency refers to semantic information errors or contradictions among the relevant data information in a graph. Recent methods capture inconsistency errors in graph data and repair them in terms of rules [86,87], logic-based incremental methods [89], etc.

In [86], the authors propose a class of FDs for graphs, referred to as GFDs. Capturing the attribute-value dependencies and topology of entities through GFDs provides an effective way to detect inconsistencies in knowledge graphs. The same team later proposed an arithmetic and comparison expression, NGD, to capture semantic inconsistencies in the graphs, and developed an incremental algorithm, IncDect [87], to detect errors in graph data and provide provable performance guarantees. Compared to GFDs, NGDs focus more on numerical inconsistency in real-life situations, and NGDs extend GFDs by supporting linear arithmetic expressions and built-in comparison predicates $\{=, \neq, >, \geq, <, \leq\}$.

In [88], the authors propose a class of constraints called Star Function Dependencies (StarFDs), which enforce value dependencies conditional on entities and their associated neighbors, unlike traditional ICs. These neighbors are identified by a star schema containing a join rule path query. This type of star function dependency strikes a balance between expressiveness and complexity. Given a set of StarFDs and graphs, entity repair detects and resolves inconsistencies differently using optimal and cost-bounded solutions, referred to as the StarRepair method. StarRepair computes the repairing process under the minimum cost by enforcing StarFDs, where the cost is determined by the size of the inconsistency.

In another line of research, ref. [89] proposes a logic-based approach to incremental graph repair, a method that does minimal change repair. The authors formalize consistency using a so-called graph condition equivalent to a first-order logic on the graph. Inconsistency is then resolved according to two repair algorithms: state-based repair independent of graph update history, and incremental repair that considers graph update history to restore consistency.

5. Detection and Repair of Compound-Type Errors

In practice, multi-source data often contain multiple error types, and fixing one type of error may introduce other types of errors. Thus, several methods focus on fixing compound errors. We summarize these methods in Table 6, where the considered types of errors are *Duplication* (i.e., entity information overlapping), *Conflict* (i.e., attribute value conflicts), *Inconsistency* (i.e., attribute value inconsistency), and *Incomplete*. As several papers consider the incomplete case in their compound-type error study, we also added "*Incomplete*" as an aspect of classification.

In [94], the authors design graph repair rules (GRRs) that capture incompleteness, conflict, and redundancy in a graph and indicate how to repair these errors. Three fundamental issues defined semantically in GRRs, namely implication, consistency, and termination, are investigated to verify whether a GRR is meaningful. The work in [94,95] proposes to deduce certain fixes for graphs based on data quality rules and truth values.They define data quality rule (GQRs), to support CFDs, recursively defined keys, and negative rules on graphs so that repairs can be deduced by combining data repair and entity resolution. In addition, they prove that deducing certain fixes is Church–Rosser and propose online and offline modes to perform fixes, respectively.

The authors of [95] also propose another class of graph association rules [96], represented by GARs, to describe regular relationships between entities in a graph. GARs are combinations of graph schemas and dependencies that can be used as predicates for relationship prediction by machine learning classifiers, capable of capturing incomplete information in schema-free graphs, predicting links in social graphs, identifying leads in digital marketing, and extending graph function dependencies to capture missing links and inconsistencies. They demonstrate that the satisfiability, implication, and association derivation problems for GARs are coNP-complete, NP-complete, and NP-complete, respectively, as well as that they maintain the same complexity bounds as the graph function dependency problem despite the improved expressiveness of GARs.

Instead of relying on various data quality rules, ref. [97] proposes a knowledge fragment cleaning method (KFCM) for cleaning up faulty knowledge fragments in a genealogical knowledge graph, consisting of three phases. The first stage detects and analyzes faulty knowledge fragments by inferring common problem patterns; the second stage supplements the entity relationship for different error patterns and conducts entity resolution; the third stage aligns entities with missing attributes based on parent–child relationships and connects isolated knowledge fragments.

In [98], the authors propose combining the idea of truth discovery methods and rule-based data repair methods to resolve the conflicts and inconsistencies. They present an automatic multi-source data repair method, AutoRepair, that uses FDS to resolve inconsistencies in multi-source data. The source reliability is used as evidence to discover and repair the errors among these violations. At the same time, the corrected results are used to estimate the source reliability. As the source reliability is unknown, the process is modeled as an iterative framework to ensure better performance.

The authors of [98] then propose incorporating DCs into the truth discovery process to resolve the conflicts together with dependencies [99]. They formulate the data repairing problem as an optimization problem and create constraints for the DCs. Compared with [98], this approach can repair the errors among related entities in different data types (e.g., categorical data and continuous data). They also give four concrete cases using different classes of DCs as examples.

Table 6. Compound-type error detection and repair methods.

Method	Duplication	Conflict	Inconsistency	Incomplete
GRRs [94]	√		√	√
GQRs [95]	√		√	
GARs [96]			√	√
KFCM [97]	√		√	√
AutoRepair [98]		√	√	
Conflicts Together with Dependencies [99]		√	√	

6. Future Research Directions

In summary, many studies have been carried out by domestic and international scholars in multi-source data error detection and repair research. These research efforts have focused on entity resolution and truth discovery, and some methods that have emerged in recent years have considered the inconsistency of multi-source data. However, several unresolved issues remain.

The detection and repair of compound-type errors in multi-source data need to be further studied. As compound-type errors commonly exist in multi-source data, error detection, and repair methods for multi-source data need to consider multiple types of errors simultaneously to obtain optimal repair solutions. However, the repair of existing compound types of errors is limited to considering only a few types of errors. Thus, there needs to be more research work that integrates the consideration of conflicting, duplicated, and inconsistent entity information on multi-source data.

The error detection based on semantic association in multi-source data needs to be studied in depth. Existing inconsistency detection methods typically use different types of data quality rules [100] to express dependencies between attributes or attribute values and treat information that violates the corresponding type of data quality rule as an error and repair it. However, with multiple data sources, information from different sources may be expressed differently. Let us suppose only exact matches of data values are considered. In that case, this can affect the judgment of the reliability of the data source and the accuracy of error detection and subsequent repair. Therefore, it is necessary to design data quality rules based on semantic association to detect various errors accurately.

Efficient repair in multi-source data needs to be further studied. Existing entity matching methods and inconsistency detection and repair methods tend to have high time complexity and can suffer from more severe efficiency problems in massive data scenarios [101]. In the present era of Big Data, modern data mining and analysis methods often include multiple iterations, thus making the efficiency disadvantage of traditional methods even more apparent. Therefore, error repair methods for multi-source data need to maximize efficiency while ensuring accuracy.

Author Contributions: Resources, H.W.; writing—original draft preparation, C.Y., H.D. and H.Z. (Hengtong Zhang); writing—review and editing, H.Z. (Hua Zhang); supervision, H.W. and G.D.; funding acquisition, G.D. All authors have read and agreed to the published version of the manuscript.

Funding: This paper was partially supported by National Natural Science Foundation of China (No. 62202132), Natural Science Foundation of Zhejiang Province (No. LQ22F020032), and National Key Research and Development Program of China (No. 2022YFE0199300).

Data Availability Statement: Not applicable.

Conflicts of Interest: The authors declare no conflict of interest.

References

1. Fan, W. Data Quality: From Theory to Practice. *SIGMOD Rec.* **2015**, *44*, 7–18. [CrossRef]
2. Arenas, M.; Bertossi, L.E.; Chomicki, J. Consistent Query Answers in Inconsistent Databases. In Proceedings of the Eighteenth ACM SIGACT-SIGMOD-SIGART Symposium on Principles of Database Systems, Philadelphia, PA, USA, 31 May–2 June 1999; pp. 68–79.
3. Cao, Y.; Deng, T.; Fan, W.; Geerts, F. On the data complexity of relative information completeness. *Inf. Syst.* **2014**, *45*, 18–34. [CrossRef]
4. Fan, W.; Geerts, F. Relative Information Completeness. *ACM Trans. Database Syst.* **2010**, *35*, 97–106. [CrossRef]
5. Fellegi, I.P.; Sunter, A.B. A theory for record linkage. *J. Am. Stat. Assoc.* **1969**, *64*, 1183–1210. [CrossRef]
6. Elmagarmid, A.K.; Ipeirotis, P.G.; Verykios, V.S. Duplicate Record Detection: A Survey. *IEEE Trans. Knowl. Data Eng.* **2007**, *19*, 1–16. [CrossRef]
7. Zhang, H.; Diao, Y.; Immerman, N. Recognizing Patterns in Streams with Imprecise Timestamps. *Inf. Syst.* **2013**, *38*, 1187–1211. [CrossRef]
8. Clifford, J.; Dyreson, C.; Isakowitz, T.; Jensen, C.S.; Snodgrass, R.T. On the Semantics of "Now" in Databases. *ACM Trans. Database Syst.* **1997**, *22*, 171–214. [CrossRef]
9. Widom, J. Trio: A System for Integrated Management of Data, Accuracy, and Lineage. In Proceedings of the Second Biennial Conference on Innovative Data Systems Research, Asilomar, CA, USA, 4–7 January 2005; Volume 5, pp. 262–276.
10. Rahm, E.; Do, H.H. Data Cleaning: Problems and Current Approaches. *IEEE Data Eng. Bull.* **2000**, *23*, 3–13.
11. Papadakis, G.; Ioannou, E.; Palpanas, T. Entity Resolution: Past, Present and Yet-to-Come. In Proceedings of the 23rd International Conference on Extending Database Technology, Copenhagen, Denmark, 30 March–2 April 2020; pp. 647–650.
12. Konda, P.; Das, S.; Doan, A.; Ardalan, A.; Ballard, J.R.; Li, H.; Panahi, F.; Zhang, H.; Naughton, J.; Prasad, S.; et al. Magellan: Toward Building Entity Matching Management Systems. *Proc. VLDB Endow.* **2016**, *9*, 1197–1208. [CrossRef]
13. Draisbach, U.; Naumann, F. A generalization of blocking and windowing algorithms for duplicate detection. In Proceedings of the 2011 International Conference on Data and Knowledge Engineering, Milano, Italy, 6 September 2011; pp. 18–24.
14. Wang, J.; Kraska, T.; Franklin, M.J.; Feng, J. CrowdER: Crowdsourcing Entity Resolution. *Proc. VLDB Endow.* **2012**, *5*, 1483–1494. [CrossRef]
15. Benjelloun, O.; Garcia-Molina, H.; Menestrina, D.; Su, Q.; Whang, S.E.; Widom, J. Swoosh: A generic approach to entity resolution. *VLDB J.* **2009**, *18*, 255–276. [CrossRef]
16. Singh, R.; Meduri, V.V.; Elmagarmid, A.; Madden, S.; Papotti, P.; Quiané-Ruiz, J.A.; Solar-Lezama, A.; Tang, N. Synthesizing Entity Matching Rules by Examples. *Proc. VLDB Endow.* **2017**, *11*, 189–202. [CrossRef]
17. Wang, H.; Ding, X.; Li, J.; Gao, H. Rule-Based Entity Resolution on Database with Hidden Temporal Information. *IEEE Trans. Knowl. Data Eng.* **2018**, *30*, 2199–2212. [CrossRef]
18. Hao, S.; Tang, N.; Li, G.; Feng, J. Discovering Mis-Categorized Entities. In Proceedings of the 34th IEEE International Conference on Data Engineering, Paris, France, 16–19 April 2018; pp. 413–424.

19. Papadakis, G.; Ioannou, E.; Niederée, C.; Fankhauser, P. Efficient entity resolution for large heterogeneous information spaces. In Proceedings of the Forth International Conference on Web Search and Web Data Mining, Hong Kong, China, 9–12 February 2011; pp. 535–544.
20. Papadakis, G.; Ioannou, E.; Palpanas, T.; Niederée, C.; Nejdl, W. A blocking framework for entity resolution in highly heterogeneous information spaces. *IEEE Trans. Knowl. Data Eng.* **2012**, *25*, 2665–2682. [CrossRef]
21. Lacoste-Julien, S.; Palla, K.; Davies, A.; Kasneci, G.; Graepel, T.; Ghahramani, Z. Sigma: Simple greedy matching for aligning large knowledge bases. In Proceedings of the 19th ACM SIGKDD International Conference on Knowledge Discovery and Data Mining, Chicago, IL, USA, 11–14 August 2013; pp. 572–580.
22. Efthymiou, V.; Papadakis, G.; Stefanidis, K.; Christophides, V. MinoanER: Schema-Agnostic, Non-Iterative, Massively Parallel Resolution of Web Entities. In Proceedings of the Advances in Database Technology—22nd International Conference on Extending Database Technology, Lisbon, Portugal, 26–29 March 2019; pp. 373–384.
23. Bilenko, M.; Kamath, B.; Mooney, R.J. Adaptive Blocking: Learning to Scale Up Record Linkage. In Proceedings of the 6th IEEE International Conference on Data Mining, Hong Kong, China, 18–22 December 2006; pp. 87–96.
24. Michelson, M.; Knoblock, C.A. Learning Blocking Schemes for Record Linkage. In Proceedings of the AAAI'06: Proceedings of the 21st National Conference on Artificial Intelligence, Boston, MA, USA, 16–20 July 2006; pp. 440–445.
25. Evangelista, L.O.; Cortez, E.; da Silva, A.S.; Meira, W., Jr. Adaptive and Flexible Blocking for Record Linkage Tasks. *J. Inf. Data Manag.* **2010**, *1*, 167.
26. Das Sarma, A.; Jain, A.; Machanavajjhala, A.; Bohannon, P. An Automatic Blocking Mechanism for Large-Scale de-Duplication Tasks. In Proceedings of the 21st ACM International Conference on Information and Knowledge Management, Maui, HI, USA, 29 October–2 November 2012; pp. 1055–1064.
27. Lin, X.; Li, H.; Xin, H.; Li, Z.; Chen, L. KBPearl: A Knowledge Base Population System Supported by Joint Entity and Relation Linking. *Proc. VLDB Endow.* **2020**, *13*, 1035–1049. [CrossRef]
28. Zeng, W.; Zhao, X.; Tang, J.; Lin, X. Collective Entity Alignment via Adaptive Features. In Proceedings of the 36th IEEE International Conference on Data Engineering, Dallas, TX, USA, 20–24 April 2020; pp. 1870–1873.
29. Meduri, V.V.; Popa, L.; Sen, P.; Sarwat, M. A Comprehensive Benchmark Framework for Active Learning Methods in Entity Matching. In Proceedings of the 2020 International Conference on Management of Data, Portland, OR, USA, 14–19 June 2020; pp. 1133–1147.
30. Kushagra, S.; Saxena, H.; Ilyas, I.F.; Ben-David, S. A Semi-Supervised Framework of Clustering Selection for De-Duplication. In Proceedings of the 35th IEEE International Conference on Data Engineering, Macao, China, 8–11 April 2019; pp. 208–219.
31. Ran, H.; Wang, H.; Rong, Z.; Li, J.; Hong, G. Map-Reduce Based Entity Identification in Big Data. *J. Comput. Res. Dev.* **2013**, *50*, 170–179.
32. Deng, D.; Tao, W.; Abedjan, Z.; Elmagarmid, A.K.; Ilyas, I.F.; Li, G.; Madden, S.; Ouzzani, M.; Stonebraker, M.; Tang, N. Unsupervised String Transformation Learning for Entity Consolidation. In Proceedings of the 35th IEEE International Conference on Data Engineering, Macao, China, 8–11 April 2019; pp. 196–207.
33. Wu, R.; Chaba, S.; Sawlani, S.; Chu, X.; Thirumuruganathan, S. ZeroER: Entity Resolution using Zero Labeled Examples. In Proceedings of the 2020 International Conference on Management of Data, Portland, OR, USA, 14–19 June 2020; pp. 1149–1164.
34. Galhotra, S.; Firmani, D.; Saha, B.; Srivastava, D. Robust entity resolution using random graphs. In Proceedings of the 2018 International Conference on Management of Data, Houston, TX, USA, 10–15 June 2018; pp. 3–18.
35. Ke, X.; Teo, M.; Khan, A.; Yalavarthi, V.K. A Demonstration of PERC: Probabilistic Entity Resolution with Crowd Errors. *Proc. VLDB Endow.* **2018**, *11*, 1922–1925. [CrossRef]
36. Ebraheem, M.; Thirumuruganathan, S.; Joty, S.R.; Ouzzani, M.; Tang, N. Distributed Representations of Tuples for Entity Resolution. *Proc. VLDB Endow.* **2018**, *11*, 1454–1467. [CrossRef]
37. Mudgal, S.; Li, H.; Rekatsinas, T.; Doan, A.; Park, Y.; Krishnan, G.; Deep, R.; Arcaute, E.; Raghavendra, V. Deep learning for entity matching: A design space exploration. In Proceedings of the 2018 International Conference on Management of Data, Houston, TX, USA, 10–15 June 2018; pp. 19–34.
38. Thirumuruganathan, S.; Li, H.; Tang, N.; Ouzzani, M.; Govind, Y.; Paulsen, D.; Fung, G.; Doan, A. Deep Learning for Blocking in Entity Matching: A Design Space Exploration. *Proc. VLDB Endow.* **2021**, *14*, 2459–2472. [CrossRef]
39. Li, Y.; Li, J.; Suhara, Y.; Doan, A.; Tan, W.C. Deep Entity Matching with Pre-Trained Language Models. *Proc. VLDB Endow.* **2020**, *14*, 50–60. [CrossRef]
40. Wang, J.; Li, Y.; Hirota, W.; Kandogan, E. Machop: An end-to-end generalized entity matching framework. In Proceedings of the Fifth International Workshop on Exploiting Artificial Intelligence Techniques for Data Management, Philadelphia, PA, USA, 17 June 2022; pp. 2:1–2:10.
41. Ye, C.; Jiang, S.; Zhang, H.; Wu, Y.; Shi, J.; Wang, H.; Dai, G. JointMatcher: Numerically-aware entity matching using pre-trained language models with attention concentration. *Knowl. Based Syst.* **2022**, *251*, 109033. [CrossRef]
42. Kushagra, S.; Ben-David, S.; Ilyas, I.F. Semi-supervised clustering for de-duplication. In Proceedings of the 22nd International Conference on Artificial Intelligence and Statistics, Naha, Japan, 16–18 April 2019; Volume 89, pp. 1659–1667.
43. Mueller, J.; Thyagarajan, A. Siamese Recurrent Architectures for Learning Sentence Similarity. In Proceedings of the Thirtieth AAAI Conference on Artificial Intelligence, Phoenix, AZ, USA, 12–17 February 2016; pp. 2786–2792.

44. Devlin, J.; Chang, M.; Lee, K.; Toutanova, K. BERT: Pre-training of Deep Bidirectional Transformers for Language Understanding. In Proceedings of the 2019 Conference of the North American Chapter of the Association for Computational Linguistics: Human Language Technologies, Minneapolis, MN, USA, 2–7 June 2019; pp. 4171–4186.
45. Li, Y.; Gao, J.; Meng, C.; Li, Q.; Su, L.; Zhao, B.; Fan, W.; Han, J. A survey on truth discovery. *SIGKDD Explor.* **2016**, *17*, 1–16. [CrossRef]
46. Yin, X.; Han, J.; Yu, P.S. Truth discovery with multiple conflicting information providers on the web. In Proceedings of the 13th ACM SIGKDD International Conference on Knowledge Discovery and Data Mining, San Jose, CA, USA, 12–15 August 2007; pp. 1048–1052.
47. Xiao, H.; Gao, J.; Li, Q.; Ma, F.; Su, L.; Feng, Y.; Zhang, A. Towards confidence interval estimation in truth discovery. *IEEE Trans. Knowl. Data Eng.* **2018**, *31*, 575–588. [CrossRef]
48. Li, Q.; Li, Y.; Gao, J.; Su, L.; Zhao, B.; Demirbas, M.; Fan, W.; Han, J. A confidence-aware approach for truth discovery on long-tail data. *Proc. VLDB Endow.* **2014**, *8*, 425–436. [CrossRef]
49. Li, Q.; Li, Y.; Gao, J.; Zhao, B.; Fan, W.; Han, J. Resolving conflicts in heterogeneous data by truth discovery and source reliability estimation. In Proceedings of the International Conference on Management of Data, Snowbird, UT, USA, 22–27 June 2014; pp. 1187–1198.
50. Yin, X.; Tan, W. Semi-supervised truth discovery. In Proceedings of the 20th International Conference on World Wide Web, Hyderabad, India, 28 March–1 April 2011; pp. 217–226.
51. Rekatsinas, T.; Joglekar, M.; Garcia-Molina, H.; Parameswaran, A.G.; Ré, C. SLiMFast: Guaranteed Results for Data Fusion and Source Reliability. In Proceedings of the 2017 ACM International Conference on Management of Data, Chicago, IL, USA, 14–19 May 2017; pp. 1399–1414.
52. Yang, Y.; Bai, Q.; Liu, Q. On the Discovery of Continuous Truth: A Semi-supervised Approach with Partial Ground Truths. In Proceedings of the Web Information Systems Engineering—WISE 2018—19th International Conference, Dubai, United Arab Emirates, 12–15 November 2018; Volume 11233, pp. 424–438.
53. Pasternack, J.; Roth, D. Knowing What to Believe (when you already know something). In Proceedings of the 23rd International Conference on Computational Linguistics, Beijing, China, 23–27 August 2010; pp. 877–885.
54. Pasternack, J.; Roth, D. Making Better Informed Trust Decisions with Generalized Fact-Finding. In Proceedings of the 22nd International Joint Conference on Artificial Intelligence, Barcelona, Spain, 16–22 July 2011; pp. 2324–2329.
55. Yu, D.; Huang, H.; Cassidy, T.; Ji, H.; Wang, C.; Zhi, S.; Han, J.; Voss, C.R.; Magdon-Ismail, M. The Wisdom of Minority: Unsupervised Slot Filling Validation based on Multi-dimensional Truth-Finding. In Proceedings of the 25th International Conference on Computational Linguistics, Technical Papers, Dublin, Ireland, 23–29 August 2014; pp. 1567–1578.
56. Li, Y.; Li, Q.; Gao, J.; Su, L.; Zhao, B.; Fan, W.; Han, J. On the Discovery of Evolving Truth. In Proceedings of the 21th ACM SIGKDD International Conference on Knowledge Discovery and Data Mining, Sydney, NSW, Australia, 10–13 August 2015; pp. 675–684.
57. Meng, C.; Jiang, W.; Li, Y.; Gao, J.; Su, L.; Ding, H.; Cheng, Y. Truth Discovery on Crowd Sensing of Correlated Entities. In Proceedings of the 13th ACM Conference on Embedded Networked Sensor Systems, Seoul, Republick of Korea, 1–4 November 2015; pp. 169–182.
58. Yao, L.; Su, L.; Li, Q.; Li, Y.; Ma, F.; Gao, J.; Zhang, A. Online Truth Discovery on Time Series Data. In Proceedings of the 2018 SIAM International Conference on Data Mining, San Diego Marriott Mission Valley, San Diego, CA, USA, 3–5 May 2018; pp. 162–170.
59. Nakhaei, Z.; Ahmadi, A.; Sharifi, A.; Badie, K. Conflict resolution in data integration using the relationship between entities. *Int. J. Inf. Commun. Technol. Res.* **2019**, *11*, 38–49.
60. Ye, C.; Wang, H.; Zheng, K.; Kong, Y.; Zhu, R.; Gao, J.; Li, J. Constrained Truth Discovery. *IEEE Trans. Knowl. Data Eng.* **2022**, *34*, 205–218. [CrossRef]
61. Dong, X.L.; Berti-Équille, L.; Srivastava, D. Integrating Conflicting Data: The Role of Source Dependence. *Proc. VLDB Endow.* **2009**, *2*, 550–561. [CrossRef]
62. Qi, G.; Aggarwal, C.C.; Han, J.; Huang, T.S. Mining collective intelligence in diverse groups. In Proceedings of the 22nd International World Wide Web Conference, Rio de Janeiro, Brazil, 13–17 May 2013; pp. 1041–1052.
63. Dong, X.L.; Berti-Équille, L.; Srivastava, D. Truth Discovery and Copying Detection in a Dynamic World. *Proc. VLDB Endow.* **2009**, *2*, 562–573. [CrossRef]
64. Pochampally, R.; Das Sarma, A.; Dong, X.L.; Meliou, A.; Srivastava, D. Fusing data with correlations. In Proceedings of the International Conference on Management of Data, Snowbird, UT, USA, 22–27 June 2014; pp. 433–444.
65. Zhao, B.; Rubinstein, B.I.P.; Gemmell, J.; Han, J. A Bayesian Approach to Discovering Truth from Conflicting Sources for Data Integration. *Proc. VLDB Endow.* **2012**, *5*, 550–561. [CrossRef]
66. Lin, X.; Chen, L. Domain-aware multi-truth discovery from conflicting sources. *Proc. VLDB Endow.* **2018**, *11*, 635–647. [CrossRef]
67. Zhi, S.; Zhao, B.; Tong, W.; Gao, J.; Yu, D.; Ji, H.; Han, J. Modeling truth existence in truth discovery. In Proceedings of the 21th ACM SIGKDD International Conference on Knowledge Discovery and Data Mining, Sydney, NSW, Australia, 10–13 August 2015; pp. 1543–1552.
68. Li, Y.; Sun, H.; Wang, W.H. Towards fair truth discovery from biased crowdsourced answers. In Proceedings of the 26th ACM SIGKDD Conference on Knowledge Discovery and Data Mining, California, CA, USA, 23–27August 2020; pp. 599–607.

69. Wang, Y.; Wang, K.; Miao, C. Truth discovery against strategic sybil attack in crowdsourcing. In Proceedings of the 26th ACM SIGKDD Conference on Knowledge Discovery and Data Mining, California, CA, USA, 23–27 August 2020; pp. 95–104.
70. Huang, H.; Fan, G.; Li, Y.; Mu, N. Multi-truth Discovery with Correlations of Candidates in Crowdsourcing Systems. In Proceedings of the Collaborative Computing: Networking, Applications and Worksharing—17th EAI International Conference, Virtual Event, 16–18 October 2021; pp. 18–32.
71. Jiang, L.; Niu, X.; Xu, J.; Yang, D.; Xu, L. Incentive mechanism design for truth discovery in crowdsourcing with copiers. *IEEE Trans. Serv. Comput.* **2021**, *5*, 2838–2853. [CrossRef]
72. Dong, X.L.; Saha, B.; Srivastava, D. Less is More: Selecting Sources Wisely for Integration. *Proc. VLDB Endow.* **2012**, *6*, 37–48. [CrossRef]
73. Nakhaei, Z.; Ahmadi, A.; Sharifi, A.; Badie, K. Conflict resolution using relation classification: High-level data fusion in data integration. *Comput. Sci. Inf. Syst.* **2021**, *18*, 1101–1138. [CrossRef]
74. Yu, Z.; Chu, X. Piclean: A probabilistic and interactive data cleaning system. In Proceedings of the 2019 International Conference on Management of Data, Amsterdam, The Netherlands, 30 June–5 July 2019; pp. 2021–2024.
75. Wang, J.; Tang, N. Towards Dependable Data Repairing with Fixing Rules. In Proceedings of the International Conference on Management of Data, Snowbird, UT, USA, 22–27 June 2014; pp. 457–468.
76. Fan, W.; Li, J.; Ma, S.; Tang, N.; Yu, W. Towards Certain Fixes with Editing Rules and Master Data. *VLDB J.* **2012**, *21*, 213–238. [CrossRef]
77. Bohannon, P.; Fan, W.; Geerts, F.; Jia, X.; Kementsietsidis, A. Conditional Functional Dependencies for Data Cleaning. In Proceedings of the 23rd International Conference on Data Engineering, Istanbul, Turkey, 15–20 April 2007; pp. 746–755.
78. Bohannon, P.; Flaster, M.; Fan, W.; Rastogi, R. A Cost-Based Model and Effective Heuristic for Repairing Constraints by Value Modification. In Proceedings of the ACM SIGMOD International Conference on Management of Data, Baltimore, MD, USA, 14–16 June 2005; Özcan, F., Ed.; ACM: Baltimore, MD, USA, 2005; pp. 143–154.
79. Kolahi, S.; Lakshmanan, L.V.S. On approximating optimum repairs for functional dependency violations. In Proceedings of the Database Theory—ICDT 2009, 12th International Conference, St. Petersburg, Russia, 23–25 March 2009; Volume 361, pp. 53–62.
80. Cong, G.; Fan, W.; Geerts, F.; Jia, X.; Ma, S. Improving Data Quality: Consistency and Accuracy. In Proceedings of the 33rd International Conference on Very Large Data Bases, Vienna, Austria, 23–27 September 2007; University of Vienna: Vienna, Austria, 2007; pp. 315–326.
81. Fan, W.; Geerts, F.; Ma, S.; Müller, H. Detecting inconsistencies in distributed data. In Proceedings of the 26th International Conference on Data Engineering, Long Beach, CA, USA, 1–6 March 2010; pp. 64–75.
82. Fan, W.; Li, J.; Tang, N.; Yu, W. Incremental Detection of Inconsistencies in Distributed Data. In Proceedings of the IEEE 28th International Conference on Data Engineering, Washington, DC, USA, 1–5 April 2012; pp. 318–329.
83. Li, P.; Dai, C.; Wang, W. Inconsistent Data Cleaning Based on the Maximum Dependency Set and Attribute Correlation. *Symmetry* **2018**, *10*, 516. [CrossRef]
84. Chu, X.; Ilyas, I.F.; Papotti, P. Holistic data cleaning: Putting violations into context. In Proceedings of the 29th IEEE International Conference on Data Engineering, Brisbane, Australia, 8–12 April 2013; pp. 458–469.
85. Rekatsinas, T.; Chu, X.; Ilyas, I.F.; Ré, C. HoloClean: Holistic Data Repairs with Probabilistic Inference. *Proc. VLDB Endow.* **2017**, *10*, 1190–1201. [CrossRef]
86. Fan, W.; Wu, Y.; Xu, J. Functional Dependencies for Graphs. In Proceedings of the 2016 International Conference on Management of Data, San Francisco, CA, USA, 26 June–1 July 2016; pp. 1843–1857.
87. Fan, W.; Liu, X.; Lu, P.; Tian, C. Catching Numeric Inconsistencies in Graphs. In Proceedings of the 2018 International Conference on Management of Data, Houston, TX, USA, 10–15 June 2018; pp. 381–393.
88. Lin, P.; Song, Q.; Wu, Y.; Pi, J. Repairing Entities using Star Constraints in Multirelational Graphs. In Proceedings of the 36th IEEE International Conference on Data Engineering, Dallas, TX, USA, 20–24 April 2020; pp. 229–240.
89. Schneider, S.; Lambers, L.; Orejas, F. A Logic-Based Incremental Approach to Graph Repair. In Proceedings of the Fundamental Approaches to Software Engineering—22nd International Conference, Held as Part of the European Joint Conferences on Theory and Practice of Software, Prague, Czech Republic, 6–11 April 2019; Volume 11424, pp. 151–167.
90. Bravo, L.; Bertossi, L.E. Logic Programs for Consistently Querying Data Integration Systems. In Proceedings of the Eighteenth International Joint Conference on Artificial Intelligence, Acapulco, Mexico, 9–15 August 2003; pp. 10–15.
91. Calì, A.; Lembo, D.; Rosati, R. On the decidability and complexity of query answering over inconsistent and incomplete databases. In Proceedings of the Twenty-Second ACM SIGACT-SIGMOD-SIGART Symposium on Principles of Database Systems, San Diego, CA, USA, 9–12 June 2003; pp. 260–271.
92. Wijsen, J. Condensed Representation of Database Repairs for Consistent Query Answering. In Proceedings of the Database Theory—ICDT 2003, 9th International Conference, Siena, Italy, 8–10 January 2003; Calvanese, D., Lenzerini, M., Motwani, R., Eds.; Springer: Siena, Italy, 2003; Volume 2572, pp. 375–390.
93. Yakout, M.; Elmagarmid, A.K.; Neville, J.; Ouzzani, M.; Ilyas, I.F. Guided data repair. *Proc. VLDB Endow.* **2011**, *4*, 279–289. [CrossRef]
94. Cheng, Y.; Chen, L.; Yuan, Y.; Wang, G. Rule-Based Graph Repairing: Semantic and Efficient Repairing Methods. In Proceedings of the 34th IEEE International Conference on Data Engineering, Paris, France, 16–19 April 2018; pp. 773–784.
95. Fan, W.; Lu, P.; Tian, C.; Zhou, J. Deducing Certain Fixes to Graphs. *Proc. VLDB Endow.* **2019**, *12*, 752–765. [CrossRef]

96. Fan, W.; Jin, R.; Liu, M.; Lu, P.; Tian, C.; Zhou, J. Capturing Associations in Graphs. *Proc. VLDB Endow.* **2020**, *13*, 1863–1876 [CrossRef]
97. Liu, G.; Li, L. Knowledge Fragment Cleaning in a Genealogy Knowledge Graph. In Proceedings of the 2020 IEEE International Conference on Knowledge Graph, Online, 9–11 August 2020; pp. 521–528.
98. Ye, C.; Li, Q.; Zhang, H.; Wang, H.; Gao, J.; Li, J. AutoRepair: An automatic repairing approach over multi-source data. *Knowl. Inf. Syst.* **2019**, *61*, 227–257. [CrossRef]
99. Ye, C.; Wang, H.; Zheng, K.; Gao, J.; Li, J. Multi-source data repairing powered by integrity constraints and source reliability. *Inf. Sci.* **2020**, *507*, 386–403. [CrossRef]
100. Fan, W.; Geerts, F.; Li, J.; Xiong, M. Discovering conditional functional dependencies. *IEEE Trans. Knowl. Data Eng.* **2010**, *23*, 683–698. [CrossRef]
101. Rezig, E.K.; Ouzzani, M.; Aref, W.G.; Elmagarmid, A.K.; Mahmood, A.R.; Stonebraker, M. Horizon: Scalable dependency-driven data cleaning. *Proc. VLDB Endow.* **2021**, *14*, 2546–2554. [CrossRef]

mathematics

MDPI

Article

An Effective Partitional Crisp Clustering Method Using Gradient Descent Approach

Soroosh Shalileh [1,2]

1 Center for Language and Brain, HSE University, Myasnitskaya Ulitsa, 20, 101000 Moscow, Russia; sshalileh@hse.ru

2 Vision Modelling Lab, HSE University, Myasnitskaya Ulitsa, 20, 101000 Moscow, Russia

Abstract: Enhancing the effectiveness of clustering methods has always been of great interest. Therefore, inspired by the success story of the gradient descent approach in supervised learning in the current research, we proposed an effective clustering method using the gradient descent approach. As a supplementary device for further improvements, we implemented our proposed method using an automatic differentiation library to facilitate the users in applying any differentiable distance functions. We empirically validated and compared the performance of our proposed method with four popular and effective clustering methods from the literature on 11 real-world and 720 synthetic datasets. Our experiments proved that our proposed method is valid, and in the majority of the cases, it is more effective than the competitors.

Keywords: clustering objective functions; clustering methods; gradient descent approach

MSC: 62G05; 68-04

1. Introduction: Background and Motivation

Clustering is a method of partitioning a set of data points into partitions such that the within-partition data points are as homogeneous as possible and the between-partitions data points are as heterogeneous as possible. The partitions are referred to as clusters. Clustering is a crucial tool in data science, knowledge discovery and artificial intelligence and has various applications in disciplines such as biology, social science, neuroscience, computer science, etc. Thus, not surprisingly, an enormous number of papers have been published addressing different aspects of clustering.

Recently, a comprehensive survey on this subject has been published [1] that extends the well-accepted taxonomy of clustering methods and reviews the trends and open challenges. The authors classified the clustering methods into (i) hierarchical and (ii) partitional clusterings. Furthermore, they categorized the hierarchical clusterings into (i-a) agglomerative and (i-b) divisive clusterings: and they categorized the partitional clusterings into (ii-a) crisp, (ii-b) mixture resolving and (iii-c) fuzzy clusterings. Figure 1 depicts the three first levels of this taxonomy.

Furthermore, the authors of this survey considered the recent research works devoted to adaptations of clustering methods to various disciplines as the recent trends in this area of research. Moreover, they listed nine open issues in clustering algorithms, and the "effectiveness" of clustering methods is one of them.

Our line of thought aligned with this survey. Therefore, the main objective of the current research was to propose an effective clustering method to improve the clusters recovery results. Therefore, inspired by the success story of the gradient descent algorithm in the supervised learning tasks [2], we proposed a generic clustering objective function and then adopted the gradient descent approach to optimize it. As a by-product of our proposed method and to increase its flexibility, we implemented it using an automatic differentiation library called JaX [3]. With this setting, any differentiable distance function can be applied, and this can be considered as an additional tool for further improvements of the clusters recovery results.

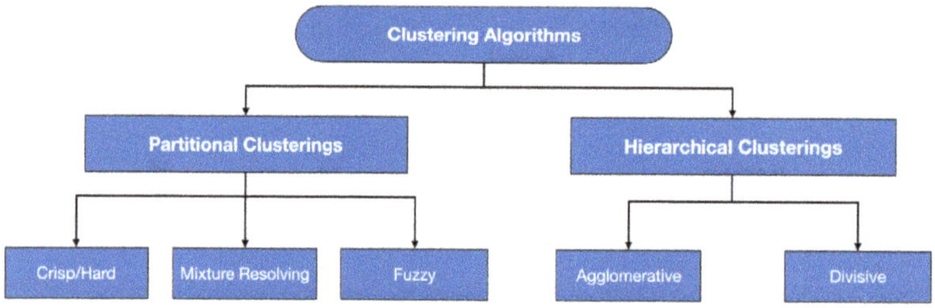

Figure 1. Clustering algorithms taxonomy introduced in [1] with three levels.

It is noteworthy to add that the current research introduces the following contributions:

- Proposing a generic clustering criterion with the possibility of utilizing any differentiable distance functions in it;
- Adapting the gradient descent approach for the task of partitional crisps clustering;
- Equipping the proposed method to automatic differentiation as a by-product for further improvements of cluster recovery results.

We empirically validated and compared the performance of our proposed method with four popular and effective clustering methods on real-world and synthetic datasets. Our experiments proved that in most cases, our proposed method enhances the cluster recovery results. More so, our flexible implementation serves as a supplementary device for further clustering results' improvements.

The rest of the paper is organized as follows. Section 2 reviews the previous work. Section 3 describes our proposed clustering. Section 4 explains the experimental setting for scrutinizing the hyperparameters of our proposed method and comparing it with four effective clustering methods from the literature. It presents (a) competitors; (b) datasets, both real-world and artificially generated; (c) criteria for assessment of the quality of experiments; and (d) the pre-processing technique. The study of the proposed methods' hyperparameters is reported in Section 5. Section 6 describes the results of our experiments. Finally, Section 7 concludes the paper and presents our future directions.

2. Previous Work

This section concisely reviews the principles of the clustering algorithms with respect to the taxonomy mentioned earlier. However, since the gradient descent clustering is not covered in [1] and it is the cornerstone of the current research, Section 2.3 reviews the scarce number of previously published gradient descent (GD) clustering papers.

2.1. Partitional Clusterings

The partitional clusterings assign data points into K clusters by optimizing some clustering criteria. This class of clustering methods can be further classified into three subclasses: (i) crisp/hard, (ii) fuzzy, and (iii) mixture-resolving clusterings. In the first subclass, each data point belongs only to one cluster, while on the contrary, in the fuzzy clustering methods, each data point can belong to more than one cluster. The third subclass, mixture resolving, assumes a world model leading to a probabilistic distribution for which its parameters should be inferred from the data. The rest of this subsection is devoted to reviewing these three subclasses.

Presumably, K-means [4] can be considered the most well-known instance of the first subclass. K-means minimizes the total squared errors of within-cluster. K-medoids [5,6] minimizes the dissimilarities of within-cluster data points while selecting some of the data points as centroids, referred to as medoids, instead of the average data points of the clusters. The density-based clusterings [7] recover the clusters by separating the dense regions from low-density regions in the feature space. For instance, the density-based spatial clustering of applications with noise [8], DBSCAN, finds core samples of high-density regions and expands clusters from them. Ordering points to identify the clustering structure [9,10], OPTICS, tackles the issue of finding the proper range parameter in DBSCAN.

Recently, a new set of (meta)heuristic clustering methods has emerged [11–15]. The main objective of this set of methods is to spontaneously recover the cluster structures and the number of clusters without prior information. These methods are mainly nature-inspired and contain an immense number of hyperparameters, which in our opinion contradicts the ultimate goal of clustering. It ought to mention that the results in [14,15] did not enhance the traditional methods' cluster recovery results. These methods can be categorized under the search-based clusterings [1] umbrella.

The deep clustering methods are another set of newly emerged methods. These methods use deep neural networks [16,17], DNNs, to learn a cluster-friendly representation of data followed by a traditional clustering algorithm to recover clusters from the obtained data representation by DNN. Various DNN algorithms have been applied to learn the cluster-friendlier data representation; Ref. [18] provided a systematic overview of this subject.

Contrary to crisp clusterings in fuzzy clusterings, the clusters overlap with a degree of membership based on fuzzy logic [19]. The initial fuzzy clusterings had problems with outliers, noise and initial partition dependencies [20]. The algorithms proposed in [21,22] tried to tackle those issues. Ref. [23] combined fuzzy C-means with mini-batch gradient descent with regularization. The authors in [24] proposed a unified combination of K-means and C-means methods. The authors in [25] proposed a novel technique to find the optimal number of clusters.

The underlying assumption of mixture-resolving clusterings is that the observed data points are generated from a mixture of probabilistic distributions whose parameters should be inferred from the dataset. These methods are model-based, and a statistical model or a priori should be known ahead of clustering. The expectation-maximization algorithm is the cornerstone of this category of methods [26,27].

2.2. Hierarchical Clusterings

This category of clusterings methods groups the data points to construct a hierarchical structure: the grouping procedure can be performed either in a bottom–up (agglomerative) or a top–down (divisive) fashion [20]. The agglomerative methods [28,29] initially start by assigning each data point to a singleton cluster and then iteratively merge every two clusters until (i) all clusters are merged into the root node or (ii) some stopping criteria are met. The root node represents the entire dataset. The divisive hierarchical methods start from a single cluster, representing the data, then in a top–down fashion splitting the clusters.

The merging or splitting decision generalizes the distance metrics of individual data points to distance metrics of subsets of data points. The distance metrics between subsets usually is referred to as linkage metrics. The single linkage—when the least interconnecting (dis)similarity between two components is considered [30], complete linkage, average linkage, McQuitty methods [31], median and centroid methods [32] are some of the prominent agglomerative (bottom–up) clustering methods employing different linkage metrics. Ward's methods [33] are another type of agglomerative clustering in which instead of linkage metrics, the merging decision is based on the optimal values of an objective function [34]. Balanced iterative reducing and clustering using hierarchies [35], BIRCH, is an online and memory-efficient agglomerative algorithm developed for large-scale datasets. The clustering using representative (CURE) addresses the drawbacks of BIRCH and is more robust to outliers, and it claims to detect different clusters' shapes and sizes.

The divisive methods are the reverse of agglomerative clustering. They start by splitting the entire dataset into smaller subsets until the predefined number of clusters is detected [36–38]. The natural splitting solution would be to analyze all possible bipartitions and select the two optimal ones. This solution is computationally expensive, and various divisive approaches have been developed to tackle this. For instance, bisecting K-means [39], reference point-based dissimilarity measure [40], and particle optimizer [41] are some of the efforts proposed to tackle this expensive computational complexity. In principle, divisive methods can be classified into monothetic and polythetic classes. The former uses the features one-by-one and was initially proposed for binary data [42,43] but later applied to multi-modal data. The latter class uses all features at once and utilizes the distance values [44,45].

2.3. *Gradient Descent Clusterings*

The majority of the previous GD-based clustering papers used it to optimize the proposed clustering objective function. For instance, the authors in [46] proposed a new graph cut clustering. They derived the graph cut using the Parzen windowing; then, they used GD for optimizing the proposed graph cut. In [47], it was employed to optimize the Gaussian kernel density estimators; similarly, ref. [48] used this optimization algorithm to learn Gaussian mixture models parameters. The methods proposed in [49,50] exploited GD to improve the K-means clustering performance; and the authors in [51] applied it for fuzzy clustering. While the previous works were devoted to partitional clustering, the authors in [52] adopted gradient descent for hierarchical clustering by embedding the representation of tree structures in hyperbolic space.

On the contrary, there are few papers in which they used GD for cluster refinement purposes or fine-tuning the parameters of the proposed methods. For instance, in [53], a fuzzy clustering method was proposed, and GD was used to fine-tune the parameters of the constructed fuzzy model to obtain a more accurate fuzzy model from the given input–output data. The authors in [54] used fuzzy clustering methods to construct the similarity matrices of each partition. Next, they aggregated partitions employing the direct sum of weighted vectors. Finally, the ultimate membership matrix was calculated by optimizing the sum of square errors through the gradient descent method.

3. Methodology

3.1. *Problem Formulation, Notation and Motivation of the Proposed Method*

Consider a set of N data points $X = \{\mathbf{x}_i\}_{i=1}^{N}$ for $\mathbf{x}_i \in \mathbb{R}^V$, where V is the dimensionality of the data points. Our goal is to partition X into K subsets, $S = \{s_k\}_{k=1}^{K}$, such that (i) the within-cluster data points are as homogeneous as possible and (ii) the between-clusters data points are as heterogeneous as possible. To accomplish our goal, as a standard practice, we associate each subset with the so-called cluster centroid $\mathbf{c}_k$ forming our set of centroids C. Then, we define the following clustering criterion:

$$F(X, S, C) = \sum_{k=1}^{K}\sum_{i=1}^{N} f(\mathbf{x}_i, \mathbf{c}_k) \tag{1}$$

where $f : X \times C \longrightarrow \mathbb{R}$ represents a (generic) distance function that will be applied to measure the distance between the data point $\mathbf{x}_i$ and the centroid $\mathbf{c}_k$.

In principle, optimizing clustering criterion (1) in a reasonable time depends on (i) the availability of any prior knowledge, including the number of clusters, (ii) the expected cluster membership type, i.e., being crisp or fuzzy, and (iii) the choice of the distance function, i.e., being differentiable or not. For instance, by defining f to be the Euclidean distance and pursuing the alternating optimization algorithm, for a given number of clusters, the popular K-means method [4] can be obtained. In contrast, using the same distance function in the one-by-one cluster extracting strategy [55], when the number of clusters is not known, leads to the i-K-means method [56]—it extended to a more complex data structure in [57] recently. Interested readers may advise [20,56] for more details on clustering methods and [58] about generic optimization algorithms.

The authors in [58], a recent and comprehensive textbook on optimization algorithms, categorized the existing algorithms into eight families of methods, as shown in Figure 2. They explained the conditions for which each family is applicable and discussed the challenges and limits of the algorithms under consideration. Among those possible options, due to the simplicity, intuitiveness, and yet proven effectiveness of the derivative-based methods, we were interested in applying them. This family can be further categorized into first-order and second-order methods, for which, in the multivariate optimization setting, the former relies on gradients, and the latter relies on Hessian information to direct the search to find an optimum.

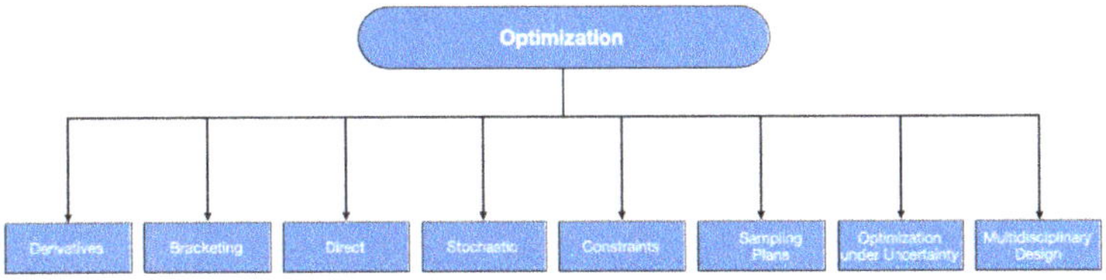

Figure 2. The first level of optimization algorithms taxonomy introduced in [58].

Although the second-order methods are proven to be more effective than first-order methods, as we observed in our preliminary experiments, they suffer from expensive computational complexity. Therefore, despite some of the disadvantages of the first-order methods such as their sensitivity to seed initialization or the step size, the possibility of being stuck in local minima or close to the global minimum, etc., we decided to proceed with first-order methods. This set of methods starts from a random initial point, and based on the fact that the negative of the gradient represents the steepest descent, iteratively modifies the initial guess to find a minimum using the gradient information.

In this work, we assumed that the clusters are crisp, and their number, K, is given. Moreover, although any differentiable distance function can be exploited, we limit our choice to the Minkowski distance with p-values limited to $1 \leq p \leq 4$. This setting enables us to adopt the celebrated gradient descent optimization algorithm, a well-known and popular member of first-order-derivative-based optimization methods, for the task of cluster recovery. Since gradient descent is an iterative method, we should update our notation by adding subscript (t) to reflect the concept of iterations. Concretely, we denote the set of cluster centroids at iteration t with $C^{(t)} = \{\mathbf{c}_k^{(t)}\}_{k=1}^K$. Similarly, we denote the set of detected clusters at iteration t with $S^{(t)} = \{s_k^{(t)}\}_{k=1}^K$.

3.2. Gradient Descent Clustering Methods

Our proposed gradient descent clustering (GDC) method consists of three constituents: (A) cluster assignment criterion, (B) cluster update rules and (C) convergence condition. In the remainder of this subsection, we explain them.

The first constituent of GDC, the cluster assignment criterion, is shown in Equation (2):

$$\underset{k}{argmin} f(\mathbf{x}_i, \mathbf{c}_k^{(t)}) < f(\mathbf{x}_i, \mathbf{c}_j^{(t)}), \ \forall j \neq k. \tag{2}$$

that is, at iteration t, the data point $\mathbf{x}_i$ will be assigned to the cluster k for which its distance to the centroid $\mathbf{c}_k^{(t)}$, is minimum.

The second constituent of GDC, i.e., the update rule, in its Vanilla form is explained in Equation (3):

$$\mathbf{c}_k^{(t+1)} = \mathbf{c}_k^{(t)} - \alpha \nabla_{\mathbf{c}_k^{(t)}} f(\mathbf{x}_i, \mathbf{c}_k^{(t)}), \tag{3}$$

where α represents the so-called step size, and $\nabla c_k^{(t)}$ is the gradient of the distance function, f, with respect to the k-th centroid at iteration t evaluated with the data point $\mathbf{x}_i$. It ought to point out that our preliminary experiments, aligned with the results of [59], showed that the per-data-point, or online, update rule is significantly more efficient than the batch version of the gradient descent algorithm; therefore, we always update the centroids in an online manner.

Furthermore, our unreported experiments were aligned with the well-known fact that the Vanilla update rule, i.e., Equation (3), is prone to slow convergence, especially at nearly flat surfaces [58]. To tackle this issue, accumulating momentum was proposed [60]. However, this accumulation may lead to overshoots at the valley floor; to avoid the overshooting, we exploit the Nesterov-accelerated momentum [61] to modify the gradient at the projected future position as follows:

$$\mathbf{v}^{(t+1)} = \beta_1 \mathbf{v}^{(t)} - \alpha \nabla_{\mathbf{c}_k^{(t)}} f(\mathbf{x}_i + \beta_1 \mathbf{v}^{(t)}, \mathbf{c}_k^{(t)}) \tag{4a}$$

$$\mathbf{c}_k^{(t+1)} = \mathbf{c}_k^{(t)} + \mathbf{v}^{(t+1)} \tag{4b}$$

where $\mathbf{v}^{(t)}$ is the so-called momentum vector, with initial values of zero, and is the accumulation of the gradient's history up to iteration t. The coefficient $\beta_1 \in [0, 1)$ is a hyperparameter that decays the momentum. We empirically study its impact and show that any value $\in [0.3, 0.6]$ leads to superior results. It is noteworthy to add that since at each iteration, we compute the gradients of f with respect to the closet centroid of $\mathbf{x}_i$, thus, adding $\mathbf{v}^{(t)}$ to $\mathbf{x}_i$ usually has a desirable impact. More precisely, consider the ideal situation for which the data and the momentum vectors point to the same direction in the (feature) space. Thus, this addition decreases the gradients, which is desirable to avoid overshooting. Meanwhile, the first term in (4a) provides additional momentum for going down the hill. However, in less ideal circumstances, this addition may have less desirable influences, and this negative influence becomes more exaggerated when some of the components of the gradient vectors (or the momentum) have constantly high values: for which they negatively influence the update direction. The adaptive gradient optimization methods [62–64] have been proposed to dull the effect of such components. We postponed applying those methods to our future studies.

One may consider at least the five following options for the last constituent of GDC, i.e., the convergence condition:

1. Applying the principles of first-order and second-order necessary conditions for optimality;
2. Monitoring the obtained results by a user, i.e., by mapping clustering results to an external source of knowledge;
3. When the value of loss function, i.e., Equation (1), is lower than a threshold, say, for instance, a percentage of data scatter;
4. When no significant improvements occur in the minimization of the loss function (or clusters inertia) in a pre-specified patience period;
5. When the number of iterations reaches its maximum.

We tried hard to establish a stopping condition using the item (1). Although in our preliminary experiments, we obtained ARI $= 0.91$ for the IRIS dataset, we failed to compute the Hessian matrix for large datasets, and therefore, we postponed this direction to our future studies. Moreover, the second and third options require domain knowledge and thus are out of the scope of the current study, and interested readers may consult Section 6.4 of [56] for more details.

We proceed in our computations with the fourth and fifth items. Nevertheless, in the synthetic datasets, where we could adjust the complexity of data, we noticed that the so-called patience period, the period in which we monitor the reduction of the clusters' inertia, significantly depends on the complexity of the dataset, developing a new method to assess the complexity of data that is required, and currently, this option is not applicable.

However, we assigned a high priority to this development in future research directions. Consequently, in the rest of our computations, we used the fifth item as the convergence condition and empirically scrutinized it.

We summarized our proposed gradient descent clustering method using the Nesterov momentum update rule in Algorithm 1, and we call it Nesterov momentum Gradient Descent Clustering (NGDC).

Algorithm 1: Nesterov momentum Gradient Descent Clustering (NGDC)

Input: X: Data set; K: number of clusters.
Hyperparameters: α: step size; T: maximum number of iterations; τ: the loss function upper bound; β_1: momentum decay coefficient.
Result: $S = \{s_k^{(t)}\}_{k=1}^{K}$ % set of K binary cluster membership vectors;
$C = \{\mathbf{c}_k^{(t)}\}_{k=1}^{K}$ % set of K centroids in feature space.
Initialize: Randomly initialize C and S.
for $t \in Range(T)$ **do**
    for $x_i \in X$ **do**
        find k using Equation (2) and set i-th entry of the $s_k^{(t)}$ to one;
        update clusters using the Equation (4);
        if *Equation* (1) $\leq \tau$ **then**
            Halt.
        end
    end
end

The Python implementation of our proposed methods, the code for applying all of the methods and the metrics under consideration, and the entire datasets used in this study are publicly available at https://github.com/Sorooshi/NGDC_method.git, accessed on 19 April 2023.

4. Experimental Setting to Validate and Compare the Performance of the Proposed Methods

We conducted our computational experiments to (A) study the characteristics of the hyperparameters of the NGDC to propose sustainable default values and (B) empirically validate and compare the performance of our proposed method with the most popular and effective clustering methods from the literature. Concerning those objectives, our computational experiment consists of the following constituents: (1) the set of methods under comparison; (2) the set of data under consideration; (3) the evaluation criterion for assessing the experimental results; (4) the pre-processing technique applied to standardize the datasets; In the rest of this section, we described each of them separately.

4.1. Competitors

We compared the performance of the NGDC with four popular clustering methods from the literature: namely, agglomerative [28], K-means [4], Gaussian mixture models [27] (GMM), and spectral [65] clustering methods. The reason behind our choice of competitors was four-fold: (i) we limit our choice only to those methods for which they have a reasonable number of hyperparameters, (ii) they require a given number of clusters, (iii) they have a proven history of applications, and (iv) their source code is publicly available. It ought to be mentioned that although clustering is still a relatively trendy research topic, however, according to [1], an overwhelming majority of recent research endeavors concentrate on the adoption of clustering methods in different disciplines: to the best of our knowledge, there are no more recent approaches that suit our selection criteria.

Agglomerative clustering starts with N singleton clusters with each data point assigned to a cluster, recursively, in a hierarchical manner. At each step, it merges the two most similar clusters until only one cluster remains. The output is a tree structure in which the root node represents the entire dataset. We provide the pseudo-code of this clustering method in Algorithm 2.

Algorithm 2: Agglomerative clustering

Initialize N singleton clusters: for $i \leftarrow 1$ to N do $c_i \leftarrow \{i\}$;
Initialize set of available clusters to be merged: $S \leftarrow \{1, 2, \ldots, N\}$;
repeat
  select two most similar clusters to merge: $(j, k) \leftarrow argmin_{j,k \in S}\, d_{j,k}$;
  create new cluster $c_l \leftarrow c_j \cup c_k$;
  extract j and k from list of available clusters: $S \leftarrow S \setminus \{j, k\}$;
  if $c_l \neq \{1, 2, \ldots, N\}$ **then**
    add l to list of available clusters to merge: $S \leftarrow S \cup \{l\}$;
  end
  for $i \in S$ **do**
    update the dissimilarity matrix $d(i, l)$;
  end
until *only one cluster remains*;

Essentially, depending on how we measure the dissimilarity between the pairs of clusters, we categorize agglomerative methods into (1) single linkage, (2) complete linkage and (3) average linkage. The single linkage minimizes the distance between the closest data points of pairs of clusters. Formally, for any two given clusters A and B and the selected distance metric $d_{i,j}$:

$$d_{SL}(A, B) = \min_{i \in A, j \in B} d_{i,j},$$

the result of this category is a minimum spanning tree: a tree that connects all of the data points in a way that minimizes the edge weights. The complete linkage minimizes the maximum distance between data points of pairs of clusters. Similarly:

$$d_{CL}(A, B) = \max_{i \in A, j \in B} d_{i,j},$$

the complete linkage results in more compact clusters in comparison with the single linkage variant. The average linkage compromises between the two previous options by minimizing the average of the distances between all data points of pairs of clusters: formally,

$$d_{AL}(A, B) = \frac{1}{N_A N_B} \sum_{i \in A} \sum_{j \in B} d_{i,j}.$$

where N_A and N_B are the cluster cardinalities of A and B, respectively. Although d_{AL} is sensitive to outliers and any changes in the measurement scale may change the clustering outputs, usually, it results in relatively compact clusters which are relatively far apart from each other. Therefore, in our experiment, we used this linkage method with the Euclidean distance metric.

Agglomerative clustering suffers from (i) expensive computational complexity $O(N^3)$—or in the best-case-scenario, $O(N^2 \log N)$, (ii) ambiguity in the definition of similarity, and (iii) it is just an algorithm, not a model, so assessing its goodness is difficult. The K-means methods address these issues.

K-means clustering uses the alternating optimization algorithm, that is, given the number of clusters K and N data points $X = \{\mathbf{x}_i\}_{i=1}^N$, at first, it initializes K random centroids $\mathbf{c}_k$; then, it alternates between the cluster assignment and centroids update steps until convergence. In the cluster assignment step, each data point $\mathbf{x}_i$ is assigned to its closest centroid:

$$z_i^* = \underset{k}{argmin}||\mathbf{x}_i - \mathbf{c}_k||_2^2,$$

The cluster centers are updated:

$$\mathbf{c}_k = \frac{1}{N_k} \sum_{i:z_i=k} x_i.$$

where N_k is the cardinality of cluster k. K-means is sensitive to random initialization. In our experiments, to make a fair comparison, we always applied all of the methods under consideration, including K-means, with ten random initializations and selected the best results with respect to cluster inertia (squared sum of the data points of a cluster with its centroid). We summarized the alternating optimization algorithm focusing on K-means clustering in Algorithm 3.

Algorithm 3: Alternating optimization algorithm (K-means)

Randomly initialize K centroids $\mathbf{c}_k$;
repeat
  $z_i = argmin_k d(\mathbf{x}_i, \mathbf{c}_k)$ for $i = 1 : N$; % E-step of EM
  $\mathbf{c}_k = \frac{1}{N_k} \sum_{i:z_i=k} \mathbf{x}_i$; % M-Step of EM
until *convergence*;

The underlying assumption of the K-means clustering is (i) all clusters have the same spherical shape and (ii) all clusters can be described by Gaussian distributions in the input space. While the former assumption is relatively restrictive, the latter implies that K-means cannot be applied to discrete data. The mixture models were developed to tackle these issues. In our opinion, the second issue can be addressed by quantitative enveloping of the categories of discrete data using dummy variables (also known as one-hot encoding). Thus, we will focus on Gaussian mixture models (GMMs) to address the first issue.

Gaussian mixture models (GMMs) clustering can be considered as a generalization of K-means clustering. It also exploits the alternating optimization strategy, which is usually referred to as the expectation maximization (EM) algorithm in this context. Given the dataset $X = \{\mathbf{x}_i\}_{i=1}^N$ and a set of parameters of multivariate normal distribution, i.e., $\boldsymbol{\theta} = \{(\boldsymbol{\Sigma}_k, \boldsymbol{\mu}_k)\}_{k=1}^K$, each iteration consists of two steps. In the first step, i.e., the E-step, we compute the expectations, or the responsibilities of latent variable z_i (associated with cluster k) for generating data point $\mathbf{x}_i$ given the current parameters:

$$r_{ik} = p^*(z_i = k|\boldsymbol{\theta}) = \frac{\pi_k p(\mathbf{x}_i|\boldsymbol{\theta}_k)}{\sum_{k'} \pi_{k'} p(\mathbf{x}_i|\boldsymbol{\theta}_{k'})} \tag{5}$$

In the M-step, we maximize the complete data log-likelihood:

$$LL(\boldsymbol{\theta}) = \mathbb{E}\left[\sum_i \log p(z_i|\boldsymbol{\pi}) + \log p(\mathbf{x}_i|z_i, \boldsymbol{\theta})\right] \tag{6a}$$

$$= \mathbb{E}\left[\sum_i \left(\log \prod_k \pi_k^{z_{ik}}\right) + \log\left(\prod_k \mathcal{N}(\mathbf{x}_i|\boldsymbol{\mu}_k, \boldsymbol{\Sigma}_k)^{z_{ik}}\right)\right] \tag{6b}$$

$$= \sum_i \sum_k \mathbb{E}[z_{ik}] \log \pi_k + \sum_i \sum_k \mathbb{E}[z_{ik}] \log \mathcal{N}(\mathbf{x}_i|\boldsymbol{\mu}_k, \boldsymbol{\Sigma}_k) \tag{6c}$$

where $z_{ik} = \mathbb{I}(z_i = k)$ is the one-hot encoding of the latent categorical value z_i, and $\pi_k = \frac{1}{N}\sum_i r_{ik}$ is the mixture weight. Depending the type of covariance, $\boldsymbol{\Sigma}$, different versions of GMMs will be obtained. In this work, we assigned a full covariance matrix to each component, and we used K-means to initialize the parameters. It ought to be mentioned that for the sake of fairness in our comparison, we assigned one cluster to each component.

Spectral clustering is a set of combined approaches based on the eigenvalue analysis of a graph's adjacency matrix $\mathbf{W}$ and K-means clustering. The goal is to partition the graph into $S_1, \ldots, S_K$ disjoint partitions which minimize some kind of cost. To this end, at first, we consider every data point $\mathbf{x}_i$ as a node, and the edge $i - j$ represents the similarity measure between two data points. A natural choice of the cost function is to calculate the edge weights of nodes in each cluster to nodes outside each cluster:

$$cut(S_1, \ldots, S_K) \triangleq \frac{1}{2} \sum_{k=1}^{K} W(S_k, \bar{S}_k) \tag{7}$$

where $W(A, B) \triangleq \sum_{i \in A, j \in B} w_{ij}$ and $\bar{S}_k = \{1, \ldots, K\} \setminus S_k$ is the complement of S_k. The cut has a trivial optimal solution when each node is assigned to a cluster. To tackle this issue, the normalized cut is proposed:

$$Ncut = \frac{1}{2} \sum_{k=1}^{K} \frac{cut(S_k, \bar{S}_k)}{V(S_k)} \tag{8}$$

where $V(S_k) \triangleq \sum_{i \in A} d_i$ denotes the total weight of set A and $d_i = \sum_{j=1}^{N} w_{ij}$ is the weighed degree of node i. Optimizing $Ncut$ is NP-hard. We can relax $Ncut$ optimization by using the Laplacian matrix defined as $\mathbf{L} \triangleq \mathbf{D} - \mathbf{W}$, where $\mathbf{W}$ is a symmetric weighted adjacency matrix and $\mathbf{D} = diag(d_i)$ is a diagonal matrix containing the weighted degree of each node, $d_i = \sum_j w_{ij}$. It is proven that the set of eigenvectors of $\mathbf{L}$ with zero eigenvalues spans K connected components of the graph: thus, one can apply K-means on the matrix $\mathbf{U}$, derived from the K eigenvectors with the smallest eigenvalue in its column, to recover the clusters.

4.2. Datasets

We scrutinized the performance of the methods under consideration using both real-world and synthetic datasets. The following two subsections describe each of them.

4.2.1. Synthetic Data

We applied the mechanism proposed in [66], which was later used in various papers, for instance [67–69], to generate our synthetic data. In this mechanism, first, we needed to determine the number of data points N, clusters K, and features V. Next, the clusters' cardinalities were determined randomly with two constraints: (a) no cluster should contain less than a pre-specified number of data points (we set this number to 30 in our experiments), and (b) the number of data points in all clusters should sum to N. Once the cluster cardinalities were determined, we generated each cluster from a multivariate normal distribution whose covariance matrix was diagonal with diagonal values derived uniformly at random from the range $[0.05, 0.1]$—they specify the cluster's spread. We generated each component of the cluster centroid uniformly random from the range $\zeta[-1, +1]$, where $\zeta \in A$ controls the cluster intermix: the smaller value of ζ, the higher the chance that data points from a cluster fall within the spreads of other clusters. Figure 3 depicts four examples of the generated datasets with $V = 10$ for $\zeta = 0.35$ and $\zeta = 0.95$ for $N = 2000$. The upper row visualizes five clusters, whereas the lower row shows 15 clusters.

As mentioned earlier, we generated synthetic data for two purposes: (A) to scrutinize the impact of the hyperparameters of our proposed methods and (B) to validate and compare the performance of our methods with other works from the literature. Concerning objective (A), with $N = 2000$ and $V = 10$, we generated datasets for two numbers of clusters $k = 5, 10$ and three distinct cluster intermix probabilities $\zeta = 0.35, 0.65, 0.95$. These (synthetic data generator's) settings led to six configurations as summarized in Table 1. We repeated each configuration ten times, yielding 60 distinct datasets. We referred to these datasets as "hyperparameter-scrutinizing data." Concerning objective (B), we studied the performance of methods under consideration for different numbers of clusters $K = 2, 10, 20$, numbers of features $V = 2, 5, 10, 15, 20, 200$, data points $N = 1000, 3000$ and cluster intermix probabilities $\zeta = 0.4, 0.8$, as summarized in Table 1. These settings led to 72 configurations, each repeated ten times, yielding 720 distinct synthetic datasets. We called these datasets as "comparison data". We ran each method with ten random seed initializations and chose the one that led to the best cluster inertia; then, we reported the averages and standard deviations of ten datasets of each configuration.

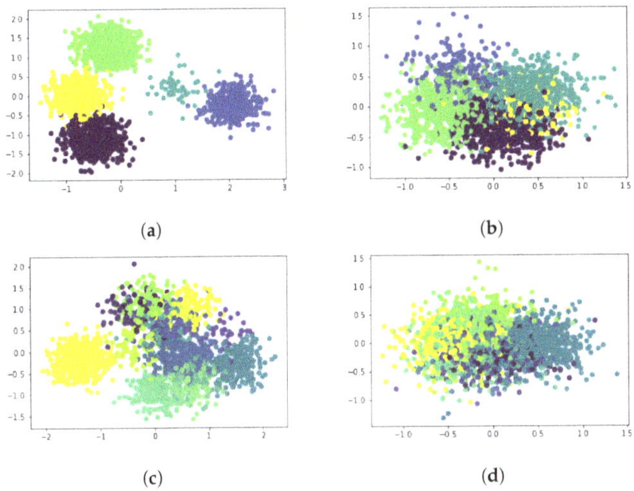

Figure 3. Scatter plots of the top two principal components of four synthetically generated data with ten features and 2000 data points at different cluster intermix probabilities $\zeta = 035, 0.95$ and two distinct numbers of clusters $K = 5, 15$. The value ζ controls the clusters' intermix: the smaller the ζ, the greater the intermix. (**a**) $\zeta = 0.95, K = 5$; (**b**) $\zeta = 0.35, K = 5$; (**c**) $\zeta = 0.95, K = 15$; (**d**) $\zeta = 0.35, K = 15$.

Table 1. Synthetic datasets configurations to study the hyperparameters of proposed methods (six configurations) and to validate and compare the methods under consideration (72 configurations): each case consists of 10 repeats summing up to 780 datasets.

Generator Parameters	Hyperparameter-Scrutinizing Values	Comparison Values
Clusters (K)	5, 15	2, 10, 20
Features (V)	10	2, 5, 10, 15, 20, 200
Data points (N)	2000	1000, 3000
Clusters intermix (ζ)	0.35, 0.65, 0.95	0.4, 0.8

4.2.2. Real-World Data

We used 11 real-world datasets to validate and compare the performance of the methods under consideration. We downloaded ten datasets from the popular UCI Machine Learning repository [70] and the Chernoff Fossile dataset from [71]. We summarized the characteristics of these datasets in Table 2.

Table 2. The real-world dataset's characteristics.

Dataset	Points	Features	Clusters
Breast Tissue	106	9	6
Ecoli	336	7	8
Fossil	87	6	3
Glass	214	9	6
Iris	150	4	3
Leaf	340	15	30
Libras Movement	360	90	15
Optical Recognition	3823	62	10
Spam Base	4601	57	2
Pen-Based Recognition	7494	16	10
Wine	178	13	3

4.3. Evaluation Metric

We assess the performance of the clustering methods utilizing the normalized mutual information, NMI [72]. The NMI is a popular metric based on the concept of entropy to quantify the similarity between the cluster recovery results, $S = \{S_k\}_{k=1}^{K}$, and the ground truth $T = \{T_l\}_{l=1}^{L}$. Concretely, given S and T, NMI relies on the so-called contingency table, a two-way table whose rows correspond to components S_k $(k = 1, 2, \ldots, K)$ of S, and the columns correspond to components T_l $(l = 1, 2, \ldots, L)$ of T, such that its (k, l)-th entry is $n_{kl} = |S_k \cap T_l|$. The marginal row and marginal column, in respect, are defined as $a_k = \sum_{l=1}^{L} n_{kl} = |S_k|$ and $b_l = \sum_{k=1}^{K} n_{kl} = |T_l|$. The probability that an object picked at random falls into S_k is $a(k) = a_k/N$. Similarly, the probability that an object picked at random falls into T_l is $b(l) = b_l/N$. Therefore, we define the entropy of S as $H(S) = -\sum_{k=1}^{K} a(k)\log(a(k))$. Similarly, we define $H(T) = -\sum_{l=1}^{L} b(l)\log(b(l))$ as the entropy of T. Thus, the mutual information (MI) between S and T is calculated using:

$$MI(S,T) = \sum_{k}^{K}\sum_{l=1}^{L} p_{kl}\log\left(\frac{p_{kl}}{a(k)\times b(l)}\right), \tag{9}$$

where $p_{kl} = n_{kl}/N$ is the probability that an object picked at random falls into both S_k and T_l $(k = 1, 2, \ldots, K;\ l = 1, 2, \ldots, L)$. Therefore, normalized mutual information is defined as

$$NMI = \frac{MI(S,T)}{max(H(S), H(T))}. \tag{10}$$

For the NMI $\in [0, 1]$, the closer its values are to one, the better the match between the clustering results and the ground truth and vice versa.

4.4. Data Pre-Processing

To pre-process the data, we used the so-called Min–Max standardization technique. Let $X = \{x_{iv}\}_{i=1}^{N}$ for $v = 1, \ldots, V$, where V is the number of features, represent the dataset. In addition, let x_{va} and x_{vb} represent the minimum and maximum of feature v for the entire dataset. The Min–Max method standardizes the data point $\hat{x_{iv}} = \frac{x_{iv} - x_{va}}{x_{vb} - x_{va}}$ such that $\hat{x_{iv}} \in [0, 1]$. Although it was empirically shown, for instance in [67], that the clustering result might differ depending on how the data were standardized, due to the intuitiveness of the output of the Min–Max technique, we chose it as the default for our experiments.

5. Scrutinizing the Hyperparameters of the NGDC Method

Our proposed method contains two hyperparameters: (i) step size α and (ii) momentum decay coefficient β_1. Moreover, similar to other gradient-descent-based algorithms, the convergence of NGDC and its sensitivity to random seed initialization needed to be scrutinized. Consequently, we designed our hyperparameter-scrutinizing datasets, consisting of 60 synthetic data configurations, and summarized them in Table 3 to scrutinize these four items empirically.

Table 3. The hyperparameters' search space of the proposed methods.

Hyperparameters	Values
Seed initialization	1, 5, 10, 20
Step size (α)	0.0001, 0.001, 0.01, 0.1, 0.2, 0.5
Number of Iterations (T)	5, 10, 20, 40
Momentum decay (β_1)	0.01, 0.1, 0.3, 0.6, 0.9, 0.99
Minkowski p-values	1, 1.5, 2, 2.5, 3, 3.5, 4

5.1. Random Seed Initialization

The NGDC method is non-deterministic, implying that different seed initializations lead to different results. In supervised learning, where the evaluation of results due to the existence of ground truth is easily feasible, it is recommended to apply the (non-deterministic) algorithm under consideration with different random seed initializations and select the one which leads to more desirable results. Although in clustering there is no ground truth available, still, this framework can be applied by considering the value of the clustering criteria or any other accessible external source of information to evaluate the results. In this work, our goal was to scrutinize the hyperparameters and validate our proposed method empirically. Thus, we ran the NGDC method with the hyperparameter-scrutinizing data with four different numbers of random seed initialization, n_init, and reported the results concerning the NMI in Table 4.

Table 4. Studying the impact of different seed initialization using NMI values at fixed $\alpha = 0.01$, $\beta_1 = 0.45$ and the maximum number of iterations equal to ten.

K	ζ	$n\_init = 1$	$n\_init = 5$	$n\_init = 10$	$n\_init = 20$
	0.35	0.540 ± 0.052	0.561 ± 0.055	0.567 ± 0.054	0.571 ± 0.056
5	0.65	0.714 ± 0.075	0.758 ± 0.076	0.856 ± 0.063	0.886 ± 0.062
	0.95	0.851 ± 0.074	0.944 ± 0.068	0.963 ± 0.049	0.993 ± 0.010
	0.35	0.400 ± 0.046	0.412 ± 0.050	0.413 ± 0.049	0.417 ± 0.048
15	0.65	0.815 ± 0.032	0.839 ± 0.024	0.848 ± 0.033	0.863 ± 0.029
	0.95	0.898 ± 0.030	0.930 ± 0.015	0.948 ± 0.012	0.953 ± 0.009

The reported results of this table strongly suggest repeating the seed initialization at least five or ten times. Although the higher the number of seeds initialization, the better the performance of NGDC, still, the reported difference between 10 and 20 seeds initialization, in our opinion, is application-dependable. In addition, if the time has higher priority than accuracy, this difference can be neglected. In the rest of our computations, we use ten seeds initialization.

5.2. Convergence and the Number of Iterations

The convergence of gradient descent algorithms in the supervised learning tasks with random initialization has been well-studied and (under specific conditions) proved to be convergent; for instance, refer to [73,74] for more details. In our opinion, this subject deserves independent research devoted to clustering, and therefore, in the current study, relying upon the results of the two papers mentioned earlier, we limited our analyses to the impact of different numbers of iterations on the quality of the recovered clusters using the NMI values.

Relying on the number of iterations has its advantages and disadvantages. The main advantages are (i) not limiting the choice of the distance functions in the central loss function shown in Equation (1), and (ii) the termination of the NGDC is guaranteed. The disadvantages are that (i) the inappropriate number of iterations may lead NGDC to be stuck in local minima or pass a global minimum; and (ii) an external source of knowledge for assessing the quality of obtained results might be required for further adjustments.

Table 5 represents the results of our investigation on the number of iterations. Taking an attentive look at these results, one can conclude that in the majority of settings, the higher the number of iterations, the larger the value of NMI. However, except for one case, i.e., $(K = 5,\ \zeta = 0.65)$, in the rest of the cases, the improvement obtained by setting the number of iterations to more than 10 is insignificant (approximately less than 1%) and can be ignored. In our opinion, this exception (the second row) includes instances of the first disadvantage discussed earlier.

Table 5. Studying the impact of different numbers of iterations using NMI at fixed $\alpha = 0.01, \beta_1 = 0.45$ and 10 random seeds initializations.

K	ζ	$T = 1$	$T = 5$	$T = 10$	$T = 20$	$T = 40$
	0.35	0.426 ± 0.045	0.567 ± 0.054	0.565 ± 0.055	0.567 ± 0.056	0.571 ± 0.055
5	0.65	0.749 ± 0.076	0.838 ± 0.097	0.856 ± 0.063	0.779 ± 0.068	0.786 ± 0.079
	0.95	0.873 ± 0.043	0.974 ± 0.037	0.976 ± 0.043	0.973 ± 0.030	0.976 ± 0.035
	0.35	0.315 ± 0.043	0.404 ± 0.051	0.418 ± 0.051	0.419 ± 0.048	0.423 ± 0.046
15	0.65	0.716 ± 0.030	0.842 ± 0.026	0.848 ± 0.033	0.860 ± 0.027	0.869 ± 0.026
	0.95	0.864 ± 0.015	0.930 ± 0.013	0.953 ± 0.009	0.954 ± 0.013	0.961 ± 0.016

5.3. Step Size

Assuming that the loss function under consideration is convex and differentiable, i.e., its gradient is Lipschitz continuous with a constant L, it is not hard to prove its convergence. However, finding the constant L to adjust the proper step size is computationally expensive, and intuitively, numerical fine-tuning the step size has become a common practice in supervised learning. Following this convention, we studied the impact of the step size with the fixed number of iterations, in our case equal to ten, and applied NGDC to each dataset with ten different seeds.

We reported the results of our investigations to fine-tune the step size in Table 6. From these results, it is not hard to conclude that the appropriate step size should be set to 0.01.

Table 6. Study of step size (α) with fixed $n\_init = max\_iter = 10$, $\mu = 0.9$ and p-value = 2. The best results are bold-faced.

Configuration		$\alpha = 0.0001$	$\alpha = 0.001$	$\alpha = 0.01$	$\alpha = 0.1$	$\alpha = 0.2$
K	ζ	**NMI**	**NMI**	**NMI**	**NMI**	**NMI**
	0.35	0.342 ± 0.060	0.524 ± 0.057	**0.539 ± 0.052**	0.003 ± 0.002	0.000 ± 0.000
5	0.65	0.734 ± 0.078	**0.806 ± 0.088**	0.766 ± 0.063	0.005 ± 0.003	0.000 ± 0.000
	0.95	0.885 ± 0.062	0.950 ± 0.034	**0.990 ± 0.011**	0.004 ± 0.001	0.000 ± 0.000
	0.35	0.287 ± 0.039	0.344 ± 0.045	**0.388 ± 0.048**	0.006 ± 0.007	0.000 ± 0.000
15	0.65	0.666 ± 0.038	0.770 ± 0.026	**0.844 ± 0.036**	0.008 ± 0.008	0.000 ± 0.000
	0.95	0.840 ± 0.020	0.913 ± 0.018	**0.953 ± 0.017**	0.015 ± 0.008	0.000 ± 0.000

5.4. NGDC Update Rule: β_1

We scrutinized and recorded the impact of the momentum (β_1) in the NGDC update rule in Table 7. As one can see, unlike the recommended value for this hyperparameter in classification tasks, usually 0.9, here smaller values of β_1, specifically in more challenging datasets, lead to better cluster recovery results. Since there is no clear-cut edge between 0.3 and 0.6, we suggested fixing the default value to 0.045.

Table 7. Study of β_1 with fixed step size = $\alpha = 0.01$, $n\_init = max\_iter = 10$ and p-value = 2. The best results are bold-faced.

Configuration K	ζ	$\beta_1 = 0.01$ NMI	$\beta_1 = 0.1$ NMI	$\beta_1 = 0.3$ NMI	$\beta_1 = 0.6$ NMI	$\beta_1 = 0.9$ NMI	$\beta_1 = 0.99$ NMI
5	0.35	0.568 ± 0.054	0.568 ± 0.055	**0.570 ± 0.054**	0.562 ± 0.056	0.539 ± 0.039	0.005 ± 0.001
	0.65	0.792 ± 0.072	0.785 ± 0.054	**0.837 ± 0.102**	0.804 ± 0.090	0.766 ± 0.063	0.013 ± 0.008
	0.95	0.975 ± 0.032	0.960 ± 0.048	0.953 ± 0.052	**0.992 ± 0.009**	0.990 ± 0.011	0.011 ± 0.005
15	0.35	**0.418 ± 0.053**	0.417 ± 0.049	0.417 ± 0.049	0.416 ± 0.048	0.388 ± 0.048	0.025 ± 0.001
	0.65	0.844 ± 0.031	**0.850 ± 0.038**	0.849 ± 0.028	**0.850 ± 0.029**	0.844 ± 0.036	0.028 ± 0.002
	0.95	0.951 ± 0.014	**0.955 ± 0.018**	0.947 ± 0.012	0.943 ± 0.018	0.953 ± 0.017	0.029 ± 0.002

5.5. Tuned Parameters

In this section, we empirically scrutinized the impact of different hyperparameters of the NGDC method to propose the default values. Considering our experimental results, we propose the following default values: (i) the step size $\alpha = 0,01$; (ii) the momentum decay coefficient, β_1, for any value in the range $[0.3, 0.6]$, we fixed it to 0.45; (iii) the number of seeds initialization, $n\_init = 10$; and (iv) the number of iterations, $T = 10$.

It ought to be mentioned that not only our proposed methods but also some of our competitors can adopt different distance functions. For instance, the K-means clustering with cosine distance has proven to be an efficient alternative to the innate Euclidean distance as reported in [75]. However, to maintain a fair comparison in the rest of our computations, we fixed $p = 2$ that imitates the innate Euclidean distance in the majority of the clustering methods.

5.6. p-Value in Minkowski Distance

As mentioned earlier, one of the contributions of our proposed method and our software implementation is its flexibility for accepting any differentiable distance function. We used the Minkowski distance with p-values bounded in $[1.0, 4.0]$ and ran the NGDC method at the hyperparameter-scrutinizing datasets to demonstrate this advantage. We reported the corresponding results in Table 8.

Table 8. Study of p-value with fixed step size $\alpha = 0.01$, $n\_init = 10$, $\beta_1 = 0.9$ and $max\_iter = 10$. The best results are bold-faced.

Configuration K	ζ	$P = 1$ NMI	$P = 1.5$ NMI	$P = 2$ NMI	$P = 2.5$ NMI	$P = 3$ NMI	$P = 3.5$ NMI	$P = 4$ NMI
5	0.35	0.056 ± 0.020	0.449 ± 0.060	**0.544 ± 0.056**	0.537 ± 0.057	0.504 ± 0.064	0.458 ± 0.068	0.391 ± 0.063
	0.65	0.353 ± 0.076	0.775 ± 0.091	0.806 ± 0.065	**0.849 ± 0.082**	0.840 ± 0.092	0.816 ± 0.070	0.772 ± 0.047
	0.95	0.705 ± 0.109	**0.982 ± 0.019**	0.970 ± 0.044	0.974 ± 0.032	0.953 ± 0.044	0.945 ± 0.038	0.942 ± 0.028
15	0.35	0.109 ± 0.014	0.340 ± 0.047	**0.384 ± 0.051**	0.376 ± 0.048	0.344 ± 0.043	0.312 ± 0.040	0.285 ± 0.035
	0.65	0.360 ± 0.055	0.826 ± 0.033	**0.848 ± 0.033**	0.834 ± 0.037	0.793 ± 0.035	0.750 ± 0.042	0.676 ± 0.039
	0.95	0.686 ± 0.047	**0.953 ± 0.010**	0.949 ± 0.016	0.936 ± 0.016	0.916 ± 0.021	0.895 ± 0.014	0.854 ± 0.028

From Table 8, one can observe that not only p-value equal to 1.5 in two configurations has an edge over the others, but also the $p = 2.5$ led to winning the competition when the cluster overlap probability is equal to 0.65 and there were five clusters.

6. Experiments

6.1. Experimental Results at Real-World Data

We reported the comparison results of the methods under consideration using 11 real-world datasets in Table 9. Considering the number of wins, the NGDC won eight competitions, which turned it into the overall winner. Agglomerative clustering, by winning three competitions, can be considered the second winner.

Table 9. Comparison on real-world datasets with $n\_init = 10$. The best results regarding NMI are bold-faced.

	K-Means	GMM	Spectral	Agglomerative	NGDC
Breast Tissue	0.515 ± 0.020	0.381 ± 0.047	0.462 ± 0.030	0.419 ± 0.000	**0.549 ± 0.017**
Ecoli	0.599 ± 0.010	0.388 ± 0.061	0.559 ± 0.007	**0.667 ± 0.000**	0.630 ± 0.024
Fossil	**1.000 ± 0.000**	0.687 ± 0.242	**1.000 ± 0.000**	**1.000 ± 0.000**	**1.000 ± 0.000**
Glass	0.338 ± 0.018	0.331 ± 0.035	0.277 ± 0.001	0.294 ± 0.000	**0.387 ± 0.031**
Iris	0.742 ± 0.000	0.629 ± 0.032	0.658 ± 0.000	**0.784 ± 0.000**	0.766 ± 0.020
Leaf	0.648 ± 0.010	0.589 ± 0.013	0.622 ± 0.017	0.621 ± 0.000	**0.653 ± 0.009**
Libras Movement	0.597 ± 0.015	0.197 ± 0.019	0.563 ± 0.016	0.563 ± 0.000	**0.602 ± 0.012**
Optical Recognition	0.761 ± 0.011	0.387 ± 0.068	0.699 ± 0.001	0.733 ± 0.000	**0.774 ± 0.019**
Spam Base	0.085 ± 0.115	0.080 ± 0.043	0.004 ± 0.000	0.001 ± 0.000	**0.259 ± 0.003**
Pen-Based Recognition	0.692 ± 0.006	0.691 ± 0.034	0.692 ± 0.000	0.635 ± 0.000	**0.708 ± 0.010**
Wine	0.846 ± 0.006	0.332 ± 0.107	**0.909 ± 0.000**	0.018 ± 0.000	0.858 ± 0.012

We ought to highlight the following intriguing observations about NGDC performance: (i) it won in approximately 73% of the real-world data; (ii) it obtained a relatively acceptable NMI equal to 0.55 at the breast tissue dataset which is approximately 4% higher than its closest competitor; (iii) similarly, using the glass dataset, it outperforms its closest competitor with approximately 5% better NMI; (iv) except for NGDC, which obtained a poor NMI value equal to 0.26, the rest of the methods under consideration failed to detect the clusters in the spam dataset. All these observations can be considered as pieces of evidence for the robustness and effectiveness of our proposed method. Nevertheless, we should emphasize that spectral clustering has a significant edge over its closest competitor, NGDC, in the wine dataset. More interestingly, except for GMM, the rest of the methods performed faultlessly on the Fossil dataset.

6.2. Experimental Results Using Synthetic Data

In this section, we compared the performance of our proposed methods with four popular and effective clustering methods described in Section 4.1 using our comparison datasets as outlined in the second half of Table 1.

We summarized the methods' performance for the case of two clusters with 1000 and 3000 data points in Tables 10 and 11, respectively. In both tables, NGDC, with slightly better results compared to its closest competitors, can be considered the overall winner. However, its unstable performance in Table 10 with 200 features and $\zeta = 0.4$, leading to NMI equal to 0.6 with a high standard deviation of 0.49, might require further investigations. The K-means and spectral clusterings each won eight settings in the total of both tables and can be considered the second winners. Moreover, considering the overall performances of methods, one may consider the settings with two features as the most challenging, especially when $\zeta = 0.4$ and $V = 200$ as the most straightforward. However, surprisingly, the GMM failed even in such simple settings, and except for a couple of other simple settings, i.e., $\zeta = 0.8$, the GMM performed poorly. Although the agglomerative also did not perform encouragingly in most settings, it still performed better than GMM.

Table 10. Comparison on synthetic datasets with 1000 data points and two clusters. The best results regarding NMI are bold-faced.

V	ζ	K-Means	GMM	Spectral	Agglomerative	NGDC
2	0.40	0.257 ± 0.212	0.041 ± 0.050	0.255 ± 0.215	0.008 ± 0.011	**0.284 ± 0.200**
	0.80	0.487 ± 0.286	0.075 ± 0.119	0.484 ± 0.282	0.180 ± 0.354	**0.499 ± 0.286**
5	0.40	**0.538 ± 0.156**	0.044 ± 0.059	0.537 ± 0.159	0.064 ± 0.184	0.523 ± 0.195
	0.80	0.876 ± 0.137	0.106 ± 0.087	**0.877 ± 0.138**	0.581 ± 0.474	0.837 ± 0.201

Table 10. *Cont.*

V	ζ	K-Means	GMM	Spectral	Agglomerative	NGDC
10	0.40	0.562 ± 0.151	0.415 ± 0.145	0.627 ± 0.138	0.006 ± 0.007	**0.685 ± 0.175**
	0.80	0.987 ± 0.033	0.976 ± 0.066	0.990 ± 0.024	0.895 ± 0.295	**0.993 ± 0.009**
15	0.40	0.869 ± 0.072	0.754 ± 0.294	**0.883 ± 0.063**	0.268 ± 0.399	0.882 ± 0.066
	0.80	**1.000 ± 0.000**	0.902 ± 0.293	**1.000 ± 0.000**	0.999 ± 0.003	**1.000 ± 0.000**
20	0.40	0.951 ± 0.039	0.310 ± 0.434	0.950 ± 0.037	0.281 ± 0.428	**0.958 ± 0.033**
	0.80	**1.000 ± 0.000**	**1.000 ± 0.000**	0.993 ± 0.008	0.997 ± 0.010	**1.000 ± 0.000**
200	0.40	**1.000 ± 0.000**	0.000 ± 0.000	0.992 ± 0.016	**1.000 ± 0.000**	0.600 ± 0.490
	0.80	**1.000 ± 0.000**	0.001 ± 0.001	**1.000 ± 0.000**	**1.000 ± 0.000**	**1.000 ± 0.000**

Table 11. Comparison on synthetic datasets with 3000 data points and two clusters. The best results regarding NMI are bold-faced.

V	ζ	K-Means	GMM	Spectral	Agglomerative	NGDC
2	0.40	0.306 ± 0.200	0.168 ± 0.112	0.306 ± 0.199	0.001 ± 0.001	**0.313 ± 0.201**
	0.80	0.584 ± 0.261	0.107 ± 0.104	0.574 ± 0.255	0.249 ± 0.381	**0.589 ± 0.260**
5	0.40	0.395 ± 0.230	0.033 ± 0.047	0.391 ± 0.228	0.002 ± 0.004	**0.403 ± 0.224**
	0.80	0.844 ± 0.140	0.339 ± 0.276	**0.858 ± 0.135**	0.463 ± 0.465	0.852 ± 0.141
10	0.40	0.750 ± 0.165	0.015 ± 0.014	0.748 ± 0.165	0.089 ± 0.264	**0.757 ± 0.165**
	0.80	0.969 ± 0.064	0.028 ± 0.030	0.970 ± 0.062	0.884 ± 0.294	**0.972 ± 0.061**
15	0.40	0.835 ± 0.111	0.018 ± 0.014	0.834 ± 0.109	0.001 ± 0.001	**0.843 ± 0.108**
	0.80	**1.000 ± 0.000**	0.118 ± 0.295	0.999 ± 0.002	0.998 ± 0.004	**1.000 ± 0.000**
20	0.40	0.918 ± 0.069	0.844 ± 0.283	**0.926 ± 0.061**	0.095 ± 0.280	0.922 ± 0.073
	0.80	0.999 ± 0.004	**1.000 ± 0.000**	0.994 ± 0.007	**1.000 ± 0.000**	0.999 ± 0.004
200	0.40	**1.000 ± 0.000**	0.001 ± 0.001	**1.000 ± 0.000**	**1.000 ± 0.000**	**1.000 ± 0.000**
	0.80	**1.000 ± 0.000**	0.000 ± 0.000	**1.000 ± 0.000**	**1.000 ± 0.000**	**1.000 ± 0.000**

We reported the results of methods under consideration with ten clusters and 1000 data points in Table 12, and we show the results of data with 3000 data points and the same number of clusters in Table 13. Concerning the number of wins, the NGDC and agglomeration each, in total, won eight settings and thus can be considered the joint winners. However, it ought to be highlighted that four out of eight wins of agglomerative clustering were obtained using the most straightforward datasets (the last two rows). Whilst NGDC also obtained completely acceptable results, it stocked at a local minimum in some cases. The closeness of NGDC results to the winners in the cases for which it did not win, for instance, $N = 1000, V = 5, 10$, can also be considered another piece of evidence for its effectiveness. The spectral and K-means clusterings, in respect, are the second and third winners. The GMM still performs poorly; however, it is slightly better than the case of the existence of two clusters.

Table 12. Comparison on synthetic datasets with 1000 data points and ten clusters. The best results regarding NMI are bold-faced.

V	ζ	K-Means	GMM	Spectral	Agglomerative	NGDC
2	0.40	0.207 ± 0.040	0.157 ± 0.045	0.193 ± 0.039	0.192 ± 0.039	**0.212 ± 0.040**
	0.80	0.432 ± 0.041	0.321 ± 0.077	0.401 ± 0.030	0.433 ± 0.038	**0.438 ± 0.043**
5	0.40	0.350 ± 0.049	0.200 ± 0.045	0.285 ± 0.026	0.199 ± 0.081	**0.358 ± 0.046**
	0.80	**0.753 ± 0.044**	0.607 ± 0.077	0.641 ± 0.061	0.711 ± 0.063	0.751 ± 0.042
10	0.40	**0.549 ± 0.077**	0.283 ± 0.072	0.460 ± 0.077	0.251 ± 0.153	0.546 ± 0.075
	0.80	**0.957 ± 0.029**	0.765 ± 0.083	0.922 ± 0.037	0.925 ± 0.027	0.956 ± 0.025

Table 12. *Cont.*

V	ζ	K-Means	GMM	Spectral	Agglomerative	NGDC
15	0.40	**0.757 ± 0.050**	0.338 ± 0.057	0.677 ± 0.075	0.363 ± 0.196	0.739 ± 0.045
	0.80	0.940 ± 0.030	0.666 ± 0.051	**0.991 ± 0.011**	0.985 ± 0.023	0.948 ± 0.031
20	0.40	**0.862 ± 0.034**	0.316 ± 0.016	0.804 ± 0.031	0.566 ± 0.125	0.843 ± 0.035
	0.80	0.993 ± 0.015	0.676 ± 0.051	**0.999 ± 0.002**	**0.999 ± 0.002**	0.970 ± 0.014
200	0.40	0.971 ± 0.027	0.023 ± 0.003	**1.000 ± 0.000**	**1.000 ± 0.000**	0.916 ± 0.020
	0.80	0.961 ± 0.027	0.023 ± 0.003	**1.000 ± 0.000**	**1.000 ± 0.000**	0.930 ± 0.027

Table 13. Comparison on synthetic datasets with 3000 data points and ten clusters. The best results regarding NMI are bold-faced.

V	ζ	K-Means	GMM	Spectral	Agglomerative	NGDC
2	0.40	0.200 ± 0.031	0.158 ± 0.041	0.193 ± 0.029	0.189 ± 0.035	**0.204 ± 0.033**
	0.80	0.410 ± 0.052	0.346 ± 0.081	0.381 ± 0.046	**0.415 ± 0.062**	0.413 ± 0.052
5	0.40	0.348 ± 0.054	0.199 ± 0.056	0.283 ± 0.041	0.169 ± 0.101	**0.355 ± 0.053**
	0.80	0.716 ± 0.057	0.685 ± 0.138	0.604 ± 0.055	**0.743 ± 0.062**	0.730 ± 0.066
10	0.40	0.579 ± 0.046	0.327 ± 0.132	0.484 ± 0.049	0.032 ± 0.045	**0.581 ± 0.042**
	0.80	0.920 ± 0.035	0.892 ± 0.041	0.877 ± 0.042	0.901 ± 0.045	**0.927 ± 0.021**
15	0.40	0.714 ± 0.051	0.552 ± 0.113	0.616 ± 0.050	0.178 ± 0.218	**0.727 ± 0.057**
	0.80	0.935 ± 0.031	0.909 ± 0.078	0.967 ± 0.039	**0.990 ± 0.008**	0.922 ± 0.034
20	0.40	**0.852 ± 0.031**	0.635 ± 0.067	0.784 ± 0.036	0.352 ± 0.263	0.845 ± 0.036
	0.80	0.956 ± 0.025	0.834 ± 0.086	**0.999 ± 0.001**	0.998 ± 0.001	0.967 ± 0.019
200	0.40	0.979 ± 0.014	0.011 ± 0.001	**1.000 ± 0.000**	**1.000 ± 0.000**	0.940 ± 0.018
	0.80	0.974 ± 0.022	0.015 ± 0.003	**1.000 ± 0.000**	**1.000 ± 0.000**	0.970 ± 0.008

We represented the methods' results for the case of 20 clusters with 1000 and 3000 data points in Tables 14 and 15, respectively. Now, the K-means, by winning nine settings, is the winner, and the agglomerative and NGDC, in respect, by winning eight and seven settings, are the second and third winners, respectively. Similar to the previous observations, we noticed similar patterns in the performance of the NGDC and agglomerative clustering concerning the relationship between data complexity and the quality of the obtained results. We also observed similar results with subtle improvements in the performances of spectral and GMM clustering methods.

Table 14. Comparison on synthetic datasets with 1000 data points and 20 clusters. The best results regarding NMI are bold-faced.

V	ζ	K-Means	GMM	Spectral	Agglomerative	NGDC
2	0.40	0.217 ± 0.023	0.160 ± 0.028	0.191 ± 0.025	0.207 ± 0.025	**0.220 ± 0.022**
	0.80	0.402 ± 0.028	0.333 ± 0.027	0.378 ± 0.024	0.403 ± 0.033	**0.408 ± 0.027**
5	0.40	0.325 ± 0.027	0.225 ± 0.026	0.286 ± 0.020	0.252 ± 0.029	**0.328 ± 0.023**
	0.80	**0.697 ± 0.048**	0.513 ± 0.078	0.601 ± 0.043	0.653 ± 0.047	0.683 ± 0.043
10	0.40	**0.494 ± 0.043**	0.271 ± 0.017	0.424 ± 0.040	0.307 ± 0.046	0.477 ± 0.029
	0.80	**0.928 ± 0.020**	0.689 ± 0.020	0.914 ± 0.018	0.904 ± 0.024	0.911 ± 0.017
15	0.40	**0.702 ± 0.031**	0.350 ± 0.017	0.631 ± 0.026	0.459 ± 0.059	0.643 ± 0.025
	0.80	0.968 ± 0.013	0.717 ± 0.039	0.974 ± 0.016	**0.979 ± 0.012**	0.949 ± 0.019
20	0.40	**0.837 ± 0.023**	0.376 ± 0.021	0.793 ± 0.029	0.617 ± 0.037	0.768 ± 0.035
	0.80	0.968 ± 0.009	0.708 ± 0.023	**0.999 ± 0.001**	**0.999 ± 0.001**	0.959 ± 0.013
200	0.40	0.963 ± 0.009	0.082 ± 0.008	**1.000 ± 0.000**	**1.000 ± 0.000**	0.900 ± 0.017
	0.80	0.973 ± 0.006	0.083 ± 0.007	**1.000 ± 0.000**	**1.000 ± 0.000**	0.926 ± 0.014

Table 15. Comparison on synthetic datasets with 3000 data points and 20 clusters. The best results regarding NMI are bold-faced.

V	ζ	K-Means	GMM	Spectral	Agglomerative	NGDC
2	0.40	0.179 ± 0.024	0.148 ± 0.026	0.174 ± 0.023	0.176 ± 0.022	**0.182 ± 0.023**
	0.80	0.390 ± 0.042	0.342 ± 0.055	0.373 ± 0.043	0.392 ± 0.045	**0.394 ± 0.042**
5	0.40	0.298 ± 0.042	0.199 ± 0.039	0.264 ± 0.038	0.218 ± 0.060	**0.303 ± 0.042**
	0.80	**0.691 ± 0.025**	0.462 ± 0.083	0.581 ± 0.031	0.648 ± 0.044	0.689 ± 0.026
10	0.40	**0.486 ± 0.040**	0.282 ± 0.059	0.396 ± 0.031	0.220 ± 0.057	0.482 ± 0.041
	0.80	0.919 ± 0.016	0.835 ± 0.029	0.889 ± 0.024	0.894 ± 0.030	**0.922 ± 0.025**
15	0.40	**0.686 ± 0.037**	0.433 ± 0.044	0.586 ± 0.045	0.258 ± 0.159	0.670 ± 0.034
	0.80	0.913 ± 0.016	0.870 ± 0.034	0.937 ± 0.023	**0.983 ± 0.011**	0.914 ± 0.016
20	0.40	**0.797 ± 0.021**	0.480 ± 0.045	0.728 ± 0.037	0.538 ± 0.087	0.787 ± 0.027
	0.80	0.975 ± 0.010	0.815 ± 0.043	0.996 ± 0.005	**0.997 ± 0.003**	0.961 ± 0.005
200	0.40	0.960 ± 0.013	0.046 ± 0.002	0.999 ± 0.001	**1.000 ± 0.000**	0.917 ± 0.016
	0.80	0.960 ± 0.019	0.061 ± 0.005	**1.000 ± 0.000**	**1.000 ± 0.000**	0.938 ± 0.017

It is noteworthy to mention that we ran NGDC with $T = 20$ and $T = 40$; however, since these increases in the number of iterations, as expected, did not lead to significant improvements, we did not report those results.

7. Conclusions and Future Work

In this work, we proposed a generic clustering criterion and adopted the GD algorithm to optimize it; our unreported experiments were aligned with the well-known fact that the Vanilla GD is prone to slow convergence, especially at nearly flat surfaces. Consequently, inspired by the Nesterov momentum, we proposed the NGDC method. As a by-product of our proposed method, we implemented the NGDC using Jax (an automatic differentiation library).

The NGDC method contains two hyperparameters: (i) step size α and (ii) momentum decay coefficient β_1. Similar to other gradient-descent-based algorithms, the convergence of NGDC and its sensitivity to random seed initialization needed to be scrutinized. Consequently, we designed the hyperparameter-scrutinizing datasets consisting of 60 synthetic data configurations (refer Table 3) to study the items mentioned earlier empirically.

Our investigations on the impact of random seed initialization showed that exploiting five or ten random initializations is sufficient; therefore, in the rest of our computations, we set this parameter to ten. Next, we studied the convergence of NGDC. The convergence of gradient-descent-based algorithms is well-studied, and it is proven that all GD-based algorithms under a specific set of conditions are convergent: although we think this subject deserves a separate study devoted to gradient descent adopted for clustering, relying on the results of previous research, we limited the current study to establish a stopping condition, i.e., the relationship between convergence and the number of iterations. Our results demonstrated that usually, NGDC converges within ten iterations; therefore, in the rest of our computations, we used ten iterations.

Following, we analyzed the impact of step size and momentum decay coefficient using our hyperparameter-scrutinizing datasets. Our computations suggested that one can set the step size equal to 0.01 and choose any values from the range $[0.3, 0.6]$ for the momentum decay coefficient; we fixed $\beta_1 = 0.45$.

Furthermore, our experiments using hyperparameters-scrutinizing datasets showed that our flexible implementation of the NGDC enables users to adopt any differentiable distance function for further improvements of the cluster recovery results. More so, we demonstrated that there were cases in which setting the p-value of Minkowski distance to 1.5 or 2.5 led to higher NMI values than the innate $p = 2$. One may consider these cases as preliminary pieces of evidence for a better scalability and generalization power of NGDC.

Once we fine-tuned the NGDC's hyperparameters, we statistically validated and compared its performance with four clustering methods from the literature on 11 real-world and 720 synthetic datasets. In the real-world data competitions, the NGDC won approximately 73% of the competitions, turning it into the prevailing winner when using real-world datasets. More so, for the breast tissue and glass datasets, in respect, it obtained approximately 4% and 5% higher NMI compared to its closest competitor, K-means. The performance of methods in the Spam and Fossile datasets needs to be highlighted. For the Fossile dataset, except for GMM with $NMI = 0.69$, the rest of the methods recovered the clusters without any mistakes. Conversely, in the Spam dataset, except for NGDC with poor $NMI = 0.26$, the rest of the methods failed to detect the clusters. Agglomerative clustering by winning three competitions and spectral clustering by winning two competitions are the second and third winners of real-world data competition.

Similar to real-world data competitions, in the synthetic data competitions, NGDC won 300 competitions and took first place. K-means won 230 datasets and took second place. Agglomerative and spectral clustering each won 210 competitions and jointly won third place. The GMM won only 20 competitions and performed poorly in most settings.

Taking a closer look at synthetic data results reveals the following points: (a) In general, we have three groups of algorithms. The first group consists of NGDC and K-means with frequently acceptable performance; the second group consists of spectral and agglomerative clusterings for which they usually performed acceptably on the settings with large number of features; and the third group contains GMM with frequent poor performances. (b) Although NGDC frequently performed acceptably; however, it constantly failed to recover completely faultless clusters when there were more than two clusters, and the number of features was equal to 200. In our opinion, these nuances in the performance of NGDC could occur due to convergence near the optimum, while the exhaustive search in the agglomeration clustering led to faultless recovery. (c) The reason for the constantly acceptable performance of the K-means might be because the underlying assumption of this algorithm and our synthetic data were both multivariate Gaussian distributions. (d) The performance of all methods under consideration in $V = 2, \zeta = 0.4, 0.8$ and $V = 5, \zeta = 0.4$ settings were moderate or even poor. This issue can be tackled by using a more powerful model and the same algorithm.

The current research is not without drawbacks, and those drawbacks form some aspects of our future research as follows.

The central purpose of the current research was to improve the effectiveness of clustering methods, and thus, we proposed a generic clustering criterion and used the JAX library to implement it: with this setting, we equipped users with the possibility of applying a diverse range of (differentiable) distance functions and adjusting the hyperparameters depending on the data under consideration. Although we empirically studied the hyperparameters of NGDC and proposed some default values, and they proved to be effective, however, due to the "no free lunch theorem," we believe developing a novel framework for employing NGDC in a semi-supervised manner can be a promising future direction.

Despite our endeavors in the current research, we failed to establish new convergence conditions and instead empirically scrutinized the impact number of iterations on the quality of recovered clusters. Theoretical analysis of NGDC convergence is another beneficial future direction. Furthermore, in the current research, we applied the Minkowski distance on our hyperparameter-scrutinizing data to demonstrate the possibility for further improvement in cluster recovery. However, we believe this subject needs a more rigorous investigation, and thus scrutinizing the impact of various distance metrics, including Minkowski metrics with different p-values, could be the third future direction.

Adopting other update rules such as RMSProb and ADAM can be considered our fourth direction. Reformulating our proposed clustering objective functions using a probabilistic approach so that we can determine the probability of clusters' membership is another promising future direction. Last but not least, extending the NGDC method to more complex data structures, for instance, to the feature-rich networks [68], is another promising future area of research.

Funding: This research received no external funding.

Data Availability Statement: The entire real-world data can be found at https://github.com/Sorooshi/NGDC_method/tree/main/Datasets/F. And the code for generating the synthetic data can be found at https://github.com/Sorooshi/NGDC_method/blob/main/gdcm/data/generate_synthetic_data.py.

Acknowledgments: Support from the Basic Research Program of the National Research University Higher School of Economics (HSE University) is gratefully acknowledged. The author is indebted to the anonymous referees for their invaluable comments taken into account in the final draft.

Conflicts of Interest: The authors declare no conflict of interest.

References

1. Ezugwu, A.E.; Ikotun, A.M.; Oyelade, O.O.; Abualigah, L.; Agushaka, J.O.; Eke, C.I.; Akinyelu, A.A. A comprehensive survey of clustering algorithms: State-of-the-art machine learning applications, taxonomy, challenges, and future research prospects. *Eng. Appl. Artif. Intell.* **2022**, *110*, 104743. [CrossRef]
2. Murphy, K.P. *Probabilistic Machine Learning: An Introduction*; MIT Press: Cambridge, MA, USA, 2022.
3. Bradbury, J.; Frostig, R.; Hawkins, P.; Johnson, M.J.; Leary, C.; Maclaurin, D.; Necula, G.; Paszke, A.; VanderPlas, J.; Wanderman-Milne, S.; et al. JAX: Composable Transformations of Python+NumPy Programs. 2018. Available online: https://github.com/google/jax (accessed on 2 February 2018).
4. Steinley, D. K-means clustering: A half-century synthesis. *Br. J. Math. Stat. Psychol.* **2006**, *59*, 1–34. [CrossRef] [PubMed]
5. Van der Laan, M.; Pollard, K.; Bryan, J. A new partitioning around medoids algorithm. *J. Stat. Comput. Simul.* **2003**, *73*, 575–584. [CrossRef]
6. Park, H.S.; Jun, C.H. A simple and fast algorithm for K-medoids clustering. *Expert Syst. Appl.* **2009**, *36*, 3336–3341. [CrossRef]
7. Campello, R.J.; Kröger, P.; Sander, J.; Zimek, A. Density-based clustering. *Wiley Interdiscip. Rev. Data Min. Knowl. Discov.* **2020**, *10*, e1343. [CrossRef]
8. Schubert, E.; Sander, J.; Ester, M.; Kriegel, H.P.; Xu, X. DBSCAN revisited, revisited: Why and how you should (still) use DBSCAN. *ACM Trans. Database Syst. (TODS)* **2017**, *42*, 1–21. [CrossRef]
9. Ankerst, M.; Breunig, M.M.; Kriegel, H.P.; Sander, J. OPTICS: Ordering points to identify the clustering structure. *ACM Sigmod Rec.* **1999**, *28*, 49–60. [CrossRef]
10. Schubert, E.; Gertz, M. Improving the Cluster Structure Extracted from OPTICS Plots. In Proceedings of the LWDA, Mannheim, Germany, 22–24 August 2018 ; pp. 318–329.
11. Agrawal, R.; Gehrke, J.; Gunopulos, D.; Raghavan, P. Automatic subspace clustering of high dimensional data. *Data Min. Knowl. Discov.* **2005**, *11*, 5–33. [CrossRef]
12. Mirjalili, S.; Lewis, A. The whale optimization algorithm. *Adv. Eng. Softw.* **2016**, *95*, 51–67. [CrossRef]
13. Nasiri, J.; Khiyabani, F.M. A whale optimization algorithm (WOA) approach for clustering. *Cogent Math. Stat.* **2018**, *5*, 1483565. [CrossRef]
14. Aliniya, Z.; Mirroshandel, S.A. A novel combinatorial merge-split approach for automatic clustering using imperialist competitive algorithm. *Expert Syst. Appl.* **2019**, *117*, 243–266. [CrossRef]
15. Ezugwu, A.E. Nature-inspired metaheuristic techniques for automatic clustering: A survey and performance study. *SN Appl. Sci.* **2020**, *2*, 1–57. [CrossRef]
16. Chollet, F. *Deep Learning with Python*; Simon and Schuster: New York, NY, USA, 2021.
17. Murphy, K.P. *Probabilistic Machine Learning: Advanced Topics*; MIT Press: Cambridge, MA, USA, 2023.
18. Min, E.; Guo, X.; Liu, Q.; Zhang, G.; Cui, J.; Long, J. A survey of clustering with deep learning: From the perspective of network architecture. *IEEE Access* **2018**, *6*, 39501–39514. [CrossRef]
19. Zadeh, L.A. Fuzzy sets. *Inf. Control* **1965**, *8*, 338–353. [CrossRef]
20. Saxena, A.; Prasad, M.; Gupta, A.; Bharill, N.; Patel, O.P.; Tiwari, A.; Er, M.J.; Ding, W.; Lin, C.T. A review of clustering techniques and developments. *Neurocomputing* **2017**, *267*, 664–681. [CrossRef]
21. Yager, R.R.; Filev, D.P. Approximate clustering via the mountain method. *IEEE Trans. Syst. Man Cybern.* **1994**, *24*, 1279–1284. [CrossRef]
22. Krishnapuram, R.; Keller, J.M. A possibilistic approach to clustering. *IEEE Trans. Fuzzy Syst.* **1993**, *1*, 98–110. [CrossRef]
23. Shi, Z.; Wu, D.; Guo, C.; Zhao, C.; Cui, Y.; Wang, F.Y. FCM-RDpA: TSK fuzzy regression model construction using fuzzy C-means clustering, regularization, Droprule, and Powerball Adabelief. *Inf. Sci.* **2021**, *574*, 490–504. [CrossRef]
24. Bouwmans, T.; Sobral, A.; Javed, S.; Jung, S.K.; Zahzah, E.H. Decomposition into low-rank plus additive matrices for background/foreground separation: A review for a comparative evaluation with a large-scale dataset. *Comput. Sci. Rev.* **2017**, *23*, 1–71. [CrossRef]

25. Chowdhury, K.; Chaudhuri, D.; Pal, A.K. An entropy-based initialization method of K-means clustering on the optimal number of clusters. *Neural Comput. Appl.* **2021**, *33*, 6965–6982. [CrossRef]
26. Verbeek, J. Mixture Models for Clustering and Dimension Reduction. Ph.D. Thesis, Universiteit van Amsterdam, Amsterdam, The Netherlands, 2004.
27. McLachlan, G.J.; Rathnayake, S. On the number of components in a Gaussian mixture model. *Wiley Interdiscip. Rev. Data Min. Knowl. Discov.* **2014**, *4*, 341–355. [CrossRef]
28. Murtagh, F.; Contreras, P. Algorithms for hierarchical clustering: An overview. *Wiley Interdiscip. Rev. Data Min. Knowl. Discov.* **2012**, *2*, 86–97. [CrossRef]
29. Murtagh, F.; Contreras, P. Algorithms for hierarchical clustering: An overview, II. *Wiley Interdiscip. Rev. Data Min. Knowl. Discov.* **2017**, *7*, e1219. [CrossRef]
30. Blashfield, R.K.; Aldenderfer, M.S. The literature on cluster analysis. *Multivar. Behav. Res.* **1978**, *13*, 271–295. [CrossRef]
31. Sneath, P.H. Thirty years of numerical taxonomy. *Syst. Biol.* **1995**, *44*, 281–298. [CrossRef]
32. Sneath, P.H.; Sokal, R.R. Numerical Taxonomy San Francisco. *Stat. Method Eval. Syst. Relationsh.* **1973**, *38*, 1409–1438.
33. Ward, J.H., Jr. Hierarchical grouping to optimize an objective function. *J. Am. Stat. Assoc.* **1963**, *58*, 236–244. [CrossRef]
34. Murtagh, F.; Legendre, P. Ward's hierarchical agglomerative clustering method: Which algorithms implement Ward's criterion? *J. Classif.* **2014**, *31*, 274–295. [CrossRef]
35. Zhang, T.; Ramakrishnan, R.; Livny, M. BIRCH: An efficient data clustering method for very large databases. *ACM SIGMOD Rec.* **1996**, *25*, 103–114. [CrossRef]
36. Boley, D. Principal direction divisive partitioning. *Data Min. Knowl. Discov.* **1998**, *2*, 325–344. [CrossRef]
37. Savaresi, S.M.; Boley, D.L.; Bittanti, S.; Gazzaniga, G. Cluster selection in divisive clustering algorithms. In Proceedings of the 2002 SIAM International Conference on Data Mining, SIAM, Arlington, VA, USA, 11–13 April 2002; pp. 299–314.
38. Chavent, M.; Lechevallier, Y.; Briant, O. DIVCLUS-T: A monothetic divisive hierarchical clustering method. *Comput. Stat. Data Anal.* **2007**, *52*, 687–701. [CrossRef]
39. Karypis, G.; Kumar, V. Multilevel k-way hypergraph partitioning. In Proceedings of the 36th Annual ACM/IEEE Design Automation Conference, New Orleans, LA, USA, 21–25 June 1999; pp. 343–348.
40. Zhong, C.; Miao, D.; Wang, R.; Zhou, X. DIVFRP: An automatic divisive hierarchical clustering method based on the furthest reference points. *Pattern Recognit. Lett.* **2008**, *29*, 2067–2077. [CrossRef]
41. Feng, L.; Qiu, M.H.; Wang, Y.X.; Xiang, Q.L.; Yang, Y.F.; Liu, K. A fast divisive clustering algorithm using an improved discrete particle swarm optimizer. *Pattern Recognit. Lett.* **2010**, *31*, 1216–1225. [CrossRef]
42. Williams, W.T.; Lambert, J.M. Multivariate methods in plant ecology: I. Association-analysis in plant communities. *J. Ecol.* **1959**, *47*, 83–101. [CrossRef]
43. Kim, J.; Billard, L. Dissimilarity measures and divisive clustering for symbolic multimodal-valued data. *Comput. Stat. Data Anal.* **2012**, *56*, 2795–2808. [CrossRef]
44. Kim, J.; Billard, L. A polythetic clustering process and cluster validity indexes for histogram-valued objects. *Comput. Stat. Data Anal.* **2011**, *55*, 2250–2262. [CrossRef]
45. Kim, J.; Lee, W.; Song, J.J.; Lee, S.B. Optimized combinatorial clustering for stochastic processes. *Clust. Comput.* **2017**, *20*, 1135–1148. [CrossRef]
46. Jenssen, R.; Erdogmus, D.; Hild, K.E., II; Principe, J.C.; Eltoft, T. Information cut for clustering using a gradient descent approach. *Pattern Recognit.* **2007**, *40*, 796–806. [CrossRef]
47. Charytanowicz, M.; Niewczas, J.; Kulczycki, P.; Kowalski, P.A.; Łukasik, S.; Żak, S. Complete gradient clustering algorithm for features analysis of x-ray images. In *Information Technologies in Biomedicine: Volume 2, Proceedings of the Information Technologies in Biomedicine ITiB, Kamien Slaski, Poland, 7–9 June 2010*; Springer: Berlin/Heidelberg, Germany, 2010; pp. 15–24.
48. Messaoud, S.; Bradai, A.; Moulay, E. Online GMM clustering and mini-batch gradient descent based optimization for industrial IoT 4.0. *IEEE Trans. Ind. Inform.* **2019**, *16*, 1427–1435. [CrossRef]
49. Sculley, D. Web-scale k-means clustering. In Proceedings of the 19th International Conference on World Wide Web, Raleigh, NC, USA, 26–30 April 2010; pp. 1177–1178.
50. Yin, P.; Pham, M.; Oberman, A.; Osher, S. Stochastic backward Euler: An implicit gradient descent algorithm for k-means clustering. *J. Sci. Comput.* **2018**, *77*, 1133–1146. [CrossRef]
51. Wang, Y.; Chen, L.; Mei, J.P. Stochastic gradient descent based fuzzy clustering for large data. In Proceedings of the 2014 IEEE International Conference on Fuzzy Systems (FUZZ-IEEE), Luxembourg, 11–14 July 2014; pp. 2511–2518.
52. Monath, N.; Zaheer, M.; Silva, D.; McCallum, A.; Ahmed, A. Gradient-based hierarchical clustering using continuous representations of trees in hyperbolic space. In Proceedings of the 25th ACM SIGKDD International Conference on Knowledge Discovery & Data Mining, Anchorage, AK, USA, 4–8 August 2019; pp. 714–722.
53. Wong, C.C.; Chen, C.C. A hybrid clustering and gradient descent approach for fuzzy modeling. *IEEE Trans. Syst. Man Cybern. Part B* **1999**, *29*, 686–693. [CrossRef] [PubMed]
54. Son, L.H.; Van Hai, P. A novel multiple fuzzy clustering method based on internal clustering validation measures with gradient descent. *Int. J. Fuzzy Syst.* **2016**, *18*, 894–903. [CrossRef]
55. Mirkin, B. The iterative extraction approach to clustering. In *Principal Manifolds for Data Visualization and Dimension Reduction*; Springer: Berlin/Heidelberg, Germany, 2008; pp. 151–177.

56. Mirkin, B. *Clustering for Data Mining: A Data Recovery Approach*; Chapman and Hall/CRC: Boca Raton, FL, USA, 2005.
57. Mirkin, B.; Shalileh, S. Community Detection in Feature-Rich Networks Using Data Recovery Approach. *J. Classif.* **2022**, *39*, 432–462 . [CrossRef]
58. Kochenderfer, M.J.; Wheeler, T.A. *Algorithms for Optimization*; MIT Press: Cambridge, MA, USA, 2019.
59. Wilson, D.R.; Martinez, T.R. The general inefficiency of batch training for gradient descent learning. *Neural Netw.* **2003**, *16*, 1429–1451. [CrossRef]
60. Qian, N. On the momentum term in gradient descent learning algorithms. *Neural Netw.* **1999**, *12*, 145–151. [CrossRef]
61. Nesterov, Y.E. A method of solving a convex programming problem with convergence rate $O(1/k^2)$. *Proc. Dokl. Akad. Nauk. Russ. Acad. Sci.* **1983**, *269*, 543–547.
62. Duchi, J.; Hazan, E.; Singer, Y. Adaptive subgradient methods for online learning and stochastic optimization. *J. Mach. Learn. Res.* **2011**, *12*, 2121–2159.
63. Kingma, D.P.; Ba, J. Adam: A method for stochastic optimization. *arXiv* **2014**, arXiv:1412.6980.
64. Zeiler, M.D. Adadelta: An adaptive learning rate method. *arXiv* **2012**, arXiv:1212.5701.
65. Von Luxburg, U. A tutorial on spectral clustering. *Stat. Comput.* **2007**, *17*, 395–416. [CrossRef]
66. Kovaleva, E.V.; Mirkin, B.G. Bisecting K-means and 1D projection divisive clustering: A unified framework and experimental comparison. *J. Classif.* **2015**, *32*, 414–442. [CrossRef]
67. Shalileh, S.; Mirkin, B. Least-squares community extraction in feature-rich networks using similarity data. *PLoS ONE* **2021**, *16*, e0254377. [CrossRef] [PubMed]
68. Shalileh, S.; Mirkin, B. Community partitioning over feature-rich networks using an extended k-means method. *Entropy* **2022**, *24*, 626. [CrossRef] [PubMed]
69. Shalileh, S.; Mirkin, B. Summable and nonsummable data-driven models for community detection in feature-rich networks. *Soc. Netw. Anal. Min.* **2021**, *11*, 1–23. [CrossRef]
70. Dua, D.; Graff, C. UCI Machine Learning Repository. 2017. Available online: https://archive.ics.uci.edu/ml/index.php (accessed on 1 January 2007)
71. Chernoff, H. The use of faces to represent points in k-dimensional space graphically. *J. Am. Stat. Assoc.* **1973**, *68*, 361–368. [CrossRef]
72. Cover, T.; Thomas, J. *Elements of Information Theory*; John Wiley and Sons: Hoboken, NJ, USA, 2006.
73. Chen, Y.; Chi, Y.; Fan, J.; Ma, C. Gradient descent with random initialization: Fast global convergence for nonconvex phase retrieval. *Math. Program.* **2019**, *176*, 5–37. [CrossRef]
74. Sutskever, I.; Martens, J.; Dahl, G.; Hinton, G. On the importance of initialization and momentum in deep learning. In Proceedings of the International Conference on Machine Learning, PMLR, Atlanta, GA, USA, 17–19 June 2013; pp. 1139–1147.
75. Magara, M.B.; Ojo, S.O.; Zuva, T. A comparative analysis of text similarity measures and algorithms in research paper recommender systems. In Proceedings of the 2018 Conference on Information Communications Technology and Society (ICTAS), Durban, South Africa, 8–9 March 2018; pp. 1–5.

mathematics

MDPI

Article

Design of an Automatic Classification System for Educational Reform Documents Based on Naive Bayes Algorithm

Peng Zhang [1,2,3], Zifan Ma [1,2], Zeyuan Ren [1,2], Hongxiang Wang [1,2], Chuankai Zhang [1,2], Qing Wan [4,*] and Dongxue Sun [5]

1 School of Mechanical Engineering, Hebei University of Technology, Tianjin 300401, China; zhangpeng@hebut.edu.cn (P.Z.); m202121203010@163.com (Z.M.); rzyhebut@126.com (Z.R.); 15822427129@163.com (H.W.); zuhom595@126.com (C.Z.)
2 National Engineering Research Center for Technological Innovation Method and Tool, Hebei University of Technology, Tianjin 300401, China
3 Yueqing Institute of Technological Innovation, Yueqing 325600, China
4 Undergraduate School, Hebei University of Technology, Tianjin 300401, China
5 Party Committee Organization Department, Hebei University of Technology, Tianjin 300401, China; 2016031@hebut.edu.cn
* Correspondence: 202221203005@stu.hebut.edu.cn

Abstract: With the continuous deepening of educational reform, a large number of educational policies, programs, and research reports have emerged, bringing a heavy burden of information processing and management to educators. Traditional manual classification and archiving methods are inefficient and susceptible to subjective factors. Therefore, an automated method is needed to quickly and accurately classify and archive documents into their respective categories. Based on this, this paper proposes a design of an automatic document classification system for educational reform based on the Naive Bayes algorithm to address the challenges of document management in the education field. Firstly, the relevant literature and document data in the field of educational reform are collected and organized to establish an annotated dataset for model detection. Secondly, the raw data are preprocessed by cleaning and transforming the original text data to make them more suitable for input into machine learning algorithms. Thirdly, various algorithms are trained and selected to determine the best algorithm for classifying educational reform documents. Finally, based on the determined algorithm, a corresponding classification software is designed to automatically classify and archive educational reform documents for analysis. Through experimental evaluation and result analysis, this research demonstrates the effectiveness and accuracy of the education reform document automatic classification system based on the Naive Bayes algorithm. This method can efficiently classify a large number of documents into their respective categories quickly and accurately, thereby improving the efficiency of educators and their information management capabilities. In the future, further exploration of feature extraction methods and machine learning algorithms can be conducted to optimize the classification performance and apply this method to practical management and decision-making in the education field.

Keywords: educational reform; manual classification; Naive Bayes algorithm; feature extraction

MSC: 68T09; 68T50

1. Introduction

With the rapid development of artificial intelligence and machine learning, the education sector has also ushered in opportunities for transformation. Traditional education systems face many challenges, one of which is the management and utilization of educational resources. Educational institutions and educators often need to deal with a large number of documents, including course materials, student assignments, teaching materials, and so on. The classification and archiving of these documents are crucial for improving educational efficiency, supporting personalized learning, and facilitating teaching assessment.

Text classification was proposed by American scholar Professor Luhn in 1957. In 1961, Maron [1] published the first paper on automatic text categorization. Text classification is to use the computer to automatically classify the text set according to a certain classification system or standard. Text classification technology has a wide range of application prospects. It is the technical support in the fields of information filtering, information retrieval, and document classification [2]. Text classification is generally divided into two categories: classification method based on knowledge engineering, and classification method based on machine learning. The classification method based on knowledge engineering refers to the classification based on expert experience and manual extraction rules. The classification method based on machine learning refers to the classification by computer self-learning and extracting rules. In view of the shortcomings of traditional text classification methods, many scholars have carried out research on text classification methods and revised and improved them. Based on the superiority of neural network algorithms in the field of natural language processing, Alina utilized a classification tool based on deep neural networks to automatically extract diagnostic and disease information at the time of surgery from electronic pathology reports monitored by the National Cancer Institute (NCI) and the Surveillance, Epidemiology, and End Results (SEER) population cancer registries, benefiting the cancer registries [3]. Liu trained a recursive neural network model to classify microblog posts related to urban flooding, establishing an online monitoring system for urban inundation triggered by flooding disasters [4]. Yang utilized artificial intelligence technology to improve the speed of encoding classroom dialogues, achieving automated classroom dialogue classification and instant feedback. They used neural network analysis models to evaluate and classify question level, answer level, and feedback level, constructing a comprehensive, rapid, and accurate method for evaluating classroom dialogue [5]. Vishaal established a recursive interleaved multi-task learning network that can be used for any general multi-label classification task related to the field of education [6]. Compared with the traditional classification methods, which mainly use supervised methods, relying on existing natural language processing tools can easily lead to error accumulation problems in the processing process. Chen proposed a Chinese text classification method based on appearance semantics and ASLA. Baidu Encyclopedia is used to extract the apparent semantics of Chinese text, and then PLSA is used to mine the potential semantics, and the correlation between the apparent semantics and the potential semantics and the category of the document is calculated. This method can deal with the classification of irregular texts such as Chinese network short texts [7]. In order to express text directly, Li proposed a short text classification model based on dense network, which uses one-hot coding, expands text feature selection by merging and random selection, and solves the problems of feature sparseness, dimensional text data, and feature representation [8]. Wang used the method of improving TF-IDF to modify the weight of word vector to optimize the text classification algorithm. Finally, the convolutional neural network was used to construct the classifier, which improved the accuracy of text classification. However, the high-order features were not properly disposed, resulting in the time complexity of learning much higher than the traditional machine learning method, which needs to be further improved [9]. With the research of deep learning for text classification, many researchers have found that the classification effect cannot be further improved by using only a single deep learning model, so scholars have proposed a method of mixing these deep learning models. Du proposed an emotion classification model based on convolution attention. This structure combines RNN with convolution-based attention model, and further superimposes the attention model to construct a hierarchical attention model for emotion analysis [10]. Peng proposed a hybrid model combining a deep ultra-deep convolutional neural network with a long short-term memory network, which is an application of deep CNN. The hybrid model shows better text effect than shallow CNN [11].

Although the existing common classification methods can meet the requirements of text classification in some aspects, there are still the following shortcomings for specific domain files (educational reform documents):

1. The classification standards are not uniform, and it is impossible to form a widely accepted and recognized classification.
2. The training sample data retrieval is difficult, the lack of standardized retrieval methods.
3. It is difficult to train pre-trained language models with domain background knowledge.

At the same time, many scholars have made contributions to the field of text classification. However, for educational-reform-related documents, manual classification by professional personnel from schools or educational institutions remains the prevailing method in today's educational environment. With a large number of educational policies, program proposals, and research reports constantly emerging, manually handling and organizing these documents is a tedious and time-consuming task. In order to solve the above problems, this paper proposes a text classification system for educational reform documents based on the Naive Bayes algorithm. The design involves several key steps: firstly, the classification standard is determined according to the "Guidelines for Application of Research and Practice Projects on Undergraduate Education and Teaching Reform at Hebei University of Technology in 2021". Next, develop a retrieval strategy to collect the relevant literature and document data in the field of education reform, and establish a well-annotated dataset for model testing. Again, preprocessing the raw data, cleaning and transforming the original text data to make them more suitable for input into machine learning algorithms. Further, training and selecting multiple algorithms to determine the most effective algorithm for classifying educational reform documents. Finally, based on the chosen algorithm, designing corresponding classification software to automatically classify and archive the analyzed educational reform documents. This system utilizes machine learning algorithms and natural language-processing techniques to automatically identify, classify, and archive different types of educational documents, greatly enhancing the efficiency and accuracy of educational management.

The development and application of this automatic classification system for educational reform documents based on the Naive Bayes algorithm will enable educational institutions and educators to better manage and utilize educational resources, thereby improving teaching effectiveness and learning outcomes. The advancement and application of this technology will bring about more intelligent and efficient management and teaching methods in the field of education, leading to overall enhancements in the quality of education delivery and outcomes.

2. Methods

In this section, the method designed for automatic classification of educational reform documents is introduced. To achieve the intended goals, it is necessary to follow several steps as illustrated in Figure 1. The key points of this method include:

1. Determine the categories for classification based on the "Guidelines for Application of Research and Practice Projects on Undergraduate Education and Teaching Reform at Hebei University of Technology in 2021".
2. Collect data from sources such as CNKI (China National Knowledge Infrastructure) and the school database for training and testing data.
3. Preprocess the data by segmenting the obtained Chinese text, and construct training and testing sets.
4. Train the model by using various algorithms to train the training set and calculate the probability analysis of each feature under each category.
5. Analyze the training results and error rates, select the optimal algorithm for further design.
6. Design corresponding software to achieve automatic classification.

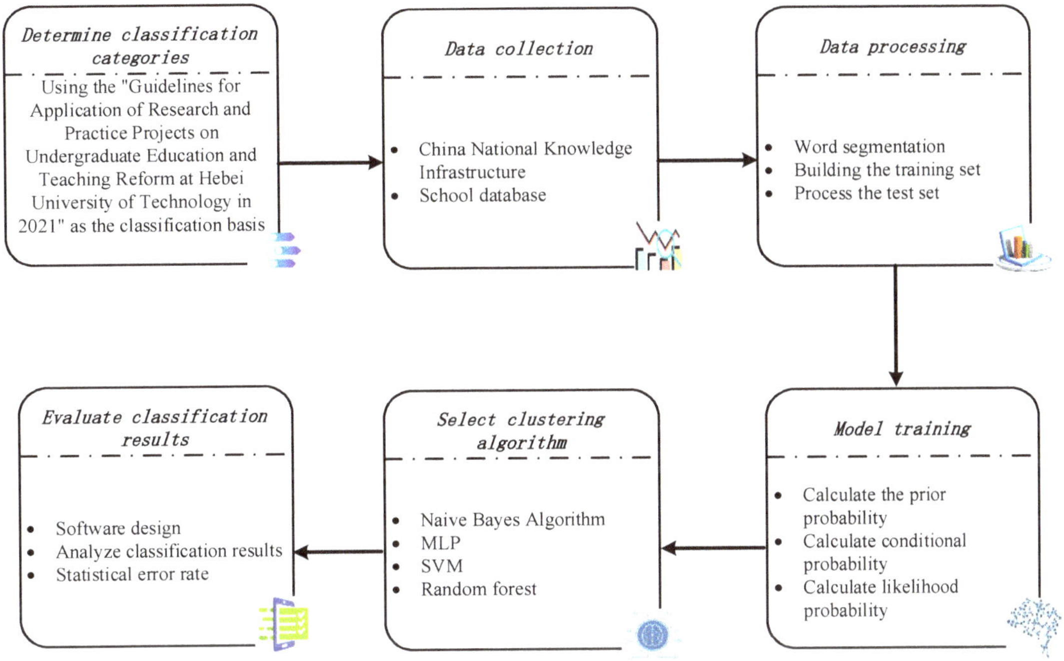

Figure 1. Representation of the methodology used to conduct this study.

The following parts of this paper are organized as follows: Section 2.1 identifies the categories for classifying documents related to educational reform; Section 2.2 determines the sources of the dataset and extracts the dataset; Section 2.3 selects various clustering algorithms, finalizes the algorithm to be used, pre-processes the initial data, and trains the selected algorithm; and Section 2.4 designs corresponding software to evaluate the model.

2.1. Categories of Documents Related to Educational Reform

To achieve precise classification of documents related to educational reform, it is essential to determine the categories of the documents. The "Guidelines for Application for Research and Practice Projects on Undergraduate Education Teaching Reform in 2021" from Hebei University of Technology provides detailed descriptions of the categories for educational teaching reform documents. Therefore, based on this guideline as the classification criteria, as shown in Figure 2, educational reform documents are divided into six categories: Special Topic on Theoretical and Practical Research of Emerging Engineering Education; Special Topic on Theoretical and Practical Research of New Liberal Arts; Research Topic of Collaborative Education Development; Research Topic of Curriculum Ideological and Political Construction; Labor Education, Aesthetic Education, Sports Research Topics; and Research on Teaching and Practice of Integrated Education. Keywords under each special topic are then counted for subsequent searching and extraction of the dataset.

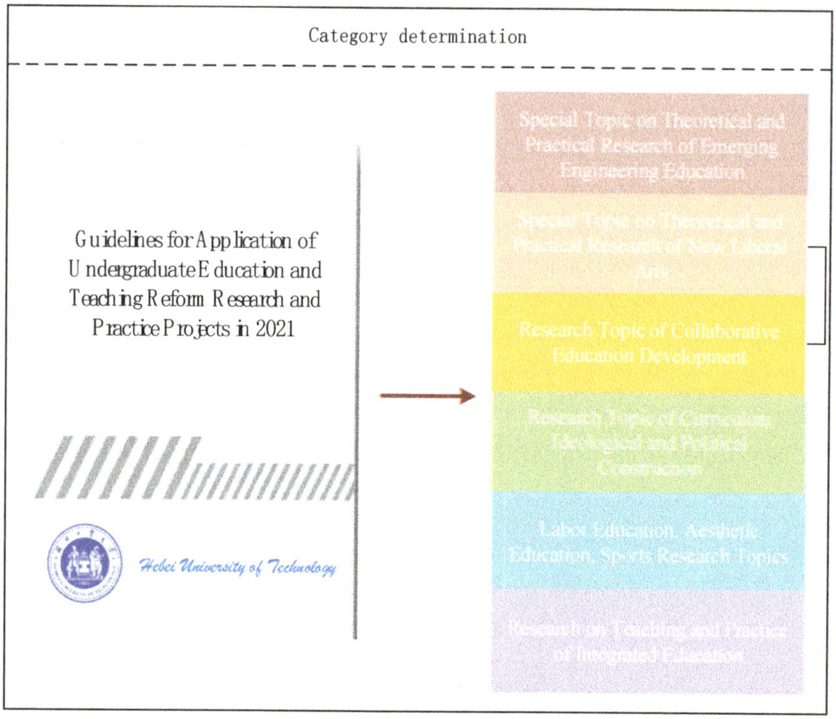

Figure 2. Category determination.

2.2. Data Set Extraction

China National Knowledge Infrastructure (CNKI) is one of the largest academic literature databases in China, gathering a vast amount of resources in the education field, including academic journals, conference papers, and master's and doctoral dissertations [12,13]. It covers a wide range of research areas related to educational reform. Its rich dataset provides a guarantee for the large training set required for the systematic design of this paper. At the same time, this paper is mainly aimed at classifying Chinese educational reform documents. As CNKI contains abundant Chinese literature, it can provide more specific information on practical applications, policies, and theoretical research related to educational reform in China. Therefore, this paper selects CNKI and the university's database as the sources of the dataset.

To accurately obtain each category of educational reform documents, this paper utilizes the advanced search mode of China National Knowledge Infrastructure (CNKI) and employs the keywords compiled in Section 2.1 as search terms. The paper uses "AND", "OR", and "NOT" operators to construct retrieval strategies for educational reform documents.

Taking the "Special Topics on Research on New Engineering Theory and Practice" as an example, a simple retrieval strategy is established as follows: "New Engineering" AND "Educational Reform" OR "Emerging Engineering" OR "New Type of Engineering" OR "Traditional Engineering" NOT "New Arts" NOT "Collaborative Education" NOT "Ideological and Political Education Construction" NOT "Labor Education, Aesthetic Education, Physical Education" NOT "Specialized and Innovative Education Teaching Integration". The goal is to retrieve educational reform documents related to "Special Topics on Research on New Engineering Theory and Practice" while being unrelated to the other five categories. The search results will be downloaded and saved into the corresponding folders for subsequent model training and evaluation. Finally, a Python program will be used to count the number of documents in the training set, with each category containing hundreds of files, as depicted in Figure 3.

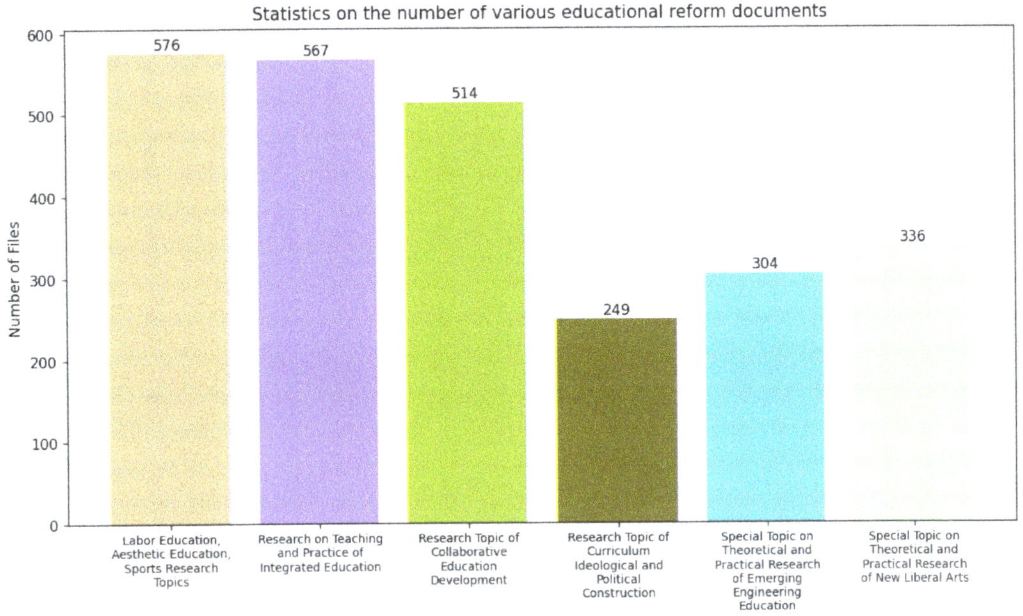

Figure 3. Statistics on the number of various educational reform documents.

2.3. *Algorithm Selection and Application*

2.3.1. Data Preprocessing

Text preprocessing plays a crucial role in text classification tasks. Its main purpose is to clean and transform raw text data to make them more suitable for input into machine learning algorithms [14,15]. Through text preprocessing, raw text data can be converted into more standardized, clean, and structured data, providing a better foundation for feature extraction and model training. The preprocessing process can reduce data noise, and improve the accuracy and efficiency of classification tasks.

For the text types involved in this article, the preprocessing mainly consists of the following steps. Firstly, Python-based natural language processing (NLP) technology is used to segment the original text data set [14,15], each sentence is processed as a unit, and the resulting sentences are segmented into word sequences. Secondly, the words after word segmentation are compared with a predefined list of stop words to remove the meaningless or too common words, such as 'the', 'is', 'in', etc. Thirdly, the part-of-speech tagging of words after word segmentation is carried out; that is, the part-of-speech of each word in the sentence is determined, such as nouns, verbs, adjectives, etc., which is helpful for the model to understand the sentence structure, the relationship between words, and semantic information. Finally, the data set after word segmentation is constructed and saved as a binary file.

After preprocessing the initial dataset, it is necessary to construct the TF-IDF (term frequency-inverse document frequency) term frequency space vector. The TF-IDF algorithm is a common statistical method used to measure the importance of words in information retrieval and data mining. The TF-IDF algorithm is used to measure the importance of a word in a corpus, and it calculates the TF-IDF value of a word using the product of term frequency (TF) and inverse document frequency (IDF) [16,17]. The specific formula is as follows:

$$TF_{w,D_i} = \frac{count(w)}{|D_i|} \tag{1}$$

$$IDF_w = \log \frac{N}{\sum_{i=1}^{N} I(w, D_i)} \tag{2}$$

$$TF - IDF_{w,D_I} = TF_{w,D_i} \times IDF_w \tag{3}$$

In the above formula, $count(w)$ represents the frequency of the term in the document, and $|D_i|$ is the total number of words in the document. TF represents the frequency of the term in the document, and a higher TF reflects that the term appears more frequently. IDF reflects the commonness of a term in the document. When a large number of documents contain a word, the IDF is lower, indicating that the word is more common [18].

The TF-IDF value of a word is equal to the product of its TF and IDF. A higher TF-IDF value for a word indicates that the word is more important in the document and better represents the document [19]. In text feature extraction, TF-IDF performs well, and is easy to implement and use. Therefore, this article selects the TF-IDF algorithm to calculate the importance of each word in the text dataset and constructs a word frequency matrix. Finally, the same processing is performed on the test set.

2.3.2. Algorithm Selection

After completing the above tasks, the next step is to select a text classification algorithm. Common algorithms used for Chinese text classification include Multilayer Perceptron (MLP), Support Vector Machine (SVM), Random Forest Algorithm, and Naive Bayes Algorithm. This article will introduce these four algorithms, conduct model testing, and ultimately determine the algorithm to be used.

Multilayer Perceptron (MLP), also known as Artificial Neural Network (ANN), is built upon a single-layer neural network by introducing one or more hidden layers, creating a neural network with multiple layers, hence the name "multilayer perceptron". The hidden layers are located between the input layer and the output layer [20,21]. The simplest MLP contains only one hidden layer, making it a three-layer structure, as shown in Figure 4.

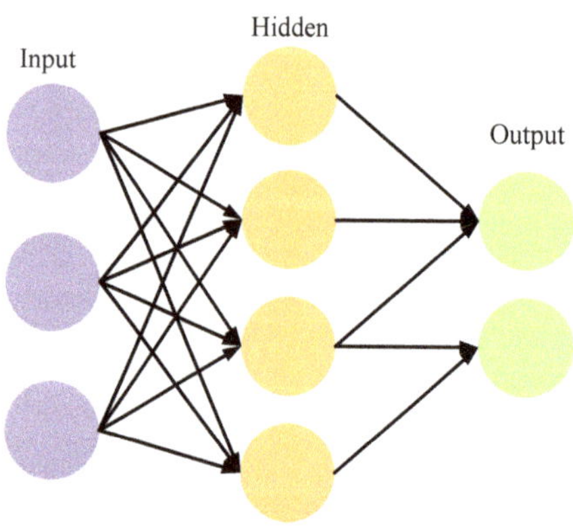

Figure 4. Schematic diagram of MLP.

MLP has powerful learning capabilities and can automatically extract features from training data for classification, making it very effective in handling complex text classification problems. Additionally, MLP can utilize multiple hidden layers to enhance the model's representational capacity. It can also leverage different activation functions and regularization methods to optimize model performance, giving it good scalability when dealing with large-scale text classification problems. However, due to the large number of parameters in MLP, the training process tends to be slow and may struggle with processing large amounts of text data. Moreover, when dealing with small amounts of training data, it is prone to overfitting.

SVM is a supervised learning algorithm widely used for classification and regression tasks [22]. The core idea of SVM is to find a hyperplane that maximizes the margin between two classes, thus achieving good classification performance. Its advantages lie in its ability to perform well in classifying data in high-dimensional spaces, making it suitable for handling high-dimensional features, as demonstrated in fields such as text classification and image recognition. SVM is suitable for small sample datasets, as it determines the decision boundary based on support vectors rather than the entire dataset, giving it an advantage in handling small sample data. Additionally, SVM can use kernel functions to map data to high-dimensional spaces, enabling nonlinear classification and providing good flexibility. However, SVM also has some drawbacks. Firstly, it incurs significant computational costs and longer training times when dealing with large-scale datasets. Secondly, SVM is sensitive to missing data and requires additional handling methods. Lastly, the original SVM algorithm is only applicable to binary classification problems, requiring extensions for multi-class problems, which increases the complexity of the algorithm.

Random Forest is a classifier that trains and predicts samples using multiple trees. It repeatedly randomly samples k samples with replacement from the original training sample set N to generate a new training sample set, and then uses the bootstrap sample set to generate k classification trees to form a random forest [23–25]. The classification result of new data is determined by the score based on the voting of the classification trees. Random Forest has the following advantages: firstly, it can handle high-dimensional data and performs well in feature selection, automatically selecting important features and reducing the burden of feature engineering. Secondly, Random Forest is efficient in handling large-scale datasets and can quickly build a large number of decision tree models. Furthermore, Random Forest exhibits good robustness to missing data and outliers, capable of handling incomplete datasets. Additionally, Random Forest uses a voting mechanism for classification or regression, which can reduce the risk of overfitting and is less susceptible to the influence of individual decision trees. However, Random Forest also has some drawbacks. Firstly, due to the ensemble of multiple decision trees, the model has poor interpretability compared to a single decision tree. Secondly, Random Forest may overfit on datasets with high noise and may require significant memory space. Moreover, Random Forest may lean towards categories with more samples when dealing with highly imbalanced datasets.

Naive Bayes algorithm is a classification algorithm based on Bayes' theorem, assuming that features are independent of each other. Under a given category, the joint probability of features equals the product of the independent probabilities of each feature. By calculating the posterior probability of each category, the category with the highest posterior probability is chosen as the prediction result [26]. Bayes' theorem is an important theorem in probability theory used to calculate the probability of an event occurring given certain conditions [27]. Its calculation formula is:

$$P(A|B) = \frac{P(B|A)P(A)}{P(B)} \tag{4}$$

In the formula, $P(A|B)$ represents the probability of event A occurring given that event B has occurred, $P(B|A)$ represents the probability of event B occurring given that event A has occurred, and $P(A)$ and $P(B)$ represent the probabilities of events A and B occurring, respectively.

The Naive Bayes algorithm has the following advantages. Firstly, it has relatively fast training and prediction speeds because it assumes independence between features, reducing the complexity of parameter estimation. Secondly, the Naive Bayes algorithm performs well on small sample datasets and can handle high-dimensional feature data, making it suitable for tasks such as text classification and spam filtering. Additionally, the Naive Bayes algorithm is robust to missing data, and can handle partially missing sample data. Finally, the Naive Bayes algorithm is not easily influenced by noisy data, and can provide good classification results even for datasets with significant noise. However, the Naive Bayes algorithm also has some disadvantages. Firstly, it assumes independence between features, which may not hold true in some cases, leading to a decrease in classification performance. Secondly, the Naive Bayes algorithm may exhibit higher error rates for datasets with large feature spaces or strong feature correlations. Furthermore, the Naive Bayes algorithm cannot handle continuous features and requires discretization.

The four algorithms mentioned above each have their own advantages and disadvantages in text classification, making it difficult to directly choose a classification algorithm. Therefore, it is necessary to build and test models for them. Four algorithm testing models were built separately, and the classification process of the testing models is shown in Figure 5.

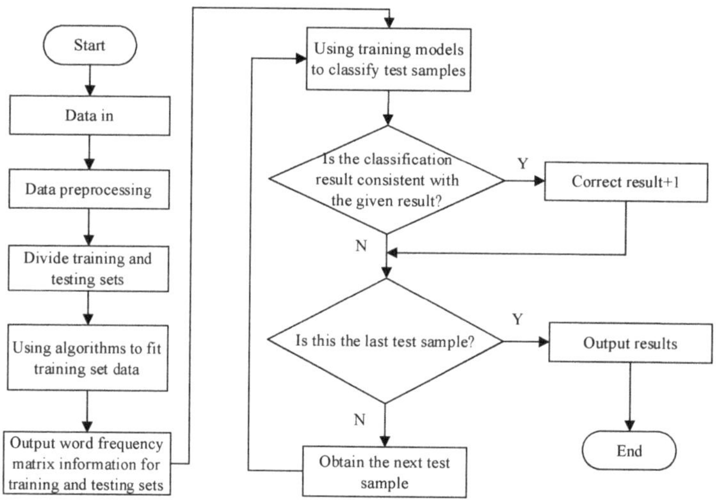

Figure 5. Classification process of the testing models.

The classification process of the test model is as follows:

1. Data preprocessing: Pre-process the data, including steps such as data cleaning, denoising, and standardization.
2. Divide the training and testing sets: Divide the pre-processed data into training and testing sets, and divide the dataset into training and testing sets in an 8:2 ratio.
3. Use algorithms to fit the training set data: Select the above four algorithms to train the data and establish a model.
4. Output word frequency matrix information: Perform word frequency statistics on the training and testing sets to generate word frequency matrix information.
5. Use training models to classify test samples: Use the established model to classify test samples.
6. Determine whether the classification result is correct: Evaluate the classification result to determine whether it is consistent with the given result. If the classification is consistent, the correct result is+1; if not correct, proceed to the next step.
7. Determine if it is the last test sample: Determine if there are still unclassified test samples, and if so, continue to classify the next test sample; if not, output the result and the classification ends.
8. Obtain the next test sample: Obtain the next test sample for classification testing, and then repeat steps 5–7.

After completing the model building and testing, it is necessary to evaluate the performance of the four models to determine the final model to be used. The evaluation index is a quantitative indicator of the performance of a model. A single evaluation indicator can only reflect a portion of the model's performance. If the selected evaluation indicator is unreasonable, it may lead to incorrect conclusions. Therefore, this study used commonly used evaluation indicators in classification tasks, including Precision, Recall, F1 score, Accuracy, Macro average (represented by Macro avg in the table), and Weighted average (represented by Weighted avg in the table) to comprehensively evaluate the model. The results are shown in Table 1, where Topic 1–Topic 6 represents the six categories from left to right in Figure 3. R-F stands for Random Forest Algorithm. N-B represents the naive Bayesian algorithm. The dataset is divided into training and testing sets in an 8:2 ratio. Therefore, Topic 1–Topic 6 obtained 58, 57, 51, 25, 30, and 33 test sets in sequence for model evaluation.

Table 1. Calculation results of various indicators.

	Precision				Recall				F1-Score				Support
	MLP	SVM	R-F	N-B	MLP	SVM	R-F	N-B	MLP	SVM	R-F	N-B	
Topic 1	0.93	0.90	0.75	0.96	0.89	0.90	0.74	0.90	0.91	0.90	0.75	0.93	58
Topic 2	0.93	0.96	0.82	0.97	0.91	0.88	0.79	0.98	0.92	0.92	0.80	0.97	57
Topic 3	0.92	0.92	0.86	0.96	0.86	0.90	0.73	0.96	0.89	0.91	0.79	0.96	51
Topic 4	0.70	0.83	0.63	0.88	0.84	0.96	0.60	0.88	0.76	0.89	0.61	0.88	25
Topic 5	0.84	0.90	0.61	0.85	0.90	0.90	0.83	0.97	0.87	0.90	0.70	0.91	30
Topic 6	0.91	0.86	0.71	0.93	0.88	0.91	0.73	0.91	0.89	0.88	0.72	0.92	33
Accuracy									0.89	0.90	0.75	0.94	255
Macro avg	0.87	0.90	0.73	0.93	0.88	0.91	0.74	0.93	0.87	0.90	0.73	0.93	255
Weighted avg	0.89	0.90	0.75	0.94	0.88	0.90	0.74	0.94	0.89	0.90	0.75	0.94	255

From Table 1, it can be seen that the Naive Bayes algorithm leads the other three algorithms in most indicators in the classification process of educational reform documents. Although the SVM algorithm is leading in some indicators in the Topic 4 classification process, the lead is not significant, and from a comprehensive performance perspective, the Naive Bayes algorithm is still significantly better than the SVM algorithm. Therefore, this study selected Naive Bayes algorithm as the classification algorithm for subsequent software design.

2.4. *Software Design*

In order to enhance the usability of the classification algorithm, this article designed auxiliary software based on relevant Python3.9 technologies for multiple steps in the process, ultimately creating an automated classification assistance system for education reform documents using the Naive Bayes algorithm.

2.4.1. Teaching Reform File Information Extraction System

The teaching reform file information extraction interface is shown in Figure 6, which is mainly used for extracting the required information from the dataset and extracting information from the documents to be classified later. The information retrieval process is divided into five steps:

1. Obtain relevant education reform documents based on the classification category from patent retrieval systems such as CNKI (China National Knowledge Infrastructure).
2. When the user clicks the "Browse" button, the system will open a file dialog box allowing the user to select the path where the files to be classified are located. The program will then display the selected directory path in the text box corresponding to that button.

3. When the user clicks the "Reading files" button, the program will read all file names in the previously selected directory and display these file names in a text box.
4. When the user clicks the "Save" button, the program will open a file dialog box allowing the user to choose a directory. The program will then iterate through all PDF files in the previously selected directory, extract the abstracts and keywords from these files, and save the abstracts and keywords to a TXT file named after the PDF file. These TXT files will be saved in the user-selected directory.
5. Implement the functionality to navigate to the next interface, which is bound to the "NEXT" button. When the user clicks this button, the program will close the current interface and call the run_next_script method to execute the next script. In the run_next_script method, the program will start the next script using the subprocess Popen method.

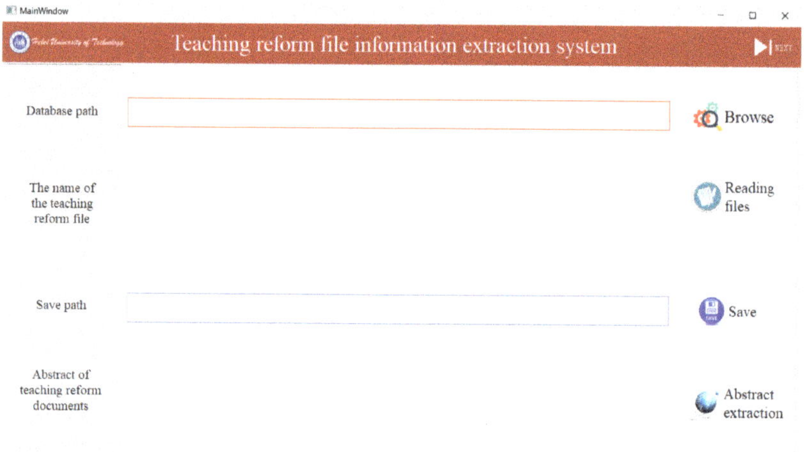

Figure 6. Teaching reform file information extraction system.

2.4.2. Automatic Classification System of Educational Reform Documents

The automatic classification system of educational reform documents consists of two modules: the "Classification" module, and the "Result statistics" module.

The "Classification" module, as shown in Figure 7, achieves the classification of the files to be processed by utilizing a model trained with the Naive Bayes algorithm. The specific implementation steps are as follows:

1. Initialize the interface, load the UI file, and connect the click events of the buttons.
2. After clicking the "Browse" button, a folder selection dialog will pop up, allowing the user to choose the folder containing the files to be classified, and display the selected path in the corresponding text box.
3. After clicking the "Reading files" button, read all the files in the selected folder and display the file names in the connected text box.
4. After clicking the "Articles classification" button, the system will start classifying the files in the selected folder. First, it will iterate through all the TXT files in the folder; next, it will open and read the content of each file, tokenize the content, and remove stop words. Then, it will construct the TF-IDF term frequency vector space, convert the tokenized text into a TF-IDF frequency matrix, and save it as a binary file. Finally, it will utilize the model built using the Naive Bayes algorithm to calculate the conditional probabilities of different categories based on the TF-IDF vectors, thus achieving the classification of the test files. The classification results will be output and written into an Excel file. The classification results will be displayed in the text box associated with the "Articles classification" button.

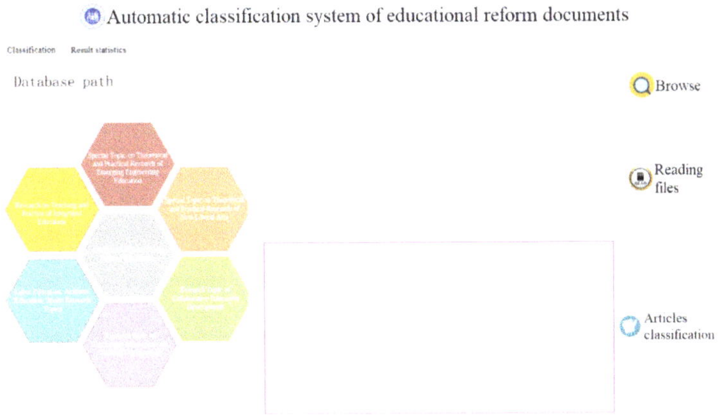

Figure 7. The classification module of Automatic classification system of educational reform documents.

The "Result statistics" module, as shown in Figure 8, mainly focuses on the statistical analysis of the classification results. The implementation steps are as follows:

1. After clicking the "Result statistics" button, read the classification results saved in the Excel file from the above interface, count the number of each category, and display the number of each category and the corresponding file names in their respective text boxes.
2. After clicking the "Pie chart" button, generate a pie chart based on the classification results to visualize the proportion of each file category within the processed folder. The corresponding results will be displayed in the output box associated with the "Pie chart" button.

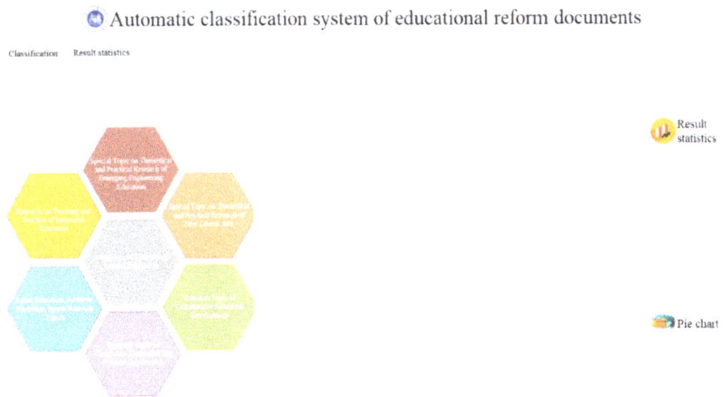

Figure 8. The Result statistics module of Automatic classification system of educational reform documents.

3. Experimental Verification, Taking the Educational Reform Documents of Hebei University of Technology as an Example

3.1. Background

In recent years, the deepening reforms in education and teaching have been continuously advancing, leading to a surge in the number of educational reform documents. This has resulted in challenges, such as a massive quantity of educational reform documents and a wide variety of document types. However, traditional manual classification methods require significant human and time costs, resulting in low efficiency and potential classification errors. Moreover, as the number of documents increases and the types become more diverse, manual classification becomes increasingly difficult. To address these issues, this paper proposes an automatic classification system for educational reform documents based on the Naive Bayes algorithm. This system is designed to assist education administrators in automatically classifying a large number of educational reform documents.

3.2. Extracting Information from Educational Reform Documents of Hebei University of Technology

Using the educational reform documents related to Hebei University of Technology from the past two years as samples, we obtained 52 educational reform documents awaiting classification from the school database and stored them in the corresponding folder for further processing.

After obtaining the files to be classified, we used the Educational Reform Document Information Extraction System to extract the abstract sections of the pending documents, as shown in Figure 9. Firstly, click "Browse" to select the folder to be processed, and the system will automatically display the path of the folder in the corresponding text box. Then, click "Reading files", and the names and file types of the files to be processed in this folder will be automatically displayed in the text box corresponding to this button. Furthermore, use the "Save" button to determine the location for saving the processed text. Finally, use the "Abstract extraction" button to extract the abstracts from the files to be processed and save them as TXT files in the location selected by the "Save" button for future processing.

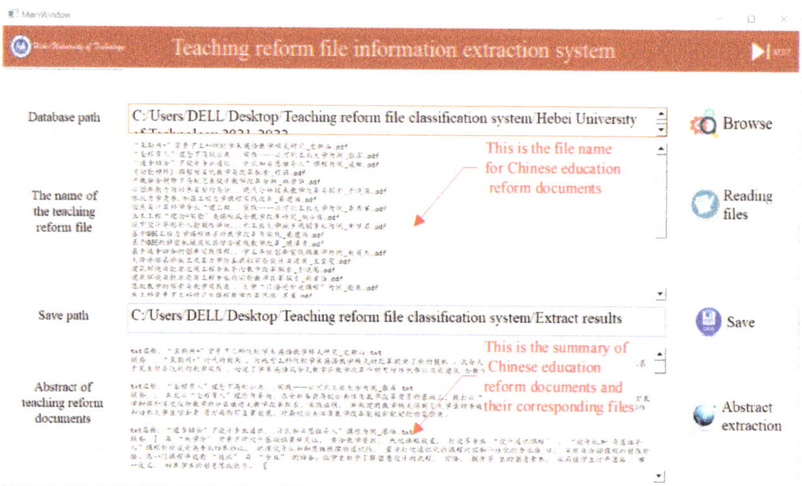

Figure 9. Information extraction results of teaching reform file from Hebei University of Technology.

3.3. Automatic Classification of Educational Reform Documents at Hebei University of Technology

First, use the "Classification" module to classify the educational reform documents of Hebei University of Technology to be processed, as shown in Figure 10.

1. Click "Browse" and select the file path saved in the previous step.
2. Click "Reading files", and the names and file types of the files to be processed in this folder will be automatically displayed in the text box corresponding to this button.
3. Utilize the model trained using the Naive Bayes algorithm to classify the documents to be processed. The classification results of the educational reform documents at Hebei University of Technology will be displayed in the text box corresponding to the "Articles classification" button.

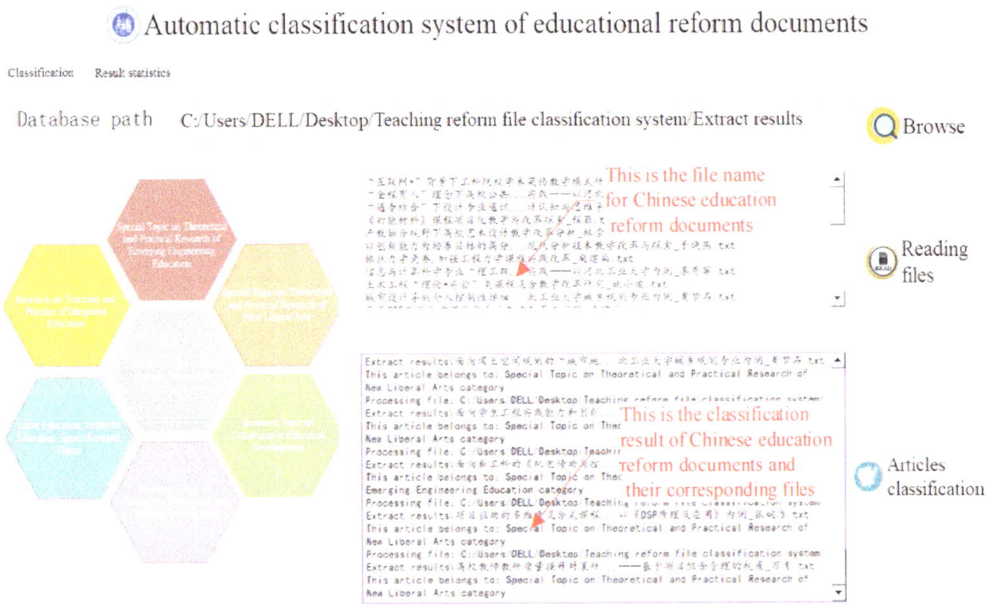

Figure 10. The classification process of teaching reform file from Hebei University of Technology.

Next, use the "Result statistics" module as shown in Figure 11. This module is mainly used to provide statistical analysis of the classification results of the educational reform documents at Hebei University of Technology. The number and names of documents in each category will be displayed in the text box corresponding to the "Result statistics" button. Additionally, a pie chart will be generated based on the classification results, allowing for an easy analysis of the distribution of each type of document within the processed folder. The corresponding results will be displayed in the output box corresponding to the "Pie chart" button. From the results, it can be seen that Hebei University of Technology has invested heavily in educational reform in the past two years, with a focus on the "Special Topic on Theoretical and Practical Research of New Liberal Arts" and the "Special Topic on Theoretical and Practical Research of Emerging Engineering Education", accounting for 46.2% and 36.5%, respectively. Therefore, this system can be used to analyze the key directions of educational reform in a certain area for the current year.

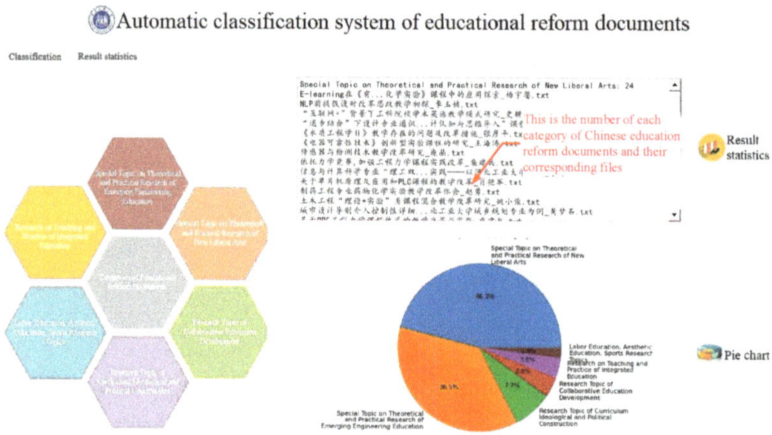

Figure 11. Statistics on the classification results of teaching reform file from Hebei University of Technology.

Finally, the educational reform documents at Hebei University of Technology from the past two years will be manually classified by professional personnel. The results of the manual classification will then be compared with the classification results of the automatic educational reform document classification system based on the Naive Bayes algorithm, and the comparison is presented in Figure 12. From Figure 12, it can be observed that the classification results of the automatic educational reform document classification system based on the Naive Bayes algorithm are largely consistent with the classifications made by professional personnel, with only a few instances of misclassification.

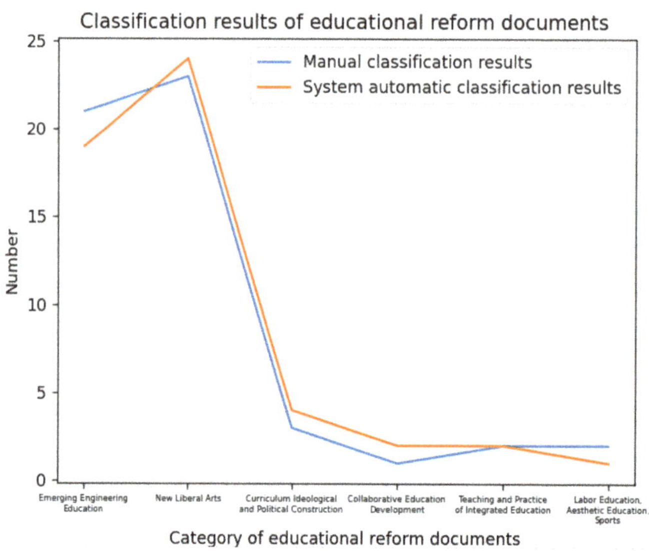

Figure 12. Comparison of classification results.

4. Verification and Discussion

Through in-depth analysis of questionnaire surveys and systematic evaluations, the universal applicability and effectiveness of the educational reform document automatic classification system based on the Naive Bayes algorithm designed in this paper have been validated.

To further demonstrate the universality and efficiency of the current design of the educational reform document automatic classification system based on the Naive Bayes algorithm, 20 relevant education professionals were invited to evaluate the system and fill out a questionnaire. The Chinese version and English version of the questionnaire are provided in Table 2. The 20 invited workers were divided into two groups based on their experience level: experienced workers, and novices. Figures 13 and 14 summarize the survey results, where EW-A represents experienced workers choosing option A, and N-A represents novices choosing option A.

Table 2. Questionnaire.

Chinese Version	English Version
您的身份:	**Identity:**
Q1:使用该系统是否对相应文件分类有帮助?	**Q1**: Does the system help in classifying the corresponding files?
□很有帮助□有一定帮助□没有帮助	**A** Very helpful. **B** Some help. **C** No help.
Q2:使用该系统是否能解决由于专业知识不足而导致分类错误?	**Q2**: Can the use of the system solve the classification errors caused by lack of professional knowledge ?
□能□一定程度上可以□不能	**A** Yes. **B** To some extent. **C** No.
Q3:使用该系统是否能提高文件分类速度?	**Q3**: Can the system improve the speed of file classification ?
□能□一定程度上可以□不能	**A** Yes. **B** To some extent. **C** No.
Q4:使用该系统是否能提高文件分类准确性?	**Q4**: Can the use of the system improve the accuracy of file classification ?
□能□一定程度上可以□不能	**A** Yes. **B** To some extent. **C** No.
Q5:该系统是否有实用价值?	**Q5**: Does the system have practical value ?
□有□有一定价值□没有	**A** Yes. **B** To some extent. **C** No.
Q6:使用该系统是否能得到期望的分类效果?	**Q6**: Can the system be used to get the desired classification results ?
□能□一定程度上可以□不能	**A** Yes. **B** To some extent. **C** No.
Q7:使用该系统时是否遇到困难,使用效果如何?	**Q7**: Do you encounter difficulties when using the system, and what is the effectiveness of its usage?
□使用简单,没有任何困难	**A** User-friendly, no difficulty.
□有一些困难,使用效果一般	**B** Some difficulties, average performance.
□完全不会使用,非常困难	**C** Not used at all, very difficult.
Q8:是否推荐其他人员使用?	**Q8**: Do you recommend other personnel to use it
□是的!我推荐□可以尝试□不推荐	**A** Yes. **B** Probably. **C** No.
其他:	Other:
	Q is question

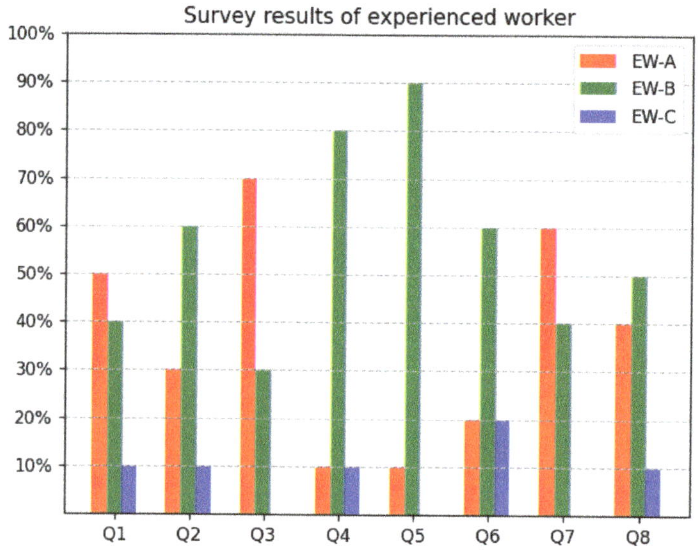

Figure 13. Survey results of experienced workers.

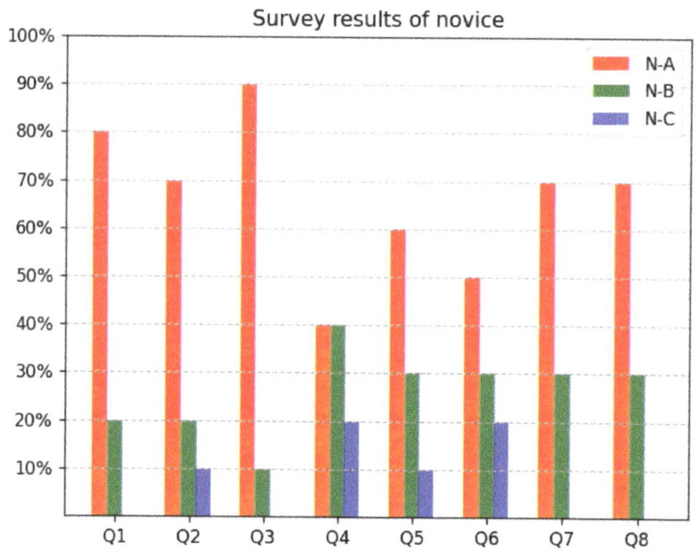

Figure 14. Survey results of novice.

4.1. Analysis of Survey Results from Experienced Worker

As shown in Figure 13, from Q1 and Q2, it can be seen that 90% of experienced workers believe that the current design of the classification system is useful and can compensate for the lack of professional knowledge reserves among workers.

According to the results of Q3, Q5, and Q7, 100% of experienced workers believe that the current design of the classification system can improve document classification speed, has practical value, and performs well in its usage.

From Q4 to Q8, it is evident that 90% of experienced workers believe that the system can improve document classification accuracy and are willing to recommend it to others.

Based on the results of Q6, 80% of experienced workers believe that the current design of the classification system can achieve the expected classification results.

4.2. Analysis of Survey Results from Novice

As shown in Figure 14, from Q1 and Q3, it can be seen that 100% of novices believe that the current design of the classification system is useful and can improve document classification speed.

According to the results of Q2 and Q5, 90% of novices believe that the current design of the classification system can compensate for the lack of professional knowledge reserves among workers and has practical value.

From Q4 to Q6, it is evident that 80% of novices believe that the system can improve document classification accuracy and achieve the expected classification results.

Based on the results of Q7 and Q8, 100% of novices believe that the current design of the classification system performs well in its usage and are willing to recommend it to others.

4.3. Discussion

To select the most suitable algorithm for classifying educational reform documents, we trained classification models based on multilayer perceptron, support vector machine, random forest algorithm, and the Naive Bayes algorithm. After data testing, we found that the classification model based on the Naive Bayes algorithm performed the best, with a prediction accuracy of about 94%.

Based on the analysis of the experimental results, our designed automatic classification system for educational reform documents based on the Naive Bayes algorithm was generally consistent with the classification of professional personnel, with only a few misclassified files. The classification results were acceptable. At the same time, applying this software can reduce the demand for professional knowledge reserves of management personnel and reduce classification errors caused by subjective factors. Therefore, this system is feasible for classifying educational reform documents.

Finally, we verified the universal applicability and effectiveness of our designed automatic classification system for educational reform documents based on the Naive Bayes algorithm through survey questionnaires. The results showed that this system is helpful for education workers, especially for novices.

5. Conclusions

Through the organization of educational reform documents and algorithm reuse, we have designed an automatic classification system for educational reform documents based on the Naive Bayes algorithm. Experimental verification has shown that the system can effectively classify educational reform documents automatically, filling the gap in the application of text classification in this category of documents and reducing the demand for professional knowledge of management personnel. The main contributions of the current research can be summarized as follows:

1. Determined the classification direction for educational reform documents based on the "Guidelines for the Declaration of Undergraduate Education Reform Research and Practice Projects in 2021".
2. Constructed retrieval strategies for educational reform documents using "AND", "OR", and "NOT" combinations based on the keywords obtained from the guidelines.
3. Conducted data cleaning, algorithm construction, training, and selection for educational reform documents, identifying the most suitable classification algorithm for this type of document.
4. Developed an automatic classification software for educational reform documents based on the naive Bayes algorithm, which significantly reduces classification time

while lowering the requirement for professional knowledge storage of classifiers, all while ensuring accuracy.

Despite the contributions of this system, its limitations are evident. Educational reform documents often involve multiple topics and fields, and sometimes a document may belong to multiple categories, making it difficult for the system to handle multi-label classification problems. This system is designed for Chinese documents only, and supports the classification of single-language documents, making it unable to accurately classify documents in other languages. Additionally, education reform is a constantly evolving field with new themes and concepts emerging regularly. Therefore, the classification system requires regular updates and maintenance to adapt to new developments in educational reform. These limitations point to future research directions. It is necessary to explore the use of more scientific algorithms for document analysis to make the results more objective and effective. Designing the software to be scalable to accommodate new educational reform topics and concepts is also important. Future research will also focus on designing classification systems for different language types and continuously improving the analysis of educational reform documents while enriching the corresponding training databases.

Author Contributions: Conceptualization, P.Z., Z.M. and Q.W.; methodology, P.Z. and Z.M.; writing—original draft preparation, Z.M.; data curation, Z.R. and Q.W.; writing—review and editing, H.W. and D.S.; visualization, C.Z.; supervision, P.Z.; funding acquisition, P.Z. All authors have read and agreed to the published version of the manuscript.

Funding: This paper was funded by the National Natural Science Foundation of China (Grant No. 51975181), the National Innovation Method Fund of China (Grant No. 2020IM020500) and Hebei Province Teaching Reform Project (Grant No. 2022GJJG042 and No. 2022GJJG038).

Data Availability Statement: The data is contained in the article and is available from the corresponding authors on reasonable request.

Conflicts of Interest: The authors declare no conflicts of interest.

References

1. Maron, M.E. Automatie indexing: An experimental in-quiry. *J. ACM* **1961**, *8*, 404–417. [CrossRef]
2. Zhang, Z.J.; Wang, Z.Q. Summary of text classification and algorithm. *Comput. Knowl. Technol.* **2012**, *8*, 825–828.
3. Alina, P.; Ioana, D.; Yoon, H.J.; Mohd, Y.J.; Tanmoy, B. Deep learning uncertainty quantification for clinical text classification. *J. Biomed. Inform.* **2024**, *149*, 104576.
4. Liu, H.; Hao, Y.; Zhang, W.H.; Zhang, H.Y.; Gao, F. Online urban-waterlogging monitoring based on a recurrent neural network for classification of microblogging text. *Nat. Hazards Earth Syst. Sci.* **2021**, *21*, 1179–1194. [CrossRef]
5. Yang, X.Z.; Wang, Q.Q.; Jiang, J.L. Analysis of classroom teacher-student dialogue based on artificial intelligence:automatic classification and sub-level construction of IRE. *E-Educ. Res.* **2023**, *44*, 79–86.
6. Vishaal, U.; Abhishek, A.; Anubha, G.; Tanmoy, C. InPHYNet: Leveraging attention-based multitask recurrent networks for multi-label physics text classification. *Knowl.-Based Syst.* **2021**, *211*, 106487.
7. Chen, Y.W.; Wang, J.L.; Cai, Y.Q.; DU, J.X. A method for Chinese text classification based on apparent semantics and latent aspects. *J. Ambient Intell. Humaniz. Comput.* **2015**, *6*, 473–480. [CrossRef]
8. Li, H.M.; Huang, H.N.; Cao, X.; Qian, J.G. Falcon: A novel Chinese short text classification method. *J. Comput. Commun.* **2018**, *6*, 216–226. [CrossRef]
9. Wang, G.S.; Huang, X.J. Convolutional neural network text classification model based on Word2vec and improved TF-IDF. *J. Chin. Comput. Syst.* **2019**, *40*, 1120–1126.
10. Du, J.C.; Gui, L.; He, Y.L.; Xu, R.F.; Wang, X. Convolution-Based Neural Attention with Applications to Sentiment Classification. *IEEE Access* **2019**, *7*, 27983–27992. [CrossRef]
11. Peng, Y.Q.; Song, C.B.; Yan, Q.; Zhao, X.S.; Wei, M. Research on Chinese text classification based on Hybrid Model of VDCNN and LSTM. *Comput. Eng.* **2018**, *44*, 190–196.
12. Yun, X.P. Research progress and prospect of emergency management based on CNKI and CiteSpace. *China Saf. Sci. J.* **2022**, *32*, 185.
13. Nan, M.Y.; Chen, J. Research Progress, Hotspots and Trends of Land Use under the Background of Ecological Civilization in China: Visual Analysis Based on the CNKI Database. *Sustainability* **2022**, *15*, 249. [CrossRef]
14. Li, X.P.; Zhou, Y. Research on information text extraction and analysis technology based on natural language processing. *Wirel. Internet Technol.* **2023**, *20*, 157–159.

15. Zhu, Y.H. Medical text mining and knowledge extraction based on natural language processing and knowledge graph. *China Comput. Commun.* **2023**, *35*, 1–3.
16. Aizawa, A. An information-theoretic perspective of tf–idf measures. *Inf. Process. Manag.* **2003**, *39*, 45–65. [CrossRef]
17. Paulsen, D.; Yash, G.; AnHai, D. Sparkly: A Simple yet Surprisingly Strong TF/IDF Blocker for Entity Matching. *Proc. VLDB Endow.* **2023**, *16*, 1507–1519. [CrossRef]
18. Wan, Q.; Xu, X.H.; Han, J. A dimensionality reduction method for large-scale group decision-making using TF-IDF feature similarity and information loss entropy. *Appl. Soft Comput.* **2024**, *150*, 111039. [CrossRef]
19. González, F.; Torres-Ruiz, M.; Rivera-Torruco, G.; Chonona-Hernández, L.; Quintero, R. A Natural-Language-Processing-Based Method for the Clustering and Analysis of Movie Reviews and Classification by Genre. *Mathematics* **2023**, *11*, 4735. [CrossRef]
20. Jitchaijaroen, W.; Keawsawasvong, S.; Wipulanusat, W.; Kumar, D.R.; Jamsawang, P. Machine learning approaches for stability prediction of rectangular tunnels in natural clays based on MLP and RBF neural networks. *Intell. Syst. Appl.* **2024**, *21*, 200329. [CrossRef]
21. Xiang, M.; Zhou, B.T.; Cheng, S.Q.; Liu, S. MCMP-Net: MLP combining max pooling network for sEMG gesture recognition. *Biomed. Signal Process. Control* **2024**, *90*, 105846.
22. Sun, H.L.; Lu, Y.F. A novel approach for solving linear Fredholm integro-differential equations via LS-SVM algorithm. *Appl. Math. Comput.* **2024**, *470*, 128557. [CrossRef]
23. Chen, C.F.; He, Q.X.; Li, Y.Y. Downscaling and merging multiple satellite precipitation products and gauge observations using random forest with the incorporation of spatial autocorrelation. *J. Hydrol.* **2024**, *632*, 130919. [CrossRef]
24. Lauzon, D.; Gloaguen, E. Quantifying uncertainty and improving prospectivity mapping in mineral belts using transfer learning and Random Forest: A case study of copper mineralization in the Superior Craton Province, Quebec, Canada. *Ore Geol. Rev.* **2024**, *166*, 105918. [CrossRef]
25. Li, C.; Managi, S. Mental health and natural land cover: A global analysis based on random forest with geographical consideration. *Sci. Rep.* **2024**, *14*, 2894. [CrossRef] [PubMed]
26. Wang, L.; Li, Z.W.; Zhu, C.D.; Li, Y.J. Research on spam filtering based on NB algorithm. *Transducer Microsyst. Technol.* **2020**, *39*, 46–48.
27. Yuan, L.H.; Li, X.W.; Xu, J. An improved anti-spam filtering method based on bayesian. *Comput. Digit. Eng.* **2020**, *48*, 513–516.

mathematics

MDPI

Article

A Study on the Identification of the Water Army to Improve the Helpfulness of Online Product Reviews

Chuyang Li, Shijia Zhang and Xiangdong Liu *

School of Economics, Jinan University, Guangzhou 510632, China; chuyangli@stu2022.jnu.edu.cn (C.L.); zsjlrz@stu2022.jnu.edu.cn (S.Z.)
* Correspondence: tliuxd@jnu.edu.cn; Tel.: +86-20-8522-6933

Abstract: Based on the perspective of identifying the water army, this paper uses the methods of machine learning and data visualization to analyze the helpfulness of online produce reviews, portray product portraits, and provide real and helpful product reviews. In order to identify and eliminate the water army, the Term Frequency-Inverse Document Frequency Model (TF-IDF) and Latent Semantic Index Model (LSI) are used. After eliminating the water army, three classification methods were selected to perform sentimental analysis, including logistics, SnowNLP, and Convolutional Neural Network for text(TextCNN). The TextCNN has the highest F1 score among the three classification methods. At the same time, the Latent Dirichlet Allocation mode (LDA) is used to extract the topics of various reviews. Finally, targeted countermeasures are proposed to manufacturers, consumers, and regulators.

Keywords: online product reviews; water army; latent semantic index; latent dirichlet allocation; convolutional neural network

MSC: 91G40; 91G80

1. Introduction

In recent years, China's technological infrastructure has continued to improve, and the Internet has become widespread in both urban and rural areas, significantly increasing network coverage. This has greatly driven the rise of e-commerce, with online shopping becoming mainstream. According to data from the "The 54th Statistical Report on China's Internet Development" [1], as of June 2024, the number of internet users in China had reached 1.099 billion, meaning the internet penetration rate hit 78.0%. The number of online shopping and online payment users rose to 905 million and 969 million, respectively, reflecting a 1.5% increase compared to December 2023. This large population of internet users has formed the foundation of China's rapidly developing consumer market, providing a strong user base for the growth of the digital economy.

Against the backdrop of rapid e-commerce growth and the development of Web 2.0 social platforms, consumers can now purchase their preferred products without leaving home. However, due to the inherent virtual nature of online shopping and the uncertainty surrounding product quality, it is difficult for consumers to obtain complete and accurate product information through online shopping. Consumers often rely on manufacturers' descriptions and other consumers' reviews to determine whether a product meets their needs. Online product reviews are not only an essential reference for consumers when selecting products or services but also a key channel through which businesses interact with users. However, the varying quality of review information and the vast quantity of reviews present a significant challenge for consumers trying to find useful information.

In addition, the growing number of fake review groups, known as the "water army", has significantly disrupted consumers' decision-making processes. In order to establish a favorable product image, many companies have started paying for higher positive review rates. Companies hire large numbers of these "water army" to pose as regular internet users or consumers, flooding the internet with concentrated posts that deliberately skew public opinion and real information, severely impacting the order of the internet [2]. This has fueled the growth of fake reviews, bringing significant negative effects to the e-commerce industry. To genuinely protect internet users' rights, government authorities have made great efforts, with the Cyberspace Administration of China focusing on cracking down on the "water army" as a key part of its regulatory efforts.

Research on identifying and eliminating the "water army" as well as distinguishing useful information, has become a hot topic.

The main contributions are as follows:

1. We introduce variables such as historical comment records of users who have been less concerned by the predecessors to enrich the evaluation index system.
2. We identify and eliminate the reviews from the water army based on the behavior characteristics of reviewers and the content characteristics of reviews.
3. We use sentiment analysis and topic analysis methods to extract the most important information in the reviews, portray the corresponding product portraits, and improve the efficiency of users browsing reviews.

2. Literature Review

When shopping online, user review information can directly influence consumers' purchasing intentions. The reviews left by buyers often hold significant reference value and provide insights into the true condition of the products. Driven by profit motives, some merchants may hire a "water army" to spread false positive reviews for their own products to increase sales or to use malicious reviews to discredit competitors' ratings. The existence of this marketing "water army" severely disrupts the normal competitive mechanisms of e-commerce platforms. Therefore, identifying these online "water armies" through relevant technological means has become an increasingly urgent issue [3].

In the last decade, early research mainly used the methods of multivariate statistical analysis or experimental design to study how online reviews exert their usefulness and test qualitative hypotheses or conclusions [4]. Combining theory and practice, 1587 reviews of 6 products on Amazon's e-commerce platform are modeled and analyzed, and the results show that the extremeness of reviews, product types, and depth of reviews have a significant impact on the helpfulness of online reviews, see Mudambi and Schuff [5]. Based on the evaluation indicators provided on the Amazon e-commerce platform, the star rating of reviews is the most important factor that has a significant impact on the usefulness of online reviews, see Korfiatis et al. [6]. The moderating effect of product brands on products through regression analysis is studied, and it found that if a review conveys more information that matches the description of the product on the website or contains less personal subjective feelings, the more useful the review will be, otherwise, the review will be less useful. In addition, there is no significant correlation between the emotional intensity shown in the reviews and the usefulness of the reviews, see Liao et al. [7]. By using the three factors of word-of-mouth, e-commerce platform, and trust tendencies as dependent variables in the process of consumers' attitudes being affected by negative online word-of-mouth, the result proved that consumers believe that rational negative word-of-mouth is more credible through structural equation models, see Tao et al. [8]. Nowadays, traditional analysis methods are no longer suitable for massive data and features. More and more experts and scholars use machine learning methods to conduct text mining on online reviews from multiple perspectives to increase the breadth and depth of research and obtain practical conclusions. The communication behavior based on the interaction characteristics between different communication subjects can be quantified; the Decision Tree Model to detect the information disseminated by the water army can be used; and an information dissemination model based on interactive behavior can be established, see Chen et al. [9]. The word2vec word vector technology of deep learning is required to build product feature words and emotional word lexicons through the construction of emotional concept pairs to score sentiment and analyze user sentiment of specific characteristics of brand products. The empirical results show that compared with the general sentiment vocabulary, this method has improved the accuracy of sentiment analysis, see Wang et al. [10]. The neural networks are utilized to learn a distributed representation for each word and the probability function of word sequences and convert each word into a low-dimensional, continuous vector, see Bengio et al. [11]. An approach that uses a combined kernel from multiple branches of a Convolutional Neural Network (CNN) with Long Short-term Memory (LSTM) layers is proposed. The model has the highest reported accuracy on the Internet Movie Database review sentiment dataset. Additionally, they presented multiple architectural variations; see Yenter and Verma [12]. Luo [13] presents a text sentiment analysis method combining Latent Dirichlet Allocation (LDA) text representation and convolutional neural network (CNN). The CNN with the gated recurrent unit (GRU) is used as a classifier to achieve highly accurate text classification, and experimental results indicate the effectiveness of such a method. Peng et al. [14] focused on detecting "e-commerce water army" through graph modeling of collusive behaviors in online reviews. Their study highlighted how these groups manipulate product reviews by forming collusive networks, impacting consumer decisions in e-commerce. The method they proposed includes analyzing collusive relationships based on user behavior and content, which helps in detecting these organized activities more accurately. Paul and Nikolaev [15] offer a systematic literature review for detecting the water army on the e-commerce platform.

In general, the existing literature on the usefulness of online product reviews is mostly measured by the length of the review, the number of words in the review, and the star rating of the review. The types of variables are relatively single. The biggest innovation of this paper is to introduce variables such as historical comment records of users who have been less concerned by the predecessors to enrich the evaluation index system and to identify and eliminate the reviews from the water army based on the behavior characteristics of reviewers and the content characteristics of reviews. Then, we use sentiment analysis and topic analysis methods to extract the most important information in the reviews, portray the corresponding product portraits, and improve the efficiency of users browsing reviews.

3. Identify and Eliminate Water Army Based on TF-IDF and LSI Models

3.1. TF-IDF and LSI Models

In order to create a good network ecosystem, the identification and elimination of the water army is very important. With the development of data science, more and more technologies have been developed and applied to the field of identifying water army, such as text-based, user-based, and influence-based features methods, see Moon et al. [16]; Budhi et al. [17]; Gaoswami et al. [18].

The Term Frequency-Inverse Document Frequency model (TF-IDF) [19] can evaluate the importance of a word for all online reviews of a product, thereby scaling text data. The term frequency indicates the frequency of items appearing in the document. TF-IDF is an unsupervised learning method that gives higher weight to terms that often appear in a particular document. However, the weight given to the terms that often appear in many documents in the corpus is not high. If a word appears frequently in a particular document but does not appear frequently in many documents, then the word is likely to be a better description of the content of the document. The purpose of TF-IDF zooming is to find words that can be used to distinguish documents, that is, the most "important" words. The "important" here is not necessarily related to the "positive" or "negative" we want to discuss. The formula for calculating the TF-IDF score of word ω in document d is:

$$tfidf(\omega, d) = tf \log\left(\frac{N+1}{N_\omega + 1}\right) + 1 \quad (1)$$

where N is the number of documents in the training set, d is a document from N, N_ω is the number of documents in which the word ω appears in the training set, and tf is the number of times the word ω appears in the query document d.

Scikit-learn 1.0.2 version is a popular machine-learning library in Python 3.8 [20]; under its framework, it has two functions for solving TF-IDF problems: TfidfTransformer and TfidfVectorizer. The former accepts the coefficient matrix generated by CountVectorizer and transforms it, and the latter accepts the text data and completes the bag of words feature extraction and TF- IDF transformation.

Latent Semantic Indexing (LSI) is an unsupervised topic model based on the singular value decomposition method used to obtain the topic of the text. Using the LSI model to analyze the potential themes of the text and the self-similarity of the text, the water army can be identified based on the content characteristics of the text. Eigenvalue decomposition can extract the eigenvalues of the square matrix. Singular value decomposition can extract the eigenvalues of any matrix, including square matrices, which have a wider range of applications. Singular value decomposition can be explained as a matrix of $m \times n$ that can be decomposed into three matrices:

$$A_{m\times n} = U_{m\times m} B_{m\times n} V^T_{m\times n} \tag{2}$$

To reduce the dimension, it can also be written:

$$A_{m\times n} \approx U_{m\times k} B_{k\times k} V^T_{k\times n} \tag{3}$$

When applied to a text topic model, m is the number of texts, n is the number of words in each text, and k is the number of topics which is generally less than the number of texts. And A_{ij} corresponds to the feature value of the j-th word in the i-th text. After singular value decomposition, U_{il} corresponds to the relevance of the i-th text and the l-th topic, V_{jp} corresponds to the relevance of the p-th word meaning of the j-th word, and B_{lp} corresponds to the relevance of the l-th topic and the p-th word meaning.

3.2. Water Army Characteristics and Identification Process

One of the behavioral characteristics of water army users is that they will post a massive number of reviews in a short period of time. In other words, if a user posts a large amount of reviews on a single-day basis, we can identify this user as a water army.

Moreover, water army often applies fixed templates, their emotional tone is relatively single and extreme, and the self-similarity of water army users' texts will be relatively high. Therefore, another way of identifying the water army is based on the self-similarity of comments. First, the TF-IDF model is used to extract the feature values of the comment texts, and then the LSI model will analyze the auto-correlation of the user's respective comment texts. Num_topics is an important parameter in the LSI model and refers to the number of topics contained in the document. We adjust Num_topics and choose the most suitable parameter value.

3.3. Data Source

According to the different attributes of products, online products are mainly divided into two categories: search goods and experience goods, see Zhai et al. [21]. Search goods refer to products that consumers can obtain as much objective information as possible about, including digital products and home appliances, through the objective description given by the manufacturer before purchasing. Experience goods refer to a category of products whose consumer reviews largely depend on subjective personal feelings, including food and makeup. Consumers depend on online reviews when buying different types of products. For example, consumers rely more on online reviews when buying experiential products. There are a large number of water armies in the review area of experiential products. In order to have an accurate model, this article chooses to analyze experiential products, taking beauty and personal care products sold on online shopping platforms as an example.

Specifically, we selected the Bioderma Make-up Removing product, which is at the top of the top-selling makeup list of the online shopping platform JD.com, as a sample. We use the Octopus crawler tool to collect reviews and the respective historical comment records. The review data, ranging from 20 May 2020, to 18 September 2024, includes the user name (partially shown by JD.com for privacy purposes), name of the product, purchase date, review rating, review title, and review content (in simplified Chinese).

3.4. Identify and Eliminate Water Army

Table 1 reveals some comments identified by the suspected water army; for readers' convenience, the original Chinese text is translated into English. It is evident that the water army used fixed review templates for mass copying and pasting, resulting in very rigid and unnatural feedback. Additionally, the number of these comments is quite staggering; the total number of comments crawled is 5510, of which 949 are from fake reviewers, accounting for a high percentage of 17%. As mentioned in the literature review, the presence of fake comments potentially skews the consumers' opinions and hides real information. Therefore, it is necessary to identify and eliminate these fake reviews.

Table 1. Reviews posted by water army.

	Review Content
1	"Always like the brand! The product packing is exquisite, not greasy on the face. Removes the makeup. Feels refreshing after use. I will definitely repurchase this brand. Bought two big bottles during promotion, can use for a long time, affordable!"
2	"Always like the brand! The product packing is exquisite, not greasy on the face. Removes the makeup. Feels refreshing after use. I will definitely repurchase this brand. Bought two big bottles during promotion, can use for a long time, affordable!"
3	"I bought this many times, and I'm still using it. I liked it."
4	"Easy makeup removal, simple and convenient, good for sensitive skin. Eyelashes and lips can be removed together. With a gentle wipe, the dirt falls off."
5	"Easy makeup removal, simple and convenient, good for sensitive skin. Eyelashes and lips can be removed together. With a gentle wipe, the dirt falls off."

4. Text Classification Model Based on Sentimental Analysis

4.1. Classification Methods

Text sentiment classification is the process of analysis, processing, induction, and reasoning for subjective texts with emotional colors; see Nandwani and Verma [22]. In other words, the most meaningful elements in the text are extracted, the emotional color is analyzed, and finally, the conclusions obtained from the analysis are applied to actual life. So far, many scholars have conducted related research in this field. Three types of sentiment analysis classification methods are summarized, namely sentiment dictionary, language analysis, and machine learning, see Lightart et al. [23]. The main process of sentiment analysis is shown in Figure 1.

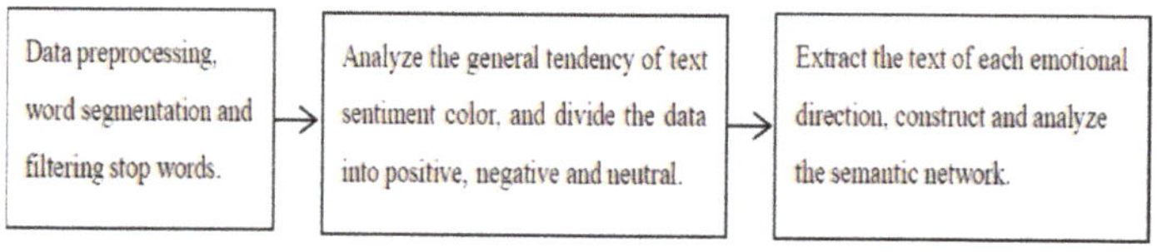

Figure 1. Sentiment analysis process.

The processing objects of sentiment analysis are generally text data, and there are significant differences between text features and numerical features, so the text needs to be expressed numerically before it can be used in algorithms.

SnowNLP 0.12.3 version, the sentiment analysis processing package in Python, uses the naïve Bayesian method to train and predict data. It has powerful functions and can perform Chinese word segmentation, analyze text emotional colors, and extract text keywords. The sentiment attribute can automatically recognize the semantics of each comment based on the emotional color score and classify it according to the corresponding score to generate new texts of the corresponding category. This score is essentially the probability of the appearance of various emotional themes and words in each comment, so the score interval is 0 to 1. The higher the score, the richer the positive emotional color conveyed in the sentence; on the contrary, the more negative the emotional color.

Convolutional Neural Networks (CNN) are commonly used in computer vision image analysis and natural language processing in the field of deep learning. CNN has three characteristics: local connection, weight sharing, and sub-sampling. The main flow of CNN text processing is shown in Figure 2.

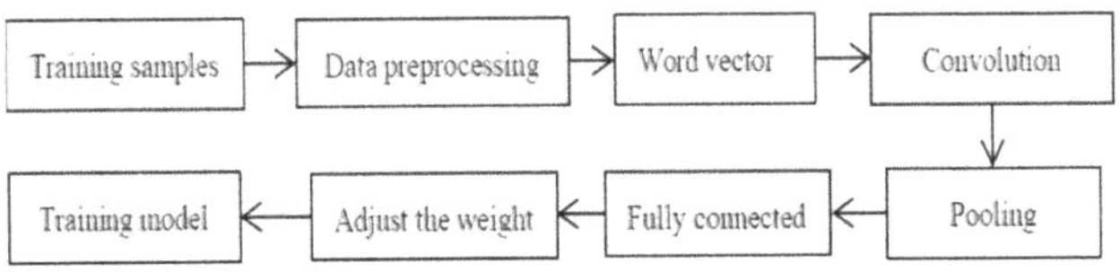

Figure 2. CNN training process.

CNN text processing is mainly used in sentiment analysis and topic classification tasks. This method directly uses the convolution kernel as a shared weight to connect the entire neural network, which has been proven to be convenient for most texts. In this paper, we employ TextCNN (PyTorch 2.0.1 version) for sentiment classification. To achieve the best fitting results, we train our model by iteratively optimizing the algorithm and continuously adjusting the model parameters. Eventually, our model parameters are as follows:

Embedding: Set to 10, representing the vector dimension for each word in the input layer.

Maximum sentence length: Set to 200, indicating the maximum length allowed when processing sentences.

Batch Size: Determined to be 100, representing the amount of data used for training in each iteration. A reasonable batch size helps balance memory usage efficiency with the stability of model training.

Epochs: Set to 100, indicating the number of times the entire dataset will be traversed for training. Sufficient training cycles help the model fully learn data features, achieving better generalization.

Learning Rate: Set to 0.001, as a smaller learning rate helps the model adjust parameters more finely during training, avoiding overfitting.

Hidden Layer Channels: Set to 12, representing the number of output channels in the convolutional layer of TextCNN.

4.2. Evaluation Metrics

In this paper, the F1 score is used to measure the accuracy of the two-class model. The F1 score is the harmonic average of precision and recall. The maximum value is 1, and the minimum value is 0.

$$F_1 = 2 \cdot \frac{precision \cdot recall}{precision + recall} \tag{4}$$

4.3. Data Preprocessing

In order to encourage consumers to post reviews to attract more potential consumers, businesses generally propose an encouragement mechanism. When the number of reviews made by consumers reaches the lower limit, they can receive several rewards. In order to improve the effectiveness of reviews, some e-commerce platforms also set a lower limit for the number of reviews. The original intention of this initiative is positive, but in the actual implementation process, many consumers may post redundant and invalid repetitive reviews. Therefore, the comment text obtained directly from the e-commerce platform will inevitably contain a large amount of invalid information. If invalid information is introduced into the subsequent analysis work, it will lead to deviations. Therefore, it is necessary to preprocess the data, filter the data, and remove the repetitive and meaningless content.

Text deduplication is to remove the repetitive and meaningless parts of the text. There are two main reasons for removing these invalid parts. On the one hand, when consumers purchase a certain product multiple times, they may directly copy and paste the reviews from the previous purchase for convenience and post the same reviews again. Some consumers copy and paste other consumers' reviews for convenience. Deduplication can keep only one of these same reviews. On the other hand, e-commerce platforms will stipulate that consumers post reviews within a certain time limit; otherwise, the system will automatically generate reviews. In addition, consumers can choose the system to automatically generate reviews when they post reviews. For example, there are a lot of "system default praise" in the product review area of JD.com. This kind of comment is obviously of no analytical value.

A total of 949 duplicate comments were deleted, and the new sample comment set contains 4561 reviews. The 4561 reviews corresponding to 4561 users are numbered 1–4561 sequentially.

Many consumers use repetitive words in reviews in order to reach the lower limit of the number of words in a review. Such repetitive and meaningless fragments generally appear at the beginning or the end of the corpus. The purpose of mechanical compression is to remove these fragments. The code character encoding module is called when mechanically compressing the text. The specific steps of mechanical compression are as follows: first, the comment text is processed in the correct order, and the words with the same prefix in the comment text are removed and then the newly generated comment text is reversed, and the words with the same prefix are removed again, and finally the text is reversed back to the normal sequence.

After completing the above preprocessing steps, in order to intuitively understand the main emotional tone conveyed in the text, we use the command 'word cloud' to generate a word cloud image of the preprocessed text. Jieba module 0.42.1 is used to split text into segmented words, incorporating stop words and a custom dictionary during the process. Stop words can eliminate unimportant words, such as conjunctions and pronouns like "you", "and" and "then". Next, rank frequently used words to generate a word cloud. Among these words, "clean", "not bad", "makeup removal", "mild", "good to use" and "repurchase" rank the highest accordingly. The majority of sentimental words in word clouds convey a positive attitude.

4.4. Experimental Results

We call the sentiment analysis processing package SnowNLP in Python to get the final scoring result of each comment, as shown in Figure 3. It can be seen from Figure 3 that the score clusters around 1, indicating an overall positive sentiment of consumers.

Suppose the sentiment score is s. The standard for the first classification is: if $s \geq 0.5$, it means that the text conveys positive sentiment, then the review will be classified as a positive review; if $s < 0.5$, it will be classified as a negative review. In addition to expressing positive emotions, positive reviews' text length is usually longer than negative reviews', and makes its TF-IDF weight higher. The positive review allows users to form a comprehensive understanding of the product. In other words, it is more effective for manufacturers, consumers, and regulators. Most of the reviews classified as negative reviews are negative experiences of the product or descriptions that have nothing to do with the product itself.

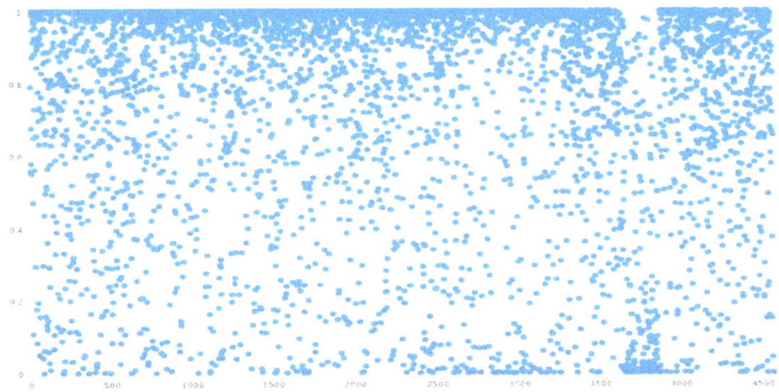

Figure 3. Sentiment analysis score chart. The horizontal axis represents the ID of 4561 users, and the vertical axis represents the score.

The sentiment attribute is judged by the built-in trained model. Consumers choose the positive and negative reviews on this online shopping platform. The positive reviews published by some consumers in order to meet the word count requirements or the positive reviews published by the system by default will be included in the negative reviews during the sentimental mining process. Such positive reviews actually do not contain positive sentimental colors. Therefore, the classification result obtained by the sentiments attribute must be different from the number of positive reviews and negative reviews displayed on the online shopping platform. Table 2 shows the classification results of the three sentiment analyses. For the TextCNN and SnowNLP sentiments analysis, the number of positive reviews is less than the number of positive reviews displayed on the online shopping platform, and the number of negative reviews is more than the number of negative reviews displayed on the platform.

Table 2. Classification results of the review types.

Review Type	The Online Shopping Platform	Textcnn	Logistic	SnowNLP
positive review	4308	4048	4535	3611
negative review	253	513	26	950

This article selects the Jieba word segmentation tool, inserts the stop word dictionary of Harbin Institute of Technology, and adds the custom stop words based on the actual situation for word segmentation. The custom stop words mainly include some network terms. Call the CountVectorizer and TfidfTransformer functions in the scikit-learn feature extraction.text library to calculate the TF-IDF weight of the text [23]. Based on the known TF-IDF weights, the logistic regression classification method under the scikit-learn framework is called, and the results are shown in Table 3.

Table 3. Logistic Classification Results.

Label	Precision	Recall	F1_Score
positive review	0.69	1.00	0.82
negative review	1.00	0.02	0.03

It can be seen from Table 3 that even though the precision for negative review hits 1, the recall rate and F1 score are extremely low. For positive reviews, the logistic classification was able to detect all positive reviews but only with 69% precision. Overall, the logistic classification is considered invalid, and further adjustments are required.

Table 4 shows the SnowNLP classification performs better than the logistic classification in a negative review. The F1_score of positive review and negative are 0.88 and 0.84, respectively, suggesting SnowNLP is a reasonable classification method.

Table 4. SnowNLP Classification Results.

Label	Precision	Recall	F1_Score
positive review	0.91	0.84	0.88
negative review	0.70	0.83	0.76

As shown in Table 5, the classification result of TextCNN is better. Basically, positive and negative reviews can be better distinguished. TextCNN outperforms previous classification models; overall, it can be considered the most effective one.

Table 5. TextCNN Classification Results.

Label	Precision	Recall	F1_Score
positive review	0.89	0.93	0.91
negative review	0.87	0.81	0.83

Table 6 displays the weight average value of each measurement among logistic, SnowNLP, and TextCNN classifications. Apparently, logistic classification is not an ideal choice. SnowNLP and TextCNN both proved to be valid, but TextCNN is slightly better.

Table 6. Classification Comparison.

Classification	Precision	Recall	Accuracy	F1_Score
Logistic	0.79	0.69	0.69	0.57
SnowNLP	0.85	0.83	0.83	0.84
TextCNN	0.88	0.89	0.89	0.88

5. The Analysis of Online Product Reviews

5.1. LDA Model

Latent Dirichlet Allocation (LDA) is an unsupervised learning model that extracts topics from text. The normal sequence of text generation is from words to topics and finally text; however, LDA attempts to reverse engineer this process [13]. According to the existing text, several topics are selected under a certain probability, and finally, under these several topics, several corresponding words are selected with a certain probability. Intuitively, the LDA model attempts to find word groups that frequently appear together in a text containing multiple topics. Each document can be understood as a "mixed" of subsets of various topics. These topics refer to the components extracted from the text, which may or may not have semantics.

Suppose there are several topic sets T in the text set D; the word set composed of all the different words contained in D is V, and there are m words and k topics in total. Consider each text d in D as a word sequence $(\omega_1, \omega_2, \cdots, \omega_n)$. The position of these n words in the sequence has no effect on the LDA algorithm. The probability that each text n in D corresponds to a different topic is $(p_{t1}, p_{t2}, \cdots, p_{tk})$ The probability of corresponding to the i-th topic in text d is defined as:

$$p_{ti} = \frac{n_{ti}}{n} \quad (5)$$

The total number of words in the text is n, n_{ti} represents the number of words corresponding to the i-th topic in the text d. The probability that the topic t in each topic set T

generates a different word is $(p_{\omega 1}, p_{\omega 2}, \cdots, p_{\omega m})$. The probability that the topic t generates the i-th word in the entire word set V is $P_{\omega i}$. Specifically,

$$P_{\omega i} = \frac{N_{\omega i}}{N} \tag{6}$$

$N_{\omega i}$ represents the number of the i-th word in the word set V corresponding to the topic t, and N is the total number of all words corresponding to the topic t. In summary, the core formula of the LDA model is:

$$p(\omega|d) = p(\omega|t) \times p(t|d) \tag{7}$$

5.2. Optimal Number of Topics in LDA Topic Modeling

The LDA model is used for topic analysis, and the probability has indicated the frequency of topic feature words in various topic texts. As shown in Table 3, TextCNN classification divides 4561 reviews into 4048 positive reviews and 513 negative reviews; we use this result to perform the LDA model. First, determine whether it is a stop word for the word segmentation result. When a stop word is encountered, it will be removed. Then, clean the text again, and convert the words into vectors, and use the LDA model to train the positive and negative word segmentation results. The output is the clustering result of several features in all kinds of texts.

When conducting LDA topic modeling, the optimal number of topics directly affects the interpretability and predictive power of the model. By analyzing the graph of average cosine similarity between positive and negative reviews, the cohesion and differentiation of each topic can be evaluated to determine the optimal number of topics. Cosine similarity represents the distance between topics, with higher cosine similarity indicating more overlap between topics and lower cosine similarity suggesting better classification performance. Figure 4 shows cosine similarity for both positive and negative reviews.

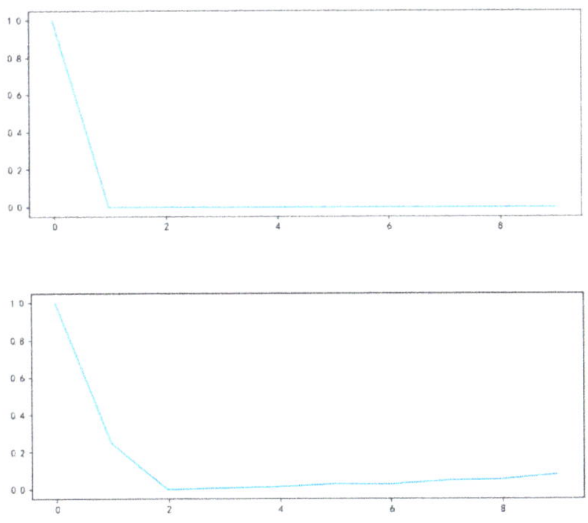

Figure 4. Cosine similarity for both positive and negative reviews. The horizontal axis measures a number of topics, and the vertical axis measures cosine similarity.

For positive reviews, the average cosine similarity increases and then stabilizes as the number of topics increases. When there are fewer topics, the similarity is lower, possibly because a small number of topics cannot fully capture the diversity of the reviews, leading to significant differences in the content within the same topic. As the number of topics increases, the similarity gradually rises, indicating that the content within each topic becomes more consistent. Once the number of topics reaches a certain point, the growth remains unchanged, suggesting that adding more topics does not bring additional information but rather increases the complexity of the model. The cosine similarity is lowest when the number of topics is 2, but with sufficient sample size, we eventually choose 3 to be the optimal number of topics for positive reviews.

For negative reviews, the average cosine similarity shows a trend of initially decreasing and then slowly increasing. The similarity for negative reviews decreases more rapidly with fewer topics, indicating that the content of negative reviews is more concentrated and consistent, requiring fewer topics to achieve higher cohesion. The similarity between topics is lowest when the number of topics is 2, so 2 is also determined as the optimal number of topics for negative reviews.

5.3. Sentiment Analysis for Both Positive and Negative Topics

As shown in Table 7, positive topics include consumer experience, product value, and after-sales. Among consumer experience, keywords such as "refreshing", "gentle", "fast", "good" and "logistics" reflect consumers' strong satisfaction with the product experience and their positive attitudes toward delivery speed. This indicates significant affirmation of the product. Under the product value topic, words like "worth", "feeling", "price", "packaging", "like" and "real" suggest strong shopping satisfaction from consumers to purchase this product. The after-sales topic includes keywords like "repurchase", "affordable", "promotions", "useful", "purchase" and "quality" indicating that consumers recognize the company's commitment to product quality and find the selling price reasonable and acceptable.

Table 7. Keywords of positive and negative topics.

Topic Trend	Topic	Keywords
Positive Topic	Consumer experience	refreshing, gentle, fast, good, logistics
	Product value	worth, feeling, price, packaging, like, real
	After sales	repurchase, affordable, promotions, useful, purchase, quality
Negative Topic	Logistics experience	poor, leaking, damage, fake, packaging
	Consumer feedback	customer service, poor, bottle, packaging, cap

Negative topics are logistics experience and consumer feedback. The first topic includes keywords such as "poor", "leaking", "damage", "fake" and "packaging" which highlight consumers' dissatisfaction with product integrity. This reveals that the company should enhance quality checks and protective measures during shipping to fundamentally improve the consumer experience. In the second topic, keywords like "customer service", "poor", "bottle", "packaging" and "cap" reflect consumer dissatisfaction with service and raise doubts about the product itself, creating a divergence from positive reviews. The product company should comprehensively consider consumer feedback to optimize the product and upgrade all aspects from production to after-sales service, striving for sustainable development and promotion of the product.

6. Conclusions

Online reviews are a necessary reference for consumers before making online shopping decisions. However, driven by interest, a large number of fake reviews have emerged online, making it difficult for consumers to obtain genuine product experiences. This study collected 5510 review data from JD.com and analyzed it using machine learning and data visualization methods, identifying 949 reviews posted by water army. After eliminating the water army, we explored the positive and negative sentiments in the rest of the reviews. The result reveals that positive sentiments significantly outnumber negative ones, indicating a generally favorable consumer evaluation of the Bioderma Make-up Removing product. Finally, through LDA topic analysis and keyword examination, our study delved into users' authentic feelings. The majority of consumers held a positive view regarding product effectiveness, packaging, and logistics speed, with some users even making repeat purchases. However, there was considerable dissatisfaction regarding product integrity, and a few users expressed doubts about the products.

Product manufacturers, consumers, and regulators can carry out the targeted work and make decisions based on the product portraits. Based on our findings, several suggestions are proposed for product manufacturers, consumers, and regulators:

First, manufacturers should focus on topic phrases extracted from negative reviews in the research and development process. For example, they consider how to enhance the effect of the product and improve the practicality of the product and the consumer experience. They also need to consider how to improve the packaging so that the product is not easily damaged during transportation and is more convenient for consumers to use. In addition, manufacturers should focus on the topic phrases extracted from the praise in the sales link, such as combining the true advantages of the product, determining the key direction of marketing, and putting an end to false propaganda.

Second, for consumers, the subject terms of various reviews help them quickly and concisely obtain effective information from a large number of reviews and improve the efficiency of online shopping.

Third, for regulators, information from reviews can be used as a reference in the supervision process to supervise whether manufacturers have false propaganda or whether consumers have unreasonable complaints.

Finally, the model can effectively identify the water army and eliminate interfering reviews. To thoroughly solve the problem of the water army, the supervisory authority should clarify the water army concept, strictly implement the supervision system, increase penalties, and create a good online shopping environment.

Our study has made some progress but still has certain limitations, outlined as follows:

Firstly, this study focuses solely on the e-commerce platform of JD.com, which is quite narrow. Obviously, water army activities across various platforms may exhibit different patterns. Future research could consider analyzing multiple platforms to explore whether differences in platforms lead to variations in the number of online reviews and the quantity of water army.

Secondly, the research methods could also be further optimized. This study uses cosine similarity to identify the water army, but there are other methods available. Exploring a combination of different approaches could enhance the accuracy of water army detection.

Author Contributions: Conceptualization, S.Z.; Methodology, C.L.; Software, C.L.; Formal analysis, X.L.; Writing—original draft, S.Z.; Supervision, X.L. All authors have read and agreed to the published version of the manuscript.

Funding: This research received no external funding.

Data Availability Statement: The data will be made available by the authors on request.

Conflicts of Interest: The authors declare no conflicts of interest.

References

1. The 54th Statistical Report on China's Internet Development. Available online: https://www.cnnic.cn/n4/2024/0829/c88-11065.html (accessed on 20 September 2024).
2. Li, X.; Jiang, J. Identifying Useful Reviews with Improved Graph Convolutional Neural Network. *Data Anal. Knowl. Discov.* **2022**, *6*, 38–51.
3. Wang, L.; Chen, D. Reach on Water Army in e-commerce Platform based on Integrated Learning. *Electron. Technol. Softw. Eng.* **2021**, *11*, 253–256.
4. Liu, Z.; Park, S. What makes a useful online review? Implication for travel product websites. *Tour. Manag.* **2015**, *47*, 140–151. [CrossRef]

5. Mudambi, S.M.; Schuff, D. Research Note: What Makes a Helpful Online Review? A Study of Customer Reviews on Amazon.com. *MIS Q.* **2010**, *34*, 185–200. [CrossRef]
6. Korfiatis, N.; García-Bariocanal, E.; Sánchez-Alonso, S. Evaluating content quality and helpfulness of online product reviews: The interplay of review helpfulness vs. review content. *Electron. Commer. Res. Appl.* **2012**, *11*, 205–217. [CrossRef]
7. Liao, C.; Cai, C.; Li, Y. An empirical study on influence factors of online reviews' helpfulness in e-commerce. *Soft Sci.* **2013**, *27*, 5.
8. Tao, X.; Song, Z.; Zhang, R.; Lv, Y. An empirical study on the effects of online negative WOM on consumers' attitude: Countermeasures of the enterprises. *Manag. Rev.* **2013**, *25*, 101–110.
9. Chen, K.; Chen, L.; Zhu, P.D.; Xiong, Y. Interaction based on method for spam detection in online social networks. *J. Commun.* **2015**, *36*, 120–127.
10. Wang, R.; Song, J.; Chen, C. Application of sentiment analysis based on Word2vec in brand awareness. *Libr. Inf. Serv.* **2017**, *61*, 6.
11. Bengio, Y.; Ducharme, R.; Vincent, P.; Jauvin, C.; Kandola, J.; Hofmann, T.; Poggio, T.; Shawe-Taylor, J. A Neural Probabilistic Language Models. *J. Mach. Learn. Res.* **2003**, *3*, 1137–1155.
12. Yenter, A.; Verma, A. Deep CNN-LSTM with combined kernels from multiple branches for IMDb review sentiment analysis. In Proceedings of the 2017 IEEE 8th Annual Ubiquitous Computing, Electronics and Mobile Communication Conference (UEMCON), New York, NY, USA, 19–21 October 2017; pp. 540–546.
13. Luo, L. Network text sentiment analysis method combining LDA text representation and GRU-CNN. *Pers. Ubiquitous Comput.* **2019**, *23*, 405–412. [CrossRef]
14. Peng, J.; Wang, Y.; Meng, Y. Detecting E-Commerce Water Army through Graph Modeling on User Multiple Collusive Relationships: A Case Study of China's Hotel Industry. *J. Theor. Appl. Electron. Commer. Res.* **2023**, *18*, 105–129. [CrossRef]
15. Paul, H.; Nikolaev, A. Fake review detection on online E-commerce platforms: A systematic literature review. *Data Min. Knowl. Discov.* **2021**, *35*, 1830–1881. [CrossRef]
16. Moon, S.; Kim, M.Y.; Iacobucci, D. Content analysis of fake consumer reviews by survey-based text categorization. *Int. J. Res. Mark.* **2021**, *38*, 343–364. [CrossRef]
17. Budhi, G.S.; Chiong, R.; Wang, Z.; Dhakal, S. Using a hybrid content-based and behaviour-based featuring approach in a parallel environment to detect fake reviews. *Electron. Commer. Res. Appl.* **2021**, *47*, 101048. [CrossRef]
18. Goswami, K.; Park, Y.; Song, C. Impact of reviewer social interaction on online consumer review fraud detection. *J. Big Data* **2017**, *4*, 15. [CrossRef]
19. Ramos, J. Using tf-idf to determine word relevance in document queries. In Proceedings of the First Instructional Conference on Machine Learning, Los Angeles, CA, USA, 23–24 June 2003; Volume 242, pp. 29–48.
20. Buitinck, L.; Louppe, G.; Blondel, M.; Pedregosa, F.; Mueller, A.; Grisel, O.; Niculae, V.; Prettenhofer, P.; Gramfort, A.; Grobler, J.; et al. API design for machine learning software: Experiences from the scikit-learn project. *arXiv* **2013**, arXiv:1309.0238.
21. Zhai, Q.; Cao, X.; Mokhtarian, P.L.; Zhen, F. The interactions between E-Shopping and Store Shopping in the Shopping Process for search goods and experience goods. *Transportation* **2017**, *44*, 885–904. [CrossRef]
22. Nandwani, P.; Verma, R. A review on sentiment analysis and emotion detection from text. *Soc. Netw. Anal. Min.* **2021**, *11*, 81. [CrossRef] [PubMed]
23. Ligthart, A.; Catal, C.; Tekinerdogan, B. Systematic reviews in sentiment analysis: A tertiary study. *Artifcial Intell. Rev.* **2021**, *54*, 4997–5053. [CrossRef]

mathematics

MDPI

Article

SCS-Net: Stratified Compressive Sensing Network for Large-Scale Crowd Flow Prediction

Xiaoyong Tan [1], Kaiqi Chen [1,2,*], Min Deng [1,2], Baoju Liu [1,2], Zhiyuan Zhao [3], Youjun Tu [3] and Sheng Wu [3]

1 Department of Geo-Informatics, School of Geosciences and Info-Physics, Central South University, Changsha 410083, China; tanxy@csu.edu.cn (X.T.); dengmin@csu.edu.cn (M.D.); baojuliu@csu.edu.cn (B.L.)
2 The Third Surveying and Mapping Institute of Hunan Province, Hunan Geospatial Information Engineering and Technology Research Center, Changsha 410018, China
3 Academy of Digital China (Fujian), Fuzhou University, Fuzhou 350108, China; zyzhao@fzu.edu.cn (Z.Z.); 241010017@fzu.edu.cn (Y.T.); wusheng@fzu.edu.cn (S.W.)
* Correspondence: chenkaiqi@csu.edu.cn

Abstract: Large-scale crowd flow prediction is a critical task in urban management and public safety. However, achieving accurate and efficient prediction remains challenging. Most existing models overlook spatial heterogeneity, employing unified parameters to fit diverse crowd flow patterns across different spatial units, which limits their accuracy. Meanwhile, the massive spatial units significantly increase the computational cost, limiting model efficiency. To address these limitations, we propose a novel model for large-scale crowd flow prediction, namely the Stratified Compressive Sensing Network (SCS-Net). First, we develop a spatially stratified module that posterior adaptively extracts the underlying spatially stratified structure, effectively modeling spatial heterogeneity. Then, we develop compressive sensing modules to compress redundant information from massive spatial units and learn shared crowd flow patterns, enabling efficient prediction. Finally, we conduct experiments on a large-scale real-world dataset. The results demonstrate that SCS-Net outperforms deep learning baseline models by 35.25–139.2% in MAE and 26.3–112.4% in RMSE while reducing GFLOPs by 53–1067 times and shortening training time by 3.1–83.2 times compared to prevalent spatio-temporal prediction models. Moreover, the spatially stratified structure extracted by SCS-Net offers valuable interpretability for spatial heterogeneity in crowd flow patterns, providing deeper insights into urban functional layouts.

Keywords: crowd flow prediction; large scale; compressive sensing; spatial heterogeneity; spatially stratified structure

MSC: 68T09

1. Introduction

With the accelerated pace of urbanization, urban population density has increased rapidly [1,2]. The improper allocation of urban infrastructure has triggered numerous issues, such as traffic congestion and crowd crush [3–5]. Crowd flow prediction, which aims to forecast the future total number of people entering or leaving a given region (i.e., inflows and outflows) [6–8], plays a crucial role in mitigating these issues. Specifically, accurate crowd flow predictions enable transportation authorities to dynamically adjust public transit resources and optimize urban infrastructure allocation. In addition, by providing early warnings of high crowd concentrations, these predictions support precautionary measures for urban public safety.

Temporal and spatial dependencies are fundamental for ensuring the predictability of crowd flow [9,10]. Since deep learning techniques have achieved significant progress in spatio-temporal prediction tasks, numerous recent studies have developed diverse neural network models to capture these dependencies [11,12]. Regarding spatial modeling, prevailing approaches are typically categorized into Convolutional Neural Network (CNN)-based models, Graph Neural Network-(GNN) based models, and attention-based models [13]. Although these methods effectively model spatio-temporal dependencies, the increasing demand for large-scale crowd flow prediction presents two major challenges: inaccuracy and inefficiency.

Firstly, inaccuracy is primarily attributable to spatial heterogeneity, which implies that spatio-temporal dependencies vary across different spatial units [14]. Existing crowd flow prediction models often overlook the influence of spatial heterogeneity. They employ unified parameters to fit the diverse crowd flow patterns across various spatial units, leading to unsatisfactory predictions [15]. Since the spatio-temporal evolution of crowd flow is closely related to human activities and regional functions [16,17], the patterns across different spatial units are not entirely unique but share certain similarities [18]. For example, workers typically commute daily between their residences and workplaces, while older adults often travel between parks and their homes during the day [19]. This regularity indicates that crowd flow patterns exhibit a spatially stratified structure, which categorizes the spatial units. Spatial units of the same type tend to display similar patterns. Since spatial heterogeneity becomes more significant at larger scales, it is crucial to understand and leverage this structure for effective modeling of spatial heterogeneity.

Secondly, inefficiency arises from the massive spatial units. Since existing crowd flow prediction models are primarily designed based on small-scale public datasets, the efficiency challenges introduced by large-scale prediction have not been adequately considered [20–22]. Specifically, due to irregular urban boundaries, CNN-based models struggle to be directly applied. A large number of unnecessary spatial units must be incorporated to fill the standardized tensor structures required for convolutional operations, leading to additional computational overhead and increased data noise. Although GNN-based and attention-based models can more flexibly adapt to diverse spatial unit distributions, their computational cost increases significantly with the expansion of spatial extent. When the number of spatial units grows by a factor of N, the computational cost of the adjacency matrix and self-attention mechanism increases by a factor of N^2, significantly reducing model efficiency. This highlights the urgent need for a more scalable and efficient model for large-scale crowd flow prediction.

In this study, we propose a novel model for large-scale crowd flow prediction, namely the Stratified Compressive Sensing Network (SCS-Net). The proposed SCS-Net consists of two key components: (1) a Spatially Stratified Module (SS-Module), which extracts the spatially stratified structure of crowd flow, and (2) several Compressive Sensing Modules (CS-Modules), which learn the shared crowd flow patterns. The main contributions of this study are summarized as follows:

- We developed a spatially stratified module to model spatial heterogeneity. This module enables posterior adaptive extraction of the spatially stratified structure from geographical environments, improving prediction accuracy.
- We developed several compressive sensing modules to enhance efficiency. By compressing redundant information among spatial units of the same type, this module facilitates the learning of shared crowd flow patterns, thereby significantly improving computational efficiency. Meanwhile, by leveraging the information lost after reconstruction, this module captures residual fluctuation patterns, further enhancing the model's predictive capabilities.

- We evaluated our proposed model for large-scale crowd flow prediction in Fuzhou, China. Experimental results demonstrated its significant advantages over baseline models in both accuracy and efficiency. Based on the interpretability analysis of the spatially stratified structure, we found that spatial heterogeneity in crowd flow patterns is closely related to the urban functional layouts in Fuzhou.

2. Related Works

Crowd flow prediction has emerged as a pivotal task in urban dynamic monitoring, aiming to uncover spatio-temporal patterns from historical crowd flow data to forecast future crowd movements. It provides essential decision support for urban management and public safety. Hoang et al. (2016) proposed the first model for Forecasting Citywide Crowd Flow (FCCF) [6]. It leverages Intrinsic Gaussian Markov Random Fields to capture seasonal and trend components in crowd flow while employing a spatio-temporal residual model to learn spatio-temporal dependencies. Since then, driven by the strong capacity of neural network architectures to model these dependencies, numerous deep learning-based approaches have been developed [23]. Based on their spatial modeling strategies, these crowd flow prediction models can be broadly classified into CNN, GNN, and attention-based models.

CNN-based models, the most prevalent in crowd flow prediction, leverage convolutional operations to capture spatio-temporal dependencies in crowd flow data. For instance, the deep-learning-based prediction model for spatio-temporal data (DeepST) [24] and Spatio-Temporal Residual Network (ST-ResNet) [7] employ 2D convolutions to model spatial dependencies, as well as temporal closeness, periodicity, and trends. Building on this, Zheng et al. (2019) introduced 3D convolutions to enhance the modeling of spatio-temporal dependencies [25]. Since crowd flow patterns are constrained by the local receptive fields of standard convolutions, several improvements have been proposed. In the spatial domain, the ConvPlus architecture expands the spatial receptive field of convolutions [26,27]. In the temporal domain, recurrent neural networks (RNNs) have been combined with convolutional structures to extend the temporal receptive field [28–31]. However, due to the inherent limitation of convolutional operations on regular grid-based data, CNN-based models struggle to adapt to complex study areas with irregularly shaped spatial units.

GNN-based models can more flexibly handle complex spatial units, such as administrative districts [32]. For spatial modeling, existing studies primarily construct graphs based on spatial proximity, road connectivity, and functional similarity to capture spatial dependencies between units [17,33,34]. Based on this, the Graph Attention Network (GAT) has been introduced to enhance GNN-based models by adaptively assigning edge weights [35]. However, defining a suitable graph is challenging, as it often relies on prior knowledge.

Attention-based models apply self-attention mechanisms to adaptively learn the intrinsic spatio-temporal structures in crowd flow data [36,37]. To better capture the influence of the geographical environments, environmental factors are also mapped into embedding vectors and integrated into the spatio-temporal attention mechanism [38,39]. However, attention-based models frequently compute pairwise attention scores between spatial units, which is considerably less efficient compared to CNN-based and GNN-based models.

Meanwhile, most of these models are designed based on small-scale datasets, such as the TaxiNYC dataset (with $10 \times 20 = 200$ grids) and the BikeNYC dataset (with $16 \times 8 = 128$ grids). Since large-scale crowd flow prediction has become a critical demand in urban dynamic monitoring [40,41], these models overlook the impact of the number of spatial units on efficiency, making them difficult to apply in practice. Specifically, spatial convolutions often require numerous additional spatial units to maintain grid regularity, while the computational cost of graph convolutions and self-attention mechanisms increases significantly with the number of spatial units. Although Jiang et al. (2021) and Su et al. (2023) introduced pyramid structures to model the multi-scale spatio-temporal dependencies of large-scale crowd flow [20,42], the efficiency of these models remains concerning.

Moreover, these models overlook the impact of spatial heterogeneity, which limits their predictive performance. Since spatial units with similar geographical environments exhibit similar patterns [43], identifying the spatially stratified structure of spatial units has become an effective approach for modeling spatial heterogeneity [44,45]. Lin et al. (2023) applied K-shape clustering to extract spatial units of the same type for spatial heterogeneity modeling [19]. However, this method is constrained by its reliance on a priori linear similarity metrics. Liang et al. (2021) proposed an unsupervised Mincut loss to posteriorly cluster spatial units [15]. However, the loss enforces spatially compact and balanced clusters, which contradicts the irregular urban functional layouts and impairs interpretability. Therefore, accurately extracting the spatially stratified structure by incorporating geographical environments is crucial for enhancing the accuracy of crowd flow prediction models.

3. Preliminaries

Definition 1 (Spatial unit). *The fundamental units that constitute the study area. The most common shape of a spatial unit is a grid.*

Definition 2 (Crowd flow). *The total number of people entering or leaving a spatial unit within a given time interval, including inflow and outflow. The crowd flow at time t is denoted as* $\boldsymbol{\mathcal{X}}_t \in \mathbb{R}^{N\times 2}$, *where N denotes the number of spatial units.*

Definition 3 (Geographical environments). *External factors related to crowd flow that characterize human activities, functions, and other attributes of spatial units. The geographical environments of the study area are represented as* $\mathbf{E} \in \mathbb{R}^{N\times D}$, *where D denotes the number of external factors.*

Definition 4 (Large-scale area). *A study area is defined as large-scale if it comprises more than 10,000 spatial units or covers at least one entire city. This definition is empirically based on (i) the typical spatial resolution (1 km × 1 km) adopted in publicly available crowd flow datasets, (ii) the area of most cities, and (iii) the application contexts of large-scale crowd flow prediction. This empirical definition provides an explicit and testable reference for distinguishing between large-scale and small-scale crowd flow prediction.*

Problem 1. *Here, we define the problem of large-scale crowd flow prediction as follows: Given historical crowd flow* $\boldsymbol{\mathcal{X}} = \{\boldsymbol{\mathcal{X}}_t\}_{t=1}^{T_1} \in \mathbb{R}^{N\times 2\times T_1}$ *for N spatial units during the time period from 1 to* T_1, *along with the geographical environments* $\mathbf{E}$, *the goal is to predict the future crowd flow* $\boldsymbol{\mathcal{X}}' = \{\boldsymbol{\mathcal{X}}_t\}_{t=T_1+1}^{T_1+T_2} \in \mathbb{R}^{N\times 2\times T_2}$ *for the time period from* T_1+1 *to* T_2.

4. Methodology

Figure 1 illustrates the framework of the proposed SCS-Net, which consists of a Spatially Stratified Module (SS-Module) and several Compressive Sensing Modules (CS-Modules). The SS-Module first clusters the spatial units based on their geographical environments to extract the spatially stratified structure. Then, for the spatial units in each cluster, a certain CS-Module compresses the redundant information in the historical crowd flow of the spatial units for efficient prediction. Finally, the parameters of SCS-Net are optimized through the prediction loss, the clustering loss, and the compressive sensing loss. We then aggregate the predictions of spatial units in different clusters to obtain the future crowd flow.

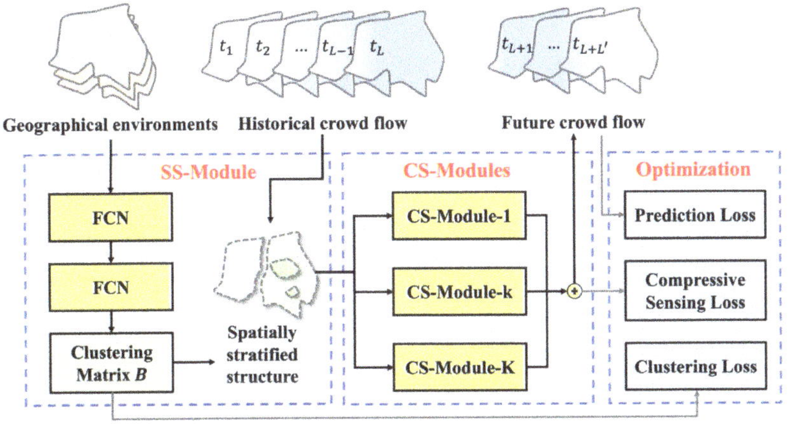

Figure 1. Framework of the proposed SCS-Net.

4.1. Spatially Stratified Module

The influence of spatial heterogeneity on crowd flow is reflected in a certain spatially stratified structure, which is closely related to geographical environments. In other words, spatial units with similar geographical environments are likely to exhibit similar crowd flow patterns. Clustering the spatial units has been proven to be a feasible approach for extracting the spatially stratified structure. However, the results of prior clustering methods are often overly generic, as they are not customized for the crowd flow prediction task.

Therefore, we integrate the process of clustering spatial units into the neural network to capture the task-specific spatially stratified structure posteriorly. Specifically, we employ two fully connected neural networks to learn the correlations between different spatial units from the geographical environments $\boldsymbol{E}$. Based on this non-linear similarity measure, the clustering matrix can be obtained. The SS-Module can be formulated by the following equation:

$$\boldsymbol{B} = Softmax\left(\sigma\left(\boldsymbol{E}\boldsymbol{W}_s^1 + \boldsymbol{b}_s^1\right)\boldsymbol{W}_s^2 + \boldsymbol{b}_s^2\right) \tag{1}$$

where $\boldsymbol{B} = \{\boldsymbol{B}_k\}_{k=1}^K \in \mathbb{R}^{N \times K}$ denotes the clustering matrix, and K denotes the number of clusters. Each column of $\boldsymbol{B}$ represents the probabilities of all spatial units belonging to a specific cluster; each row of $\boldsymbol{B}$ corresponds to the classification vector of a spatial unit, representing its probabilities of belonging to each cluster. Spatial units with more similar geographical environments will have more similar classification vectors. $\sigma(\cdot)$ denotes the ReLU activation function; $Softmax(\cdot)$ denotes the Softmax activation function; $\boldsymbol{W}_s^1$, $\boldsymbol{b}_s^1$, $\boldsymbol{W}_s^2$, and $\boldsymbol{b}_s^2$ are all learnable parameters.

4.2. Compressive Sensing Module

In large-scale crowd flow prediction, existing CNN, GNN, and attention-based models are all constrained by the computational cost of spatial modeling. To address this, we introduce the idea of compressive sensing from the signal processing field. Compressive sensing extracts key information in the sparse domain (e.g., frequency-domain signals) from discrete sampling signals, enabling efficient reconstruction of the original signal. In crowd flow, such key information corresponds to the shared patterns. We develop a flexible and efficient prediction architecture with linear complexity, namely the CS-Module, as illustrated in Figure 2.

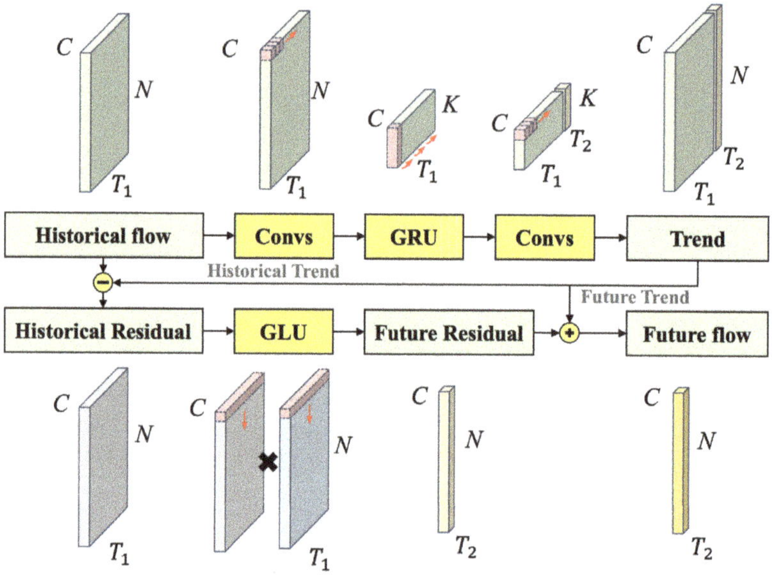

Figure 2. Architecture of the CS-Module.

The CS-Module consists of four steps: information compression, pattern prediction, trend reconstruction, and residual learning. Specifically, for the k-th column of the clustering matrix B_k, the information compression step first applies two convolutional layers to compress the redundant information of different spatial units in the historical crowd flow and learn the shared crowd flow patterns. This process can be formulated by the following equation:

$$\mathcal{P}_k = Conv_C(B_k \odot \mathcal{X}) = \sigma\left(B_k \odot \mathcal{X} * W_C^1 + b_C^1\right) * W_C^2 + b_C^2 \tag{2}$$

where $\mathcal{P}_k = \{\mathcal{P}_{k,t}\}_{t=1}^{T_1} \in \mathbb{R}^{L \times 2 \times T_1}$ denotes the L shared patterns in the embedding space, with each shared pattern containing a portion of the key information, similar to an eigenvector in a matrix; $Conv_C(\cdot)$ denotes the operation process of the information compression step. This process considers three key components: the similarities across different crowd flow series, the temporal dependencies within each series, and the correlations between inflow and outflow series; $\odot$ denotes the Hadamard product, which controls the proportion of information from $\mathcal{X}$ flowing into the k-th CS-Module based on B_k; $*$ represents the convolution operator; W_C^1, b_C^1, W_C^2, and b_C^2 are all learnable parameters. The convolution kernel size is set to 3 with a padding of 1 to ensure the length of the time slices remains unchanged.

The information compression step simplifies the prediction task of numerous spatial units in the physical space into the prediction task of L shared patterns in the embedding space, significantly improving the efficiency of crowd flow prediction. Second, the pattern prediction step applies a Gated Recurrent Unit (GRU) to capture the temporal dependencies in the shared patterns and predict their future evolution. This process can be formulated as the following equation:

$$R_t = \sigma(\mathcal{P}_{k,t} W_{pr} + H_{t-1} W_{hr} + b_r) \tag{3}$$

$$Z_t = \sigma(\mathcal{P}_{k,t} W_{pz} + H_{t-1} W_{hz} + b_z) \tag{4}$$

$$\widetilde{H_t} = tanh(\mathcal{P}_{k,t}W_{ph} + (R_t \odot H_{t-1})W_{hh} + b_h) \quad (5)$$

$$H_t = Z_t \odot H_{t-1} + (1 - Z_t) \odot \widetilde{H_t} \quad (6)$$

$$\mathcal{P}_{k,t+1} = H_t W_G + b_G \quad (7)$$

where R_t and Z_t denote the reset gate and update gate of the GRU, respectively; $\widetilde{H_t}$ represents the candidate hidden states; H_{t-1} and H_t are the hidden states at times $t-1$ and t, respectively; $tanh(\cdot)$ denotes the tanh activation function; W_{pr}, W_{hr}, b_r, W_{pz}, W_{hz}, b_z, W_{ph}, W_{hh}, b_h, W_G, and b_G are all learnable parameters. Through iterative prediction, the future shared crowd flow patterns $\mathcal{P}'_k = \{\mathcal{P}_{k,t}\}_{t=T_1+1}^{T_1+T_2} \in \mathbb{R}^{L\times 2\times T_2}$ can be obtained.

Based on this, the trend reconstruction step applies two convolutional layers to perform the inverse process of the information compression step, i.e., mapping the historical and future shared patterns into the crowd flow in the physical space. This process can be formulated as the following equation:

$$[\mathcal{T}_k || \mathcal{T}'_k] = \sigma\Big([\mathcal{P}_k || \mathcal{P}'_k] * W_R^1 + b_R^1\Big) * W_R^2 + b_R^2 \quad (8)$$

where $\mathcal{T}_k \in \mathbb{R}^{N\times 2\times T_1}$ and $\mathcal{T}'_k \in \mathbb{R}^{N\times 2\times T_2}$ represent the reconstructed historical and future crowd flow of the spatial units in the k-th cluster. Considering that $\mathcal{P}_k$ and $\mathcal{P}'_k$ represent the shared crowd flow patterns, the reconstructed $\mathcal{T}_k$ and $\mathcal{T}'_k$ can represent the crowd flow trend. W_R^1, b_R^1, W_R^2, and b_R^2 are all learnable parameters, where the convolution kernel size is 3 and the padding is 1 to ensure the length of the time slices remains unchanged.

It is evident that the reconstructed crowd flow retains only the key trends while losing the details of the spatial units. To fully leverage the information in the crowd flow data for improving predictions, the residual learning step employs a Gated Linear Unit (GLU) to capture the fluctuation patterns of the residuals between the historical crowd flow and the trends and to predict the future residuals for each spatial unit. This process can be formulated as the following equation:

$$\mathcal{R}_k = B_k \odot \mathcal{X} - \mathcal{T}_k \quad (9)$$

$$\mathcal{R}'_k = \Big(\mathcal{R}_k W_r^1 + b_r^1\Big) \odot sigmoid\Big(\mathcal{R}_k W_r^2 + b_r^2\Big) \quad (10)$$

where $\mathcal{R}_k$ and $\mathcal{R}'_k$ denote the historical and future residuals, respectively; $sigmoid(\cdot)$ denotes the sigmoid activation function; and W_r^1, b_r^1, W_r^2, and b_r^2 are all learnable parameters.

By integrating the trend and residual predictions from the CS-Modules corresponding to different clusters, the final crowd flow predictions $\hat{\mathcal{X}}' \in \mathbb{R}^{N\times 2\times T_2}$ can be formulated as the following equation:

$$\hat{\mathcal{X}}' = \sum_{k=1}^{K} (\mathcal{T}'_k + \mathcal{R}'_k) \quad (11)$$

4.3. Optimization

In our proposed SCS-Net, we design three types of losses to guide the model's training: the prediction loss, the clustering loss, and the compressive sensing loss. The prediction loss aims to minimize the discrepancy between the predicted crowd flow and the actual future crowd flow, ensuring the accuracy of the predictions. The prediction loss $\mathcal{L}_p$ can be formulated as the following equation:

$$\mathcal{L}_p = \frac{\left|\left|\mathcal{X}' - \hat{\mathcal{X}}'\right|\right|_2^2}{N \times 2 \times T_2} \tag{12}$$

where $||\cdot||_2$ denotes the L2 norm. The clustering loss aims to promote the sparsity of the classification vectors of spatial units, ensuring the effectiveness of the SS-Module. The clustering loss $\mathcal{L}_c$ can be formulated as the following equation:

$$\mathcal{L}_c = \left|\left|\boldsymbol{B}^T\boldsymbol{B} \odot \frac{1}{\boldsymbol{B}^T\boldsymbol{B}1} - \boldsymbol{I}\right|\right|_2 \tag{13}$$

where $1 \in \mathbb{R}^{K\times 1}$ is a row vector with all elements equal to 1, and $\boldsymbol{I} \in \mathbb{R}^{K\times K}$ is an identity matrix. When the classification vectors of different clusters are orthogonal and those within the same cluster are sparse, $\boldsymbol{B}^T\boldsymbol{B}$ tends to be a diagonal matrix. $\frac{1}{\boldsymbol{B}^T\boldsymbol{B}1}$ serves as a diagonal normalization of $\boldsymbol{B}^T\boldsymbol{B}$. The compressive sensing loss aims to promote the completeness of the reconstructed crowd flow information and the accuracy of the shared pattern predictions, ensuring the effectiveness of the CS-Modules. The compressive sensing loss can be decomposed into two parts, $\mathcal{L}_{S1}$ and $\mathcal{L}_{S2}$, and formulated as the following equation:

$$\mathcal{L}_{S1} = \frac{\left|\left|\mathcal{X} - \sum_{k=1}^{K} \mathcal{T}_k\right|\right|_2^2}{N \times 2 \times T_1} \tag{14}$$

$$\mathcal{L}_{S2} = \frac{\left|\left|\sum_{k=1}^{K} (\mathcal{P}'_k - Conv_C(B_k \odot \mathcal{X}'))\right|\right|_2^2}{K \times 2 \times T_2} \tag{15}$$

To train the proposed SCS-Net, the overall loss, composed of the three losses mentioned above, will be minimized to optimize the SCS-Net's parameters. The overall loss can be formulated as the following equation:

$$\mathcal{L} = \mathcal{L}_p + \lambda_c \mathcal{L}_c + \mathcal{L}_{S1} + \lambda_S \mathcal{L}_{S2} \tag{16}$$

where $\mathcal{L}$ denotes the overall loss. Considering the scale discrepancies among different loss terms, $\lambda_c \in [0,1]$ and $\lambda_S \in [0,1]$ are introduced to balance the importance of the loss terms.

5. Experiments

5.1. Dataset

In this study, we conducted experiments on a large-scale real-world dataset, the CrowdFZ dataset. This dataset is derived from Android device location data in Fuzhou, China, provided through a collaboration with Chinese telecom operators. The data have a population sampling rate of approximately 20%, with a random sampling process, and each record finely reflects a user's location. Therefore, we believe that this dataset is sufficiently capable of representing large-scale real-world crowd movements. Based on this, we divided Fuzhou into grids with a spatial resolution of 0.01 degrees in both latitude and longitude, resulting in a total of 11,418 spatial units, as shown in Figure 3. We then aggregated the inflow and outflow within each grid at 30 min intervals from 1 January 2023 to 28 February 2023 to construct the CrowdFZ dataset.

Additionally, we collected the 2022 Point-of-Interest (POI) data and the 2023 road network data of Fuzhou to describe the geographical environments. The POI data were sourced from Gaode Map (https://lbs.amap.com/ (accessed on 11 May 2024)), while the road network data were obtained from OpenStreetMap (https://download.geofabrik.de (accessed on 21 November 2024)). The geographical environments include 22 external factors, denoted as $D = 22$. Specifically, we used the POI data to calculate the number of facilities in each spatial unit for the following categories: tourist attractions, transportation facilities, educational and cultural institutions, healthcare services, sports and fitness centers, leisure and entertainment venues, dining establishments, shopping locations, hotels and accommodations, life services, residential and commercial buildings, business enterprises, automotive services, and financial institutions, totaling 14 external factors. Using the road network data, we computed the distance from each spatial unit to primary roads, secondary roads, tertiary roads, and residential roads, as well as the length of these four types of roads within each spatial unit, totaling eight external factors.

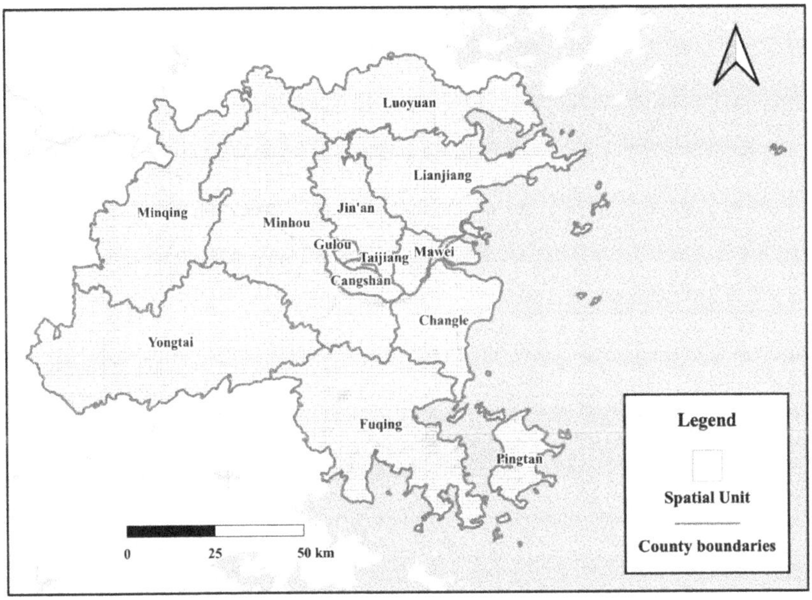

Figure 3. Spatial distribution of the spatial units in the CrowdFZ dataset of Fuzhou.

5.2. Experiment Setting and Evaluation Metric

To ensure the fairness of the comparison, we adopted almost identical experimental settings for our proposed SCS-Net and the deep learning baselines. Specifically, we used the historical crowd flow data from the previous six time slices ($T_1 = 6$) to predict the next one or three time slices ($T_2 = 1$ or 3). The last two weeks of the CrowdFZ dataset were used for testing, while 80% of the remaining data were randomly selected for training and 20% for validation. Min-max normalization was applied to scale the crowd flow and geographical environments into the range [0,1]. Moreover, the batch size was set to 16. The number of hidden states was set to 64. The convolution kernel size was set to 3. The random seed was set to 2025. We employed the Adam optimizer to optimize the model parameters with an initial learning rate of 0.001 and a maximum of 500 epochs. We applied the early stopping strategy to avoid overfitting, setting a patience of 10, which means training stopped if the validation loss did not improve for 10 consecutive epochs. The experiments were conducted using the PyTorch 1.13 framework on an NVIDIA Tesla V100 GPU server.

In particular, for the key hyperparameters of our proposed SCS-Net, we conducted a manual search over the following ranges: the number of clusters $K = \{1, 2, 3, 4, 5, 6\}$, the number of shared patterns $L = \{4, 8, 12, 16, 20\}$, the weight for the clustering loss $\lambda_c = \{0.1, 0.01, 0.001, 0.0001, 0.00001\}$, and the weight for the compressive sensing loss $\lambda_S = \{0.1, 0.01, 0.001, 0.0001, 0.00001\}$. As shown in Figure 4, SCS-Net demonstrates relatively stable performance with small MAE and RMSE fluctuations across most parameter configurations. Based on the optimal parameter configuration, we selected $K = 3$, $L = 16$, $\lambda_c = 0.0001$, and $\lambda_S = 0.001$ as the default setting.

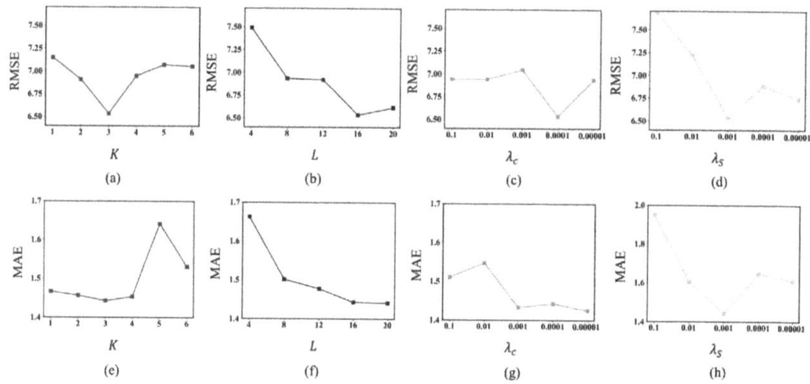

Figure 4. Results of the parameter sensitivity analysis. (**a–d**) RMSE of SCS-Net under different hyperparameter configurations. (**e–h**) MAE of SCS-Net under different hyperparameter configurations.

In the experiments, we evaluated the models' performance using two common metrics: Mean Absolute Error (MAE) and Root Mean Square Error (RMSE). They can be formulated as the following equations:

$$MAE = \frac{\left|\left|\mathcal{X}' - \hat{\mathcal{X}}'\right|\right|_1}{N \times 2 \times T_2} \tag{17}$$

$$RMSE = \frac{\left|\left|\mathcal{X}' - \hat{\mathcal{X}}'\right|\right|_2}{\sqrt{N \times 2 \times T_2}} \tag{18}$$

where $||\cdot||_1$ denotes the L1 norm.

5.3. Model Accuracy

To evaluate the accuracy of our proposed SCS-Net for large-scale crowd flow prediction, we selected the following 11 baseline models for comparison. To ensure a fair comparison, we kept the hyperparameters of the baseline models as consistent as possible with those of the proposed SCS-Net. This includes settings such as batch size, number of hidden states, number of CNN layers, number of RNN layers, convolution kernel size, random seed, optimizer, learning rate and patience in early stopping strategy. Based on these aligned configurations, we then performed additional hyperparameter tuning for each baseline model to optimize their performance.

- HA: Historical Average is a classic non-parametric time series prediction method that uses the average of historical crowd flow as the predictions.
- GRU [46]: Gated Recurrent Unit is a classic deep learning time-series prediction model capable of capturing long-term temporal dependencies.
- DLinear [47]: DLinear is an advanced time series prediction model that decomposes historical data into trend and residual components, efficiently capturing long-term temporal dependencies through simple linear layers. The kernel size of the moving average operation was set to 5.

- ConvGRU [48]: Convolutional Gated Recurrent Unit is a classic CNN-based spatio-temporal prediction model that extends GRU with convolutional structures to capture spatio-temporal dependencies.
- STResNet [7]: Spatio-Temporal Residual Network is a widely recognized CNN-based crowd flow prediction model that employs residual units to capture spatio-temporal dependencies. The number of ResUnits was set to 3.
- AGCRN [49]: Adaptive Graph Convolutional Recurrent Network is a representative GNN-based spatio-temporal prediction model that extends GRU with adaptive graph convolution to capture spatio-temporal dependencies. The dimension of node embedding was set to 16.
- DeepCrowd [20]: DeepCrowd is the first model applied to large-scale crowd flow prediction. It constructs a pyramidal architecture by stacking ConvLSTM layers to capture large-scale spatial dependencies. The number of pyramidal ConvLSTM layers was set to 3.
- ASTCN [36]: Attentive Spatial–Temporal Convolutional Network is a representative attention-based crowd flow prediction model that introduces causal 3D convolutions and attention mechanisms to capture spatio-temporal dependencies. The number of ST blocks was set to 1.
- TLAE [50]: Temporal Latent Auto-Encoder is a representative prediction model incorporating compressive sensing, which achieves efficient predicting by compressing and reconstructing time series data. However, compared to SCS-Net, TLAE performs less comprehensive time-series modeling and overlooks residual learning. The latent dimension was set to 16.
- STRN [15]: Spatio-Temporal Relation Network is an advanced CNN-based crowd flow prediction model that introduces Mincut loss to extract the spatially stratified structure for modeling spatial heterogeneity. The number of regions was set to 3.
- BigST [51]: BigST is an advanced large-scale spatio-temporal prediction model that uses a pre-training strategy to extract long-term temporal representations and introduces a linearized global spatial convolution network to efficiently capture spatial dependencies. The size of time window in the long sequence feature extractor was set to 24. The dimension of random features was set to 32.

The accuracy comparison results of our proposed SCS-Net and the baseline models on the CrowdFZ dataset are shown in Table 1. Overall, SCS-Net significantly outperforms the baseline models across all metrics. Specifically, for the deep learning baseline models, the MAE increases by 35.5% to 120.3% and the RMSE increases by 26.3% to 74.7% in single-step predictions, while the MAE increases by 58.6% to 139.2% and the RMSE increases by 33.6% to 112.4% in multi-step predictions. This demonstrates the superior performance of SCS-Net in large-scale crowd flow prediction.

Among the baseline models, the spatio-temporal prediction models outperform the time series prediction model, highlighting the importance of spatial dependency in large-scale crowd flow prediction. As the model architectures become more complex, the RMSE generally decreases. ASTCN and DeepCrowd, which have the most sophisticated structures, achieve the lowest RMSE among the baseline models. This is attributed to their incorporation of spatial downsampling techniques, which expand the spatial receptive field. These two models partially mitigate the impact of spatial heterogeneity, thereby enhancing performance. Although STRN models spatial heterogeneity, it enforces spatially compact and balanced clusters in the spatially stratified structure. This constraint misaligns with the urban functional layouts, ultimately limiting its accuracy.

However, the comparison results among the baseline models reveal an unusual phenomenon in the MAE metric. Specifically, the simpler models, ConvGRU and TLAE, achieve the lowest MAE among the baseline models, whereas the more complex ASTCN and DeepCrowd, which excel in RMSE, perform less satisfactorily in MAE. Unexpectedly, the GRU even achieves a lower MAE than ASTCN and DeepCrowd. To investigate this anomaly, we visualize the MAE distributions of single-step predictions for SCS-Net, TLAE, ASTCN, DeepCrowd, ConvGRU, and GRU (Figure 5). To enhance readability, we applied a natural logarithmic transformation, $ln(1+x)$, to the MAE values. The results indicate that most MAEs are concentrated in the low-value range, as most spatial units exhibit relatively low human activity intensity in large-scale crowd flow prediction. Although ASTCN and DeepCrowd have larger medians and quartiles compared to the other models, their peak values are significantly lower. This suggests that ASTCN and DeepCrowd demonstrate a distinct advantage in predicting spatial units with higher human activity intensity (H-units) but struggle with those with lower human activity intensity (L-units). This may be attributed to the causal 3D convolutions in ASTCN and the pyramid ConvL-STMs in DeepCrowd, which enable both models to capture longer-range spatio-temporal dependencies and thus effectively fit the complex crowd flow patterns in H-units. However, H-units contribute more to the loss function. The two models tend to overfit in H-units and poorly generalize to the simpler patterns in L-units. Since most spatial units are L-units, the advantages of ASTCN and DeepCrowd are difficult to demonstrate in the first-order MAE metric, leading to better RMSE but worse MAE. In contrast, due to their simpler structures, TLAE, ConvGRU, and GRU prioritize the simpler crowd flow patterns in L-units, resulting in the underfitting of H-units. As second-order RMSE is more sensitive to peak values, these models achieve better MAE but worse RMSE.

Table 1. Accuracy comparison results of SCS-Net and baseline models on the CrowdFZ dataset. Δ_M and Δ_R represent the MAE and RMSE increase in the baseline models relative to SCS-Net, respectively. The underlined values indicate the best metrics among the baseline models. The bold values indicate the best metrics among all models.

Model	$T_2 = 1$				$T_2 = 3$			
	MAE	Δ_M	RMSE	Δ_R	MAE	Δ_M	RMSE	Δ_R
HA	3.1847	120.7%	20.3833	212.0%	3.9934	133.0%	25.6272	219.3%
GRU	2.1654	50.1%	11.412	74.7%	2.9217	70.5%	17.0506	112.4%
DLinear	2.1398	48.3%	11.5169	76.3%	3.0281	76.7%	17.5576	118.8%
ConvGRU	1.9551	35.5%	10.4633	60.2%	2.9022	69.3%	12.806	59.6%
STResNet	3.2986	128.6%	10.922	67.2%	4.0994	139.2%	16.0819	100.4%
AGCRN	2.9574	105.0%	10.7298	64.2%	3.9031	127.7%	16.6018	106.8%
DeepCrowd	2.1502	49.0%	8.9211	36.5%	3.0979	80.8%	10.7258	33.6%
ASTCN	2.8359	96.6%	8.2524	26.3%	3.0012	75.1%	10.7272	33.7%
TLAE	2.2912	58.8%	9.9185	51.8%	2.7184	58.6%	13.3906	66.8%
STRN	3.1779	120.3%	8.9634	37.2%	4.5195	163.7%	13.9061	73.3%
BigST	2.9839	106.8%	10.0191	53.4%	3.4222	99.7%	12.4788	55.5%
SCS-Net	**1.4427**	-	**6.5334**	-	**1.7139**	-	**8.0263**	-

Additionally, we visualized the prediction errors of an H-unit and an L-unit on 24 February 2023 (Figure 6). To maintain readability, we selected four representative models for comparison. H-unit A corresponds to Shangxiahang Historic District, a major tourist and commercial area in Fuzhou, while L-unit B corresponds to Gu'an Village, a small rural village in Fuzhou. The results show that ConvGRU and GRU exhibit larger error fluctuations in H-unit A, whereas their errors remain relatively stable in L-unit B. In contrast, ASTCN exhibits the opposite trend, further validating our understanding of this anomaly. Moreover, as shown in Figure 6, SCS-Net effectively captures the significant differences in crowd flow patterns between spatial units A and B, demonstrating its capability to handle spatial heterogeneity. As a result, it achieves the best overall performance.

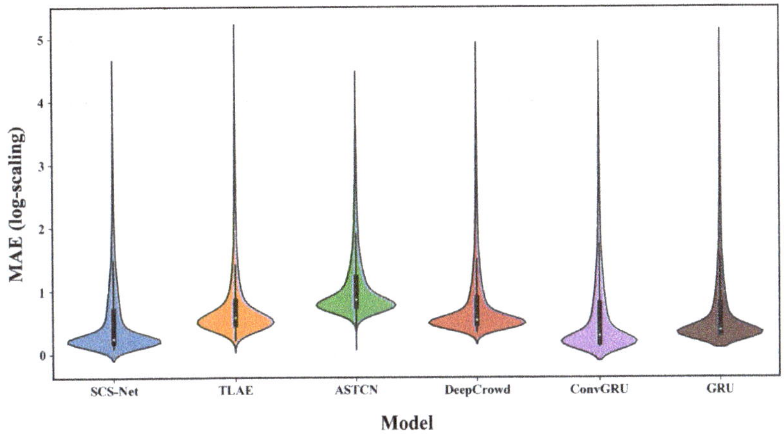

Figure 5. MAE distributions of SCS-Net, TLAE, ASTCN, DeepCrowd, ConvGRU, and GRU after log-scaling. For each column, the outer curve illustrates the probability density distribution, the thick black bar in the center represents the interquartile range (IQR), the thin black lines extending from it denote the 95% confidence interval, and the white dot indicates the median.

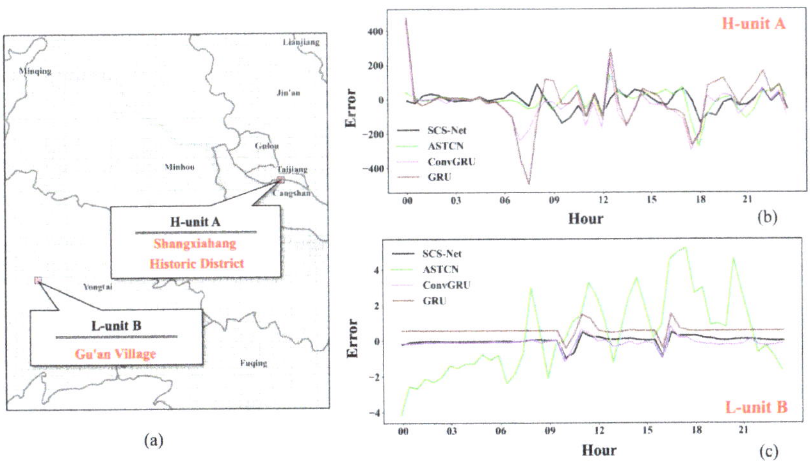

Figure 6. Prediction errors of SCS-Net, ASTCN, ConvGRU, and GRU on H-unit A and L-unit B on 24 February 2023. (**a**) Locations of H-unit A and L-unit B. (**b**) Prediction errors for H-unit A. (**c**) Prediction errors for L-unit B.

5.4. Model Efficiency

To evaluate the efficiency of our proposed SCS-Net and the baseline models for large-scale crowd flow prediction, we introduced Giga Floating-Point Operations (GFLOPs) and training time (minutes) as evaluation metrics to assess model efficiency. The GFLOPs measures the total number of floating-point operations performed by the model per batch (batch size = 1). The training time reflects the actual time required for the models to converge during training. The efficiency comparison results are shown in Figure 7. Overall, the GFLOPs and the training time are correlated. SCS-Net significantly outperforms most baseline models. Although the GFLOPs and training time of HA and DLinear are considerably lower than that of SCS-Net, the poor predictive performance of these two linear time series prediction models limits their application to large-scale crowd flow prediction tasks. Meanwhile, TLAE also has lower GFLOPs and training time and achieves relatively good accuracy. However, when SCS-Net is deployable, it remains the better choice. In contrast, the CNN, GNN, and attention-based spatio-temporal prediction models have GFLOPs approximately 53 (ASTCN) to 1067 (DeepCrowd) times higher than SCS-Net and training times that are about 3.1 times (ASTCN) to 83.2 times (AGCRN) longer, leading to substantially higher costs. Considering that SCS-Net is not constrained by prior graph structures, nor by the shape or distribution of spatial units, this demonstrates its superior applicability to large-scale crowd flow prediction.

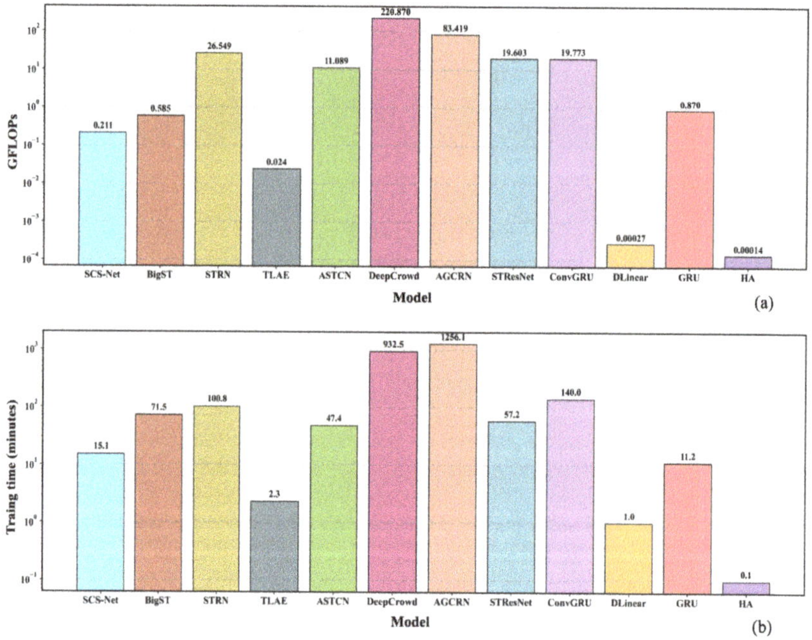

Figure 7. Efficiency comparison results of SCS-Net and baseline models on the CrowdFZ dataset. (**a**) Comparison of GFLOPs. (**b**) Comparison of training time.

5.5. Ablation Experiment

To validate the effectiveness of the SS-Module and CS-Modules in our proposed SCS-Net, we designed three variants of SCS-Net and conduct ablation experiments on the CrowdFZ dataset.

- SCS-Net-g: Replaces the CS-Modules with a GRU, retaining the model's predictive function while removing its capacity to perceive shared crowd flow patterns.
- SCS-Net-k: Replaces the SS-Module with K-means clustering based on geographical environments, providing a prior spatially stratified structure.
- SCS-Net-c: Removes the SS-Module entirely, making the model incapable of capturing the spatially stratified structure.

The comparison results of our proposed SCS-Net and its variants are shown in Table 2. Among the three variants, SCS-Net-g, which removes the compressive sensing component, experiences the most significant performance degradation. This highlights the critical contribution of the CS-Modules to the superior performance of SCS-Net. Specifically, the CS-Modules learn shared crowd flow patterns, preventing SCS-Net from being disturbed by redundant information among spatial units, thereby enhancing its sensitivity to individual spatial unit differences. Moreover, the results of SCS-Net-k and SCS-Net-c are close, indicating that prior K-means clustering fails to effectively capture the spatially stratified structure suitable for large-scale crowd flow prediction. In contrast, the SS-Module adaptively learns this structure in a posterior manner during the prediction process, further enhancing the model's predictive performance.

Table 2. Comparison results of SCS-Net and its variants on the CrowdFZ dataset. Δ_M and Δ_R represent the MAE and RMSE increase in the variants relative to SCS-Net, respectively. The bold values indicate the best metrics among all models.

Model	$T_2 = 1$				$T_2 = 3$			
	MAE	Δ_M	RMSE	Δ_R	MAE	Δ_M	RMSE	Δ_R
SCS-Net-g	2.3623	63.7%	10.7731	64.9%	2.7451	60.2%	15.2769	90.3%
SCS-Net-k	1.6072	11.4%	8.1463	24.7%	1.9194	12.0%	9.8755	23.0%
SCS-Net-c	1.5249	5.7%	7.7657	18.9%	2.141	24.9%	9.6372	20.1%
SCS-Net	**1.4427**	-	**6.5334**	-	**1.7139**	-	**8.0263**	-

5.6. Analysis of the Spatially Stratified Structure

The spatially stratified structure not only improves the accuracy of crowd flow prediction but also offers deeper insights into spatial heterogeneity of human mobility. To explore this, we visualized the spatial distributions of clusters produced by the prior K-means and the posterior SS-Module, and Fuzhou's actual road network, as shown in Figure 8. Overall, both clustering methods produce clusters with similar meanings: Cluster 1 (C-1) represents H-units with high crowd activity, while Cluster 0 (C-0) and Cluster 2 (C-2) correspond to L-units with low and even lower activity, respectively. The distribution of C-0 is relatively consistent between the two methods, but C-1 and C-2 show notable differences. Compared to Fuzhou's road network, the C-1 from K-means aligns with the core urban area, whereas the C-1 from the SS-Module matches the built-up areas, reflecting the city's urban development boundary. Since the ablation experiments show that the SS-Module's clustering better captures the spatially stratified structure for crowd flow prediction in Fuzhou, this suggests that effectively handling large-scale, city-level tasks requires the ability to distinguish and model the crowd flow patterns in built-up and non-built-up areas.

To further investigate which external factors play a key role in identifying the spatially stratified structure, we built regression models using the random forest algorithm to relate the external factors to each cluster from the SS-Module. We then visualized the distribution of normalized feature importances for these clusters, as shown in Figure 9. Overall, road network-related factors dominate the feature importance across all three clusters. Specifically, distance to primary roads, distance to residential roads, and residential road length are critical for identifying C-0 and C-2, likely reflecting proximity to built-up areas. In contrast, identifying C-1, which represents built-up areas, requires considering more factors, including residential road length, distance to residential roads, distance to primary roads, life services, shopping locations, educational and cultural institutions, and tourist attractions. These factors are closely related to transport accessibility and diverse urban functions, offering potential value for urban spatial planning in Fuzhou. The prior K-means clustering fails to capture the complex relationships between crowd flow and these factors, thereby limiting its ability to improve prediction performance.

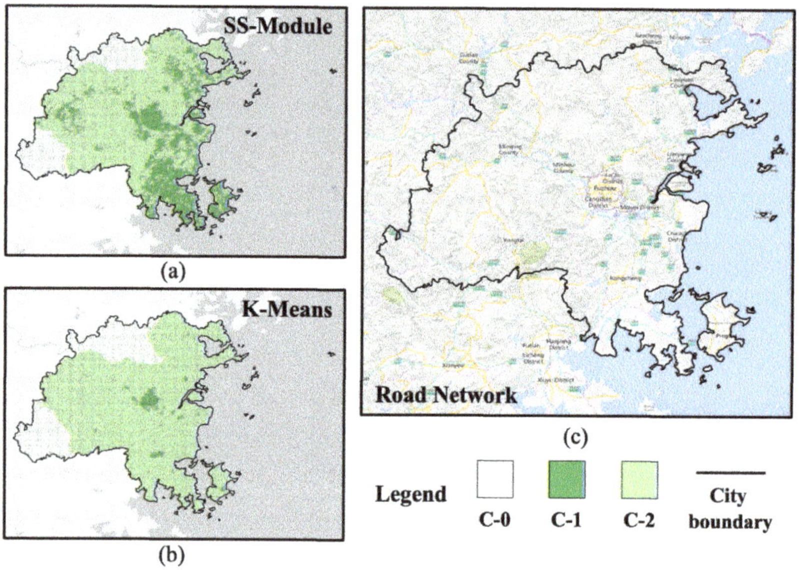

Figure 8. Comparison of clustering results between K-means and the SS-Module. (**a**) Spatial distribution of clusters produced by K-means. (**b**) Spatial distribution of clusters produced by the SS-Module. (**c**) Actual road network of Fuzhou. In the legend, "C-0", "C-1", and "C-2" represent Cluster 0, Cluster 1, and Cluster 2 in both clustering results, respectively.

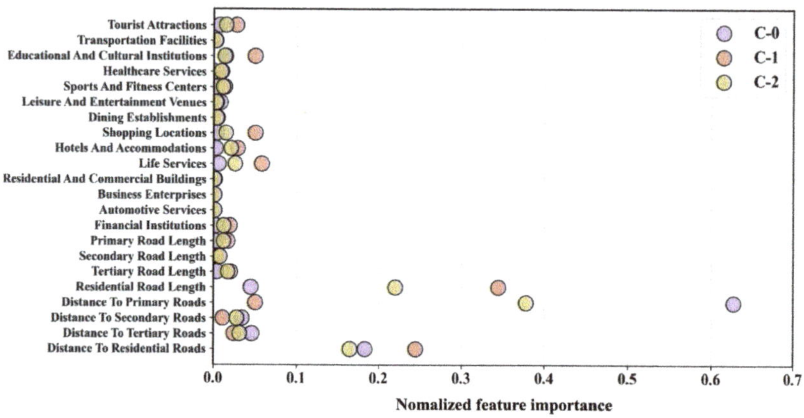

Figure 9. Random forest normalized feature importances for each cluster in the SS-Module.

6. Conclusions

In this paper, we propose SCS-Net for accurate and efficient large-scale crowd flow prediction. In the model, we develop a Spatially Stratified Module (SS-Module) that adaptively extracts the underlying spatially stratified structure in a posterior manner, thereby improving prediction accuracy. Based on this, several Compressive Sensing Modules (CS-Modules) are developed to compress redundant information in crowd flow and learn shared crowd flow patterns, enhancing model efficiency. We conduct extensive experiments on a large-scale real-world crowd flow prediction dataset. The results show that SCS-Net achieves superior accuracy, outperforming deep learning baseline models by 35.25–139.2% in MAE and 26.3–112.4% in RMSE. In terms of efficiency, the GFLOPs and the training time of the prevalent spatio-temporal prediction models are approximately 53 to 1067 times and

3.1 to 83.2 times higher than SCS-Net, respectively. Additionally, ablation experiments on several variants of SCS-Net validate the effectiveness of the SS-Module and CS-Modules. Further analysis of the spatially stratified structure reveals that spatial heterogeneity in crowd flow patterns is closely related to the urban road network.

However, there are several limitations in this study. First, the generalizability and applicability of our proposed SCS-Net need to be further validated through experiments in additional study areas. Second, since quantifying predictive uncertainty is also crucial for the applications of crowd flow prediction, we plan to incorporate techniques such as Monte-Carlo dropout, quantile regression, and deep ensembles in the future work to enhance the model's robustness and interpretability. Moreover, for long-term and large-scale crowd flow prediction tasks, we will explore more efficient and effective solutions, as modeling more temporal slices may reduce model efficiency and lead to vanishing gradient issues. Meanwhile, future crowd flow is influenced not only by historical trends but also by data incompleteness (e.g., sparsity and missing values) and anomalous events (e.g., concerts and public holidays). Capturing the impact of these external disruptions is another challenge we aim to address. This will further support urban management and public safety.

Author Contributions: Conceptualization, X.T. and K.C.; methodology, X.T.; software, X.T.; validation X.T. and K.C.; formal analysis X.T.; data curation X.T., B.L., Z.Z., Y.T. and S.W.; writing—original draft preparation, X.T.; writing—review and editing, X.T., K.C. and M.D.; visualization, X.T.; supervision, K.C., M.D. and B.L.; funding acquisition, K.C., M.D. and B.L. All authors have read and agreed to the published version of the manuscript.

Funding: This research was funded by the National Natural Science Foundation of China (grant number 42430110 and 42171459) and the Natural Science Foundation of Hunan Province (grant number 2024JJ1009).

Data Availability Statement: The datasets presented in this article are not readily available due to privacy restrictions and cooperation agreements with Chinese telecom operators. Requests for access to the datasets should be directed to the corresponding author. We confirm that all figures and tables in this article were originally created by the authors with data or results from this study. There are no copyright issues associated with these figures and tables, and no permissions are required for their use or reference.

Acknowledgments: This work was carried out in part using computing resources at the High-Performance Computing Platform of Central South University.

Conflicts of Interest: The authors declare that they have no conflicts of interest.

References

1. Sun, L.; Chen, J.; Li, Q.; Huang, D. Dramatic Uneven Urbanization of Large Cities throughout the World in Recent Decades. *Nat. Commun.* **2020**, *11*, 5366. [CrossRef]
2. Mahtta, R.; Fragkias, M.; Güneralp, B.; Mahendra, A.; Reba, M.; Wentz, E.A.; Seto, K.C. Urban Land Expansion: The Role of Population and Economic Growth for 300+ Cities. *npj Urban Sustain.* **2022**, *2*, 5. [CrossRef]
3. Zheng, Y.; Capra, L.; Wolfson, O.; Yang, H. Urban Computing: Concepts, Methodologies, and Applications. *ACM Trans. Intell. Syst. Technol.* **2014**, *5*, 1–55. [CrossRef]
4. Chen, K.; Chu, G.; Yang, X.; Shi, Y.; Lei, K.; Deng, M. HSETA: A Heterogeneous and Sparse Data Learning Hybrid Framework for Estimating Time of Arrival. *IEEE Trans. Intell. Transp. Syst.* **2022**, *23*, 21873–21884. [CrossRef]
5. Wang, P.; Zhang, Y.; Hu, T.; Zhang, T. Urban Traffic Flow Prediction: A Dynamic Temporal Graph Network Considering Missing Values. *Int. J. Geogr. Inf. Sci.* **2023**, *37*, 885–912. [CrossRef]
6. Hoang, M.X.; Zheng, Y.; Singh, A.K. FCCF: Forecasting Citywide Crowd Flows Based on Big Data. In Proceedings of the 24th ACM SIGSPATIAL International Conference on Advances in Geographic Information Systems, Burlingame, CA, USA, 31 October–3 November 2016; pp. 1–10.
7. Zhang, J.; Zheng, Y.; Qi, D. Deep Spatio-Temporal Residual Networks for Citywide Crowd Flows Prediction. In Proceedings of the AAAI Conference on Artificial Intelligence, San Francisco, CA, USA, 4–9 February 2017; Volume 31. [CrossRef]

8. Dai, G.; Huang, H.; Peng, X.; Zhang, B.; Fu, X. ARFGCN: Adaptive Receptive Field Graph Convolutional Network for Urban Crowd Flow Prediction. *Mathematics* **2024**, *12*, 1739. [CrossRef]
9. Zhang, J.; Zheng, Y.; Qi, D.; Li, R.; Yi, X.; Li, T. Predicting Citywide Crowd Flows Using Deep Spatio-Temporal Residual Networks. *Artif. Intell.* **2018**, *259*, 147–166. [CrossRef]
10. Xie, P.; Li, T.; Liu, J.; Du, S.; Yang, X.; Zhang, J. Urban Flow Prediction from Spatiotemporal Data Using Machine Learning: A Survey. *Inf. Fusion* **2020**, *59*, 1–12. [CrossRef]
11. Wang, P.; Zhang, T.; Zhang, H.; Cheng, S.; Wang, W. Adding Attention to the Neural Ordinary Differential Equation for Spatio-Temporal Prediction. *Int. J. Geogr. Inf. Sci.* **2024**, *38*, 156–181. [CrossRef]
12. Chen, K.; Deng, M.; Lei, K.; Liu, Q.; Shi, Y. Adaptive Multi-View Neural Network for Network-Wide and Segment-Wise Traffic Speed Estimation With Heterogeneous Missing Cases. *Trans. GIS* **2025**, *29*, e13295. [CrossRef]
13. Xu, L.; Chen, N.; Chen, Z.; Zhang, C.; Yu, H. Spatiotemporal Forecasting in Earth System Science: Methods, Uncertainties, Predictability and Future Directions. *Earth-Sci. Rev.* **2021**, *222*, 103828. [CrossRef]
14. Luo, P.; Song, Y.; Zhu, D.; Cheng, J.; Meng, L. A Generalized Heterogeneity Model for Spatial Interpolation. *Int. J. Geogr. Inf. Sci.* **2023**, *37*, 634–659. [CrossRef]
15. Liang, Y.; Ouyang, K.; Sun, J.; Wang, Y.; Zhang, J.; Zheng, Y.; Rosenblum, D.; Zimmermann, R. Fine-Grained Urban Flow Prediction. In Proceedings of the Web Conference 2021, Ljubljana, Slovenia, 19–23 April 2021; pp. 1833–1845.
16. Huang, W.; Li, S.; Liu, X.; Ban, Y. Predicting Human Mobility with Activity Changes. *Int. J. Geogr. Inf. Sci.* **2015**, *29*, 1569–1587. [CrossRef]
17. Zhang, Y.; Wu, S.; Zhao, Z.; Yang, X.; Fang, Z. An Urban Crowd Flow Model Integrating Geographic Characteristics. *Sci. Rep.* **2023**, *13*, 1695. [CrossRef] [PubMed]
18. Lei, K.; Chen, K.; Deng, M.; Tan, X.; Yang, W.; Liu, H.; Huang, C. CSSKL: Collaborative Specific-Shared Knowledge Learning Framework for Cross-City Spatiotemporal Forecasting in Cellular Networks. *Int. J. Geogr. Inf. Sci.* **2025**, 1–38. [CrossRef]
19. Lin, Y.; Huang, J.; Sun, D. A Novel Recurrent Convolutional Network Based on Grid Correlation Modeling for Crowd Flow Prediction. *J. King Saud Univ.-Comput. Inf. Sci.* **2023**, *35*, 101699. [CrossRef]
20. Jiang, R.; Cai, Z.; Wang, Z.; Yang, C.; Fan, Z.; Chen, Q.; Tsubouchi, K.; Song, X.; Shibasaki, R. DeepCrowd: A Deep Model for Large-Scale Citywide Crowd Density and Flow Prediction. *IEEE Trans. Knowl. Data Eng.* **2021**, *35*, 276–290. [CrossRef]
21. Zhang, X.; Sun, Y.; Guan, F.; Chen, K.; Witlox, F.; Huang, H. Forecasting the Crowd: An Effective and Efficient Neural Network for Citywide Crowd Information Prediction at a Fine Spatio-Temporal Scale. *Transp. Res. Part C Emerg. Technol.* **2022**, *143*, 103854. [CrossRef]
22. Wang, P.; Zhang, H.; Liu, J.; Lu, F.; Zhang, T. Efficient Inference of Large-Scale Air Quality Using a Lightweight Ensemble Predictor. *Int. J. Geogr. Inf. Sci.* **2025**, *39*, 900–924. [CrossRef]
23. Medina-Salgado, B.; Sánchez-DelaCruz, E.; Pozos-Parra, P.; Sierra, J.E. Urban Traffic Flow Prediction Techniques: A Review. *Sustain. Comput. Inform. Syst.* **2022**, *35*, 100739. [CrossRef]
24. Zhang, J.; Zheng, Y.; Qi, D.; Li, R.; Yi, X. DNN-Based Prediction Model for Spatio-Temporal Data. In Proceedings of the 24th ACM SIGSPATIAL International Conference on Advances in Geographic Information Systems, Burlingame, CA, USA, 31 October–3 November 2016; pp. 1–4.
25. Zheng, C.; Fan, X.; Wen, C.; Chen, L.; Wang, C.; Li, J. DeepSTD: Mining Spatio-Temporal Disturbances of Multiple Context Factors for Citywide Traffic Flow Prediction. *IEEE Trans. Intell. Transp. Syst.* **2020**, *21*, 3744–3755. [CrossRef]
26. Lin, Z.; Feng, J.; Lu, Z.; Li, Y.; Jin, D. DeepSTN+: Context-Aware Spatial-Temporal Neural Network for Crowd Flow Prediction in Metropolis. In Proceedings of the AAAI Conference on Artificial Intelligence, Honolulu, HI, USA, 27 January–1 February 2019; Volume 33, pp. 1020–1027. [CrossRef]
27. Go, H.; Park, S. A Study on Deep Learning Model Based on Global–Local Structure for Crowd Flow Prediction. *Sci. Rep.* **2024**, *14*, 12623. [CrossRef]
28. Jin, W.; Lin, Y.; Wu, Z.; Wan, H. Spatio-Temporal Recurrent Convolutional Networks for Citywide Short-Term Crowd Flows Prediction. In Proceedings of the 2nd International Conference on Compute and Data Analysis, DeKalb, IL, USA, 23–25 March 2018; pp. 28–35.
29. Yuan, X.; Han, J.; Wang, X.; He, Y.; Xu, W.; Zhang, K. A Novel Learning Approach for Citywide Crowd Flow Prediction. In Proceedings of the 2019 Computing, Communications and IoT Applications (ComComAp), Shenzhen, China, 26–28 October 2019; pp. 341–346.
30. Ren, Y.; Chen, H.; Han, Y.; Cheng, T.; Zhang, Y.; Chen, G. A Hybrid Integrated Deep Learning Model for the Prediction of Citywide Spatio-Temporal Flow Volumes. *Int. J. Geogr. Inf. Sci.* **2020**, *34*, 802–823. [CrossRef]
31. Tang, G.; Li, B.; Dai, H.-N.; Zheng, X. SPRNN: A Spatial–Temporal Recurrent Neural Network for Crowd Flow Prediction. *Inf. Sci.* **2022**, *614*, 19–34. [CrossRef]
32. Wang, X.; Zhou, Z.; Zhao, Y.; Zhang, X.; Xing, K.; Xiao, F.; Yang, Z.; Liu, Y. Improving Urban Crowd Flow Prediction on Flexible Region Partition. *IEEE Trans. Mob. Comput.* **2020**, *19*, 2804–2817. [CrossRef]

33. Cardia, M.; Luca, M.; Pappalardo, L. Enhancing Crowd Flow Prediction in Various Spatial and Temporal Granularities. In Proceedings of the Companion Proceedings of the Web Conference 2022, Virtual Event, Lyon, France, 25–29 April 2022; pp. 1251–1259.
34. Ul Abideen, Z.; Sun, X.; Sun, C. Crowd Flow Prediction: An Integrated Approach Using Dynamic Spatial–Temporal Adaptive Modeling for Pattern Flow Relationships. *J. Forecast.* **2025**, *44*, 556–574. [CrossRef]
35. Li, F.; Feng, J.; Yan, H.; Jin, D.; Li, Y. Crowd Flow Prediction for Irregular Regions with Semantic Graph Attention Network. *ACM Trans. Intell. Syst. Technol.* **2022**, *13*, 1–14. [CrossRef]
36. Guo, H.; Zhang, D.; Jiang, L.; Poon, K.-W.; Lu, K. ASTCN: An Attentive Spatial–Temporal Convolutional Network for Flow Prediction. *IEEE Internet Things J.* **2022**, *9*, 3215–3225. [CrossRef]
37. Ali, A.; Zhu, Y.; Zakarya, M. Exploiting Dynamic Spatio-Temporal Correlations for Citywide Traffic Flow Prediction Using Attention Based Neural Networks. *Inf. Sci.* **2021**, *577*, 852–870. [CrossRef]
38. Xie, Y.; Niu, J.; Zhang, Y.; Ren, F. Multisize Patched Spatial-Temporal Transformer Network for Short- and Long-Term Crowd Flow Prediction. *IEEE Trans. Intell. Transp. Syst.* **2022**, *23*, 21548–21568. [CrossRef]
39. Zheng, Z.; Gu, J.; Zhou, Q.; Lu, X. Prediction in Long-Term Evolution: Exploiting the Interaction between Urban Crowd Flow Variation and POI Transition Patterns. In Proceedings of the 2023 IEEE International Conference on Data Mining (ICDM), Shanghai, China, 1–4 December 2023; pp. 1559–1564.
40. Jiang, R.; Cai, Z.; Wang, Z.; Yang, C.; Fan, Z.; Chen, Q.; Song, X.; Shibasaki, R. Predicting Citywide Crowd Dynamics at Big Events: A Deep Learning System. *ACM Trans. Intell. Syst. Technol.* **2022**, *13*, 1–24. [CrossRef]
41. Yuan, Y.; Ding, J.; Feng, J.; Jin, D.; Li, Y. UniST: A Prompt-Empowered Universal Model for Urban Spatio-Temporal Prediction. In Proceedings of the Proceedings of the 30th ACM SIGKDD Conference on Knowledge Discovery and Data Mining, Barcelona, Spain, 25–29 August 2024; pp. 4095–4106.
42. Su, C.; Wu, C.; Lian, D. GridFormer: Spatial-Temporal Transformer Network for Citywide Crowd Flow Prediction. In *Frontiers in Artificial Intelligence and Applications*; Gal, K., Nowé, A., Nalepa, G.J., Fairstein, R., Rădulescu, R., Eds.; IOS Press: Amsterdam, The Netherlands, 2023; ISBN 978-1-64368-436-9.
43. Zhu, A.; Lu, G.; Liu, J.; Qin, C.; Zhou, C. Spatial Prediction Based on Third Law of Geography. *Ann. GIS* **2018**, *24*, 225–240. [CrossRef]
44. Deng, M.; Yang, W.; Liu, Q.; Jin, R.; Xu, F.; Zhang, Y. Heterogeneous Space–Time Artificial Neural Networks for Space–Time Series Prediction. *Trans. GIS* **2018**, *22*, 183–201. [CrossRef]
45. Zhang, C.; Zhang, H.; Qiao, J.; Yuan, D.; Zhang, M. Deep Transfer Learning for Intelligent Cellular Traffic Prediction Based on Cross-Domain Big Data. *IEEE J. Sel. Areas Commun.* **2019**, *37*, 1389–1401. [CrossRef]
46. Chung, J.; Gulcehre, C.; Cho, K.; Bengio, Y. Empirical Evaluation of Gated Recurrent Neural Networks on Sequence Modeling. *arXiv* **2014**, arXiv:1412.3555.
47. Zeng, A.; Chen, M.; Zhang, L.; Xu, Q. Are Transformers Effective for Time Series Forecasting? In Proceedings of the AAAI Conference on Artificial Intelligence, Washington, DC, USA, 7–14 February 2023; Volume 37, pp. 11121–11128. [CrossRef]
48. Ballas, N.; Yao, L.; Pal, C.; Courville, A. Delving Deeper into Convolutional Networks for Learning Video Representations. *arXiv* **2015**, arXiv:1511.06432.
49. Bai, L.; Yao, L.; Li, C.; Wang, X.; Wang, C. Adaptive Graph Convolutional Recurrent Network for Traffic Forecasting. *Adv. Neural Inf. Process. Syst.* **2020**, *33*, 17804–17815.
50. Nguyen, N.; Quanz, B. Temporal Latent Auto-Encoder: A Method for Probabilistic Multivariate Time Series Forecasting. In Proceedings of the AAAI Conference on Artificial Intelligence, Virtual Event, 2–9 February 2021; Volume 35, pp. 9117–9125. [CrossRef]
51. Han, J.; Zhang, W.; Liu, H.; Tao, T.; Tan, N.; Xiong, H. BigST: Linear Complexity Spatio-Temporal Graph Neural Network for Traffic Forecasting on Large-Scale Road Networks. *Proc. VLDB Endow.* **2024**, *17*, 1081–1090. [CrossRef]

MDPI AG
Grosspeteranlage 5
4052 Basel
Switzerland
Tel.: +41 61 683 77 34

Mathematics Editorial Office
E-mail: mathematics@mdpi.com
www.mdpi.com/journal/mathematics

www.ingramcontent.com/pod-product-compliance
Lightning Source LLC
Chambersburg PA
CBHW061521210926
51850CB00008B/1989